Véronique Plata-Stenger
Social Reform, Modernization and Technical Diplomacy

Work in Global and Historical Perspective

Edited by
Andreas Eckert, Sidney Chalhoub, Mahua Sarkar,
Dmitri van den Bersselaar, Christian G. De Vito

Work in Global and Historical Perspective is an interdisciplinary series that welcomes scholarship on work/labour that engages a historical perspective in and from any part of the world. The series advocates a definition of work/labour that is broad, and especially encourages contributions that explore interconnections across political and geographic frontiers, time frames, disciplinary boundaries, as well as conceptual divisions among various forms of commodified work, and between work and 'non-work'.

Volume 8

Véronique Plata-Stenger

Social Reform, Modernization and Technical Diplomacy

The ILO Contribution to Development
(1930–1946)

DE GRUYTER
OLDENBOURG

ISBN 978-3-11-077714-7
e-ISBN (PDF) 978-3-11-061632-3
e-ISBN (EPUB) 978-3-11-061658-3
ISSN 2509-8861

Library of Congress Control Number: 2020933814

Bibliographic information published by the Deutsche Nationalbibliothek
The Deutsche Nationalbibliothek lists this publication in the Deutsche Nationalbibliografie;
detailed bibliographic data are available on the Internet at http://dnb.dnb.de.

© 2021 Walter de Gruyter GmbH, Berlin/Boston
This volume is text- and page-identical with the hardback published in 2020.
Cover: 1942-07, Osvald Stein (third from right) and other ILO officials on mission in Chile.
ILO historical archives. Ref: e46264
Typesetting: 3W+P GmbH, Rimpar
Print and binding: CPI books GmbH, Leck

www.degruyter.com

To Nicolas, Raphaël and Mila

Acknowledgments

This book is a revised and translated version of my doctoral thesis defended at the University of Geneva in 2016. Many people supported this book's project. The translation of the manuscript would not have been possible without the financial support of the General Fund of the University of Geneva, the Faculty of Arts and the History Department of the University of Geneva, La Maison de l'Histoire, and the Research Division of the International Labour Organization.

I am grateful to Sonia Doyle, who accepted the challenge of translating the manuscript; and Elizabeth Doyle, for revising the translation.

This research would not have been possible without the financial support of the Swiss University Conference (CSHE), the Boninchi Foundation in Geneva and the Swiss National Science Foundation (SNSF).

I would like to thank Sandrine Kott, my thesis supervisor, whose constant support, dynamism, openness, frankness, experience and wise advice were decisive factors in the realisation of this research. I would also like to thank Ludovic Tournès, who was an attentive and demanding co-director, whose remarks and advice made it possible to further improve my research. I also wish to express my gratitude for the time they have given to me.

I would like to thank the ILO archivists, Remo Becci, Renée Berthon and Jacques Rodriguez. I am grateful for their warm welcome, their advice and for the ideas we exchanged between two boxes of archival files. I would also like to thank the civil servants of the ILO DOSCOM Service whom I have had the pleasure of working with during these years of research. I extend my thanks to Jacques Oberson for his welcome to the archives of the League of Nations, as well as the UN archivists in Geneva; Romain Ledauphin of the UN archives in New York and Mary Ann Quinn of the Rockefeller Foundation archives in New York. I would also like to thank Pierre Roehrich for sharing his family history with me and allowing me to consult his grandfather Maurice Thudichum's archives.

Contents

List of Tables —— XV

List of Acronyms —— XVII

Introduction —— 1
    A Transnational and Social Approach to International Organisations —— 2
    The ILO, Technical Assistance and the Seeds of International Development —— 7
    Archival Materials —— 15
    Research Structure —— 16

First Part
Development as a Universalisation Strategy

Chapter I
Europe's Economic Recovery: the Emergence of a Matrix Thinking on Development —— 21

1	Albert Thomas, Reformism and the First World War —— 23
1.1	Planning Under Socialist Reformism —— 23
1.2	The Experience of the First World War —— 25
2	International Planning and the ILO's Hopes for European Economic Reconstruction Leadership —— 28
2.1	Expanding ILO Authority to the Economy —— 29
2.2	Public Planning and Economic Management —— 31
2.2.1	The ILO: A Sounding Board for European Planist Experiments —— 31
2.2.2	The American Rationalist Movement: A Possible Model —— 33
2.3	International Public Works: A Solution to the European Crisis —— 37
3	Research on Planning as a Trans-Atlantic Project —— 44
3.1	The USA Joins the ILO —— 45
3.2	Recruiting American Experts —— 49
3.3	Difficult Collaborations with the Rockefeller Foundation —— 56
	Conclusion —— 59

Chapter II
After the "Spirit of Geneva" Comes the "Spirit of Santiago": Early Regional Cooperation in Latin America —— 61

1		Opposing Models: "Europeanism" vs "Universalism" —— 62
1.1		The European Origins of the ILO —— 62
1.2		Pan-Americanism and the Creation of Regional Labour Offices —— 64
2		The Regionalisation of International Labour Office Activities —— 68
2.1		Regional Cooperation Serving International Cooperation —— 69
2.2		More Space for Non-European Countries —— 70
2.3		Organising the 1936 Regional Conference in Santiago de Chile —— 74
3		The Beginnings of the ILO's Regional Programme in Latin America —— 80
3.1		Social Insurance: ILO's Key to Latin America —— 80
3.2		Migration for Colonisation: Population Redistribution and Development —— 83
		Conclusion —— 89

Chapter III
The Limits of the ILO's Universalist Ambition in Asia and the Problem of Underdevelopment —— 91

1		Two-tier Social Justice: Imperial Domination and "Special Regimes" —— 94
1.1		Exporting the "Civilising Mission" —— 94
1.2		Putting in Place "Special Regimes" —— 95
1.3		Loosening the Colonial Grip: Indian Workers' Delegations to the ILO —— 97
2		The ILO's Attempts to Regulate Economic Competition —— 101
2.1		Combating Social Dumping —— 101
2.2		Breaking Down the Walls of Protectionism: the ILO as an Instrument of US Economic Diplomacy in Asia —— 104
2.3		The Office's Economic Research Missions —— 109
2.3.1		John Riches' Mission to Samoa —— 111
2.3.2		Harold Butler's Mission to India —— 114
3		Early Technical Assistance in Asia: The Case of China —— 117
3.1		Labour Inspection Reform —— 118
3.2		Vocational Training and Economic Reconstruction —— 120
		Conclusion —— 122

Second Part
Development Tools and Practices: Between Knowledge Building, Expertise and Diplomacy

Chapter IV
The ILO's Contribution to the Internationalisation of the Standard of Living —— 125

1	Raising the Standard of Living in Industrialised Countries —— 127
1.1	Wages and Minimum Wage —— 127
1.2	From Detroit to Europe: International Comparison of Purchasing Power —— 133
2	Extending Research Towards Less Developed Countries —— 140
2.1	The Impetus Given by the Santiago Conference —— 141
2.2	Collaborations with the Institute of Pacific Relations —— 142
2.3	The ILO's 1938 Study on the Workers' Living Standard —— 146
	Conclusion —— 154

Chapter V
Technical Assistance "Experts": ILO Brokers Around The World —— 155

1	Socialisation at the Office and the Emergence of a Sense of Belonging —— 158
1.1	ILO Civil Servants Engaged in Technical Assistance —— 158
1.2	International Civil Servants: A Homogeneous Social Group? —— 161
1.3	Institutional Arrangements for International Socialisation —— 163
2	The Professionalisation of Civil Servants Before their Entry to the Office —— 165
2.1	Professional Trajectories in National Spaces —— 165
2.2	The Importance of Administrative Careers —— 171
2.3	The Experience of War and the Networks of Social Reform —— 172
3	Professionalisation Within the Office —— 174
3.1	A Predisposition to International Openness —— 175
3.2	In-Depth Knowledge of National and International Social Legislation —— 176
3.3	A Sense of Diplomacy —— 181
3.4	Professional Trajectories and Continuity After the Second World War —— 185
	Conclusion —— 187

Chapter VI
The Social Reconstruction of Europe's Periphery: Technical Assistance to Greece and Romania —— 189

1	European Modernity and the Development of Social Policy —— 192	
1.1	The Difficult Reconstruction of Central and Eastern Europe —— 192	
1.2	The Pursuit of a European Social Model and its Limits —— 195	
2	The Challenges of Technical Assistance —— 201	
2.1	Legitimising State Action and Building Territorial Unity in Romania —— 201	
2.2	Social Insurance Reform in Greece: A Point of Contention Between the Office and the League of Nations —— 202	
3	The Effects of Technical Assistance —— 205	
3.1	The Limits of the Unification of Social Insurance Law (1933) in Romania —— 205	
3.2	Czech Experts to Support the Development of Social Insurance in Greece —— 208	
	Conclusion —— 212	

Chapter VII
On the Roads of Venezuela: Experiences and Representations of International Expertise —— 214

1	Contexts and Challenges of Technical Assistance in Venezuela —— 216	
1.1	Caracas: A Breeding Ground for Social Reformers —— 216	
1.2	Contact Point: Venezuelan Internationalists in Geneva —— 219	
1.3	In Search of International Support —— 220	
2	The Day-to-Day Running of the Missions —— 225	
2.1	A Universalist Approach to Reform Projects —— 225	
2.2	Field Surveys —— 232	
2.2.1	"Hot, Ragged, Dirty" Venezuela —— 234	
2.2.2	Inequality and Standards of Living —— 236	
2.3	Oppositions to the Labour Code —— 238	
3	The Work of Experts in Crisis —— 242	
3.1	Feelings of Exile, Physical and Psychological Constraints —— 243	
3.2	When the Status of Expert Conflicts with Institutional Loyalty —— 245	
	Conclusion —— 249	

Chapter VIII
Technical Assistance and the Formulation of an International Development Policy During the Second World War —— 252
1 Between Continental Defence and Regional Development —— 253
1.1 The Office Moves to Montreal —— 253
1.2 Social Security and Regional Solidarity —— 256
1.3 Technical Assistance in Support of the Allied War Effort —— 264
2 The Post-War Social Agenda and Development —— 272
2.1 Initial Reflections on Reconstruction —— 272
2.2 New York 1941 and Philadelphia 1944 —— 275
Conclusion —— 282

General Conclusion —— 284

Images —— 291

Unprinted Materials —— 297

Printed Materials, Archives of the International Labour Office —— 301

Bibliography —— 303

Index —— 327

List of Tables

1. Civil Servants Hired for Missions of Technical Assistance (1930–1939)
2. Civil Servants Profiles
3. ILO Missions of Technical Assistance in the Interwar Period
4. National and International Actors Involved in the Organisation of ILO Missions of Technical Assistance
5. Chronology of the Stages of Wilfred Jenks' Journey
6. List of Montreal Staff (27 November 1940)
7. ILO's Missions of Technical Assistance in the Field of Social Security (1939–1945)

List of Acronyms

AFL	American Federation of Labor
BIS	Bank for International Settlements
CEEU	Commission of Enquiry for European Union, League of Nations
CESNU	United Nations Economic and Social Council
EFO	The League's Economic and Financial Organisation
FAO	United Nations Food and Agriculture Organisation
GATT	General Agreement on Tariffs and Trade
HO	Health Organisation, League of Nations
IALL	International Association for Labour Legislation
IBRD	International Bank for Reconstruction and Development
ICC	International Chamber of Commerce
ICRC	International Committee of the Red Cross
IFTU	International Federation of Trade Unions
IIIC	International Institute of Intellectual Cooperation
ILO	International Labour Organization
IMF	International Monetary Fund
IMI	International Management Institute
IPR	Institute of Pacific Relations
OCIAA	Office of the Coordinator of Inter-American Affairs
PAU	The Pan-American Union
PEP	Political and Economic Planning Group
PMC	Permanent Mandates Commission
SSB	Social Security Board
SSRC	Social Science Research Council
UN	The United Nations
UNRRA	United Nations Relief and Rehabilitation Administration

Introduction

In 1931, Isma'il Sidqi, then Prime Minister of the Egyptian Cabinet, made a request to Albert Thomas, Director of the International Labour Office, for a mission to be sent to assist the government in implementing social reforms.[1] At this time, as it was not a member of the International Labour Organization (ILO), contacts with Egypt were extremely rare. By accepting the Egyptian government's invitation, Thomas hoped to stimulate the introduction of new social laws and show the ILO's support of social policy development in Egypt, while gathering information on the country's working conditions. When Harold Butler, Deputy Director of the International Labour Office, landed in Egypt in February 1932, he found a country in the midst of social and economic change.[2] In Cairo, the government asked Butler to help formulate a social policy programme suitable to industry in its "current stage of development".[3] Butler submitted a detailed report outlying the proposed legislative and administrative reforms. He also recommended a series of reforms inspired by the experiences of European countries as well as the principles laid out in the international labour Conventions. This mission of "technical assistance", as it would later be known, would lead the International Labour Office to take on an entirely new advisory function. By making international civil servants available to governments to implement new labour laws, the International Labour Office was experimenting with a novel practice in international cooperation, which would expand in the post Second World War era as part of international development programmes.[4]

---

[1] Letter from Isma'il Sidqi to Albert Thomas, September 30, 1931. CAT 5-26-1-1 "Relations, Informations. Egypte", in the International Labour Office Archives, Geneva (hereafter ILOA).
[2] Mitchell, T. 2002. *Rule of Experts: Egypt, Techno-Politics, Modernity.* Berkeley: University of California Press.
[3] "Mr. Butler's visit to Egypt, February 1932". XT 69/3/1, ILOA.
[4] *Assistance technique en vue du développement économique. Plan d'un programme pour l'extension de la collaboration par l'entremise de l'Organisation des Nations Unies et des institutions spécialisées.* Report prepared by the Secretary-General in consultation with the deputy heads of the specialised agencies concerned, through the Administrative Committee on Coordination pursuant to Resolution 180 (VIII), New York, UNO, 1949; Boris, G. 1950. "Assistance technique et point IV: origine, principe, buts", *Politique étrangère* 5/6: 533–550; Wilcox, F. O. 1950. "The United Nations Program for Technical Assistance", *Annals of the American Academy of Political and Social Science* 268, 45–53; Sharp, W. 1953. "The Institutional Framework for Technical Assistance", *International Organization* 7(3): 342–379; Lengyel, P. 1960. "Le rôle de l'assistance technique dans le développement économique", *Tiers Monde* 4: 461–490 ; Owen, D. 1950. "The United Nations Program of Technical Assistance", *The Annals of the American Academy of Political and Social Science* 270, 109–117, and "The United Nations Expanded Program of Technical As-

A Transnational and Social Approach to International Organisations

Created in 1919 by the victors of the First World War as part of the Treaty of Versailles, the ILO was a technical organisation, institutionally tied to the League of Nations.[5] It was and is still composed of an executive body known as the Governing Body (GB); the International Labour Conferences (ILC), where international labour Conventions and Recommendations are adopted; and the permanent secretariat, the International Labour Office. The latter, sometimes referred to as the Office, was tasked with implementing ILO policy, under the control of the Director and the GB. It originally acted as an international documentation centre. One of its main duties was therefore to collect, produce, and disseminate social information through scientific articles, reports and studies. In this context, international civil servants were regularly sent on missions to gather documentation, establish relations and develop any activity likely to strengthen the organisation's position. ILO action was and is still based on social dialogue as a key factor in moving towards progress and as instrumental in allowing the different components of the labour world to manage economic and social change. The ILO tripartite structure – where workers, employers and governments participate jointly in leadership – is a living embodiment of this social dialogue, ensuring that the views of all social partners are taken into account within the ILO's programmes and overall policy.[6]

The foundation of the ILO rested on the conviction that universal and lasting peace could be accomplished only if it was based on social justice. In the interwar period, its work consisted primarily in crafting international labour standards.[7] Until the end of the 1920s, ILO activity focused on the protection of work-

---

sistance – A Multilateral Approach", *The Annals of the American Academy of Political and Social Science* 323, 25–32; Wilcox, F. O. 1950. "The United Nations Program for Technical Assistance", *Annals of the American Academy of Political and Social Science* 268, 45–53; Blelloch, D. 1957. "Bold New Programme: A Review of United Nations Technical Assistance", *International Affairs* 33(1): 36–50; Blelloch, D. 1958. *Aid for Development*, Fabian Research Series, n°195, The Fabian Society; Rens, J. 1961. "L'Organisation internationale du travail et la coopération technique internationale", Revue internationale du travail 83(5): 441–466.

5 Ghebali, V.-Y., Ago, R., Valticos, N. 1987. *L'Organisation internationale du travail.* Genève: Georg.

6 Béguin, B. 1959. *Le Tripartisme dans l'Organisation internationale du travail.* Genève: Droz.

7 Bonvin, J.-M. 1998. *L'Organisation internationale du travail. Étude sur une agence productrice de normes.* Paris: PUF.

ers within Europe.⁸ At this time, though certain Asian, Latin American and Middle Eastern countries were members of the ILO, their importance remained limited. Moreover, far from disappearing, the colonial system was gaining new legitimacy. However, the 1930s crisis forced the ILO to reconsider the breadth of its work, and to redefine it. The rise of ultranationalisms in Europe,⁹ of authoritarian regimes in Asia, the rapid fluctuation between democracy and dictatorship that marked Latin America's history during this period, competing models of economic and social modernisation driven by the USSR, Italy and Germany,¹⁰ the resurgence of imperial policies, the implementation of protectionist measures which led to the disintegration of social protection, along with the consolidation of cartels that participated in exacerbating commercial tensions, were all perceived as signs of economic unravelling foretelling the end of globalisation.¹¹

Analysing the transformations brought forth by the Great Depression, a historiography of international organisations has long insisted on the failure of the League of Nations, on its incapacity to propose coordinated economic recovery measures and to prevent the Second World War.¹² However, this research proposes, as was partially carried out for the League of Nations,¹³ to test this interpretative framework by demonstrating that the 1930s crisis and the Second World War did not put an end to international cooperation, and did not entirely para-

---

8 Guérin, D. 1996. *Albert Thomas au BIT, 1920–1932. De l'internationalisme à l'Europe*. Genève: Euryopa; Van Daele, J. 2005. "Engineering Social Peace: Networks, Ideas, and the Founding of the International Labour Organization", *International Review of Social History* 50(3): 435–466; Plata-Stenger, V. 2016. "Europe, the ILO and the wider world (1919–1954)", EGO | European History Online: http://ieg-ego.eu/en/threads/transnational-movements-and-organisations/international-organisations-and-congresses/veronique-plata-stenger-europe-the-ilo-and-the-wider-world–1919–1954. [last accessed 17.09.2019]
9 Hobsbawm, E. 2008. *L'Âge des extrêmes : histoire du court XXᵉ siècle : 1914–1991*. Bruxelles: André Versaille.
10 Fritzsche P. and Hellbeck, J. 2009. "The New Man in Stalinist Russia and Nazi Germany", in Fitzpatrick S. and Geyer, M. eds. 2009. *Beyond Totalitarianism. Stalinism and Nazism Compared*, 302–344. Cambridge: Cambridge University Press.
11 James, H. 2002. *The End of Globalization: Lessons from the Great Depression*. Cambridge: Harvard University Press.
12 See Steiner, Z. 2005. *The Lights That Failed. European International History, 1919–1933*, Oxford: Oxford University Press; Steiner, Z. 2011. *The Triumph of the Dark. European International History, 1933–1939*. Oxford: Oxford University Press.
13 Clavin, P. 2013. *Securing the World Economy: The Reinvention of the League of Nations, 1920–1946*. Oxford: Oxford University Press; Borowy, I. 2009. *Coming to Terms with World Health: The League of Nations Health Organisation 1921–1946*. Frankfurt am Main: Peter Lang; Pedersen, S. 2007. "Back to the League of Nations: Review Essay", *American Historical Review* 112(4): 1091–1117.

lyse the ILO. This work focuses in particular on the profound changes that took place in the wake of the Great Depression, beginning with the intensification of ILO activities in less industrialised countries, and the emergence of new practices in international cooperation. Originally a European institution, the ILO was forced to universalise its mandate, while in Europe, national borders were gradually closing. For the first time since the First World War, the Great Depression posed challenges on a global scale, provoking a globalising "turning point" for the ILO.[14]

These changes affecting the ILO broadly relate to the capacity of international organisations to establish themselves as international actors, and to overcome opposition between nation-states. On this topic, the debate has long been dominated by political scientists and by Anglo-Saxon international relations specialists, divided into two prevailing perspectives: the realist perspective, which denies international organisations their participation as full-fledged players; and the functionalist perspective, which considers international organisations as part of a network composed of international elites with a set of practices and skills that can be universalised.[15] As such, the historiographical renewal of the ILO is intimately tied to a willingness to analyse the capacity of international organisations to regulate international relations.[16] A significant part of the research

---

[14] Reference here is to Anne Rasmussen's expression regarding the changes that occured in the international movement at the beginning of the twentieth century, which she defines as a "turning point" in internationalism. 2001. "Tournant, inflexions, ruptures : le moment internationaliste", *Mil neuf cent. Revue d'histoire intellectuelle* 1(19): 27–41.

[15] For the realistic position, see Jervis, R. 1998. "Realism in the Study of World Politics", *International Organization* 52(4): 971–991. For a functionalist perspective, see Martin, L. L. and Simmons, A. B. 1998. "Theories and Empirical Studies of International Institutions", *International Organization* 52(4): 729–757; Finnemore, M. and Sikkink, K. 1998. "International Norm Dynamics and Political Change", *International Organization* 52(4): 887–917; Cox, R. W. et al. 1974. *The Anatomy of Influence: Decision Making in International Organization*. New Haven: Yale University Press, 402–409; Claude Jr., I. L. 1964. *Swords into* Plowshares: *The Problems and Progress of International Organization*. New York: Random; Haas, E. B. 1964. *Beyond the Nation-State: Functionalism and International Organization*. Stanford: Stanford University Press; Mitrany, D. 1943. *A Working Peace System: An Argument for the Functional Development of International Organization*. London: The Royal Institute of International Affairs, 1943. On David Mitrany and his influence, see Devin, G. 2008. "Que reste-t-il du fonctionnalisme international? Relire David Mitrany (1888–1975)", *Critique internationale* 1(38): 137–152.

[16] Van Daele, J. 2008. "The International Labour Organization (ILO) in Past and Present Research", *International Review of Social History* 53(3): 485–511. Literature on the ILO has grown considerably in recent years. Among the latest publications, see Droux, J., Kott, S. eds. 2013. *Globalizing Social Rights. The International Labour Organization and Beyond*. ILO Centuries Series, Basingstoke: Palgrave Macmillan; Lespinet-Moret, I. and Viet, V. eds. 2011. *L'Organisation in-*

aims to restore this organisation's place within the dense fabric of social and political interactions taking place across various geopolitical spaces, using the tools of the transnational approach to do so.[17] Historian Sandrine Kott (2011) invites us to consider these organisations as "globalisation laboratories" and to understand them as "open social spaces", where transnational connections and alliances are established.[18] Transnational history aims to examine connections and transfers occuring across borders, as well as the "circulatory regimes" that can result from them[19]. However, the transnational analysis does not exclude governments as actors in this circulation of models and ideas.[20] Indeed, it can help define a quality of actor, person and/or organisation working beyond state borders, while not necessarily acting independently from the state. Regarding technical assistance, this book shows that transnational circulation occured with the knowledge of the state, which sometimes even encouraged it. Thus, circulation contributed as much to strengthening the nation-state as the latter did to foster transnational circulation.

---

ternationale du travail : origine, développement, avenir. Rennes: PUR; Van Daele, J. et al. 2010. *ILO Histories. Essays on the International Labour Organization and Its Impact on the World During the Twentieth Century*. Bern: Peter Lang; Rodger, G., Swepston, L., Lee, E., Van Daele, J. 2009. *The International Labour Organization and the Quest for Social Justice, 1919–2009*. Geneva: ILO; See also the special issue of 2008: "Albert Thomas, société mondiale et internationalisme. Réseaux et institutions des années 1890 aux années 1930", *Les Cahiers Irice* 2(2). For a more general perspective, see MacKenzie, D. C. 2010. *A World Beyond Borders: An Introduction to the History of International Organizations*. North York: University of Toronto Press; Reinalda, B. 2009. *Routledge History of International Organizations: From 1815 to the Present Day*. London: Routledge, 338–344; Iriye, A. 2004. *Global Community, The Role of International Organizations in the Making of the Contemporary World*. Berkeley: University of California Press.

17 Sluga, G. 2011. "Editorial – The Transnational History of International Institutions", *Journal of Global History* 6(2): 219–222. In French, see the special issue directed by Sandrine Kott in 2011. "Une autre approche de la globalisation : socio-histoire des organisations internationales (1900–1940)", *Critique internationale* 3(52). For a reflection on the methods, tools and objects of transnational analyses, see Saunier, P.-Y. 2013. *Transnational History. Theory and History*. Basingstoke: Palgrave; Iriye, A. and Saunier, P.-Y. eds. 2009. *The Palgrave Dictionnary of Transnational History. From the mid–19th Century to the Present Day*. Basingstoke: Palgrave; Clavin, P. 2005. "Defining Transnationalism", *Contemporary European History* 14(4): 421–439.

18 Kott, S. 2011. "Les organisations internationales, terrains d'étude de la globalisation. Jalons pour une approche socio-historique", *Critique internationale* 3(52): 9–16.

19 Saunier, P.-Y. 2008. "Les régimes circulatoires du domaine social 1800–1940 : projets et ingénierie de la convergence et de la différence", *Genèses* 2(71): 4–25. See also Saunier, P.-Y. 2004. "Circulations, connexions et espaces transnationaux", *Genèses* 4(57): 110–126.

20 For a non-governmental definition of the transnational approach, see Clavin, P. 2005. "Defining Transnationalism", *Contemporary European History* 14(4): 421–439.

Drawing on the tools of the transnational approach offers great heuristic scope to examine the ILO's capacity to provide international solutions that are able to circumvent opposition among its member states.[21] While the ILO is not an international actor, insofar as it depends on the decisions of its member states, a closer look at how it functions shows that it is not totally dependent on these decisions. Driven by a "nebula" of actors and with the help of experts that were often aggregated in "epistemic communities",[22] the International Labour Office played a specific role in mobilising transnational networks; reflecting, promoting and developing certain themes;[23] increasing its influence in national spaces;[24] and diffusing international labour standards in specific areas.[25]

The uniqueness of this book stems from its focus on the activities of the civil servants at the International Labour Office. The impetus to approach an international institution from this angle stemmed from a second methodological decision. Indeed, attentive to the logic that drove the creation of these very institutions, I chose to prioritise the socio-historical lens. Insofar as it closely considers actors' relationships to these insitutions, this actor-driven approach seemed relevant to understanding the multiple dynamics at work in shaping international organisations.[26] For historians studying the archives of these international organisations, their complexity is undeniable. In the words of Albert Thomas, they are

---

21 Legro, J. W. 1997. "Which Norms Matter? Revisiting the "Failure' of Internationalism", *International Organization* 51(1): 31–63.
22 Haas, P. M. 1992. "Introduction: Epistemic Communities and International Policy Coordination", *International Organization* 46(1): 1–35; Van Daele, J. 2005. "Engineering Social Peace: Networks, Ideas, and the Founding of the International Labour Organization", *International Review of Social History* 50(3): 435–466. Kott, S. 2008. "'Une communauté épistémique' du social? Experts de l'OIT et internationalisation des politiques sociales dans l'entre-deux-guerres", *Genèses* 2(71): 26–46.
23 Keck, M. E. and Sikkink, K. 1998. *Activists beyond Borders: Advocacy Networks in International Politics.* Ithaca; London: Cornell University Press.
24 For case studies articulating the national and international, see Hidalgo-Weber, O. 2017. *La Grande-Bretagne et l'Organisation internationale du travail (1919–1946) : Une nouvelle forme d'internationalisme*. Paris: L'Harmattan; Kott, S. 2011. "Dynamiques de l'internationalisation : L'Allemagne et l'Organisation internationale du Travail (1919–1940)", *Critique internationale* 3(52): 69–84.
25 Droux, J., Kott, S. eds. 2013. *Globalizing Social Rights. The international Labour Organization and Beyond*; Rodogno, D., Gauthier, S., and Piana, F. 2013. "What Does Transnational History Tell Us about a World with International Organizations?", in Reinalda, Bob (Ed.), 2013. *Routledge Handbook of International Organizations*, 94–105. Routledge: London.
26 Nay, O. 2011. "Éléments pour une sociologie du changement dans les organisations internationales", *Critique internationale* 4(53): 9–20.

"living things".²⁷ This also means that he considered the ILO to be an entity destined to grow and evolve. Thomas saw the International Labour Office as action-oriented in nature. He was one of the guiding forces behind the Office taking new initiatives and going beyond its original functions. This evolution makes the Office a particularly compelling object of study in the context of the 1930s and 1940s.

The ILO, Technical Assistance and the Seeds of International Development

One of the major changes that occurred at the ILO in the 1930s was the intensification of its activities in the European and American peripheries. Analysing the ILO's attempts at universalising its activites allows us to reframe them within the history of development.²⁸ It redefines the 1930s and 1940s as catalysts for promoting certain ideas on economic and social progress, along with new demands and experiences preceding the political and intellectual changes that would come after the Second World War.²⁹

Much has been written about development, but historians have only been truly interested in this issue since the 1990s.³⁰ Although some of them have

---

27 Thomas, A. 1921. "Organisation internationale du Travail : origine, développement, avenir", *Revue internationale du travail* 1(1): 21. ILOA.
28 Rist, G. 2007. *Le Développement: Histoire d'une croyance occidentale*. Paris: Presses de la Fondation nationale des sciences politiques; Hettne, B. 2009. *Thinking about Development*. London: Zed Books; Wolfgang, S. ed. 2010. *The Development Dictionary. A Guide to Knowledge as Power*. London; New York: Zed Books; Legouté, J. R. 2015. "Définir le développement : historique et dimensions d'un concept plurivoque", *Economie politique internationale. Cahier de recherche* 1(1): 5.
29 Arturo Escobar's definition of development is particularly useful to anyone wishing to analyse it in a dialectical perspective. Escobar insists on the necessity of understanding development as the result of an encounter between a certain number of ideas (rationalisation, modernity, industrialisation, technology), institutions (international organisations, national planning organisations, research institutes) and practices (statistical compilation, technical studies production, recourse to expertise). Escobar, A. 1995. *Encountering Development. The Making and Unmaking of the Third World*, 40. Princeton, Oxford: Princeton University Press.
30 Cullather, N. 2000. "Development? It's History", *Diplomatic History* 24(4): 641–653. For an overview of research on the history of development, see Unger, C. R. 2010. "Histories of Development and Modernization: Findings, Reflections, Future Research", http://hsozkult.geschichte. hu-berlin.de/forum/2010–12–001 [last accessed 17.09.2019]; Hodge, J. M. 2015. "Writing the History of Development (Part 1: The First Wave)", *Humanity Journal* 6(3): 429–463; Hodge, J. M.

shown that already in the interwar period some protagonists of the so-called "civilising" mission used the language of "development",[31] historiography usually sees the beginning of the Cold War as the trigger for development, referring in particular to the founding speech of US President Harry S. Truman on 20 January 1949, in which he announced, as the fourth principle of US foreign policy, the dissemination of technological know-how for the benefit of "underdeveloped" nations. In the 1950s, the domination of American social sciences contributed to infusing the notion of development with American post-war liberalism.[32] This resulted in development being viewed under a strictly economic lens, in relation to various economic theories of the times, in particular that of growth and modernisation, which had become, due to Walt W. Rostow's contributions, the dominant theoretical framework.[33] The modernisation process was also seen as a bulwark against communism, as evidenced by the subtitle Rostow gave his book: "A Non-Communist Manifesto". As a consequence, historical research themes were primarily concerned with the historical experiences of Western (American) modernisation. Development was perceived as an American instrument used to spread the market economy and liberal democracy to Third World countries.[34] Given the United States' importance in the implementation of international cooperation from the 1940s onwards, this lens has also been applied in studies on international organisations.[35]

2016. "Writing the History of Development (Part 2: Longer, Deeper, Wider)", *Humanity Journal* 7(1): 125–174.
31 Plata-Stenger, V., Schulz, M. 2019. "Introduction." *Relations internationales*, 177(1): 3–13.
32 Latham M. E. 2000, *Modernization as Ideology: American Social Science and "Nation Building" in the Kennedy Era*, Chapel Hill: University of North Carolina Press.
33 Rostow, W. W., 1960. *The Stages of Economic Growth. A Non-Communist Manifesto*. London; New York: Cambridge University Press. The 1940s also saw Development Economics gradually establish itself as a discipline in its own right in the American academic field. In 1961, UNESCO published a commented bibliography of technical co-operation programmes, containing a large number of American references. *Coopération internationale et programmes de développement économique et social*. Bibliographie commentée par Jean Viet, Comité international pour la Documentation des sciences sociales, Unesco, 1961.
34 Gilman, N. 2003. *Mandarins of the Future: Modernization Theory in Cold War America*. Baltimore: Johns Hopkins University Press; Ekbladh, D. 2009. *The Great American Mission: Modernization and the Construction of an American World Order*. Princeton: Princeton University Press; Engerman, D. C. and Unger, C. R. 2009. "Introduction: Towards a Global History of Modernization", *Diplomatic History* 33(3): 375–385; Latham, M. E. 2011. *The Right Kind of Revolution: Modernization, Development, and U.S. Foreign Policy from the Cold War to the Present*. Ithaca: Cornell University Press.
35 Staples, A. 2005. *The Birth of Development: How the World Bank, Food and Agriculture Organization, and World Health Organization Changed the World, 1945–1965*. Kent: Kent State Univer-

Since then, various researchers have criticised the American origin of modernisation and development.³⁶ Although the crucial role played by international organisations in shaping international development policy has long been overlooked, some recent work by Patricia Clavin and Margherita Zanasi for the League of Nations, as well as Guy Fiti Sinclair for the ILO, and Eric Helleiner for the GATT, recognise the importance of the interwar period, as a moment where development thinking was first articulated by international organisations.³⁷ This book deepens the analysis of the ILO's specific contribution and shows among other things that the United States, an ILO member since 1934, already played a role in shaping ILO's economic ideas. On this point, recent research on the history of the United States challenges the classic periodisation between the interwar and post-1945 periods.³⁸ I however argue that the idea of development that emerged in the 1930s cannot be reduced to an American-style modernisation

---

sity Press; Rist, G. 2007. *Le Développement: Histoire d'une croyance occidentale*. Paris: Presses de la Fondation nationale des sciences politiques; Stokke, O. 2009. *The UN and Development*. Bloomington: Indiana University Press. Helleiner, E. 2009. "The Development Mandate of International Institutions: Where Did It Come From?", *Studies in Comparative International Development* 44(3): 189–211.

36 Colonial historians were the first to question the centrality of the American framework in modernisation theories. Cooper, F. and Packard, R. eds. 1997. *International Development and the Social Sciences: Essays on the History and Politics of Knowledge*. Berkeley; Los Angeles [etc.]: University of California Press. See also Tournès, L. 2013. "Philanthropic foundations and the exportation of development". Conference paper presented at the "International organisations and the politics of development: historical perspective". Conference organised by the Geneva Graduate Institute and the Fondation Pierre du Bois in collaboration with the University of Geneva. Geneva, 6–7 December 2013; Murphy, N. C. 2006. *The United Nations Development Programme: A Better Way?* Cambridge: Cambridge University Press; Jolly, R., Emmerij, L. and Ghai, D. P. eds. 2004. *UN Contributions to Development Thinking and Practice*. Bloomington: Indiana University Press.

37 Zanasi, M. 2007. "Exporting Development: The League of Nations and Republican China", *Comparative Studies in Society and History* 49(1): 143–169; Helleiner, E. 2014. *Forgotten foundations of Bretton Woods: International development and the making of the postwar order*. Ithaca; London: Cornell University Press; Plata-Stenger, V. 2014. "Le Bureau international du travail et la coopération technique dans l'entre-deux-guerres", *Relations internationales* 157(1): 55–69; Fiti Sinclair, G. 2016. "International Social Reform and the Invention of Development": https://ssrn.com/abstract=2842441[last accessed 12.09.2019]; Fiti Sinclair, G. 2017. *To Reform the World: International Organizations and the Making of Modern States*. Oxford: Oxford University Press.

38 Tournès, L. 2013. "Philanthropic foundations and the exportation of development". Conference paper presented at the "International organisations and the politics of development: historical perspective". Conference organised by the Geneva Graduate Institute and the Fondation Pierre du Bois in collaboration with the University of Geneva.

project and that, for the ILO, development was conceived much more as a social engineering project.

By underlining the importance of the interwar period, this research also challenges the widely shared notion that development was above all tied to decolonisation and that it was primarily a Third World concern.[39] The fact that development finds its source in the colonial and post-colonial eras is largely recognised among specialists.[40] However, this study insists on the need to broaden the geographic framework of development.[41] It stresses the diversity of regions invested by the ILO in the interwar period; from Central and Eastern Europe to the colonies, including China, Egypt – as evidenced by Butler's missions – and a number of Latin American countries.[42]

---

[39] After the Second World War, the issue of development/underdevelopment was at the centre of the debate in the social sciences. Rist, G. 2007. *Le Développement : Histoire d'une croyance occidentale*, Paris: Presses de la Fondation nationale des sciences politiques; Norel, P. 1986. *Nord-Sud: Les enjeux du développement*. Paris: Syros.

[40] Cooper, F. and Packard, R. eds. 1997. *International Development and the Social Sciences: Essays on the History and Politics of Knowledge*. Berkeley; Los Angeles [etc.]: University of California Press. See also the special issue of the *Journal of European Modern History* edited by Andreas Eckert, Stephan Malinowski and Corinna Unger in 2010: "Modernizing Missions: Approaches to "Developing" the Non-Western World after 1945" 8(1). Some studies have also drawn interesting parallels between international development, humanitarian intervention and the practices of nineteenth-century European empires: Duffield, M. and Hewitt, V. 2009. *Empire, Development & Colonialism: The Past in the Present*. Suffolk: Boydell & Brewer.

[41] Recent publications and ongoing research projects examine the relations between "North" and "South" and "East" and "South" with regards to international development. Christian, M., Kott, S., Matejka, O. 2018. *Planning in Cold War Europe. Competition, Cooperation, Circulations* (1950s-1970s). Oldenbourg: De Gruyter.

[42] Recent research has paved the way for an analysis of international organisations which takes into account non-European regions between the two world wars. However, these have tended to focus mainly on the League of Nations. McPherson, A. and Wehrli, Y. 2015. *Beyond Geopolitics: New Histories of Latin America at the League of Nations*. New Mexico: University of New Mexico Press; Andrade, J. C. Y. 2014. *L'OIT et l'Amérique du Sud (1919–1939). La construction d'un laboratoire social regional*. Phd Diss. Paris, École des hautes études en sciences sociales; Pernet, C. 2013. "Developing Nutritional Standards and Food Policy: Latin American Reformers Between the ILO, the League of Nations Health Organization, and the Pan-American Sanitary Bureau", in Droux, J., Kott, S. eds. *Globalizing Social Rights. The International Labour Organization and Beyond*, 249–61; Pernet, C. "L'OIT et la question de l'alimentation en Amérique latine (1930–1950): Les problèmes posés par la définition internationale des normes de niveau de vie" in Lespinet-Moret, I. and Viet, V. eds. *L'Organisation internationale du travail : origine, développement, avenir*, 167–78; Herrera León, F. and Wehrli, Y. 2011. "Le BIT et l'Amérique latine durant l'entre-deux-guerres: problèmes et enjeux", in Lespinet-Moret, I. and Viet, V. eds. *L'Organisation internationale du travail : origine, développement, avenir*, 157–166.

Although the question of development increasingly rouses the interest of historians of international organisations, research projects on the ILO are rare. The main reason is that the ILO has for a long time been considered an organisation devoted solely to the production of international standards. This being said, the role of the ILO in development is better known to us today, thanks to the work of Daniel Roger Maul for the post-1945 period and Guy Fiti Sinclair for the interwar period.[43] In his study, the latter insisted on the extension of the ILO's social reform mission to non-European countries, the broadening of its competence in the economic field and the development of technical assistance. Fiti Sinclair's research represents an important contribution to the history of development, but it has a number of limitations, mainly concerning his approach to international organisations. Adopting an institutional lens, Sinclair tends to view the ILO as a monolithic organisation, free of conflict and tension. However, the various discourses at the ILO reveal a rather divided view of development.[44] The other limitation stemming from limited consultation of ILO archives, is the relative emphasis placed on the interests, rationales and skills of the actors acting on behalf of the ILO. Examining the organisation through its actors allows us, on the one hand, to specify the challenges and modalities associated with the extention of ILO activities, both geographically and technically; and, on the other hand, to better understand the scope and meaning of ideas on development and technical assistance. This is the approach taken in this book.

Intensifying relations and exchanges with less developed countries (formerly known as "less industrialised" countries) directly confronted the ILO with a new problem: the implementation of international labour standards – developed on a model shaped by the experiences of Western European industrialised societies – could only be done with great difficulty and significant limitations. This gave rise, in turn, to a reflection on the limits of the normative approach; hence the emergence of a discourse on the necessity of developing practical actions to promote social progress and the improvement of living and working conditions.

---

43 Maul, D. 2012. *Human Rights, Development and Decolonization: The International Labour Organization, 1940–70.* Basingstoke, Palgrave Macmillan. Geneva: International Labour Organization; Plata, V. 2014. "Le Bureau international du travail et la coopération technique dans l'entre-deux-guerres", *Relations internationales* 157(1), 55–69; Fiti Sinclair, G. 2016. "International Social Reform and the Invention of Development". SSRN: https://ssrn.com/abstract=2842441. [last accessed 12.09.2019]; Fiti Sinclair, G. 2017. "A Civilizing Task: The International Labour Organization, Social Reform and the Genealogy of Development", *Journal of the History of International Law*, 1–53; Fiti Sinclair, G. 2017. *To Reform the World. International Organizations and the Making of Modern States.* Oxford: Oxford University Press.
44 Plata-Stenger, V. 2018. "L'OIT et le problème du sous-développement en Asie dans l'entre-deux-guerres", *Le Mouvement Social* 263(2): 109–122.

This reflection was anchored in a set of practices, which incidentally predate the ILO's own existence. Indeed, before contributing to its internationalisation, the ILO drew inspiration, first and foremost, from the European social reformist movement. It was the bearer of a particular view on development, based on the belief that a world order could be built on common legal principles, equally applicable to all peoples and cultures. It was also founded on the notion that societies can be transformed by science, a hypothesis that rests at the heart of the social engineering project developed since the end of the nineteenth century in Europe and the United States. The ILO's development thinking rested on three principles: international organisation of the economy with the aim of improving the living standards of workers, economic and social planning, and modernisation.[45] This analysis focuses on these themes, for three core reasons. First, because they significantly mobilised ILO international civil servants during the 1930s and earlier, and were the source of major scientific and documentary production. Second, because they reflect the aspirations and demands of a large portion of ILO members at the time, especially the workers, namely that the organisation be used as an instrument to regulate and organise the economy. Third, because these themes did not disappear with the end of the Second World War and continued to infuse the ILO's rationale during the implementation of its post-war action program, both for the reconstruction of Europe and for development.[46]

---

[45] Regarding the economic ideas developed by the ILO, see Aglan, A., Feiertag, O., and Kevonian, D. eds. 2011. *Humaniser le travail. Régimes économiques, régimes politiques et Organisation internationale du Travail 1929–1969*. Bruxelles, Bern: PIE Lang; Endres, A. M., and Fleming, G. A. 2002. *International Organizations and the Analysis of Economic Policy, 1919–1950*. Cambridge: Cambridge University Press. For a study of economic networks and their interactions with international organisations in the interwar period, see Clavin, P. and Wessels, J.-W. 2005. "Transnationalism and the League of Nations: Understanding the Work of its Economic and Financial Organisation", *Contemporary European History* 14(4): 465–492, Decorzant, Y. 2011. *La Société des Nations et la naissance d'une conception de la régulation économique internationale*, Bruxelles: Peter Lang; Clavin, P. 2013. *Securing the World Economy*.

[46] Historians of Europe have recently tried to link development to European history, not only for the post-war period, but also for the beginning of the twentieth century, and even to some extent, the end of the nineteenth century. These researchers invite us not only to go beyond the category of reconstruction, but also to understand how the idea of development was designed in Europe and then disseminated in developing countries. Grabas, C. and Nützenadel, A. 2014. *Industrial Policy in Europe after 1945: Wealth, Power and Economic Development in the Cold War*, Basingstoke: Palgrave Macmillan. A conference on this topic was organised by Michele Alacevich, Sandrine Kott and Mark Mazower: "Development and Underdevelopment in Post-War Europe". The Heyman Center for the Humanities, Columbia University, 10 October 2014. Paul N. Rosenstein-Rodan's article was perhaps the first to recall the importance of Central

Another important contribution made by this book is the attention paid to practices, often overlooked by historiographies on development. Analyses that have stressed the importance of the interwar period and the 1940s as a laboratory for practices on international development predominantly focus on the technical activities of the League of Nations.[47] Regarding the ILO, little exists on the subject.[48] Although development only became enshrined as an institutionalised practice after the Second World War, examining ILO activities shows that some tools first emerged in the 1930s, before development programmes genuinely took shape. For instance, the ILO became a space to gradually build knowledge and craft scientific techniques of development. The study of the modes of knowledge production on development is a little-known field and existing research has primarily focused on poverty and gross domestic product (GDP) measurement.[49] Another significant contribution made by this research is therefore to shed light on the ILO's role as a space where development science was gradually built. This study also focuses on the missions of technical assistance organised by the International Labour Office, which reflect the key role played by advice and expertise in the diffusion of an international social normativity. These missions were born of growing ties between the implementation of social standards, measures to combat the effect of the Great Depression and increasing government involvement in economic organisation. In the 1930s the ILO, much like

---

Europe as a field for development: Rosenstein-Rodan, P. N. 1944. "The International Development of Economically Backward Areas", *International Affairs* 20(2) 157–165. For a historiographical discussion, see Mazower, M. 2011. "Reconstruction. The Historiographical Issues", in Mazower, M., Reinisch, J., Feldman, D. eds. *Post–war Reconstruction in Europe. International Perspectives, 1945–1949*, 17–28. Oxford: Oxford University Press.

47 Osterhammel, J. 1979. "Technical Co-Operation between the League of Nations and China", *Modern Asian Studies* 13(4): 661–680; Zanasi, M. 2007. "Exporting Development: The League of Nations and Republican China", *Comparative Studies in Society and History* 49(1): 143–169; Beyersdorf, F. 2011. "'Credit or Chaos'? The Austrian Stabilisation Programme of 1923 and the League of Nations", in Laqua, D. ed. *Internationalism Reconfigured. Transnational Ideas and Movements between the World Wars*, 135–157. London: Tauris.

48 Dupuy, M. 1956. *L'Assistance technique et financière aux pays insuffisamment développés*. Ed. A. Pedone: Paris; Johnston, G. 1970. *The International Labour Organisation. Its Work for Social and Economic Progress*. London: Europa Publications; Alcock, A. 1971. *History of the International Labour Organisation*, 134–148. London: Palgrave Macmillan; Ghebali, V.-Y. 1975. "Organisation internationale et guerre mondiale. Le cas de la société des nations et de l'organisation internationale du travail pendant la seconde guerre mondiale." PhD. dissert., Science politique, Grenoble 2, 47–48.

49 Speich Chassé, D. 2008. "Traveling with the GDP Through Early Development Economics History", *Working Papers on the Nature of Evidence: How Well Do Facts Travel?*", n°33. http://eprints.lse.ac.uk/22501/1/3308Speich.pdf. [last accessed 12.09.2019].

the League of Nations, conceived of the economy as a problem specific to social action, requiring scientific analysis and political regulation. It is precisely in this context that the International Labour Office's missions of technical assistance are analysed, missions through which the Office promoted the diffusion of modern social practices and standards, state involvement in economic organisation and the institutionalisation of social policy.[50] However, strictly speaking the interwar period saw no development programmes such as those that emerged in the 1940s.[51]

Analysing the missions of technical assistance shines light on the transnational dimension of the construction of the welfare state.[52] This study pays particular attention to issues such as the methods used, as well as collaborative or oppositional dynamics surrounding exchange practices. However, this book assesses the impacts of technical assistance from the perspective of the International Labour Office and offers little insights on the effects of social reforms in certain countries. It instead sheds light on the available resources and means mobilised by international experts, which remain under explored today.[53] It is striking how little attention has been given to individual actors, to the "experts" themselves, located as they were at the very heart of the modernisation process.[54] A detailed analysis of these practices aims to elucidate the means by

---

[50] Théry, I. 2005. "Expertises de service, de consensus, d'engagement : essai de typologie de la mission d'expertise en sciences sociales", *Droit et Société* 2(60): 311–329.

[51] As William C. Kirby points out with regard to the League's experts: "Never was there articulated a developmental philosophy behind all their activities. There was, however, a consistent pattern of advice regarding economic, technical, and educational development in favor of a state-managed, centralised approach to economic development emphasising the promise of scientific and engineering expertise." Kirby, W. C. 2000. "Engineering China: Birth of the Developmental State, 1928–1937", in Yeh, W.-H. ed. *Becoming Chinese: Passages to Modernity and beyond*, 147–148. Berkeley: University of California Press.

[52] There are a number of publications that explore the construction of the welfare state in Europe on an international scale. For those studying the role of the ILO, see Kettunen, P. 2013. "The ILO as a Forum for Developing and Demonstrating a Nordic Model", in Droux, J., Kott, S. eds. *Globalizing Social Rights. The international Labour Organization and Beyond*, 210–230; Kott, S. 2010. "Constructing a European Social Model: The Fight for Social Insurance in the Interwar Period", in Van Daele, J. et al. *ILO Histories. Essays on the International Labour Organization and Its Impact on the World During the Twentieth Century*, 173–196.

[53] Backouche, I. 2006. "Expertise", *Genèses* 65(4): 2–3. This journal devoted two special issues to the theme of expertise, in 2006 and 2008.

[54] There are some exceptions. Webster, D. 2011. "Development Advisors in a Time of Cold War and Decolonization: The United Nations Technical Assistance Administration, 1950–1959", *Journal of Global History* 6(2): 249–272; Hodge, J. M. 2010. "British Colonial Expertise, Post-Colonial Carreering and the Early History of International Development", *Journal of Modern European His-*

which international experts came to influence reform processes. This requires us, however, to go beyond a purely instrumental view of international expertise, and to look to knowledge models. This approach is directly inspired by the contributions made by the postmodern critique of the late 1970s, which marked an important evolution in the study of development. The most critical authors, such as Gilbert Rist, Arturo Escobar, Wolfgang Sachs and Serge Latouche, insisted on the necessity of deconstructing the framework surrounding ideas on development, which they saw above all as a component of Western imperialism.[55] Though it is clear that the International Labour Office's technical assistance functioned as a system, dominated by representations of Western countries and marked by a civilising ideology, this research focuses in particular on the material and psychological conditions out of which experts emerged, the type of expertise they were asked to provide, and the strategies they put in place to insure the promotion of ILO models. A sociological study of expertise is hence proposed, with the aim of uncovering the social resources that gave these agents the authority to act on an international scale, focusing in particular on their training and professional careers in the national space.

Archival Materials

The archives held at the ILO in Geneva constitute the main body of sources used in this research. Since development was not an institutionalised practice in the 1930s and 1940s, I began by collecting the materials on the general activities of the ILO (series G), in particular one of its sub-series, which contains all the missions of international civil servants and related activities (series G 900). This initial work made it possible to identify the ILO's missions of technical assistance. The information collected was then systematically cross-referenced with the official reports of ILO Directors, as well as the minutes of ILCs and GB meetings

---

tory, Special Issue on "Modernizing Missions: Approaches to 'Developing' the Non-Western World after 1945" 8(1): 24–46; Zanasi, M. 2007. "Exporting Development: The League of Nations and Republican China", *Comparative Studies in Society and History* 49(1): 143–169; Mitchell, T. 2002. *Rule of experts: Egypt, techno-politics, modernity*. Berkeley [etc.]: University of California Press.

55 Rist, G. 2007. *Le Développement: Histoire d'une croyance occidentale*. Paris: Presses de la Fondation nationale des sciences politiques; Escobar, A. 1995. *Encountering Development. The Making and Unmaking of the Third World*, 40. Princeton, Oxford: Princeton University Press; Wolfgang, S. ed. 2010. *The Development Dictionary. A Guide to Knowledge as Power*. London; New York: Zed Books; Latouche, S. 2005. *L'Occidentalisation du monde. Essai sur la signification, la portée et les limites de l'uniformisation planétaire*. Paris: La Découverte.

between 1929 and 1949. The relatively small number of missions of technical assistance carried out during this period encouraged me to adopt a global approach. However, due to the limitations of the available information, I was not able to analyse all missions with equivalent qualitative treatment. However, some of them, which involve inter-institutional collaboration, were further investigated in other archival collections held at UNESCO in Paris and at the Rockefeller Archive Center in New York. From these missions, it was possible to explore a rich and complex set of themes, which in turn mobilised a considerable number of ILO archives, ranging from the Cabinet files, the various Divisions and Sections files, to the reports and studies produced by ILO civil servants, as well as articles published in specialised journals and the *International Labour Review*. In order to reflect the importance of the actors, a central aspect of this research, I have also carried out a systematic examination of the personal files of ILO civil servants, which allowed me to propose a typology of the expert engaged in technical assistance between the two world wars and, more generally, to understand the role of international organisations in the construction of new socio-professional identities. This information was supplemented by the consultation of private archival funds, which made it possible to place international civil servants in specific environments and to restore the logic of their national trajectory before entering the ILO. Finally, I also had the opportunity to consult the National Archives and Records Administration archives in Washington, in particular the holdings of the Labor Department and the Social Security Board (SSB). These archives were intended to provide a better understanding of the collaborations between the ILO and the United States administration, particularly in the context of the Second World War. However, these funds, which are largely dedicated to domestic activities, provide little information on these aspects, and ILO files generally contain duplicates of existing documents in the ILO archives.

Research Structure

This book is structured using two thematic sections. The first analyses the links between the emergence of a development discourse and the technical and geographical expansion of the ILO. In this section, I argue that the ILO universalisation strategy goes hand in hand with a growing concern for the application of international conventions in less industrialised countries within and outside Europe, the rebalancing of the world economy and, more generally, for the ILO's place and purpose in an expanding world. This last point is important and makes it possible to consider the emergence of development ideas and technical assistance as an aspect of the international technical diplomacy that the ILO was trying to build at that time. Chapter 1 demonstrates that Europe was a particularly important experiential laboratory for the ILO. The discourse of the Office Directors and its work on the elaboration of an international normativity on national and international social planning reveals the seeds of a reflection on the role of public investment in resource development in Europe and its less developed regions. For Albert Thomas, state intervention and public works were the keys to national and international economic development and social progress. He tried to persuade ILO members, albeit with limited success, of the necessity to organise an international public works programme as a way not only to fight massive unemployment, but also to develop consumption and production, especially in Eastern Europe. The way in which the Office sought to lead Europe out of the economic crisis attests to the emergence of a matrix thinking on development. Chapter 2 analyses the development of collaborations with Latin America that were at the heart of new institutional practices, such as ILO regional conferences. Chapter 3 focuses on the Office's work in Asia. It shows how the ILO participated in the construction of the "under-development" issue, while seeking to export social progress to Asia. The strengthening of international cooperation with this region in the 1930s was above all motivated by a desire to find solutions to the risks of economic and social dumping in less developed countries. The evolution of the Office's perception of social problems in the colonies, especially India, sheds light on the will to inscribe the question of colonial labour within the broader frameworks of production modernisation, as well as nutrition and housing improvement. Madeleine Herren (2013), examining the case of India, exposed how this colony managed to use the international platform offered by the ILO to articulate new demands and achieve a certain form of political independence.[56] My analysis strives to pursue this matter further by linking the ILO's colonial activities with the theme of development. While, in the 1930s, the ILO attempted to "modernise" practices without questioning colonial exploitation – a phenomenon already perceived by other colonial historians[57] – its reflections took place in an ambiguous context, marked by European imperialism and its "civilising mission" on the one hand, and the desire to liberalise trade (a central aspect of US internationalism) and to integrate the colonies into the international economy on the other hand.

---

56 Herren, M. 2013. "Global corporatism after World War I, the Indian case", in Droux, J., Kott, S. eds. *Globalizing Social Rights. The international Labour Organization and Beyond*, 137–152.
57 Cooper, F. 1997. "Modernizing Bureaucrats, Backward Africans, and the Development Concept", in Cooper, F. and Packard R. eds. *International Development and the Social Sciences*, 64–192. Berkeley: University of California Press.

The second section of the book is concerned with the emergence of development tools and practices. Chapter 4 focuses on how the Office scientifically defined and constructed the notion of "standard of living", which became central in the debates on how the ILO could develop economic exchanges and drive the integration of less developed countries into the international economy. An analysis of statistical research on workers' standard of living, along with the first attempts to define the concept and the elaboration of methods allowing international comparison of living standards illustrates how a science of development was gradually being formulated by the International Labour Office. Chapter 5 takes a closer look at the actors that were mobilised for the missions of technical assistance. A study of international civil servants' profiles and careers, along with the prevailing logic that led to their recruitment is crucial if we are to understand the Office's use of technical assistance. Chapters 6 and 7 provide two case studies, namely the missions to Romania and Greece in 1930, as well as Venezuela between 1936 and 1938. These case studies aim to provide a concrete vision of the ILO's practice of technical assistance. In turn, the difficulties stemming from the geographic displacement of the actors' cultural backgrounds at the time provide a reflection on the limits of technical assistance, and on the impact it may have had on the civil servants involved. This research ends with the Second World War, where the Office's technical assistance efforts continued. Chapter 8 interrogates the impact of the war on technical assistance and measures the extent to which the conflict provided new intellectual and institutional grounds for the ILO's involvement in development after 1945.

First Part
Development as a Universalisation Strategy

Chapter I
Europe's Economic Recovery: the Emergence of a Matrix Thinking on Development

> What the crisis has managed to delay and hamper is the confident development of mutual international obligations, the voluntary cooperation of all states – one so painstainkingly established, after centuries of conflict and war, but made even more difficult by these kinds of instinctive retractions, where nations withdraw into themselves, where peoples rush into isolated units.[1]

This excerpt from Albert Thomas' 1932 report reflects the moral crisis of internationalism and speaks to what a number of historians of international relations have interpreted as the end of international cooperation in the 1930s. Giving way to discouragement, Thomas recognised that the Great Depression had hampered the expansion of social policy. This statement was followed by self-criticism, which he felt was essential if the ILO was to emerge unscathed from the storm, and stay afloat.[2] Certainly, the crisis had had a direct impact on the institution. In his opinion however, far from demonstrating its futility, it rendered the ILO more vital than ever. This discourse was directly tied to a decline in the number of international conventions that were being ratified. Having culminated at 79 between 1928 and 1929, their number began spiralling downward, with 44 ratifications between 1929 and 1930, 38 in 1930, and 28 by the end of 1933.[3] For an organisation whose very mission was the diffusion of an international normativity, this trend was extremely worrisome. For the International Labour Office it became clear that the standardisation of labour conditions brought forth by the adoption of international standards elaborated since 1919 was on the verge of being swept away. Thomas, who perceived that the Office's usefulness could no longer be measured solely by the progress of ratified conventions, urged the ILO to formulate concrete remedies to the Great Depression. International economic organisation and economic and social planning were the issues he wished to situate at the core of this debate.

The appeal of planist ideas in the 1930s caused a change in how the Office came to perceive the role of social policy. Labour issues were seen as part of a national economic recovery strategy, designed first and foremost on a European scale. The Office's discourse also reveals the seeds of a reflection on the role of

---

1 Director's Report, ILC, 1932, 899, ILOA.
2 *Ibid.*, 875.
3 *Ibid.*, 877.

public investment in resource development in less developed regions, particularly in Central and Eastern Europe. The way in which the International Labour Office formulated its social policies in times of crisis attests to the emergence of a matrix thinking on development. Planning, technocratic approaches to economic and social problems, along with the idea of development itself, converged at the heart of the ILO's thoughts on the means to help Europe exit the economic crisis. As a key actor in its internationalisation, observing the ILO can thus reveal the scope of the movement in favour of international planning. As of 1931, Thomas ushered the ILO towards the promotion of an international policy of public works, presented as a means to tackle the mass unemployment generated by the Great Depression, as well as a model for economic and social development.

In this chapter, I aim to shed light on the role played by the International Labour Office and its Directors in the development and dissemination of a discourse on economic and social planning, well before the emergence of the theories on development that would come after the Second World War. In the 1930s, Albert Thomas and his successor, Harold Butler, promoted a rational organisation of state-run economies.[4] The present inquiry will begin by highlighting Thomas' intellectual and political trajectory, which was profoundly marked by the planning experiments introduced in Europe by the First World War. His experiments, focused on employment, the organisation of production and the development of consumption, deeply influenced the Office's perception and analysis of the economic crisis. This heterodox position then naturally leads me to study the various influences that infused the Office's discourse on economic planning. The actors and institutions that inspired the ILO are of particular interest here. Until Thomas' death in 1932, the Office's discourse was directly and heavily influenced by French sociology and reformist socialism.[5] The American rationalist movement, in particular its Taylorist branch, was also an important source of inspiration.[6] This analysis will question the pertinence of planist ideas after Thomas'

---

4 A few studies on the Office's economic ideas already exist. Aglan, A., Feiertag, O., Kevonian, D. eds. 2011. *Humaniser le travail. Régimes économiques, régimes politiques et Organisation internationale du travail, 1929–1969.* Brussels, Bern: PIE Lang; Endres, A. M., Fleming, G. A. 2002. *International Organizations and the Analysis of Economic Policy, 1919–1950.* Cambridge: Cambridge University Press.

5 Dhermy-Mairal, M. 2015. "Durkheimisme scientifique et durkheimisme d'action. François Simiand et le Bureau international du travail (1920–1930)", *Revue Française de Sociologie*, 4(56): 673–696. See also "Les Sciences sociales et l'action au Bureau international du travail (1920–1939) ", PhD diss., 2015, EHESS.

6 Cayet, T. 2010. *Rationaliser le travail, organiser la production: le Bureau international du travail et la modernisation économique durant l'entre-deux-guerres.* Rennes: Presses universitaires de Rennes.

death and the subsequent nomination of British liberal Harold Butler in his place. In the context of this new direction, I will further analyse the increasing influence of the United States on ILO's economic programme.

1 Albert Thomas, Reformism and the First World War

The International Labour Office's position in favour of an organised economy was closely tied to its Director's personality, which gave an entirely novel raison d'être to the Office by making it an institution prioritising economic organisation as a condition for social progress. Thomas' thinking stemmed directly from his intellectual trajectory prior to the First World War and from his experience in economic planning during the war.

1.1 Planning Under Socialist Reformism

The emergence of the planist movement in Europe found its source in the experiences of early nineteenth-century European industrial societies. At this time, capitalism and the industrial revolution had shaken these societies and provoked an unprecedented mobilisation in favour of state intervention in the struggle against the evils of industrialisation and poverty. The state's capacity to meet society's needs rapidly became a gauge of its modernity. Ideas on modernisation, the rational organisation of societies and increasing state intervention thus joined the reformist theories of the nineteenth century.[7] Albert Thomas' career and the intellectual influences he embraced were representative of this phenomenon. In his way, on his own scale, Thomas played a central role in the promotion, first in France, then internationally, of the values of socialist reformism as a model for economic and social development.

In 1914 Thomas was 36 years old and already well accomplished intellectually and politically.[8] Having enrolled at the École normale supérieure (ENS) on

---

[7] Nemo, P. 2013. *Histoire des idées politiques aux Temps modernes et contemporains*. Paris: PUF.
[8] Among the writings on Albert Thomas, see Cabanes, B. 2014. *The Great War and the Origins of Humanitarianism, 1918–1924*. Cambridge: Cambridge University Press, Chapter 2; 2008. "Albert Thomas, société mondiale et internationalisme. Réseaux et institutions des années 1890 aux années 1930", *Les Cahiers Irice* 2(2) special issue; Fine, M. 1977. "Albert Thomas: a reformer's vision of modernization, 1914–1932", *Journal of Contemporary History* 12(3): 545–564; Rebérioux, M., Fridenson, P. 1974. "Albert Thomas, pivot du réformisme français", *Le Mouvement social* 87: 85–97; Schaper, B. W. 1960. Albert Thomas, trente ans de réformisme social. Paris: PUF.

Ulm Street in 1899, an amateur of history, labour issues and socialist doctrines, Thomas obtained his diploma in history in 1902. During his university years, he established relations with the economist Edgard Milhaud and the geographer Fernand Maurette, both of whom would soon become pillars of economic research at the International Labour Office, alongside Arthur Fontaine, the future first chairman of the ILO Governing Body. It was also within the framework of the ENS that Thomas was influenced by the great figures of French socialism of the late nineteenth century, such as Lucien Herr, Charles Andler and Jean Jaurès, with whom he collaborated on the magazine *L'Humanité* from 1904 onwards. The ENS also provided him with the intellectual material to develop his ideas in economic matters. Thomas became familiar with the economics of Adam Smith, Marx and Engels. He studied the utopian socialism of Saint-Simon, which he would himself describe in 1925 as one of "construction and organisation".[9] At the heart of Saint-Simonian thought, which undeniably marked Thomas, is the idea that, through the use of scientific and technical knowledge, society can and should be organised, planned and constructed, just as a machine is by an engineer.[10] This way of thinking generally nourished reformist socialism, with its desire to correct the negative effects of capitalism, through the rational organisation of the economy.[11]

Moreover, while Thomas was inspired by French socialist thought and drew his references from the social experience in France, it is precisely this reformist socialist movement that would influence him irreversibly, more specifically the works of the German Social Democrat Eduard Bernstein.[12] Bernstein's theories on social modernisation and the role of the state were a possible response to French socialism, which was divided on Marx's theories at the time, particularly that of the decline of the state. The influence of Bernstein's ideas on Thomas and on what would become the reformist branch of French socialism is important in that it determined a certain vision of development organised around the state. A revisionist theorist, Bernstein defended progressive reforms as the only possible path to the peaceful realisation of the socialist ideal. Thomas explicitly referred to himself as such in 1919 when, at a banquet of the *Socialist Review*, he declared: "We will forever be revisionists. We will always seek and try to see exactly

---

9 Schaper, B. W. 1960, 20.
10 Dominique, G., Amy, J. 2002. "Biology-inspired Sociology of the Nineteenth Century: A Science of Social 'Organization'", *Revue française de sociologie* 43(1): 123–155.
11 Hobsbawm, E. 2008. *L'Âge des extrêmes: histoire du court XXe siècle: 1914–1991*, 126. Bruxelles: A. Versaille.
12 Jousse, E. 2008. "Du révisionnisme d'Eduard Bernstein au réformisme d'Albert Thomas (1896–1914)", *Les Cahiers Irice* 2(2): 39–52.

how socialist doctrine, how the socialist hypothesis can explain exactly the new facts of economic evolution, and adapt to them."[13]

Thomas met Bernstein in 1902, through Charles Andler, on a research trip to Germany. This stay, during which he frequented revisionist and reformist circles in Germany, profoundly marked him, as did the spectacle of a rapidly developing society, the impact of industrial production on working conditions and the aspirations of German trade union organisations.[14] This trip resulted in a book entitled *Le Syndicalisme allemand. Résumé historique, 1848–1903*, published in 1903. More than his theories, it is Bernstein's practical proposals that seduced Thomas, who became a fervent proponent of his ideas upon his return to France, when he successively directed *La Revue syndicaliste* (1905–1910) and then *La Revue socialiste*. However, Bernstein's reformism was never diffused as such in France, it was rather reinterpreted and adapted to the national context.[15] Bernstein's ideas served as long as they provided support for the political ambition of some young French socialists to integrate the newly formed French Section of the Workers' International (SFIO) into the Republic. Thomas put his socialist commitment into practice as early as 1904, as the first socialist member of Champigny's municipal council, and again in 1910 and 1914, as deputy of the Seine. The importance of the municipal experience was made clear by the fact that it was his first opportunity to propose certain ideas on economic organisation from a socialist perspective. More specifically, he advocated for the municipal management of all economic services of public interest, an essential step towards the creation of a socialist society. In the same spirit but on a different scale, between 1912 and 1913, he defended the nationalisation of the railways before the National Assembly. Thomas was then reporting officer for the railways' budget.[16]

1.2 The Experience of the First World War

Thomas' ideas on economic organisation were first widely applied during the First World War. As Minister of Armaments between 1916 and 1917, he developed

---

[13] Schaper, B. W. 1960, 69. Original quote in French: "Nous serons éternellement des révisionnistes. Nous chercherons toujours et nous tâcherons de voir exactement comment la doctrine socialiste, comment l'hypothèse socialiste peut expliquer exactement les faits nouveaux de l'évolution économique, et s'adapter à eux."
[14] Letter from Thomas to Desjardins, January 17, 1903. Cited in change Schaper, B. W. 1960, 28.
[15] Jousse, E. 2008. 51.
[16] Fridenson, P., Griset, P. eds. 2018. *L'industrie dans la Grande Guerre: colloque des 15 et 16 novembre 2016*, 222. Paris: Comité pour l'histoire économique et financière de la France.

new methods in many areas of economic and social activity and demonstrated the possibilities for the labour movement to participate directly in the economic development of the country.[17] War thus played a central role in widening pre-war reformist perspectives, without ever becoming the dominant current within French socialism.

The reconversion of the peacetime economy to war production and the introduction of industrial planning marked the loss of influence of the liberal ideology "as a source of legitimisation of economic power".[18] This movement was both European and American. The liberal Lloyd George in Great Britain and the industrialist Walther Rathenau in Germany experimented with the organisation of production at the same time as Thomas. In the United States, the war saw the emergence of the first generation of planners, who created new administrative and economic institutions such as the Industrial Commission and the Industrial Relations Commission.[19] However, Thomas was mainly inspired by the German model. As Martin Fine noted (1977): "At this time, the United States was not as yet viewed as a model for war-time industrial mobilisation".[20]

In particular, war required the coordination of industrial activities. As minister, Thomas organised and modernised war production. The supervision of armaments led to the introduction of modern production and management techniques. Thomas centralised orders for raw materials, promoted the construction and coordination of war factories in the name of production efficiency, and organised the recruitment and training of workers in mass production techniques. Thomas' position was clearly technocratic and based on the conviction that class oppositions could be overcome by the scientific organisation of production.[21] Rationalisation was also at the heart of his programme and he advocated the mechanisation of war factory work through the introduction of overhead cranes, levers and assembly lines.[22] At the same time, the economic policy Thomas pursued

---

17 Hardach, G. 1977. "La mobilisation industrielle en 1914–1918: production, planification et idéologie", in Fridenson, P., Becker, J., & Berstein, S. *1914–1918: L'autre front* (Cahiers du "Mouvement social" 2), 81–109. Paris: Les Ed. ouvrières.
18 *Ibid.*, 81.
19 Reagan, P. D. 1999. *Designing a New America. The Origins of the New Deal Planning, 1890–1943*. Amherst: University of Massachusetts Press.
20 Fine, M. 1977. "Albert Thomas: a reformer's vision of modernization, 1914–1932", *Journal of Contemporary History* 12(3): 547.
21 Maier, C. S. 1970. "Between Taylorism and Technocracy: European Ideologies and the Vision of Industrial Productivity in the 1920s", *Journal of Contemporary History* 5(2): 27–61.
22 Hennebicque, A. 1977. "Albert Thomas et le régime des usines de guerre", in Fridenson, P., Becker, J., & Berstein, S. *1914–1918 : L'autre front* (Cahiers du "Mouvement social" 2), 126–30. Paris: Les Ed. ouvrières.

was firmly committed to improving working conditions. For example, he facilitated the creation of several social institutions and the modernisation of social policies in factories, particularly those directly affecting women: allowances for working mothers, nurseries, breastfeeding rooms in factories and dispensaries in the event of industrial accidents.[23] The institutions he helped create enabled the working class to actively participate in the conversion to mass production methods and Taylorism.[24]

In his new role, Thomas was surrounded by a small group of experts, technicians and economists, such as Mario Roques, the future Director of the Office's correspondence office in Paris, Arthur Fontaine and William Oualid. In 1916, he chose the French socialist Marius Viple as chief of cabinet, who in 1920 would be appointed to the same post at the International Labour Office. During the war, Thomas also surrounded himself with Durkheimers, including François Simiand, Maurice Halbwachs and Hubert Bourgin.[25] Maurice Halbwachs joined Thomas at the Ministry of Armament as an expert on requisitioned raw materials.[26] As early as 1915, Simiand became Thomas' deputy chief of staff. The economic and social conceptions developed by Thomas were thus strongly influenced by Durkheimian sociology. In 1920, Thomas brought together several of these personalities with whom he had collaborated during the war. There is thus continuity between the networks of socialism and Durkheimian sociology and, accordingly, the development of reformist socialism during the war and the Office's activities.

---

23 Downs, L. L. 1995. *Manufacturing Inequality: Gender Division in the French and British Metalworking Industries, 1914–1939*. Ithaca: Cornell University Press; Downs, L. L. 2003. "Les marraines élues de la paix sociale? Les surintendantes d'usine et la rationalisation du travail en France (1917–1935)", in Prost, A. ed. *Guerres, paix et sociétés : 1911–1946*, 219–242. Paris: Éditions de l'Atelier.
24 Fine, M. 1977. "Albert Thomas: a reformer's vision of modernization, 1914–1932", *Journal of Contemporary History* 12(3): 549.
25 Dhermy-Mairal, M. 2015. "Durkheimisme scientifique et durkheimisme d'action. François Simiand et le Bureau international du travail (1920–1930)", *Revue Française de Sociologie*, 4(56): 673–696. Mario Roques, Maurice Halbwachs and François Simiand were involved in a series of initiatives related to the reform movement, where they made their first steps as social experts. Halbwachs and Roques, but also Fernand Maurette, were members of the Société des Visiteurs, composed of doctors, engineers, sociologists and lawyers. This organisation's mission was to conduct social surveys on the standard of living of families. Dab, S. 1999. "Bienfaisance et socialisme au tournant du siècle: la Société des Visiteurs, 1898–1902", in Topalov, C. ed. *Laboratoires du nouveau siècle. La nébuleuse réformatrice et ses réseaux en France, 1880–1914*, 219–235. Paris: EHESS.
26 Becker, J.-J. 2008. "Albert Thomas, d'un siècle à l'autre. Bilan de l'expérience de guerre", *Les Cahiers Irice* 2(2): 9–15.

The end of the war steered the debate directly to economic reconstruction. Thomas continued to disseminate his ideas on the organisation of production, rationalisation and reformist trade unionism, while promoting collaboration between management and workers. But Thomas was increasingly isolated, with 1917 marking the beginning of his decline on the French political scene. The crisis in Ribot's Cabinet, the rejection of the government's socialists, Thomas' exclusion from the ruling sphere and finally Georges Clemenceau's appointment to the presidency of the Council of Ministers, deprived him of any possibility of holding a leadership position in French public life.[27] In fact, only the reformist wing of the party upheld the celebration of industrial mobilisation as a legacy of socialist policy. By the end of the war, these ideas had lost their strength. For French industrialists, the establishment of state control over economic activity was an experiment that was never meant to extend beyond the period of national defence. While most of Thomas' reforms did not survive the post-war period, their ephemeral existence had forged his conviction that the economy could and should be organised nationally and internationally. In particular, the Allied cooperation persuaded him of the need to abandon free trade as an economic doctrine.[28] Thomas' 1920 appointment as Director of the International Labour Office gave his career an unexpected boost, along with a new opportunity to promote economic organisation, this time within the framework of international cooperation.

2 International Planning and the ILO's Hopes for European Economic Reconstruction Leadership

In the 1930s, the ILO constituted an essential space for the expression of planist ideas, partly under the influence of Thomas, then animated by the desire to place the ILO at the centre of the debates and to develop a planning model based on tripartite cooperation. Thomas' 1932 report constitutes an interesting document in analysing the Office's response to the Great Depression. Taking stock of activities carried out throughout the year, these annual reports also have a forward-looking dimension. From this point of view, the discourse on the economic crisis developed by Thomas can be considered an attempt to "shape economic reality"

---

[27] For an analysis of the relationship between Clemenceau and Thomas, see Schaper, B. W. 1960, 155–172.
[28] See his speech at the thirteenth national congress, held in Lille on 13 and 14 May 1926. *Fédération nationale des coopératives de consommation*, 198. Paris: impression l'Émancipatrice.

in order to promote a certain social policy, and its positioning as a strategy to (re)conquer the international legitimacy that had been lost.[29]

2.1 Expanding ILO Authority to the Economy

For Thomas, the Great Depression was, above all, an unemployment crisis, which the Office estimated at 20 million people in 1931. This diagnostic was not new and had already been at the heart of the Office's economic policy since the 1920s.[30] The Office had in fact always defended an integrated approach to social and economic problems and the 1932 report speaks once again to this link. For Thomas, mass unemployment could be explained by an unequal distribution of wealth and the imbalance between production and consumption. The conclusion he reached was the following: emerging from the crisis was impossible without an in-depth transformation of the economy. What Thomas advocated was a transformation of capitalism, the creation of a new economic order that distanced itself from laissez-faire. According to him, the Great Depression had in fact demonstrated that the markets alone could not provide the necessary conditions for economic growth and social welfare. Several international meetings also bear witness to this trend. In 1931, the International Chamber of Commerce (ICC) and the International Union of the League of Nations publicly declared themselves in favour of an international economic organisation. Likewise, Catholic circles were taking part in the debate with the publication of the encyclical *Quadragesimo Anno*, which called on the various nations to engage in international economic cooperation. At its July 1931 congress, the Labour and Socialist International expressed the hope that an alternative to the laissez-faire capitalist system would be found.[31] The great challenge for Thomas would be to demonstrate that this new economic order he so dearly wished to see realised could not be accomplished without taking into consideration the issue of labour, which is to say, without the ILO. He saw in the 1930s' economic crisis an opportunity to regain authority on the economic front.

---

[29] Maris, B. 2002. "Légitimation, autolégitimation, discours expert et discours savant", in Maris, B. ed. *La Légitimation du discours économique*, 109–121. Toulouse: Presses universitaires du Mirail.
[30] Feiertag, O. 2008. "Réguler la mondialisation: Albert Thomas, les débuts du BIT et la crise économique mondiale de 1920–1923", *Les Cahiers Irice 2(2):* 127–155; Liebeskind-Sauthier, I. 2005. "L'Organisation internationale du travail face au chômage: entre compétences normatives et recherche de solutions économiques, 1919–1939". PhD diss., University of Geneva.
[31] Director's Report, ILC, 1932, 926, ILOA.

Indeed, the economy remained a field in which the Office did not, a priori, have any authority, despite the fact that it had looked to impose itself on this front since the 1920s, namely by studying national policies to reduce unemployment, promoting the introduction of unemployment insurance, addressing issues of national monetary policy, and establishing international statistics on unemployment.[32] These actions were widely criticised by employer delegates, who disapproved of the Office's pretense at bringing economic solutions to the problem of unemployment. The international production of an economic discourse hence collided with the interest of national actors and highlighted the potential power that this "addition to 'the international agenda'" might yield. [33] While it did not lead to political change, it nonetheless imposed on those actors an obligation to analyse the issues raised by the Office. The production of economic expertise by the Office during these first few years was thus inseparable from a strengthening of the right "to express an opinion on the functioning of the economy in order to understand its mechanisms in relation to the problems of the world of labour".[34] The issue was crucial on two other levels. First, at the very same time, discussions had started regarding a possible reform of the League of Nations and the possibility of turning it into an economic organisation. However, in Thomas' view, the ILO should be given this jurisdiction.[35] Second, the economic and social crisis had spurred an institutional crisis at the ILO. The development models carried forth by Germany, the USSR, Japan and Italy directly contrasted with the democratic model it defended. The withdrawal of Germany in 1933, of Italy in 1937, and of Japan in 1938 would confirm Thomas' apprehensions, which were that the ILO was no longer a vital political space. But in 1932, the die had not yet been cast. This explained the energy with which Thomas insisted that ILO representatives use the Office to seek common economic solutions. He believed that, if it did not, the future of the ILO would

---

32 Guérin, D. 1996. *Albert Thomas au BIT, 1920–1932. De l'internationalisme à l'Europe*, 37. Genève: Euryopa; Rodgers, G., Lee, E., Swepston, L., Van Daele, J. eds. 2009. *The ILO and the Quest for Social Justice, 1919–2009*, 172–178. Geneva: International Labour Organization; Endres, A. M., Fleming, G. A. 1996. "International economic policy in the interwar years: The special contribution of ILO economists", *International Labour Review* 135(2): 207–225. ILOA.
33 Gobin, C., Deroubaix, J.-C. 2010. "L'analyse du discours des organisations internationales. Un vaste champ encore peu exploré", *Mots. Les langages du politique*, Mots. Les langages du politique, [Online], 94 | 2010, online on 06 November 2012. URL: http://journals.openedition.org/mots/19872 [last accessed 17.09.2019].
34 Lespinet-Moret, I., Liebeskind-Sauthier, I. 2008. "Albert Thomas, le BIT et le chômage: Expertise, catégorisation et action politique internationale", *Les Cahiers Irice* 2(2): 175.
35 Note, May 9, 1927. CAT 6B–3–2 "Questions économiques, monétaires financières. Oct.1925-Mai.1927", ILOA.

be threatened, and with it, that of social peace. Drawing on Hesiod's words, "leave not the house half-built, or the rooks will come and settle in it and caw", Thomas called on the delegates to expand the ILO's jurisdiction to the economic domain.[36]

2.2 Public Planning and Economic Management

2.2.1 The ILO: A Sounding Board for European Planist Experiments

The emergence of progressive thinking on economic and social policy provided the ILO with a new opportunity to become a space of discussion on international economic issues from the employment and unemployment perspective.[37] The context generated by the Great Depression was particularly favourable to the idea of an organised economy, regarded as a necessary condition for material development.[38] The technocratic discourse was presented in the interwar period as "a very influential background ideology", both nationally and internationally.[39] The various national experiences provided ample evidence of experimentation with economic planning around the world, signs that a major shift in consciousness against global economic chaos was taking place.[40] This change reflected more broadly what Karl Polanyi called the end of the "nineteenth century civilisation", characterised by the balance of power systems, the international gold standard, the self-regulated market and the liberal state.[41] Macroeconomic management was gaining in popularity and several European capitalist democracies, along with the United States, were prioritising public investment policies.

Thomas' 1932 annual report placed a great deal of emphasis on national planning experiences, which were of particular interest to some national trade union organisations, severely affected by mass unemployment. Thomas mentioned in particular the experiences of Italy and the USSR, which demonstrated the state's organisational capacities. Thomas' report quotes the *Planwirtschaft* by

---

36 Director's Report, ILC, 1932, 25, ILOA.
37 Rodgers, G., Lee, E., Swepston, L., Van Daele, J. eds. 2009. *The ILO and the Quest for Social Justice, 1919–2009*, 172–178.
38 Scott, J. C. 1998. *Seeing Like a State: How Certain Schemes to Improve the Human Condition Have Failed*. New Haven: Yale University Press.
39 Schot J., Lagendijk, V. 2008. "Technocratic Internationalism in the Interwar Years: Building Europe on Motorways and Electricity Networks", *Journal of Modern European History* 6(2): 196–216.
40 Director's Report, ILC, 1935, 10, ILOA.
41 Polanyi, K. 1944. *La grande transformation : aux origines politiques et économiques de notre temps*. Paris: Gallimard.

economist and sociologist Emile Lederer, namely the conviction that planning was possible in a capitalist system. It was above all the *Allgemeiner Deutscher Gewerkschaftsbund* (ADGB) which played the most important role in disseminating ideas on economic and social reform in Germany and internationally.⁴² One of the leading intellectuals in this movement was Wladimir Woytinsky, head of the statistics department of the ADGB. The latter was attempting to equip German trade unions with a political and economic action programme.⁴³ In democracies, planism mobilised both the anti-liberal right and the left. In Great Britain, socialists saw it as a means of transforming capitalist societies, while conservatives and right-wing nationalists used it to develop corporatist economic policy.⁴⁴ Progressive civil servants were also part of the original Political and Economic Planning (PEP) group, a kind of non-partisan think tank reflecting on economic planning and the role of the consumer in what could be a new economic policy. From 1930 onwards, economist John Maynard Keynes also began making proposals for investment and public works, and the Office's civil servants recognised him as an authority.⁴⁵ In his 1932 report, Thomas also cited findings of the British Finance and Industry Committee (Macmillan Report) presented to parliament in July 1931, which he saw as an expression of a new state of mind in Britain.⁴⁶ In Belgium, Catholic organisations were mobilising in favour of corporatism.⁴⁷ Both

---

42 Liebig, G. 1997. "How the German trade unions could have stopped Hitler", *Executive Intelligence Review*, 24(16): 20–39.
43 In 1932, he published an article in the *International Labour Review* in which he argued in favour of expansionary monetary policies and public works programmes as means to bring about an international employment recovery. In 1935, he took up these ideas in a technical study carried out for the Office on the social consequences of unemployment. Woytinsky, W. 1932. "Un remède à la crise : La création d'emploi par une action internationale", *ILR*, 25(1): 1–23, ILOA; Woytinsky, W. 1935. Three Sources of Unemployment: The Combined Action of Population Changes, Technical Progress and Economic Development, Studies and Reports, Series C (Unemployment). Geneva, International Labour Office, ILOA.
44 Ritschel, D. 1991. "A Corporatist Economy in Britain? Capitalist Planning for Industrial Self-Government in the 1930s", *The English Historical Review* 106(418): 41–65.
45 On the ILO's interpretation of Keynes' ideas, see Endres, A. M., Fleming, G. A. 2002. *International Organizations and the Analysis of Economic Policy, 1919–1950*, 90–93. Cambridge: Cambridge University Press.
46 This report stipulates that there is no automatic monetary adjustment and that, on the contrary, measures must be taken to ensure coordination between financial and industrial policy. Martin, P. W. 1931. "Finance and Industry: The International Significance of the Macmillan Report", *ILR* 24(4): 359–375, ILOA.
47 Luyten, D. 2005. "Un corporatisme belge, réponse à la crise du libéralisme", in Dard, O., Deschamps, É. eds. *Les Relèves en Europe d'un après-guerre à l'autre. Racines, réseaux, projets et postérités*, 197–213. Bruxelles: Peter Lang.

the Catholic parties and the far right defended the latter. Socialist unions, however, under the impetus of Jef Rens, who was to become an Office collaborator in 1944, rejected this model. Indeed, they perceived it as an attack on universal suffrage and the right to strike. Rens defended above all the positions of Henri de Man, a socialist member of the Belgian Labour Party (POB) and theorist of planning. Thomas was also inspired by de Man's proposals, in particular those based on the notion that production could be organised with the interests of the workers in mind. In France, both the French Section of the Workers' International (SFIO) and Léon Blum rejected planism.[48] After 1935, the People's Front would not put forth any major nationalisation plan or programme.[49] There was, however, a moderate planism, which, without calling capitalism into question, required greater control by the state, particularly with credit. On this ground, a certain convergence of ideas emerged between socialists and certain industrialists. Thus was born a French social-democratic technocracy which, in the Saint-Simonian tradition, played an important role in the Groupe X-Crise, a laboratory for reflection, research and the production of economic expertise created in 1931, whose ideas would be internationalised through a number of meetings, such as the Plan Conferences from 1934 to 1937 and the Franco-Swedish Pontigny Conference.[50] The creation in 1933 of the Scientific Institute for Economic and Social Research (ISRES), under the direction of the economist Charles Rist, also involved in French monetary stabilisation projects in Central Europe in collaboration with the League of Nations,[51] further points to an intensification of economic research in France, paired with a desire to guide public policy.[52]

2.2.2 The American Rationalist Movement: A Possible Model

The International Labour Office was drawn to planist ideas in its search for concrete guidelines for an international planning policy. The United States appeared as a possible model and the Office sought the collaboration of American Taylo-

---

48 Nemo, P. 2013. *Histoire des idées politiques aux Temps modernes et contemporains*, 987–988. Paris: PUF.
49 Biard, J.-F. 1985. *Le Socialisme devant ses choix : la naissance de l'idée de plan*. Paris: Publication de la Sorbonne.
50 Dard, O. 1995. "Voyage à l'intérieur d'X–Crise", *Vingtième siècle* 3(47): 132–146; Fischman, M., Lendjel, E. 2000. "La contribution d'X–Crise à l'émergence de l'économétrie en France dans les années trente", *Revue européenne des sciences sociales* 38(118): 115–134.
51 Racianu, I. 2012. "La mission de Charles Rist en Roumanie (1929–1932)", in Feiertag, O., Margairaz, M. eds. *Les Banques centrales à l'échelle du monde*, 59–78. Paris: Presses de Sciences Po.
52 Tournès, L. 2006. "L'institut scientifique de recherches économiques et sociales et les débuts de l'expertise économique en France (1933–1940), *Genèses* 4(65): 49–70.

rist networks, with which it had been working since the 1920s to internationalise knowledge on rationalisation.[53]

It is useful here to recall that the need for a rational organisation of the economy defended by the Office cannot be understood without taking into account the impact Taylorism had on Albert Thomas, particularly through the progressive ideas disseminated by the Taylor Society.[54] Thomas did not distinguish between the idea of rationalisation and that of organisation: "rationalised economies and organised economies are one and the same".[55] Based on an original approach to Taylorism that included theories of labour productivity, technological efficiency and entrepreneurial organisation, scientific management theories were an integral part of the Office's questionings concerning the impact of modern organisational techniques on the development of mass production and consumption.[56] Thomas' involvement in the scientific organisation of the labour movement was directly linked to his attempt to bridge economic modernisation and social reform, and to develop "a tripartite approach to social change".[57] Thomas also saw rationalisation as a way to unite the interests of workers and employers and to exit what Charles S. Maier called the zero-sum game, allowing workers to share in the benefits of economic development.[58] The relations forged between the International Labour Office and American Taylorists led to the creation of the International Management Institute (IMI) in Geneva in 1927. The same year, the Office sent a report to the 1927 conference organised jointly by the League of Nations and the ILO, where it emphasised the need for coordination to apply rationalisation and scientific organisation techniques to industry, agriculture, trade and finance.[59]

In the meantime, Thomas was seeking more information from the United States regarding the relationship between public works, public investment and

---

53 Cayet, T. 2010. *Rationaliser le travail, organiser la production: le Bureau international du travail et la modernisation économique durant l'entre-deux-guerres*. Rennes: Presses universitaires de Rennes.
54 Nyland, C. 2001. "Critical Theorising, Taylorist Practice, and the International Labor Organization", CMS Conference, Manchester School of Management, UMIST, England. Unpublished.
55 Schaper, B. W. 1960, 317.
56 Nyland, C. 2001. "Critical Theorising, Taylorist Practice, and the International Labor Organization", 10.
57 Cayet, T. 2010. *Rationaliser le travail*. See the introduction.
58 Maier, C. S. 1970. "Between Taylorism and Technocracy: European Ideologies and the Vision of Industrial Productivity in the 1920s", *Journal of Contemporary History* 5(2): 43.
59 Walter-Busch, E. 2006. "Albert Thomas and scientific management in war and peace, 1914–1932", *Journal of Management History* 12(2): 222.

unemployment.[60] At this point in time, the United States had not yet fully implemented a public works policy. That being said, public works were considered useful as a short-term tool to combat unemployment fluctuations. In 1927, Percival Martin, a member of the Office's scientific division, travelled to New York on a Laura Spelman Rockefeller Memorial Scholarship.[61] At Columbia University, he became familiar with the theories of under-consumption developed by the progressive economist, Wesley C. Mitchell, among the founders of the New School for Social Research. In an article published in October 1929 on the organisation of industrial relations in the United States, Martin specifically defended an interventionist approach to restore high levels of employment.[62] That same year, he supervised the editing of a series of articles by International Labour Office and League of Nations civil servants entitled "The International Control of Economic Conditions" by Pitman's in the *Economics Educator* series. In 1929, Martin was awarded a new scholarship to attend Columbia University and undertake an economic study of unemployment.[63] These fact-finding missions, which provided a better understanding of American viewpoints on under-consumption and tax intervention as a means of circumventing the shortcomings of private spending, would directly inspire Thomas in his defence of an international public investment policy as a solution to the European crisis.

With the onset of the Great Depression, the Office and Taylorist progressives broadened the scope of their reflection. Between 1929 and 1932, American Taylorists collaborated on the launch of public works by Franklin Delano Roosevelt, then governor of New York State – they would later play a central role in the development of the New Deal – and sought to promote their ideas in Europe.[64] Scientific management was gradually being reinvested in favour of social economic

---

[60] Endres, A. M., Fleming, G. A. 2002. *International Organizations and the Analysis of Economic Policy, 1919–1950*, 85. Cambridge: Cambridge University Press.

[61] Personal file, P 19, ILOA. This mission is also mentioned in Tournès, L. 2015. *Les États-Unis et la Société des Nations (1914–1946). Le système international face à l'émergence d'une superpuissance*, 171. Bern: Peter Lang.

[62] Martin, W. P. 1929. "La technique de l'équilibre économique. Son rôle dans la prospérité américaine", *ILR* 20(4): 521–540. ILOA.

[63] Personal file, P 19, ILOA. Among his publications, see *The Flaw in the Price System* (1924). London: *P. S. King*. Original from the *University of Michigan*; *The limited market: its cause, remedy and consequences* (1926), London: George Allen & Unwin; *Unemployment and Purchasing Power* (1929). London: P. S. King; *The problem of maintaining purchasing power: a study of industrial depression and recovery* (1931). London: P.S. King.

[64] Bertrams, K. 2008. "Une inspiration tout en contrastes. Le New Deal et l'ancrage transnational des experts du planning, 1933–1943", Genèses 71(2): 64–83.

planning,⁶⁵ especially at the World Social and Economic Planning Congress, held in Amsterdam in August 1931, which Thomas attended in person. This congress, one of the most important meetings of social planners, was organised by the International Industrial Relations Institute (IRI), which brought together social workers, engineers, business leaders and trade unionists to discuss the changing labour conditions of workers in the face of new production methods.⁶⁶ Under the patronage of Mary Van Kleeck, Director of the Department of Industrial Studies of the Russell Sage Foundation (RSF), a member of the Taylor Society and head of the congress programme, many European and American scientists and economists, reformists and Taylorists alike, gathered in support of government intervention in combating the unemployment generated by the crisis.⁶⁷

All discussions within the congress began with a common reflection on a paradox: the existence of unemployment in a context of increased production.⁶⁸ The congress then considered a set of principles on which economic planning could be based. Thomas, concerned with the future of the growing number of unemployed workers in Europe, advocated compliance with international standards. Harlow S. Person, General Secretary of the Taylor Society, defended the American planning model, which he presented as an evolution of Taylorism, taking the organisation of corporate production to the scale of entire economy. This congress also saw the first participation of Soviet experts, who had come to describe the workings of the five-year plan. V. Obolensky-Ossinsky defended the Soviet model as the best way to fight the crisis of capitalism. The presence of these experts testified to the interest shown in the Soviet experience. While Western liberal capitalism stagnated, the USSR, with its economic recovery programmes, was experiencing a rapid and massive process of industrialisation.⁶⁹ This performance had also led to an increase in the number of research trips by economists and social workers, particularly from the United States, to the USSR.⁷⁰ In Europe as in the United States, the idea thus gradually spread of borrowing the Soviet

---

65 Cayet, T. 2010. *Rationaliser le travail*. See Chapter 7; Cayet, T. 2011. "Le planning comme organisation du travail", in Lespinet-Moret, I., Viet, V. eds. *L'Organisation internationale du travail : origine–développement–avenir:* 79–89. Rennes: PUR.
66 *World Social Economic Congress, under the auspices of the International Industrial Relations Association*, 1931. The Hague: International Industrial Relations Association.
67 Nyland, C. 2001. "Critical Theorising, Taylorist Practice, and the International Labor Organization", 12. CMS Conference, Manchester School of Management, UMIST, England. Unpublished.
68 Johnston, G. A. 1932. "Social Economic Planning", *ILR* 25(1): 58–78. ILOA.
69 Between 1929 and 1940, its industrial production increased threefold. Hobsbawm, E. 2008. *L'Âge des extrêmes: histoire du court XXᵉ siècle: 1914–1991*, 136. Bruxelles: A. Versaille.
70 Feuer, L. S. 1962. "American Travelers to the Soviet Union 1917–32: The Formation of a Component of New Deal Ideology", *American Quarterly* 14(2): 119–149.

planning method and transplanting it to the capitalist environment, without however calling into question its foundations.[71]

2.3 International Public Works: A Solution to the European Crisis

For Albert Thomas, the diversity of economic organisation models proposed on both sides of the Atlantic testified to the still isolated nature of these experiences. While seeking to encourage the international movement in favour of planning, he wished to define more clearly the social objectives of a planned economy and, from 1930 onwards, proposed a policy of major public works as a means of combating unemployment and revamping the economy. Thus, between the first and second decades of the interwar period, the Office did not fundamentally alter its strategic action plan for times of crisis and remained centred on the issues of employment and unemployment. Although unemployment remained central to the analysis, the focus shifted, for it no longer sufficed to propose remedies. Indeed, it had become essential to determine the economic conditions and effects of social policy.

The public works proposals made by Thomas between 1930 and 1932 underscore a significant evolution in the Office's understanding of the economic role of social policies, along with the European and global orientation of its concerns. Until the late 1920s, the Office had not yet advocated the use of public works to combat unemployment and did not support a long-term interventionist policy.[72] While a 1919 ILO resolution mentioned public works as a measure to mitigate the effects of short-term economic fluctuations, the Office considered unemployment insurance to be a more effective tool. Economic research at that time also focused more on monetary policy and its impact on unemployment.[73] The 1926 conference marked a change by recommending research development on the compensatory effect of public works.[74] At the 1930 ILC, Thomas put forward a

---

[71] Cayet, T. 2010. *Rationaliser le travail*, 166–182.
[72] Endres, A. M., Fleming, G. A. 2002. *International Organizations and the Analysis of Economic Policy, 1919–1950*, 82 and following. Cambridge: Cambridge University Press. For an analysis of the League's position, see Fior, M. 2008. *Institution globale et marchés financiers. La Société des Nations face à la reconstruction de l'Europe (1918–1931)*, 232–233. Bern: Peter Lang.
[73] This problem had already been raised by Thomas in Genoa, in 1922. According to him the reconstruction of the international monetary system should take into account the effects on employment. In 1932 he took up this idea and stated that it was impossible to achieve economic reconstruction without the restoration of a stable monetary system.
[74] "Les travaux publics, facteur de stabilisation économique" *ILR* 38(6): 793–825, ILOA.

series of measures to reduce unemployment, but also to stimulate economic activity.[75] For example, he called for a more equitable distribution of international wealth and an international public works programme. The 1929 economic crisis further strengthened his commitment to European regional cooperation.[76] His proposals were guided by the desire to see the emergence of a new Europe, one more united and more integrated, anchored in the principles of collaboration and solidarity between states, an idea he had begun cultivating as early as 1925.[77]

At the time, many saw the significant difference in economic development between Western, Central and Eastern Europe as an important source of insecurity.[78] The economic discrepancies between Eastern and Western Europe were blatant, especially after the publication of *Les Deux Europes* by French economist Francis Delaisi. In his book, Delaisi came to the conclusion that there were, in fact, two Europes: one was industrialised (Europe A), democratic and suffered from an overproduction crisis, while the other was agrarian (Europe B), run by autocratic governments and lacking the necessary capital to modernise its economy.[79] For supporters of European integration, Europe's future depended on its ability to unite. Aristide Briand's project, as presented to the League of Nations in May 1930, brought the question of the creation of the United States of Europe to the international stage. Thomas welcomed Briand's initiative, though he criticised its abstract nature.[80] Nevertheless, he took this opportunity to promote a public works programme specifically designed for the economic development of Central and Eastern Europe.

In April 1931, Thomas submitted a report to the ILO Governing Body addressing the possibility of using the Commission of Enquiry for European union (CEEU) to discuss ways of combating unemployment. In it he suggested the launch of a vast programme of European public works, which, in his opinion, would put the millions of unemployed people back to work. For instance, its pro-

---

75 Director's Report, ILC, 1930, ILOA.
76 Guérin, D. 1996. *Albert Thomas au BIT, 1920–1932. De l'internationalisme à l'Europe*, 68–69. Genève: Euryopa.
77 Schaper, B. W. 1960. *Albert Thomas, trente ans de réformisme social*, 320. Paris: PUF.
78 Schirmann, S. 2000. *Crise, coopération économique et financière entre États européens, 1929–1933*. Paris: Comité pour l'histoire économique et financière de la France; Berger, F. "Les milieux économiques et les États vis-à-vis des tentatives d'organisation des marchés européens dans les années trente", in Bussière, É., Dumoulin, M., Schirmann, S. eds. 2006. *Europe organisée, Europe du Libre-échange (Fin XIXe siècle–Années 1960)*, 71–105. Brussels: Peter Lang.
79 Delaisi, F. 1929. *Les Deux Europes : Europe industrielle et Europe agricole*. Paris: Payot.
80 Lagendijk, V. 2008. *Electrifying Europe: The Power of Europe in the Construction of Electricity Networks*, 90–106. Amsterdam: Aksant.

posal to introduce an automatic coupling system in European railways would provide jobs to 600,000 workers for five years.[81] Thomas also saw it as a way of encouraging the start-up of economic activity, in particular by moving dormant capital from industrial countries to the economies of Central and Eastern Europe. Investing foreign capital in these countries would, according to Thomas, boost the agricultural economy, which was the main source of labour and income.

The Great Depression gave international visibility to the problems of the agricultural economy in Central Europe and the Balkans. In these areas, between 1930 and 1932, the purchase price of wheat fell by 50 per cent from the 1929 level.[82] The effects on countries the majority of whose exports dealt with agricultural products was dramatic, a situation aggravated by deflationary pressure caused by the abandonment of the gold standard. Farmers in Central and Eastern Europe quickly found themselves unable to sell their products and buy manufactured goods from Western Europe. Added to the agricultural crisis was the problem of international debt, which these countries could no longer repay.[83] As a result of this situation, governments shifted their focus to protecting their economies, a choice that contributed to increasing tensions within countries, but also among European nations.

The importance attached to agricultural problems can be measured by the attempts of several Central and Eastern European countries to form an agrarian bloc in the 1930s to support their economies. In an attempt to find solutions to what appeared to be a dual crisis of agriculture and foreign debt, Yugoslavia, Romania and Hungary held an initial conference in Warsaw in August 1930, then a second one in October 1930 in Bucharest, recommending to the League of Nations that the industrial countries of Europe buy their grain at preferential rates and evaluate the potential for a regional organisation of the agricultural economy.[84] However, Central and Eastern European economies quickly became the object of rivalries between the powers of Western Europe.[85]

The crisis and its effects on the economies of Central and Eastern Europe were also mobilising International Labour Office civil servants. The Office's agriculture department was developing its research regarding the consequences of the economic crisis on the wages, employment and living conditions of agricul-

---

81 Schaper, B. W. 1960. *Albert Thomas, trente ans de réformisme social*, 324. Paris: PUF.
82 Clavin, P. 2000. *The Great Depression in Europe, 1929–1939*, 100. London: Macmillan Press.
83 *Ibid.*, 148.
84 Schirmann, S. 2000. *Crise, coopération économique et financière entre États européens, 1929–1933*, 91. Paris: Comité pour l'histoire économique et financière de la France.
85 *Ibid.*, 123.

tural workers. The crisis would foster a shift in the ILO's perception of agricultural concerns.[86] Whereas in the 1920s it considered them on par with industrial labour, by the late 1930s, it recognised the specificity of agricultural work. This change took place within the framework of the Tripartite Committee on Agriculture, set up in November 1936, whose task was to provide a better understanding of agricultural problems, and to provide guidelines for the development of research, which was taking on a new dimension. As noted by Amalia Ribi Forclaz (2011), "food, labour, health and the economy were thus connected in a much more integrated and universalist approach to social agricultural problems".[87] This mobilisation for raising the standard of living of agricultural workers was not, however, driven solely by the desire to provide assistance to Central and Eastern European countries in order to save the agricultural economy. It was also aimed at stifling the growing influence of Germany in trade relations with this region.[88]

For Thomas, an international public works policy could revive economic activity throughout Europe, but also in Asia and in Latin America. His proposals were conceived both regionally and globally.[89] Emphasis should be placed here on just how audacious these proposals were in the trying context of 1931. In addition, while shaking up government discussions, Thomas was involving the ILO on issues that were not strictly speaking related to working conditions.[90] The reactions of the members of the GB were rather mixed. Léon Jouhaux, a French worker delegate, recalled the importance of reducing working time for workers and regretted that the Office's Director did not address the issue. European employers' representatives questioned the economic viability of public

---

[86] Ribi Forclaz, A. 2011. "A New Target for International Social Reform: The International Labour Organization and Working and Living Conditions in Agriculture in the Inter-War Years", *Contemporary European History* 20(3): 307–329.
[87] Ibid., 326.
[88] Gross, S. G. 2015. *Export Empire: German Soft Power in Southeastern Europe, 1890–1945*. Cambridge: Cambridge University Press.
[89] Feiertag, O. 2011. "Humaniser la crise économique (1929–1934): l'expertise du BIT dans la crise de mondialisation des années 1930", in Aglan, A., Feiertag, O., Kevonian, D. *Humaniser le travail. Régimes économiques, régimes politiques et Organisation internationale du travail, 1929–1969*, 30–32. Brussels, Bern: PIE Lang. This idea had been raised at the 1927 Economic Conference and would be taken up again by the Office at the 1933 London Monetary and Economic Conference. CAT 2-27-2-6 "Résumé d'un discours sur la Conférence économique internationale, Londres", ILOA. D 764/100/13 "Procès-verbal de la Conférence monétaire et économique mondiale de Londres, CA, session 64, octobre 1933", ILOA.
[90] Guérin, D. 1996. *Albert Thomas au BIT, 1920–1932. De l'internationalisme à l'Europe*, 77–89. Genève: Euryopa.

works.[91] Thomas' report was nevertheless sent to the CEEU, which decided in May 1931 to refer the two aspects of the memorandum to two sub-committees.[92] The sub-committee on credits, which met in June 1931, expressed strong criticism of Thomas' project. Its president, Joseph Avenol, Assistant Secretary General of the League of Nations, insisted on the lack of available capital, while Pietro Stoppani, member of the Economic Section of the League of Nations, opposed the idea of an internationalisation of public works, which he wished to maintain at a national level of action.[93] Although League of Nations economists argued in favour of a liberal conception of the economy, the problem of financing public works stalled progress on the project of international economic cooperation.

After two failures at the ILO and the League of Nations, Thomas decided to promote Francis Delaisi's project, a five-year plan for the economic reconstruction of Europe. This plan presented itself as the solution to the economic underdevelopment of Central and Eastern Europe and the crisis of overproduction in industrialised countries. During a conference held at the Chair of the Carnegie Endowment European Centre in Paris on 16 December 1932, Delaisi, a French trade unionist and economist, clearly outlined the main features of his plan.[94] It was based on the transfer of modern means of production to workers in Central and Eastern Europe, together with a policy of public investment. In concrete terms, Delaisi proposed to extend the road network by 400,000 kilometres over five years. The construction of new roads would make it possible to increase farmers' purchasing power, by reducing transportation costs, and to revive factory activity in industrial countries. The Bank for International Settlements (BIS) would be responsible for paying expenses and collecting loan payments. As for the League of Nations, it would be called upon to oversee and ensure that this international credit system worked in the interest of both parties.

A few months earlier, Thomas had included Delaisi's proposals in his 1932 annual report. In it he drafted a European public works plan for the establishment of a network of motorways and railways, as well as a project for the distri-

---

91 Société des amis d'Albert Thomas, 1957. *Un grand citoyen du monde : Albert Thomas vivant. Études, témoignages, souvenirs*, 86. Genève: Bureau international du travail.
92 Shipper, F. 2008. *Driving Europe: Building Europe on Roads in the Twentieth Century*, 99. Amsterdam: Aksant.
93 Guérin, D. 1996. *Albert Thomas au BIT, 1920–1932*, 72.
94 Delaisi, F., Mousset, A., Clerc, H., von Beckerath, H., Hantos, E., Osuski, S. 1933. *L'Europe centrale et la crise*. Paris: Publications de la conciliation internationale, Centre Europe de la Dotation Carnegie.

bution of electrical energy.⁹⁵ These proposals involved employment policy, infrastructure development and financial assistance. Finally, Thomas insisted again on the need to encourage public works policies beyond Europe. However, at that time, the ILO did not clearly perceive the problem of unemployment that prevailed in the underdeveloped world.⁹⁶ Thomas' concern was above all that Europe could not emerge from the crisis without a global development movement, which involved colonisation plans among others. Thomas was all the more receptive to this idea as concrete proposals had been made along these lines. Giuseppe de Michelis, the Italian government delegate and Director of the International Institute of Agriculture, for instance, proposed a rational organisation plan for the world economic system centred on the global distribution of people and labour and the supply of raw materials and food production in industrialised countries.⁹⁷ The Office's participation in the International Congress of Economic and Social Sciences, held in Paris in July 1937, would be in line with these concerns. In particular, the Office would defend the idea of developing public works in collaboration with indigenous peoples in the development of settlements.⁹⁸ So it was well before the Second World War that the Office had begun to spread the idea of international collaboration for the exploitation of the world's resources. This fact would be recalled by several members of the Office's Crisis Committee, which would meet in London in April 1942 to discuss the role of the ILO in post-war reconstruction plans.⁹⁹

Thomas' energy for planning led to the adoption of a resolution on the economic crisis by 73 votes to 7 at the ILC in April 1932. The resolution encouraged

---

[95] A series of studies developing a transnational approach to the construction of these infrastructures were published as part of a Dutch research programme on the role of technology in European integration: "Transnational Infrastructures and the Rise of Contemporary Europe". https://www.nwo.nl/onderzoek –en –resultaten/onderzoeksprojecten/i/50/150.html [last accessed 12.09.2019]. See also Shipper, F. 2008. *Driving Europe*; Lagendijk, V. 2008. *Electrifying Europe*; Anastasiadou, I. 2011. *Constructing Iron Europe: Transnationalism and Railways in the Interbellum*. Amsterdam: Amsterdam University Press.
[96] Rodgers, G., Lee, E., Swepston, L., Van Daele, J. eds. 2009. *The ILO and the Quest for Social Justice, 1919–2009*, 178.
[97] Director's Report, ILC, 1932, 917, ILOA. For a detailed analysis of the relationship between de Michelis and Albert Thomas and on the evolution of the ILO's thinking on unemployment and migration, see Rosental, P.-A. 2006. "Géopolitique et État-providence. Le BIT et la politique mondiale des migrations dans l'entre-deux-guerres", *Annales. Histoire, Sciences Sociales* 1(61): 99–134.
[98] EP 1000/5 "Economic problems: Congrès des économistes de langue française – Congrès international des sciences économiques et sociales. 01/1937–12/1937", ILOA.
[99] "Vers une "paix du peuple" La réunion de la commission de crise du BIT. Londres, avril 1942", *ILR* 46(1): 1–48. ILOA.

the Office to collect information on public works and adopted the principle of tripartite collaboration on production and international trade issues.[100] The death of Thomas on 7 May 1932 did not put an end to the Office's initiatives in favour of an international European reconstruction programme. At the Stresa conference in 1932, the Office submitted a report on the possibilities of developing public works projects in Central and Eastern Europe. The Committee on Economic and Agricultural Affairs recognised the usefulness of such initiatives, which would bolster the efforts of countries that agreed to purchase Danube cereals at preferential rates.[101] A Europe-wide public works programme would facilitate the disposal, storage and development of new infrastructure in Danube countries.[102] However, the lack of agreement on how to finance this initiative prevented any political progress, paving the way for a rapprochement between Central and Eastern Europe, and Germany.[103] Despite the failure of Stresa, the Office continued to organise several missions to Central and Eastern Europe to popularise the idea of public works.[104] Then, the 1933 ILC voted in favour of a resolution to be addressed to the economic and monetary conference that was about to open in London, calling in particular for "the return of locked-in capital to circulation by all appropriate means, including the adoption of a public works policy".[105] This resolution, which enshrined the notion that the progress of labour is inseparable from the global economy, was put to the vote by ILO representatives at the London conference: Léon Jouhaux, Atul Chatterjee, the Indian government delegate and H. C. Oersted, the employers' delegate from Denmark. The adoption of this resolution should not obscure the still vivid opposition to public works expressed at the conference, particularly by governments (with the exception of France and the United States) and employers' representatives, who, although

---

[100] Martin, P. W. "World Economic Reconstruction: An Analysis of the Economic Resolution adopted by the International Labour Conference", *ILR* 26(2): 199–223. ILOA.
[101] Schirmann, S. 2000. *Crise, coopération économique et financière entre États européens, 1929–1933*, 193.
[102] *Ibid.*
[103] Gross, S. G. 2015. *Export Empire: German Soft Power in Southeastern Europe, 1890–1945*, 158. Cambridge: Cambridge University Press; Clavin, P. 2000. *The Great Depression in Europe, 1929–1939*, 104.
[104] In 1932, Harold Butler travelled to Warsaw, Prague and Greece; in 1934, to Romania, Bulgaria and Yugoslavia, where he multiplied public interventions. G900/3/12 "Director's visit to Poland November 1932". G900/3/12/1 "Director's visit to Warsaw. November 1932. Polish correspondent's report and press cuttings on the mission". G 900/3/20 "Director's visit to Eastern Europe. 1934", ILOA._
[105] ILC, *Record of proceedings*, 1933, 510–511, ILOA.

they supported the ILO's public works policy, considered it to be very costly.[106] In 1937, the ILC voted for two more recommendations on public works, one on international cooperation (No. 50) and the other on national planning (No. 51).[107] It was also decided to create an international commission on public works, the task of which was to centralise information on national public works programmes. This commission met only once before the war, in June 1938.

Thus, after 1933, public works were no longer seen just as a measure to combat unemployment or as a factor of economic stabilisation through the regularisation of employment that they allowed, but also as an instrument for the development of economic exchanges. The idea put forward was that the growth of investment in the domestic market could lead to an increase in imports and, by extension, a revival of the world economy. As Fernand Maurette noted: "Thus, from these angles, the primary purpose of public works is not so much to produce labour and eliminate unemployment as to restore capital to circulation."[108]

3 Research on Planning as a Trans-Atlantic Project

The idea of organising economic exchanges internationally was soon supported by the United States, which joined the ILO in 1934. This influence was reflected in the increase in number of Butler's missions to the United States, the appointment of American experts to the ILO and the intensification of research conducted in collaboration with American scientific networks. The strengthening of these American collaborations, despite their limitations, suggests that the promotion of an international planning policy at the ILO was now part of a broader trans-Atlantic cooperation project.

---

106 Louis, M. 2018. "Le parent pauvre de la gouvernance économique mondiale? L'OIT face aux crises de 1929 et de 2008", *Le Mouvement Social* 263(2): 45–59.
107 ILC, *Record of proceedings*, 1937. Text of the recommandation, 808, ILOA.
108 Draft note to the conference by Fernand Maurette, June 23, 1933. XE 1/8/1 "International economic organisation – League of Nations, 1933–1937", ILOA. Original quote in French: "Ainsi l'objet premier des travaux publics considérés sous ces angles n'est pas tant de produire du travail et de supprimer du chômage que de remettre du capital en circulation."

3.1 The USA Joins the ILO

The first mission of Harold Butler, who became the second Director of the International Labour Office in 1932, was to secure the United States' membership with the ILO. The latter was favoured by the Great Depression and the institutionalisation, from 1933 onwards, of the New Deal.[109] Unlike Thomas, very little is known about Butler. He entered the public service very early (1907) and studied at Eton College, Balliol College, and Oxford.[110] He was a member of All Souls College between 1905 and 1912. A friend of John Maynard Keynes, Butler developed an early interest in economics. From 1908 to 1917, he worked as assistant secretary of the industrial department and collaborated with the interior office. In 1916, he was appointed Secretary of the Foreign Trade Department of the Ministry of Foreign Affairs and, following the reorganisation of the Ministry of Labour in 1917, was appointed Assistant Secretary of Labour.[111] After the war, in Great Britain Butler defended a position radically opposed to that of Thomas in France. He did not wish to see the model of a state-run economy triumph. He thus advocated a return to liberal policy and the decentralisation of control over industry. However, the 1930s brought about significant intellectual change and directed Butler's thinking towards pre-Keynesian planning.[112]

Butler's efforts to bring the United States into the ILO can be seen in light of this changing context. The stages of the United States' accession to the ILO have been sufficiently studied to make a discussion of this point unnecessary here.[113] It is sufficient to recall that in the wake of the Great Depression, several American personalities from progressive and internationalist circles were defending greater cooperation with the ILO in order to find solutions to combat the unemployment crisis. Furthermore, the appointment of Roosevelt and the establishment of the New Deal led social reformers in the federal administration to

---

109 Ostrower, G. B. 1975. "The American Decision to Join the International Labor Organization", *Labor History* 16(4): 495–504.
110 Personal file, P 7, ILOA.
111 Hidalgo-Weber, Olga, 2017. *La Grande-Bretagne et l'Organisation internationale du travail (1919–1946). Une nouvelle forme d'internationalisme*, 50–51. Paris: l'Harmattan.
112 2009. *Edward Phelan and the ILO: Life and views of an international social actor*, 7. Geneva, International Labour Office.
113 Lorenz, E. C. 2001. *Defining global justice: The History of U.S. International Labor Standards Policy*. Notre Dame, Ind.: University of Notre Dame Press; Alcock, A. 1971. *History of the International Labour Organisation*. London: Macmillan; Moynihan, D. 1960. *The United States and the International Labor Organization, 1889–1934*. Medford, Mass.; Myers, J. 1933. "American Relations with the International Labour Office, 1919–1932", *Annals of the American Academy of Political and Social Science* 166: 135–145.

seek further support from the ILO, in which they saw an instrument for advancing their national development policy. Roosevelt shared this impression and also saw it as a way to internationalise the principles and methods of the New Deal.[114] In his book *The Lost Peace*, published in 1941, Butler recalls his meeting with Roosevelt in 1933: "He was astonishingly well informed about the ILO and all its works, and had evidently made up his mind that America should play its part in them."[115] Butler was not the sole reason behind the United States' accession. Many American internationalists active in the academic world, especially at Colombia University, carried out intense advocacy work for the ILO in the United States. These include James T. Shotwell; Carter Goodrich, government delegate on the Governing Body from 1937; and Samuel McCune Lindsay, professor of social legislation at Columbia University, also former president of the American Academy of Political and Social Science from 1900 to 1902 and member of the American Economic Association.[116]

While 1934 marks the beginning of official relations with the ILO, it should be recalled that the United States had been involved in the activities of international organisations unofficially since the 1920s. On several occasions between 1919 and 1933, the United States sent observers to ILO conferences. It is also worth noting that, in 1920, Thomas managed to open a correspondence office in Washington, led successively by Ernest Greenwood between 1920 and 1923 and by Leifur Magnusson from 1924 to 1938. In 1920, Thomas also recruited an American to head the Office's Scientific Division, Dr. Royal Meeker.[117] Thomas had always been committed to developing relations with the United States, but he entrusted this mission to Butler. As Edward C. Lorenz (2001) notes: "The quintessential British civil servant, appeared less foreign to Americans than a bearded French socialist."[118]

Between 1926 and 1935, Butler visited the United States five times. These trips primarily served a diplomatic function and enabled the Office to develop

---

114 Van Goethem, G. 2010. "Phelan's War: The International Labour Organization in Limbo (1941–1948)", in Van Daele, J. et al. eds. 2010. *ILO Histories. Essays on the International Labour Organization and Its Impact on the World During the Twentieth Century*, 314–340. Bern: Peter Lang. For an American perspective, see Ekbladh, D. 2010. *The Great American Mission: Modernization and the Construction of an American World Order*, Princeton, NJ: Princeton University Press.
115 Butler, H. 1941. *The Lost Peace: A Personal Impression*, 54. London: Faber and Faber.
116 Shotwell, J. T. 1934. *Origins of the International Labour Organization*, New York: Columbia University Press. See also the correspondence between McCune Lindsay and Butler, XR 61/4/8 "Relations with Columbia University (Prof. Samuel McCune Lindsay) 1928–1932", ILOA.
117 Personal file, P 192, ILOA.
118 Lorenz, E. C. 2001. *Defining global justice*, 96.

a network of relations, but also to exchange knowledge and experience in social policy with American experts and civil servants. The creation of the IMI is one of the direct consequences of these networking efforts. Butler's missions also aimed to study the economic and social development of the United States and to feed the Office's scientific output. For example, the 1926 trip, funded by a scholarship from the Laura Spellman Rockefeller Memorial, led to a publication on American industrial relations.[119] According to Butler, American workers addressed the problem of industrial relations differently than in Europe, a divergence based on a particular conception of industrial development. The American Federation of Labor (AFL) advocated in particular a policy of encouraging production, maintaining wages as well as working conditions and collective bargaining rather than more active collaboration between trade unions and government in the development of social legislation.[120] The Great Depression, however, favoured the emergence of a movement to centralise and adopt new labour legislation. This trend, combined with the establishment of the New Deal, would facilitate the participation of US trade union organisations in the ILO.[121]

On a mission to the United States in 1930, Butler was directly confronted with the crisis of the American economic system. He visited the United States again in November 1933 and autumn 1934, at which time he strengthened his relations with the Roosevelt administration, particularly with Frances Perkins. Appointed Secretary of the Labor Department in 1933, Perkins, who developed a social policy programme similar to that of the ILO, played a central role in bringing the United States closer to the organisation.[122]

---

119 Butler, H. 1927. *Les Relations industrielles aux États-Unis*. Études et documents, série A (Vie Sociale), no. 27, Bureau international du travail, Genève, ILOA.
120 On the relations between the AFL and the ILO, see McKillen, E. 2010. "Beyond Gompers: The American Federation of Labor, the Creation of the ILO, and US Labor Dissent", in Van Daele, J. et al. eds. 2010. *ILO Histories*, 41–66.
121 Lindsay, S. M. 1934. "The *Problem of American Cooperation*", in Shotwell, J. T. ed. *The Origins of the International Labor Organization*, 331–332. New York: Colombia University Press.
122 RL 61/1/1 "US Secretary of Labour. Washington, 1933–1945", ILOA. Perkins was born in Boston on 10 April 1882. After graduating from Mount Holyoke College, she studied sociology at Columbia University, the University of Pennsylvania and the University of Chicago. She has also studied in various European institutions. Between 1910 and 1933, she participated in various commissions in New York City. She visited the ILO in 1936. See file XH 6/61/7 "United States: Miss Perkins' visit to the ILO in Geneva, 1936", ILOA. She resigned from her position as Secretary of Labor in May 1945. That same year she was appointed head of the government delegation to the International Conference in Geneva. After the war, she supported collaboration between the ILO and the UN. See the biography of Downey, Kirsten. 2009. *The Woman behind the New Deal*, Knopf Doubleday Publishing Group.

Several of Butler's contributions on the United States recovery measures appeared in the *International Labour Review* between 1931 and 1934.[123] In his 1934 article, he emphasised the federal government's role in improving employment and wage conditions in certain industries. He also noted a shift in the attitude of industry regarding government intervention in the economy.[124] While it remained difficult to assess the impact of the recovery programme on consumption, Butler concluded that the reduction in working hours had indeed led to an increase in the volume of employment, as well as an increase in the overall purchasing power of employees. After 1934, International Labour Office studies on planning multiplied rapidly.[125] It is interesting to note that the Office's scientific output at this time contrasted with that of the League of Nations, which did not have a particular interest in planning. In 1935, Alexander Loveday, director of the League of Nations Finance Committee, wrote to Butler:

> I am not particularly enthusiastic about the economics of Roosevelt's recovery programme, while I believe that his social reform programme – which I do not venture to criticise, excepting, perhaps as being hustle history – is more generally tacitly accepted by the business world than the business world ever admit.[126]

The encouraging planning results in the United States and the space left by the League of Nations motivated Butler to strengthen the economic research focus within the International Labour Office.[127] While the Office had been interested

---

123 Butler, H. 1931. "Les répercussions sociales de la crise économique en Amérique du Nord", *ILR* 23(3): 309–333; Butler, H. 1933. "Le programme de redressement économique aux États-Unis", *ILR* 28(6): 799–815; Butler, H. 1934. "L'œuvre de redressement économique aux USA", *ILR* 24(1): 1–24. ILOA.
124 Butler, H. 1934. "L'œuvre de redressement économique aux USA", 8.
125 A new series of articles on this subject appeared in the *International Labour Review* between 1934 and 1937. Mitnizky, M. "Effet d'une politique de travaux publics sur le mouvement des affaires et l'emploi", *ILR* 30(4): 463–486; Ohlin, B. 1935. "Economic recovery and labour market problems in Sweden: I–II" *ILR* 31(4): 498–511 and 670–699; Grebler, L. 1936. "La construction d'habitations, les fluctuations, du cycle économique et l'intervention des pouvoirs publics", *ILR* 33(3): 337–355; Martin, P. W. 1936. "L'état actuel du planning économique. I. Exposé international des interventions gouvernementales", *ILR* 33(5): 658–687; Martin, P. W. 1937. "L'état actuel du planning économique. II. Les problèmes", *ILR* 35(2): 188–209; Riches, E. J. 1937. "Agricultural planning and farm wages in New Zealand", *ILR* 35(3): 293–328; Ickes, H. 1937. "Public works in the United States of America", *ILR* 35(6): 775–802; Mosse, R. 1937. "The theory of planned economy: a study of some recent works", *ILR* 36(3): 371–393.
126 Letter from Loveday to Butler, January 4, 1935. XL 3/3 "A. Loveday, 1924–1938", ILOA.
127 At the end of 1932, an economic research group was formed under the direction of Percival Martin and Fernand Maurette. In 1934, the Research Division disappeared and the technical sec-

since the end of the 1920s in American labour, after the United States joined the ILO in 1934, the Office's research programme took on a more political tone and developed in close collaboration with the Roosevelt administration.[128]

3.2 Recruiting American Experts

The need to reconsider labour in relation to economic problems had highlighted the need to strengthen the ILO's economic expertise, which had led to the emergence of a new institutional culture at the International Labour Office. Under Harold Butler, the development of international labour Conventions became secondary to economic research, an orientation he had proposed as early as 1930:

> I do not feel that we can continue to rely on Conventions as the principle test of our activity and progress. I think we ought to take this opportunity of shifting our centre of gravity, so to speak, from the purely social to the economic sphere by devoting the whole of our attention to the effects on the workers of the world Depression, and the analysis of some of the principle factors from the purely industrial point of view. [...] The real issues in industry are going to be the method and extent of rationalisation, the necessity of high wages to maintain purchasing power, the effects of the tariff war from the workers point of view. [...] I think we should go and try to create a body of coherent thought from the labour standpoint.[129]

In 1935, despite the presence at the Office of several civil servants with a thorough knowledge of economic issues, predominantly of European origin, Butler decided to entrust the work of the Office's Economic Section to socialist economist Lewis Lorwin, an important figure in the American planning movement. Lorwin first came into contact with the Office in 1926 during a visit to Geneva where he met Thomas and Butler, without establishing a close relationship

---

tions became more autonomous. This decentralisation had the effect of giving more latitude to the sections and, above all, of reducing Maurette's influence on research carried out by the Office and more generally in the French socialist and reformist tradition so well established under Thomas. The Economic Studies Department, which until 1938 was divided into two categories: general economic issues and agricultural issues, brought together, including research assistants, about 20 people between 1934 and 1939.

128 Cayet, T. 2011. "Regards croisés sur une adhésion : l'Organisation internationale du travail et le New Deal", in Aglan, A., Feiertag, O., Kevonian, D. eds. 2011. *Humaniser le travail. Régimes économiques, régimes politiques et Organisation internationale du travail, 1929–1969*, 39–54. Bruxelles ; Bern: PIE Lang.

129 Alcock, A. 1971. *History of the International Labour Organisation*, 123. London: Macmillan.

with the ILO. It was only in 1934 that Lorwin reconnected with the Office, when Butler offered him a position as economic adviser.[130]

Lorwin's recruitment marks the return of Americans to senior positions at the Office, part of a twofold strategy: on the one hand, it would help strengthen collaboration with the United States by developing relations with progressive political and scientific circles, while on the other, it would ensure better dissemination of the Office's economic work in the United States, where the organisation was still largely unknown to the public. The hiring of Lorwin was therefore not solely a scientific decision; it also had obvious political appeal.

Louis Levine, who in 1925 changed his name to Lewis Levitzki Lorwin,[131] was born in Russia in 1883. After secondary school in Cherkassy, Ukraine, he entered the University of Kiev, where he studied sociology between 1903 and 1905. He then travelled to the United States, where he studied sociology, political economy and history at Colombia University. He also studied anthropology, specialising in statistics and finance. In 1912, he obtained the title of Doctor of Philosophy with a thesis on revolutionary trade unionism in France.[132] The choice of this subject of study attests to a strong interest in socialism – which would later get Lorwin in trouble, suspected and supervised by the FBI from 1948 onwards[133] – and a profound knowledge of the history of workers' internationalism.[134] Between 1912 and 1916, as cooperation between trade union organisations and the federal government grew, he took a keen interest in the modalities of government involvement in industrial relations, a subject that was published in 1935 in collaboration with Arthur Wubnig, an economist and future collaborator of the Office whom he

---

130 Letter from Butler to Lorwin, December 14, 1934. Box 5 "uncatalogued correspondence, 1931–1939", in Archives Lewis Lorwin, Columbia University, New York. (hereafter Arch. ALL). Personal file, P 2963, ILOA.

131 This change was motivated by the existence of many people with this name at the time. Lorwin cites in particular a communist author with whom he wished not to be confused. Box 2 "uncatalogued correspondence 1908–1919", Arch. LL. See also Storrs, L. R.Y. 2012. *The Second Red Scare and the Unmaking of the New Deal Left*, note 17, 365. Princeton: Princeton University Press.

132 Box 2 Uncatalogued correspondence 1908–1919. *The Labor Movement in France: A Study in Revolutionary Syndicalism*, New York, Columbia University, 1912, in Arch. LL.

133 Following the FBI investigation, Lorwin would be forced to resign from the Office of International Trade, US Department of Commerce, where he worked alongside the socio-economist Dublin Keyserling, also harassed by the MacCarthy Administration. Storrs, Landon R.Y. 2012, 118 and following.

134 He also published a book on the AFL, which was a major international success: Lorwin, L. L. 1972. *The American Federation of Labor*. New Jersey: Augustus M. Kelley Publishers.

met during his activities at the Brookings Institution.[135] During the First World War, Lorwin developed a reputation as an expert in government agencies, particularly the State Department. He also collaborated as an economic expert with the War Labor Policies Board, established in 1918.[136] The war offered breakthroughs in the careers of several American economists with a reformist tendency, some of whom would come to collaborate on the New Deal in the 1930s.[137]

After the war, between 1922 and 1929, Lorwin undertook several trips to the USSR as a correspondent for the *Chicago Daily News*. In the 1920s, these kinds of trips were rather rare, but like the study missions organised in the West, they contributed to the professionalisation of economic experts.[138] According to sociologist Lewis S. Feuer (1962), the circulation of a nebula of American experts in the USSR between the two world wars (economists, educators, writers, social workers, humanitarian missionaries) directly contributed to forging the pragmatic ideology, which the socio-economists involved in the New Deal would later claim as their own.[139] These trips demonstrate the importance of the Soviet experience for Lorwin, as a model of interventionist economic policy.[140] In 1935, shortly after his move to Geneva, Butler called upon his expertise, sending him back to the USSR on a study mission.[141]

---

135 Lorwin, L. L., Wubnig, A. 1935. *Labor Relations Boards*, Washington: The Brookings Institution.
136 Letter from Lorwin to Butler, February 25, 1935. Box 5 "uncatalogued correspondence 1931–1939", Arch. LL.
137 Fourcade, M. 2006. "The Construction of a Global Profession: The Transnationalisation of Economics", *American Sociology* 112(1): 145–194; Rodgers, D. T., 1998. *Atlantic Crossings: Social Politics in a Progressive Age*. Cambridge Mass., London: The Belknap Press of Harvard University Press; Fraser, S., Gerstle, G. eds. 1989. *The Rise and Fall of the New Deal Order: 1930–1980*. Princeton: Princeton University Press; Barber, W. J. 1988. *From New Era to New Deal: Herbert Hoover, the Economists, and American policy, 1921–1933*. New York: Cambridge University Press.
138 For empirical studies on American economic expertise missions in the West, see Rosenberg, E. 1999. *Financial Missionaries to the World: The Politics and Culture of Dollar Diplomacy, 1900–1930*. Cambridge: Harvard University Press; Seidel, R. N. 1972. "American Reformers Abroad: The Kemmerer Missions in South America, 1923–1931", *The Journal of Economic History* 32(2): 520–545.
139 Feuer, L. S. 1962. "American Travelers to the Soviet Union 1917–1932: The Formation of Component of New Deal Ideology", *American Quarterly* 14(2): 119–149.
140 Lorwin, L. L. 1945. *Time for Planning: A Social-Economic Theory and Program for the Twentieth Century*. New York: Harper.
141 G 900/1935 "Visit of Mr. Lorwin and Mr. Abramson to USSR. September 1935". Lorwin, Lewis, 1936. "The Present Phase of Economic and Social Development in the USSR", *ILR* 33(1): 5–40, ILOA.

The onset of the Depression in the United States gave a new impetus to the American planning movement, which was seeking to play a role in the development of a national economic policy. Some of its members went so far as to encourage the creation of a national economic council. Lorwin was an active promoter of this idea. Since 1929, he had been trying to mobilise American economists and influential progressive figures from the press community around such a project. These contacts served as a conduit for Lorwin's ideas in the American press. So it was that, in 1931, he published an article entitled "A Federal Economic Council".[142] On 28 March 1931, he also submitted a memorandum on this subject to the economist Edward Eyre Hunt, specialist in European reconstruction and former delegate of the Commission for Relief in Belgium.[143]

That same year, under the patronage of the Brookings Institution, of which he became a member in 1925, Lorwin published a study entitled *Advisory Economic Councils*, which contained, among other things, about ten pages on the provisional economic council in Germany, the first European country to have set up such a body in 1920. In Lorwin's vision, this body would make it possible to steer the position of economists in the direction of government reform, an idea which he clearly stated at a meeting organised after the Amsterdam Congress of 1931 by the Twentieth Century Fund and the Industry and Commerce Section of the Social Science Research Council (SSRC), two social science research centres in which Lorwin was involved.[144] His study on national economic councils was relatively successful in the United States within progressive circles. It provided Lorwin with an opportunity to intervene in political and scientific discussions on the problem of the country's economic organisation.[145] However, among academic, professional and even social science research institutions, there was no consensus on the idea of a national economic council.[146] In this context, some representatives of the planning movement, such as Lorwin, would invest in the international stage to promote a planned economy policy for the United States, from abroad.

---

142 This article, which received good reviews, was not widely distributed, however, as the newspaper never sold more than 40,000 copies between the wars. Peterson, M. D. 1999. *Coming of Age with the New Republic, 1938–1950*, 6. Columbia: University of Missouri.
143 Memorandum from Lorwin to Edward Eyre Hunt, March 28, 1931. Box 4 "uncatalogued correspondence", Arch. LL.
144 Minutes of the Information conference of economists, under the joint auspices of the XXth Century Fund and of the section on Industry and Trade of the Social Science Research Council, on Economic aspects of a national programme. December 18, 1931. Box 4, in Arch. LL.
145 This study was based on information gathered during a research trip to Europe in 1931.
146 Letter from Robert M. La Follette, Jr., chairman of the Commitee on manufactures, United States Senate, May 8, 1931. Box 4, Arch. LL.

Lorwin was then especially interested in spreading one of his new ideas about world economic planning more widely. It was therefore logical that he should attend the Amsterdam Congress of 1931. Prior to the congress, Lorwin established contact with IRI through Mary van Kleeck, to whom he had submitted the proceedings of a 1930 conference by the Foreign Policy Association that called for the creation of a global economic planning office, "which would undertake the task of trying to map a course of world development", and "would seek to make possible the economic cooperation of various systems of economy and thereby promote world peace".[147] Seduced by this idea, which was close to IRI objectives, and keen to include members of the Brookings Institution among the speakers in Amsterdam, van Kleeck invited Lorwin to participate in the congress. He was quickly placed at the heart of organising for this event, coming into contact with several personalities from progressive American circles to establish the broad outlines of the discussions, particularly with regard to the project of creating a global economic organisation. Reactions to this point, however, were mixed, as evidenced by an exchange with James T. Shotwell – who would become one of the active promoters for the creation of an Economic League of Nations from 1938 onwards – reported by Lorwin:

> As to a world economic council, he had the impression that it was based on a kind of federation of existing associations. Such a federation seems to him lacking in life and motive power of its own. [...] Dr. Shotwell's general reaction was that to attempt any such organisation now would be premature, that there should be a series of congresses preceding it, and that it might be considered five years from now.[148]

Lorwin took used the Amsterdam meeting as an opportunity to present a progressive five-year global plan based on the following propositions:
(1) The growing economic unity of the world calls for a new sense of world solidarity based upon equal opportunity for all nations, and makes every attempt to perpetuate the division of the nations of the world into victors and vanquished, exploiters and exploited, a crime against human welfare.
(2) That just as the League of Nations had modified concepts of national sovereignty, so should national economic policy be formulated with an eye to its impact on the world economy.
(3) The costs of the World War "must be borne by the whole world".
(4) The leading nations must provide "immediate relief and... long range action on a large scale" to repair the world's debtor-creditor relations.

---
147 Letter from Lorwin to Mary van Kleeck, November 13, 1930. Box 4, Arch. LL.
148 Letter from Lorwin to Mary van Kleeck, December 24, 1930. Box 4, Arch. LL.

(5) In addition to the virtues of "hard work, collective efficiency and public thrift," maintaining the living standards of the advanced countries and "on a leveling up of standards and an increase of mass purchasing power in the less developed but potentially promising countries of the world". [149]

Lorwin refuted the dichotomy opposing economic nationalism to global cooperation by proposing a policy that reconciled the social and economic needs of nations with private investment abroad, a prerequisite for the creation of a global economic society. He had already defended these ideas in 1933, three years before the publication of Keynes' *General Theory of Employment, Interest and Currency* in "Economic Nationalism and World Cooperation", published in *Pacific Affairs*.[150] At Amsterdam, Lorwin proposed the following measures:
(1) A moratorium on war debts and reparations.
(2) A series of international loans from the "chief lending countries" to promote productivity and increase "world purchasing power".
(3) A series of "international agreements for the division and control of the world market by producers of raw commodities and some manufactured goods".
(4) Establishment of a World Planning Board, possibly under the auspices of the League of Nations.[151]

Lorwin's project, despite its utopian nature, bears witness to the emergence of a new shared conviction that the dislocations caused by the Great Depression could be overcome by a systematic analysis of economic and social problems, as well as by international macroeconomic planning. In 1935, despite the obvious similarities between the ideas he defended and the policies brought forth by the New Deal, Lorwin decided to accept the position of economic adviser offered by Butler, perhaps because his position was too radical. Indeed, although he was at the crossroads of several American planist networks, which for him mostly constituted "resource spaces" to build legitimacy and authority, Lorwin stood mostly alone. This probably explains why in 1935 he was involved in the

---

149 Claude, M. 2015. "Lewis L. Lorwin and "The Promise of Planning": Class, Collectivism, and Empire in U.S. Economic Planning Debates, 1931–1941". Phd diss., 47–48. Georgia State University.
    https://scholarworks.gsu.edu/history_theses/88 [last accessed 12.09.2019].
150 Lorwin, L. L. 1933. "Economic Nationalism and World Cooperation", *Pacific Affairs* 6(7): 361–372.
151 Claude, M. 2015. "Lewis L. Lorwin and "The Promise of Planning": Class, Collectivism, and Empire in U.S. Economic Planning Debates, 1931–1941", 47–48.

ILO rather than in the development of the New Deal in the United States. Two letters indicate this may have been the case. In 1931, Lorwin was disappointed with the report published by the commission organised around Senator La Follette for the creation of a national economic council. In a letter to economist John Maurice Clark of Columbia University, he criticised its vague content, too restrictive in its definition of planning, too focused on business interests and completely ignoring the interests of unions.[152] Finally, in a letter written in 1941 to the Russian economist John F. Normano, Lorwin firmly positioned himself against the New Deal.[153]

Lorwin's influence at the Office could be felt on several fronts. His recruitment efforts led other American economists to collaborate with him, such as the temporary appointment in 1936 of his close friend, co-member of the Brookings Institution, Arthur Wubnig.[154] As soon as Lorwin arrived, he established the economic research programme and directed it towards promoting a global policy of economic development based on the improvement of workers' standard of living. In developing the programme for the year 1935 to 1936, Lorwin noted: "It was important to emphasise again that the improvement of the living standards of the working populations of the world is the central problem of the organisation and all the work of the Office has a direct or indirect bearing on this problem."[155] Lorwin was also responsible for writing the economic part of Butler's annual report. Lorwin's knowledge of the American labour movement also seems worth mentioning, although Butler did not appear to be overly interested in his connections to it. In fact, Butler was mainly interested in Lorwin's economic ideas, especially those concerning industrial modernisation, trade and the organisation of the international economic system in collaboration with trade unions.

During his years at the International Labour Office, Lorwin served as a receptor of American ideas at the Office, as well as a relay for Office proposals in the United States. He was responsible for disseminating the Office's work among American scientific networks, in particular through the Institute of Pacific Relations (IPR), where he served as an American delegate in 1929 and 1933. He also relayed ideas on international planning in the United States. He organised

---

[152] Letter from John Maurice Clark, October 23, 1931. Box 1 "Catalogued correspondence", Arch. LL.
[153] Letter from Lorwin to John F. Normano, November 19, 1941. Box 6 "uncatalogued correspondence 1935–1962", Arch. LL.
[154] Letter from Lorwin to Butler, Feruary 25, 1935. Box 5, Arch. LL.
[155] EP 200/01/2 "Economic problems – Statements on the question of standard of living to be submitted to the Governing body at its 87th session. 03/1939–03/1939", ILOA.

conferences at American universities on several occasions. In 1936, under the influence of Lorwin, who had recently been appointed president of the association, the National Economic and Social Planning Association – whose objective was to disseminate information on planning through the monthly *Plan Age* – became one of the Office's broadcasting bodies.[156] In 1939, apparently because of conflicting relations with other International Labour Office members, Lorwin decided to leave the organisation and returned to the United States, where he continued to defend his ideas on international planning.

3.3 Difficult Collaborations with the Rockefeller Foundation

The entry of the United States into the ILO in 1934 also gave rise to a proliferation of collaborative projects with American scientific networks. The Rockefeller Foundation was particularly interested in the activities of the Office, where it sought to disseminate, as it did at the League of Nations, an American scientific culture.[157] The rapprochement between the Office and the Rockefeller was made possible by Lorwin's presence at the Office, as well as that of former fellows, like Percival Martin, John Riches and Hans Staehle. Unlike with the League of Nations, however, the Rockefeller's influence on the Office between the two World Wars remained limited.

The idea of nurturing closer ties between the two organisations emerged in 1933 under the impulse of Butler, who wanted to develop research projects with the Rockefeller Division of Social Sciences.[158] In the fall of the same year, Butler went on a mission to New York to pursue discussions with the Rockefeller concerning an international survey on economic stabilisation in agriculture and industry and its social consequences.[159] Despite these initial discussions, the Rockefeller's position was not as committed as it seemed. Economist Edmund Day, Director of the Social Science Research Division, was reluctant to enter into any collaboration with the ILO, as this organisation clearly competed with the

---

[156] Letter from F. Hinrichs, Acting President of the National Economic and Social Planning Association to Lewis Lorwin, March 24, 1936. Box 6 "Uncatalogued correspondence 1935–1962", Arch. LL.
[157] Tournès, L. 2012. "La philanthropie américaine, la Société des Nations et la coproduction d'un ordre international (1919–1946)", *Relations internationales* 3(151): 25–36.
[158] Tournès, L. 2015. *Les États-Unis et la Société des Nations (1914–1946) : Le système international face à l'émergence d'une superpuissance*, 170. Bern etc: P. Lang.
[159] XT 61/4/1 "Director's visit to USA and Mexico (Oct.–Nov. 1934). Papers taken on mission. Jacket V", ILOA.

League of Nation's Economic and Financial Organisation (EFO). Above all, however, the United States was about to join the ILO and the Rockefeller Foundation remained anxious not to "awaken isolationist enthusiasm in Congress" and not to thwart President Roosevelt's project with an overly hasty commitment.[160] Following strong opposition from the American workers' delegates in Geneva, Butler was forced to abandon his project of collaborating with the Rockefeller Foundation. Besides, this project provoked the anger of trade unionists, in particular John Lewis, President of the miners' federation and future president of the Congress of Industrial Organisations (CIO).[161] Among the reasons for their opposition, Ludovic Tournès (2015) explains that American workers did not distinguish between the Rockefeller Foundation and the Industrial Relations Counsellors – an institute dedicated to the study of industrial relations in the United States, created in 1921 by John D. Rockefeller, Jr. and Raymond Fosdick and immediately perceived by the unions as a rival body.[162]

In April 1935, despite opposition from American workers' representatives, Lorwin, then in the United States, met Edmund Day to re-launch the question of an economic survey to be conducted with the support of the Rockefeller. From this interview the idea emerged that collaboration was still possible, especially on the issues of business cycles and social insurance, two areas in which the Rockefeller Foundation wished to develop its research.[163] In October 1935, Van Sickle, then in charge of economic security research, travelled to Geneva to obtain information on the ILO's social insurance, living standards, wages and unemployment programmes.[164] This visit came shortly after the adoption of the Social Security Act (SSA) in August 1935, the first sign of the emergence of a welfare state in the United States.

Although the context was rather favourable to trans-Atlantic collaborations, Butler was still reluctant to develop specific economic research projects with the Rockefeller Foundation.[165] In December 1936, Percival Martin and Lorwin sought to convince Butler to launch informal discussions with the Rockefeller Foundation to finance studies on national reconstruction policies, particularly from an unemployment perspective, in order to monitor the attitudes of the various gov-

---

[160] Tournès, L. 2015. *Les États-Unis et la Société des Nations (1914–1946)*, 171.
[161] Folder 973: International Labor Office, 1936–1940, Box 108, series 100 S (International-Social Sciences), RG 1.1 (Projects), Rockefeller Archive Center, New York (hereafter RAC).
[162] Tournès, L. 2015. *Les États-Unis et la Société des Nations (1914–1946)*, 171.
[163] Letter from Lorwin to Butler, April 19, 1935. CAT 61–1–1, ILOA.
[164] Letter from Tracy B. Kittredge to Butler, September 24, 1935. CAT 61–1–1, ILOA.
[165] Note from Kittredge, October 2, 1936. RG 1.1/100/108/973, RAC.

ernments towards a policy of increased wages and reduced working hours.[166] On 29 January 1937, without Butler's knowledge, Martin, Lorwin and Tracy B. Kittredge, administrator at the Rockefeller Foundation, jointly reviewed the research project proposal. Through Kittredge's intervention, who believed that the Office's Director was ready to make a commitment the very same year, the Foundation's Executive Committee was authorised by the Board of Trustees to fund a three-year collaboration with the Office for a comparative study of economic measures and their social impact. A sum of $75,000 was allotted to this research project, in particular to measure the effects of wage policies on unemployment, the effectiveness of public works projects in combating unemployment, the economic consequences of the development of social insurance schemes and, finally, the effect of protectionist measures on industrial and agricultural workers. At this stage, however, as confirmed by correspondence between Van Sickle and Kittredge, Butler had still not given his approval to file an official request with the Rockefeller.[167]

Finally, in July 1937, Butler himself cancelled the project. The break between the two organisations actually took place a few months earlier, during a telephone conversation between Van Sickle, Day and Butler, which highlighted the different understanding of the nature and objectives of economic research within the two organisations. According to Day, the Office should take greater responsibility in evaluating national planning policies. Such a study would have been perceived by countries run by totalitarian regimes as a direct critique of their policies, which went against the political neutrality Butler sought to display. As Van Sickle notes, "Butler blew alternatively hot and cold, at one moment indicating his desire to secure Foundation support and the next moment definitely negative".[168] Despite his interest in the development of economic research, Butler also feared opposition from the ILO's Governing Body, particularly from American workers. This research project would also have provoked opposition from representatives of European workers who suspected that Britain and the United States were seeking, above all, to multiply economic studies in order to sabotage the social policy measures they demanded.[169] According to Percival Martin, Butler shared their fears, worried that the Rockefeller would support the research project for the sole purpose of demonstrating to trade union organisations the economic impossibility of their social demands. Thus, between the two world wars, the relations between the Rockefeller and the Office did not

---

[166] Note from Kittredge, December 17, 1936. RG 1.1/100/108/973, RAC.
[167] Letter from Van Sickle to Kittredge, April 19, 1937. RG 1.1/100/108/973, RAC.
[168] Note from Van Sickle, July 29, 1937. RG 1.1/100/108/973, RAC.
[169] Ibid.

lead to tangible collaborations. These unsuccessful attempts nevertheless constitute an interesting parenthesis in the history of trans-Atlantic collaborations involving the Office.

Conclusion

In the 1930s, the ILO's matrix reflection on development revolved around three main ideas: economic and social planning, international economic organisation, and social justice. They formed the basis for the modern philosophy of development that was emerging at the ILO. These ideas were enmeshed in complex currents and experiences. The Office's economic and social conceptions were intimately linked to Albert Thomas' experience and the influence of French reformist and American Taylorist networks within the Office. Rationalism and the practices developed by European and American reformist movements in the nineteenth and twentieth centuries, the First World War and early experiences of economic and social organisation by the state, authoritarian planning models, along with the American Taylorist and planist movements together form a set of ideas and experiences that shaped the Office's thinking.

The Office's stance on organised economies and planning in the 1930s is fundamental in understanding the development model that was being put in place. Since the Great Depression, the Office's understanding of social policy had profoundly shifted. It ceased to be conceived solely as a shield protecting the worker from the fluctuating free economy and became a weapon in favour of continuous economic and social progress through the organisation of the economy. This shift would also eventually reach the League of Nations, culminating in 1939 with the publication of a report entitled "The Development of International Co-operation in Economic and Social Affairs", better known today as the Bruce Report, which outlined the organisation's new objectives, and whose conclusions would later be taken up by the UN Economic and Social Council (CESNU), created in 1946.[170]

An analysis of how the Office reflected on the effects of and the remedies to the Great Depression highlights the wide variety of issues addressed. This diversity attests to the context of the 1930s, which was particularly conducive to ex-

---

[170] *The Development of International Co-operation in Economic and Social Affairs*. Special Committee on the Development of International Cooperation in Economic and Social Affairs, 1939. Geneva: League of Nations; Ghebali, V.–Y. 1972. "Aux origines de l'Ecosoc–l'évolution des commissions et organisations techniques de la Société des Nations", *Annuaire français de droit international* 18(1): 469–511.

periments in economic organisation. I have focused in particular on the Office's proposals for public works. International cooperation in this field was not only seen as a response to the unemployment crisis, but as a new way to develop industrial production, economic exchanges, boost employment and improve the living conditions of workers. Under Albert Thomas' leadership, the main objective was to propose possible paths for the economic reconstruction of Europe. The entry of the United States would broaden the ILO's prospects.

Chapter II
After the "Spirit of Geneva" Comes the "Spirit of Santiago": Early Regional Cooperation in Latin America

The 1930s not only led the ILO to reflect on its position and its role within Europe, it also prompted the organisation to reconsider its place in the world, along with the means to be developed to fortify its relations with countries outside Europe. In his 1932 annual report, Albert Thomas thus called for strengthening collaborations with non-European countries.[1] However, considering how little weight the demands of developing countries still had at the ILO in comparison with those of industrialised countries – whose social policies were more developed and whose influence on the international scene was much more significant – it seemed the time had not yet come for any significant commitment in this direction. This balance of power would only truly begin shifting after the entry of the United States into the ILO in 1934 and following the first Latin American regional conference in 1936. The regionalisation of ILO activities is one of the manifestations of the "shift in balance" that took place at the ILO in the 1930s, when Latin American countries began playing a greater role internationally.[2]

Before the Second World War, as it sought to build new spaces for dialogue closer to the social and economic realities of its member states, the ILO organised two regional conferences in Latin America that heralded the beginning of a new practice of international technical cooperation. Beyond particular regional trajectories, this chapter aims to analyse the ILO's influence in promoting forms of regional technical cooperation. Doing so helps reframe the consequences of this reconfiguration in the broader context of new reflections on ways to encourage social progress and the adoption of stricter social standards in less industrialised countries. After highlighting the limits of the participation of non-European countries in ILO activities, this chapter offers an analysis of the regionalisation process that took place within the organisation, focusing on the case of Latin American countries, which played a central role in promoting a Latin American perspective and more broadly influencing the ILO's globalisa-

---

1 Director's Report, ILC, 1932, 879, ILOA.
2 Director's Report, ILC, 1938, 71, ILOA.

https://doi.org/10.1515/9783110616323-006

tion process.³ This will lead me to probe the impact of this reconfiguration on ILO activities, stressing two main areas of collaboration: social insurance and migration for colonisation.

1 Opposing Models: "Europeanism" vs "Universalism"

The regionalisation of ILO activities was part of a Eurocentric reflection on the limits of international cooperation. From 1930 onwards, criticism of the ILO's predominantly European character became systematic. Faced with an international context plagued by rising tensions, one in which the global economic crisis meant the gradual closure of borders and the emergence of regional blocs, the ILO became aware of the limits of its action in Europe and in the rest of the world. In this conjuncture, Latin America, where the first regional offices had opened as early as the late 1920s, acted as a catalyst in the decentralisation of the ILO's activities away from Europe.

1.1 The European Origins of the ILO

Although Albert Thomas, who gave the International Labour Office a vital force, never ignored the importance of forging links all over the world, the social issues tackled by the Office were to a large extent limited to European industrial societies.⁴ The background of the international civil servants working for the Office reinforced the organisation's European character.⁵ In 1925, although the Office boasted 25 different nationalities among its staff, French and British nationals held the best positions, and the organisation's two official languages were English and French. In 1932, of the 420 employees, only 18 had non-European backgrounds. Outside Europe, the organisation remained little known. Office publications were not widely distributed and the organisation had very little contact with labour movements, such as organisations not affiliated with the International Federation of Trade Unions (IFTU), whose members predominantly repre-

---

3 Antony Alcock was one of the first to highlight the new importance of non-European countries to the ILO. Alcock, A. 1971. *History of the International Labour Organization*, 135. London: Macmillan.
4 Guérin, D. 1996. *Albert Thomas au BIT 1920–1932: de l'internationalisme à l'Europe.* Genève: Euryopa, 61.
5 Plata, V. 2010. *Le Recrutement des fonctionnaires du Bureau international du travail en 1920 : Une approche prosopographique.* Master diss., University of Geneva.

sented workers' delegates to the ILO.⁶ Thus, despite its universalistic claims, the ILO, like the League of Nations, was largely dominated by European culture and representations. As a result, it aroused little interest outside Europe, and struggled to provide tangible proof of its proclaimed universalism.

The low level of participation of Latin American countries in the works that came out of the Geneva conferences demonstrated the limited reach of its action.⁷ Between 1919 and 1933, only Chile and Uruguay were represented at the conference each year, followed closely by Venezuela and Brazil. Besides, most government delegates were posted abroad and did not necessarily maintain close relations with their respective governments. The ability of these Latin American delegations to disseminate information on ILO activities is questionable, as both workers' and employers' representatives were often missing. Of those in attendance, the workers' representatives were not necessarily speaking on behalf of labour organisations, which were practically non-existent in Latin America in the 1920s and 1930s.⁸ Although the organisation of the International Labour Conferences (ILC) in Geneva was in itself a barrier to these countries' participation due to the cost and duration of trans-Atlantic travel at this time (the return trip would take delegates a month and a half), the overall lack of interest in ILO activities was palpable, as the organisation was considered to be far removed from the realities of non-European countries.

This feeling was reinforced by the fact that international conventions, conceived on the model of the world's most industralised nations, did not reflect the economic and social conditions of the less developed countries, which often failed to ratify them.⁹ The debates that arose at the beginning of the

---

6 Tosstorff, R. 2010. "Albert Thomas, the ILO and the IFTU", in Van Daele, J. et al. eds. ILO Histories. Essays on the International Labour Organization and Its Impact on the World During the Twentieth Century, 91–114. Bern: Peter Lang.

7 A list of Latin American countries that were members of the ILO between 1919 and 1950: Argentina, Bolivia, Brazil, Chile, Colombia, Cuba, Salvador (from 1919 to 1939 and since 1948), Guatemala (from 1919 to 1938 and since 1945), Haiti, Honduras (from 1919 to 1938 and since 1955), Peru, Paraguay (from 1919 to 1937 and since 1956), Uruguay and Venezuela (from 1919 to 1957 and since 1958). See the database of ILO member countries, http://www.ilo.org/ilolex/french/mstatesf.htm. [last accessed 17.09.2019].

8 Note, however, the exception of Mexico and Argentina, where there were central workers' organisations. RL 86/0 "Relation of the ILO with central and south America. General", ILOA.

9 In 1930, Latin America only had light industries, despite an initial period of industrialisation from the late nineteenth century until the depression of the 1930s. For a general overview of the economic development of Latin America since 1830, see the dated but still very useful monograph by Léon, P. 1969. Économies et sociétés de l'Amérique Latine. Essai sur les problèmes du développement à l'époque contemporaine, 1815–1967. Paris: Regards sur l'Histoire.

1930s on the "European" nature of the international labour Conventions bears witness to this. The corollary of this debate was the growing emphasis on the need to develop a social policy catering to the conditions of less industrialised countries. At the 1934 ILC, several delegates echoed this concern. The ILCs were thus gradually becoming a place where this "dissociation" from Europe could be expressed, and the opposition between the ILO's universalist model and national and regional particularities articulated.[10]

1.2 Pan-Americanism and the Creation of Regional Labour Offices

This movement was reinforced by the growing interest in regional integration projects outside Europe, to which the 1929 pan-European project of Aristide Briand certainly gave new impetus. While their promoters saw them as a means of adjusting the ILO's social protection paradigms to non-Western contexts, these projects also testify to the feeling of "collective insecurity" which then dominated international meetings and which could be explained in part by the rise of extreme nationalisms[11] and the League of Nation's failures regarding economic cooperation and military security.[12]

In the field of social policy, new proposals for regional labour organisation were concretely challenging the ILO's universalist discourse. The fourth Balkan Congress, which met in Thessaloniki, Macedonia, in November 1933, recommended a text proposing a draft convention for the organisation of a labour office in the Balkans.[13] At the Montevideo Pan-American Conference of 1933,[14] or-

---

10 On international conferences as spaces for the construction and confrontation of models in a Cold War context, see Kott, S. 2011. "Par-delà la guerre froide. Les organisations internationales et les circulations Est-Ouest (1947–1973) ", *Vingtième Siècle. Revue d'histoire* 1(109): 129–143.
11 Éric Bussière also considers the importance of this context in the development of regional cooperation under the auspices of the League of Nations. See Bussière, E. 2005. "Premiers schémas européens et économie internationale durant l'entre-deux-guerres", *Relations internationales* 123(3): 51–68.
12 Guieu, J.-M. 2009. "L'"insécurité collective'. L'Europe et la Société des Nations dans l'entre-deux-guerres", *Bulletin de l'Institut Pierre Renouvin*, 2(30): 21–43.
13 Letter from Adrien Tixier to Wilfred Jenks, August 25, 1934. RL 01/4 "Coordination between regional labour organisation and the ILO", ILOA.
14 At the end of the nineteenth century, Pan-American conferences were organised for the first time. The first, held in 1889, led to the creation of the International Bureau of American Republics, which in 1910 became the Pan-American Union (PAU). Although dominated by American politics, it represents the first time inter-American relations were institutionalised. Smith, J. 2000. "The First Conference of American States (1889–1890) and the Early Pan American Policy

ganised by the Pan-American Union (PAU), a proposal submitted by the representative of Mexico, which had only been a member of the ILO since 1931 despite rapprochement efforts by Albert Thomas dating back to the 1920s, [15] aimed directly at the creation of a regional labour office.[16] Mexico had already made a similar proposal at the 1928 Pan-American Conference.[17] This pan-American labour office would have the dual function of collecting and exchanging social information, and would therefore compete with the International Labour Office in Geneva.[18] The Montevideo conference also adopted a series of recommendations on the institution of unemployment insurance and the establishment of a public works programme. Resolutions were also passed asking governments to examine the possibility of establishing mandatory health-accident-disability-pension insurance laws. The creation of an inter-American institute for the development of the cooperative movement, which would be institutionally linked to the PAU, was also planned. The Montevideo Conference thus voted on a comprehensive programme for the development of social policies, without any mention of collaboration with the ILO.

The Montevideo Conference attests to significant efforts aimed at connecting elites and fostering dialogue on social policy issues of particular interest to Latin

---

of the United States", in Sheinin, D. ed. *Beyond the Ideal: Pan Americanism in Inter-American Affairs*, 19–32. Westport: Greenwood press. For a transnational approach to Pan-American conferences, see Guy, D. 1998. "The Pan American Child Congresses, 1916 to 1942: Pan Americanism, Child Reform, and the Welfare State in Latin America", *Journal of Family History* 23(3): 272–291. For a history of international relations between the United States and Latin American countries, see Smith, J. 2005. *The United States and Latin America. A history of American diplomacy, 1776–2000*. New York: Routledge; Schoultz, L. 2003. *Beneath the United States: A History of U.S. Policy Toward Latin America*. Cambridge Massachusetts: Harvard University Press; Sheinin, D. ed. 2000. *Beyond the ideal: Pan Americanism in Inter-American affairs*. Westport, Conn.: Greenwood Press; Smith, P. H. 2000. *Talons of the Eagle: Dynamics of U.S.-Latin American Relations*. New York: Oxford University Press; Molineu, H. 1986. *US Policy toward Latin America: from Regionalism to Globalism*. Colorado: Westview Press.

15 Herrera León, F. 2011. "México y la Organización Internacional del Trabajo: Los orígenes de una relación, 1919–1931", *Foro Internacional*, 204: 336–355.

16 XR 62/1/1 "Pan-American Conference (Montevideo, Dec.1933)", ILOA.

17 Such a proposal had already been made by Argentina at the American Congress in Tucuman, in 1916. D 600/923/2/6/2 "VI Conférence Pan Américaine de la Havane. Janvier 1928. Mr. Poblete Troncoso's mission to above conference", ILOA.

18 Letter from Harold Butler to Leifur Magnusson, Decembre 27, 1933. XC 61/1/2 "United States. Correspondent's Office Washington. L. Magnusson. Jacket 1 to 4", ILOA. This project also provided for a tripartite commission for the recruitment of administrative and technical staff, a governing body and Pan-American conferences.

American countries.¹⁹ This phenomenon was reinforced by the global economic crisis, which was causing profound upheavals marked by new political organisations, the growing desire for economic development and the emergence of new social ideologies.²⁰ In Mexico, Chile and Argentina, where since the 1920s reformist tendencies were emerging in intellectual and parliamentary circles, political elites were thus seeking to promote a European-inspired policy of social reform, and perhaps even to globalise the movement, as proposals for regional labour organisation indicate. As of 1933, inter-American collaboration also grew in popularity under Roosevelet and his Good Neighbor Policy. The relative success of this policy also coincided with the development of pan-Americanism, which had begun defining North-South relations and served as the basis for the development of a new modernisation theory between American politicans and Latin American specialists.²¹ It is worth mentioning that since the early 1930s, there had been a proliferation of publications on pan-Americanism in widely read publications such as *World Affairs*, participating in the creation of a "professional" discourse on Latin America, and attesting to the growing interest of American social sciences in this region.

In Montevideo in 1933, supported only by Mexican and Cuban delegates, the project of a pan-American labour office failed to be implemented. The Latin American delegates from Brazil and Venezuela reaffirmed their commitment to the ILO, as illustrated by this statement made by the Brazilian delegate, Carlos Chagas: "The social reasons which must serve as a basis for legislation to assist the working classes and for the regulation of relations between employers and workers, and more broadly the principles which must inspire national legislators in matters related to labour, are universal in character." ²²

---

19 Social policy issues were first discussed in the PAU's programme of activities at the 1924 Santiago Conference. Some annual publications are available at

http://archive.org/search.php?query=creator%3 A%22Pan+American+Union%22 [last accessed 17.09.2019].

20 On the development of social policies in Latin America, refer to the collective work of Bel, C., Lewis, C. M. eds. 1993. *Welfare, Poverty and Development in Latin America*. London: The Macmillan Press. See in particular Lewis, C. M. "Social Insurance: Ideology and Policy in the Argentine, c.1920–1966": 175–200.

21 Berger, M. T. 2000. "A Greater America? Pan Americanism and the Professional Study of Latin America, 1890–1990", in Sheinin, D. ed., *Beyond the Ideal*, 79–94.

22 Original quote in French: "Les raisons d'ordre social qui doivent servir de base à la législation d'assistance des classes ouvrières et à la réglementation des relations entre patrons et travailleurs, et en général les principes qui doivent inspirer les législateurs nationaux en matière de travail, ont un caractère universel". XR 62/1/1 "Pan–American Conference (Montevideo, Dec.1933)", ILOA.

This statement was made at the instruction of Affonso Bandeira de Mello, Director-General at the Brazilian Ministry of Labour, who was regularly present in Geneva. The project did not receive support from the United States either, as some representatives of the Roosevelt administration were already in contact with the International Labour Office. Harold Butler would ensure that the Roosevelt administration opposed any new initiative to create a pan-American organisation that would dublicate efforts made by the Office in Geneva.[23] The support of the United States was confirmed in Montevideo through Frances Perkins' intervention with the Secretary of State, Cordell Hull, the delegate to the conference, in order to avoid the adoption of the Mexican project, the creation of which would have complicated the negotiations on the accession of the United States to the ILO.[24] The latter were not opposed to the development of social policy in Latin America, quite the contrary. The US government viewed this movement favourably, insofar as it echoed its desire to improve economic relations with this region.[25] In this regard, the ILO, where European powers could counterbalance the influence of Latin American countries, could serve as an instrument in the development of Roosevelt's economic security policy.[26] Taking into account the influence of communism in Mexico and Nazism in Argentina and Brazil, support for the ILO also constituted a clear stand in favour of the democratic model of social policies.[27]

---

[23] Letter from Butler to Leigfur Magnusson, Decembre 27, 1933. XC 61/1/2 "United States. Correspondent's Office Waschington. L. Magnusson. Jacket III: 1932–1935", ILOA.

[24] According to a confidential report, the United States expressed its negative opinion to the subcommission where the Mexican project was discussed, even though it was not an official member. XR 62/1/1 "Pan–American Conference (Montevideo, Dec.1933)", ILOA.

[25] For Joseph Smith, the United States did not conceive pan-Americanism in a context of regional cooperation but "as a function of US political and economic expansionism in the Americas". Latin America was thus perceived above all as a market for accessible raw materials capable of absorbing the surplus of American agricultural and industrial production. Smith, J. 2000. "The First Conference of American States (1889–1890) and the Early Pan American Policy of the United States", in Sheinin, D. ed. *Beyond the Ideal: Pan Americanism in Inter-American Affairs*, 20. Westport, Conn.: Greenwood Press.

[26] In 1940 the inter-ministerial meeting held in Havana marked the establishment of inter-American economic cooperation with the erection of a trade wall, the objective of which was to counter the German economic threat by paying for the surplus production of the 21 Latin American Republics. See "The cartel plan and the Havana Conference". Z 10/3/1 "2nd regional Conference of American Sates, Cuba 1939", ILOA.

[27] An article in the *New York Times* of December 9, 1933 wrote about Cordell Hull's speech in Montevideo: "[He] has contrived in one shrewd gesture to throw the weight not only of the United States but of the two American continents into the world psychological balance for peace".

Resolutions passed in Montevideo provoked an unprecedented mobilisation at the International Labour Office. After the conference, diplomatic missions multiplied. Between 1934 and 1936, Butler visited Latin America twice, thus relaunching the policy initiated by Thomas ten years earlier.[28] In 1934 Butler went to Mexico and there was assured by president Abelardo L. Rodríguez and General Calles that Mexico would "go cool on any project for a Pan American labor office".[29] Stephen Lawford Childs,[30] then a member of Butler's cabinet, along with Adrien Tixier, head of the Social Insurance Section, also visited several Latin American countries between 1934 and 1935 to survey governments on ways to strengthen the ILO's presence on the continent.[31]

2 The Regionalisation of International Labour Office Activities

Faced with the challenge posed to the ILO by the pan-American labour office project, International Labour Office civil servants began reflecting explicitly on the possibilities of integrating regional cooperation into the broader framework of international cooperation.[32] These reflections underscore the growing importance of non-European countries within the ILO at this time, as it was beginning to provide concrete institutional solutions to their demands.

New York Times, December 9, 1933. XR 62/1/1 "Pan-American Conference (Montevideo, Dec.1933)", ILOA.

28 CAT 1–25–2 "Organisation voyage Amérique latine", July-August 1925; RL 86/0 "Relation of the ILO with central and south America. General", ILOA.

29 Letter from Butler to Phelan, October 26, 1934. XT 61/4/1 "Director's visit to USA and Mexico (October-November 1934)", ILOA.

30 Stephen Lawford Childs (1895–1943) was a British international civil servant. Before joining the ILO, he worked for the League's High Commissioner for Refugees. After Butler's departure in 1938, Childs left the ILO and returned to the British Foreign Office. He died in a plane crash between Iran and Iraq in 1943. On his mission in connection with the 1936 regional conference, see XD 12/1/1 "Regional Conference of American States members of the ILO. Santiago de Chile (December 1935-January 1936). Jacket II", ILOA.

31 Singleton, L. 2013. "The ILO and Social Security in Latin America, 1930–1950", in Herrera León, F., Herrera González, P. eds. *América Latina y la Organización Internacional del Trabajo: Redes, coopéración técnica e institucionalidad social, 1919–1950*, 243–74. México City: UMSNH, UM, UFF.

32 Plata-Stenger, V. 2015. "To Raise Awareness of Difficulties and to Assert their Opinion". "The International Labour Office and the Regionalization of International Cooperation in the 1930s", in McPherson, A., Wehrli, Y. eds. *Beyond Geopolitics: New Histories of Latin America at the League of Nations*, 97–113. New Mexico, University of New Mexico Press.

2.1 Regional Cooperation Serving International Cooperation

Until the mid-1930s regional arrangements remained controversial within international organisations.[33] While the Covenant of the League of Nations explicitly referred to regional agreements, mistrust was pervasive. These projects were seen as weakening international cooperation, especially the manifestly hegemonic ones proposed by Japan and Nazi Germany. The ILO chose to adopt an intermediate position, as evidenced by the 1934 report by ILO legal adviser, Wilfred Jenks:

It might be well for the Office to be more ambitious to control such tendencies in their early stages than it has been in the past. For this purpose, it might be well to prepare a model of constitution for regional labour organisations, which could be circulated among interested persons as soon as regional organisation has become a serious possibility in any area.[34]

For Jenks, regional cooperation had to be promoted only insofar as it strengthened the ILO's political position. Regional cooperation was also to be coordinated at all levels, including research programmes and regional conference programmes. Jenks further insisted that the provisions proposed by the ILO should not be amended in its constitution, but rather inserted into the constitutions of the regional organisations. Only in 1946, with the constitutional revision of the ILO, would the practice of regional conferences be normalised in Article 38.

While regional cooperation projects addressing social policies were seen as a good thing by the International Labour Office, as they attested to the liberal spirit that reigned in "peripheral" countries, civil servants of the Office were also well aware of less desirable potential consequences, the more important being doubts about the universality of the organisation. For Adrien Tixier, recognition of regional units could also encourage coalitions against certain conventions. Referring to the ILO's experience with Scandinavian countries, he noted: "Thus, to please Denmark, a country of voluntary insurance, Sweden and Norway, which have compulsory insurance systems, frequently abstain from voting our conventions."[35] The creation of regional institutions would also call into

---

[33] Rens, Jef. 1959 "Latin America and the International Labour Organisation. Forty years of collaboration 1919–1959", in *International Labour Review* 80(1): 6. For an analysis of the discussions on "decentralisation" at the League of Nations, see Richard, A.-I. 2012. "Competition and Complementarity: Civil Society Networks and the Question of Decentralising the League of Nations", *Journal of Global History* 7(2): 233–256.
[34] RL 01/4 "Coordination between regional labour organisation and the ILO", ILOA.
[35] Letter from Adrien Tixier to Wilfred Jenks, August 1934. RL 01/4, "Coordination between regional labour organisation and the ILO", ILOA.

question the ILO's competence on specific issues, such as equal treatment of domestic and foreign workers, in particular regarding social insurance benefits. Finally, Tixier was preoccupied by the participation of workers' organisations in these regional labour offices. He feared that the regional labour office projects of which the Office was aware would operate mainly under government control, representing their interests above all. He thought in particular of the pan-American labour office, where, with the exception of Argentina and Mexico, the labour forces that were only beginning to organise[36] had little to no influence on their governments.[37] Butler's annual report to the 1934 International Labour Conference reflects the discussions taking place at the ILO at the time, concluding with these words:

> The great majority of labour problems are no doubt universal and not regional in character. In matters such as hours of work, social insurance, health and safety, there should be one world standard, and any exceptions in favour of particular countries or regions should be laid down by the Conference itself as the authority, which sets the general standard.[38]

While in itself the development of regional cooperation was perceived as a positive sign, civil servants at the Office hoped this movement would not lead to formally calling into question the universal character of the ILO. This position remains faithful to that expressed as early as 1930 by Albert Thomas.[39]

2.2 More Space for Non-European Countries

That being said, the ILO was to carry out a series of institutional reforms in hopes of strengthening collaboration with countries outside Europe. The aim was, first and foremost, to broaden representation on the Governing Body. In

---

36 On the role of American trade union organisations in the development of Latin American trade unionism and its integration into a US-led Pan-American federation, see Alexander, R. J., Parker, E. M. 2009. *International Labor Organisations and Organised Labor in Latin America and the Carribean: A History*. Santa Barbara: ABC-CLIO; Touraine, A. 1988. "L'évolution du syndicalisme en Amérique latine", *Revue française de sociologie* 29(1): 117–142. On the history of the AFL, see Lorwin, L. L. 1972. *The American Federation of Labor*. New Jersey: Augustus M. Kelley Publishers.
37 Already in 1925, Thomas noted: "our relations with Latin American workers' organisation remain fragmented and scarce". These organisations, he remarked, "are oftentimes still weak. Few have had direct or indirect contact with our Conference". Director's Report, ILC, 1925, 1032, ILOA.
38 Director's Report, ILC, 1934, 73, ILOA.
39 Director's Report, ILC, 1930, 7, ILOA.

1934, an amendment to Article 393 regarding the composition of the GB adopted in 1922 entered into force. This amendment increased the composition of the GB from 24 to 32 members, 16 of whom had to be non-European.[40] Other reforms were not successful due to the League of Nation's budget downsizing policy, over which the ILO had no decision-making power whatsoever.[41] Moreover, in 1936, the Committee of Experts on the application of conventions suggested, in vain, to hire more non-European experts. It also proposed taking more binding measures and authorising the Office to contact governments directly, so that they could specify the difficulties preventing them from fully implementing the conventions.[42] In 1934, however, the ILO adopted a budget aimed at developing its activites in non-European regions, a decision closely linked to the United States' recent entry into the ILO. In particular, there was an increase in funding for the development of relations with Latin American countries.[43] Until the ILO relocated in Montreal, the decisions of the Financing Committee point to the ILO's strategy, as influenced by the United States, to move closer to Latin American countries.[44] Finally, the ILO decided to create a Section of non-European countries within the International Labour Office,[45] whose function was to centralise and

---

40 Ghebali, V.-Y. 1975. *Organisation internationale et guerre mondiale. Le cas de la société des nations et de l'organisation internationale du travail pendant la seconde guerre mondiale*. PhD. dissert., Science politique, Grenoble 2, 40–50.

41 In 1933 a committee headed by the Belgian government delegate Ernest Manhaim made some suggestions of an essentially financial nature, proposing, for instance, the adoption of a system that would make it possible to distribute the travel expenses of delegates to the conference more equitably among all member states, or the pooling of these same expenses for delegates and alternates, in order to reduce the burden on nationals of non-European countries. GB's report, 63rd session, June 1933, 270, ILOA.

42 D 775/100/2 "ILO Governing Body sess. 75 (Geneva, Apr. 1936): documents, item 2 – Appointment of additional experts, more particularly from extra-European countries, the Committee of Experts on the application of conventions (GB.75/2/68): E, F", ILOA.

43 D 769/100/15 "ILO Governing Body sess.69: documents, item 15, report of the Finance Committee; Contribution of the United States of America to the ILO", ILOA. The budget estimates for 1935 increased to 215,000 Swiss francs from 173,000 in 1934. These expenses cover credit for correspondents, the development of relations with non-European countries (20,000 Swiss francs for 1935 from the United States contribution, compared with 0 in 1934 and 1933), press agencies, contributors to Spanish and Italian journals, contributors to the *Recueil de jurisprudence*, translations and remuneration of articles, convening experts, reports and various collaborations.

44 D 787/100/8 "Diplomatic. ILO Governing Body sess.87 (Geneva, Apr 1939), documents, item 8 – Report of the Finance Committee: Budget Estimates for 1940", ILOA.

45 Similarly, a Latin American office was created in 1923 at the League in response to requests by Latin American delegates for better representation of their interests in the Secretariat. Wehrli, Y. 2003. "*Créer et maintenir l'intérêt*" : *la liaison entre le Secrétariat de la Société des Nations et l'Amérique Latine (1919–1929)*, Master diss., University of Geneva, 76–77.

disseminate information while developing research in three distinct geographical areas: Asia, Latin America and the Middle East. In 1936, some ten civil servants ran this Section. However, for budgetary reasons, its activites rapidly decreased until 1939, when they ceased altogether.

The running of this Section relied solely on the strengths already present within the Office and did not have its own programme. It thus functioned above all as a kind of showcase for the ILO's globalising activities.[46] Nevertheless, its members produced a series of studies in various fields, such as the working conditions of agricultural workers in India, conditions in the household industry in certain parts of Japan, working hours in China, and the living and working conditions of some indigenous peoples of Latin America. It also sent translations of the Director's and annual reports to all Latin American trade union organisations with which the Office had relations.[47] In 1936, the Confederation of Mexican Workers (CTM) benefited from a free and permanent supply of Spanish and English editions of all its publications.[48] The Office also wished to strengthen its non-European staff. On this point, however, little concrete progress was made due to budget deficits recorded year after year. The ILO was also concentrating its resources on the expansion of its correspondants network. New branch offices were opened in Mexico in 1935, Cuba in 1936, Chile, Venezuela and Peru in 1937, as well as Ecuador, Colombia and Uruguay in 1938. These offices were added to those of Rio de Janeiro, opened in 1929, and Buenos Aires, in 1931.

Finally, research missions multiplied in the 1930s, particularly in the field of social insurance.[49] During his trip to South America in 1934, Tixier witnessed the extent of the social insurance movement in Brazil, Argentina, Chile and Urugay.

---

[46] In 1936 the members of this section were Mack Eastman (Canada), Caldwell (Australia), Rao (India), Kamii (Japan) and Wilson (USA) for Asia, Djamalzadeh (Iraq) for the Middle East and Moisés Poblete Troncoso (Chile), Vasquez (Colombia) and Guillen-Monfrote (Spain) for Latin America.

[47] Since 1919 the ILO had published a Spanish version of the ILC's proceedings. The Director's Report was published in Spanish as of 1928. The Spanish version of the *International Labour Review* was published in Madrid as of 1923. The *ILR* also had subscribers in Spain and its colonial territories in Morocco. The *ILR* took its final title of *Revista Internacional del Trabajo* with the first issue of 1930. In 1945, Spanish became an official language of the ILO. Bollé, P. 2012. "La *Revue internationale du travail*, le BIT, l'OIT: fragments d'une histoire", *ILR* 152, special issue: 1–14.

[48] RL 41/3/2 "Relations with the Confederacion de Trabajadores de Mexico. Vicente Lombardo Toledano. Rodolfo Puna Soria", ILOA.

[49] Plata-Stenger, V. 2017. "L'OIT et l'assurance sociale en Amérique latine dans les années 30 et 40: enjeux et limites de l'expertise internationale", *Revue d'histoire de la protection sociale*, 10(1): 42–61.

Despite significant progress, he noted that these countries' legislation did not always comply with the principles enshrined in international labour conventions.[50] For instance, regarding accident benefits (with the exception of Uruguay and, to a lesser extent, Chile), experts and administrators, favoured a lump-sum compensation system, while the ILO had adopted a convention in 1925 which established as a principle the payment of beneftits in the form of a permanent disability or death pension (Article 5 of Convention No.17). The same applied to the principle of compulsory social insurance, which Tixier felt was being adopted relitavely slowly.[51] As for compulsory accident insurance, this model had been introduced in Uruguay in 1934 – while in Argentina, Chile and Brazil, insurance remained optional. Except for Chile, health insurance was also optional in all South American countries. In Mexico, a commission of the Department of Labour, charged with drafting a law on social insurance, was created in 1934. It supported compulsory social insurance against workplace accidents and occupational hazards including disease, sickness, maternity, old age, invalidity and unemployment. This development owed much to Professor Federico Bach, one of the authors of the commission's draft proposal, also an International Labour Office correspondent who was in regular contact with Harold Butler. This first attempt at reform would however fail. It was not until 1943 that a social secturity law was adopted in Mexico.[52]

For national administrators and experts, Tixier's mission acted as a reminder of the social insurance principles established in international conventions.[53] Tixier specifically insisted on the refractory position of the Office concerning the management of social insurance by private companies, which he did not regard as truly social institutions.[54] Finally, he believed that one of the major problems at work in Latin America was the lack of organisation and rationalisation of insurance systems. According to him, laws and regulations binding the financial management of insurance institutions was overly vague. Within the Social Insur-

---

50 G 900/30/5 "Mr. Tixier's mission to South America, Autumn 1934", ILOA.
51 Tixier, A. 1935. "Le développement des assurances sociales en Argentine, au Brésil, au Chili et en Uruguay" (I), *ILR* 32(5): 647–673 and 797–827.
52 The ILO contributed to this in 1941 by sending experts from the Social Insurance Section to establish the financial basis for social insurance. SI 12–61–1 "Social security: correspondence with R. Watt, American Federation of labour, USA, 1943 Conference paper RW on AFL trade union attitude towards the Wagner-Murray-Dingall Bill (social security legislation); 1942 note O. Stein on social security trends in Argentina, Brazil, Chile, Mexico; 1941 Paper RW on social insurance", ILOA.
53 G 900/30/5 "Mr. Tixier's mission to South America, Autumn 1934", ILOA.
54 Tixier, A. 1935. "Le développement des assurances sociales en Argentine, au Brésil, au Chili et en Uruguay" (I), *ILR* 32(5): 647–673.

ance Section, Tixier's mission in Latin America played a central role in the development of a reflection on the need to develop more concrete action for the adoption of social insurance systems in less developed countries, a perspective which was at the heart of this Section's orientation towards technical assistance. For Tixier, the Office's activities suffered from important shortcomings. First, it was of little use to countries that did not already have general social insurance systems in place, and which lacked the specialists and/or the tools needed to draft new legislation.[55] In the 1934 to 1935 activities programme, he announced the Section's new orientation: "After ten years of comparing various national legislations, I believe that the Insurance Section must begin producing truly technical studies."[56]

2.3 Organising the 1936 Regional Conference in Santiago de Chile

However, it was not until the regional conferences, organised in 1936 in Santiago, Chile and in Havana in 1939, that sustainable technical cooperation between the ILO and Latin American countries began. This institutional development was implemented under Butler's direction, who, in 1933, had already confessed the following to Raul Migone, civil servant in the Argentinian Ministry of Foreign Affaires and ILO correspondent in Buenos Aires: "Indeed, I believe that, through action developed on the spot and by addressing the issues of particular interest to these countries, we will have to try by all means to strengthen our relations with the countries of Latin America."[57]

The invitation to organise the first regional conference in Latin America was presented during the 1935 ILC by the Chilean government delegate Garcia Oldini, sent directly by president Arturo Alessandri Palma. According to Moisés Poblete Troncoso, the Chilean responsible for relations between the Office and Latin America, this invitation was linked to a weakening of the president's position in the face of workers' organisations, particularly after the strike of southern agricultural workers in 1934.[58] As of October 1935, the country having ratified 33

---

[55] G 900/30/5 "Mr. Tixier's mission to South America, Autumn 1934", ILOA.
[56] XO 1/7/1 "Social Insurance Section (1932–1938)", ILOA. Original quote in French: "Après dix ans d'études comparatives des législations nationales je crois que la section des assurances doit entrer dans la phase des études véritablement techniques."
[57] Letter from Butler to Migone, December 28, 1933. XR 62/1/1 "Pan-American Conference (Montevideo, Dec.1933)", ILOA.
[58] Note from Moisés Poblete Troncoso, May 23, 1935. XD 12/1/1 "Regional Conference of American States members of the ILO. Santiago de Chile (December 1935-January 1936)", ILOA.

conventions, the Governing Body unanimously accepted Chile's invitation later that year. Several factors may explain this enthusiasm. This particular conference was perceived by the ILO as a new opportunity to prove to non-European countries that it was a truly universal organisation. Moreover, the presence of the United States, committed to a policy of rapprochement with Latin America, directly contributed to guiding the ILO in favour of inter-American cooperation. It was believed that such a conference would also stimulate the ratification of international labour standards in Latin America. Finally, according to Tixier, this conference was an opportunity to support progressive forces in Latin America and to consolidate the ILO's role in the development of trade unions, while counterbalancing government control over workers' organisations, which was particularly prevalent in Brazil and Uruguay.[59] In 1936, at the first Regional Conference held in Santiago, Evert Kupers, president of the Dutch Federation of Trade Unions and workers' representative on the GB, recalled the importance the ILO placed on this issue:

> The workers in this part of the world must learn however that they must not expect everything of legislation and that all their hopes should not be placed in the action of Governments in their favour. The workers must understand that here, as in many European countries, if they wish to improve the standard of living, shorten hours of work and raise their cultural and physical standards, they must help themselves. For this purpose, they must first of all develop strong trade union organisations. The International Labour Organization rests on three pillars – Governments, employers' organisations and workers' organisations.[60]

Following the approval of the GB to organise a conference in Santiago, Chile, an organising committee was set up. It was composed of Butler, Phelan, Childs and the heads of several Office Sections.[61] Before the conference, Butler sent civil servants to several Latin American countries. In September 1935, Poblete Troncoso went to Santiago to settle the practical and political questions raised by the conference. On the margins of the conference, in November 1935, to prepare for his visit to Brazil, Uruguay and Argentina, as well as to encourage the authorities to send tripartite delegations to Santiago, Butler also sent Childs on a trip to Latin America.[62] The most vehement opposition came from Argentina, then

---

[59] Adrien Tixier's Report, January 22, 1935, RL 86/0 "Relation of the ILO with central and south America. General", ILOA.
[60] *Minutes of the Santiago Conference*, 1936, 187, ILOA.
[61] XD 12/1/1 "Regional Conference of American States members of the ILO. Santiago de Chile (December 1935-January 1936), Jacket II", ILOA.
[62] Ibid.

plunged in military authoritarianism. At this time, according to Alejandro Unsain, the Office's new correspondent, the majority of members of government believed that the ILO was "bound up with socialism by an umbilical cord".[63] During his mission in Argentina, Childs told Butler of the considerable difficulties he encountered: "It has required a lot of pushing and tough lunching and it was a narrow shave."[64] Moreover, and despite an invitation sent by the Office, the PAU was not represented at the conference.[65] Mexico did not send a delegation, and only the Mexican ambassador in Santiago was present. ILO's action was thus weakened from the outset by this lack of support, but also by the instability of its relations, due in large part to the frequent political reconfigurations in Latin America, where, according to notes made by the Spanish civil servant Xavier Bueno in 1931, "an influential man can be exiled overnight".[66]

The practical organisation of these two conferences generated significant recruitment and accommodation research work for ILO staff. These tasks were the responsibility of a small group of civil servants who left as scouts a few weeks before the beginning of the conference. The success of the 1936 conference was mainly due to two civil servants: Moisés Poblete Troncoso and the Swiss Maurice Thudichum. In his private archives, Thudichum reported on the prepa-

---

63 Letter from Alejandro Unsain to Stephen Lawford Childs, May 5, 1934. XC 2/1/2 "Argentina. Correspondent at Buenos Aires. Mr. A. Unsain", ILOA.

64 Letter from Childs to Butler, December 13, 1935. XD 12/1/1 "Regional Conference of American States members of the ILO. Santiago de Chile (December 1935-January 1936), Jacket II", ILOA. The situation was complicated by the poor relations between Migone, former ILO correspondent in Buenos Aires, the Minister of the Interior, Melo, a conservative, and Carlos Saavedra Lamas, a politician and President of the League's General Assembly between 1936 and 1937. In particular, Migone had supported the appointment of Albert Thomas in 1920, while Saavedra Lamas considered this appointment incompatible with Thomas' former ministerial functions. See the letter from Childs to Butler, Decembre 5, 1935.

65 Among the AFL members, some continued to defend the idea of a pan-American workers' organisation in favour of the United States. In 1929, Matthew Woll, vice-president of the PAU, stated in the *American Photo Engraver*, of which he was one of the editors: "The Pan-american Federation of labor has proclaimed its unqualified sovereignty over the labor movements of the New World. It has proclaimed what amounts to an international Monroe Doctrine for all the Americas." CAT 5–31–3 "Relations et informations. *États*-Unis d'Amérique. Efforts pour rapprocher l'American Federation of Labor de la Fédération syndicale internationale, d'une part et de l'Organisation internationale du Travail, d'autre part", ILOA.

66 Xavier Bueno's Report, 1931. RL 86/0 "Relation of the ILO with Central and South America. General", ILOA. Xavier Bueno, a Spanish national, was born on August 4, 1883. He began a career as a journalist and publicist before becoming head of section at the Ministry of Labour in Madrid. He joined the ILO in 1925 in the National Information and Relations Section. In 1932, he was transferred to the press office. He left the ILO on 31 January 1940. See his personal file P 1848, ILOA.

rations for the event and noted the role played by Protestant missionary networks in the recruitment of conference staff. [67]

The first Regional Conference of American member states of the ILO was held from 2 to 14 January 1936, and brought together all the Latin American countries as well as Canada and the United States.[68] Unlike conferences in Geneva, it brought together influential figures in the field of social policy. The presence of the Brazilian Affonso Bandeira De Mello, whose role was highlighted in Montevideo, should be noted. Director-General at the Ministry of Labour and Secretary-General of the National Labour Council, he was a member of the ILO GB and was appointed vice-president for the government group in Santiago. At the opening session, the Chairperson of the Governing Body, the Canadian Walter Riddell, emphasised the scope of the Santiago Conference, which he described as a manifestation of globalisation at the ILO: "The Santiago Conference is a practical expression of its present worldwide outlook."[69] However, the conference shed light on the ambiguity that resulted from the ILO's regional involvement. Indeed, in his 1936 report, Butler acknowledged that the development of social legislation in Latin America had been poorly assessed in Geneva, and that American social problems were of a unique nature.[70] The conference also broadly reproduced the opposition between the universalist model and the Latin American perspectives on labour, as shown by the intervention of the Venezuelan government delegate Luis Yepes:

> Through it the problems peculiar to our Continent will be studied and understood and a spirit of solidarity and comprehension will emerge which will prevent the introduction and adoption of doctrines and laws alien to American mentality which do not meet the needs of our environment. The result of past activities has been a most, unsatisfactory solution of South America's social problems. The mere copying of European and North American methods has not proved favourable, but through the work of this Conference we shall become better acquainted with American labour ideals; we shall get a better knowledge of our own mentality and ability to secure that measure of justice to which we are entitled.[71]

---

[67] Maurice Thudichum's private archives, held by his grandson Pierre Roehrich in Geneva. Four collections *in quarto* of two hundred pages each entitled *Notes diverses, généalogiques et autres* covering the period 1913 to 1960, plus a fifth collection of notes entitled *Vagabondages dans le souvenir*, which contains his memoirs written between 1951 and 1961.
[68] Costa Rica, which is not a member of the ILO, was also present as an observer. For a report of this conference, see 1936, *ILR* 33(4) and (5): 512–531 and 688–727.
[69] Ibid., 516.
[70] *Minutes of the Santiago Conference*, 1936, 304, ILOA.
[71] Ibid., 97.

The workers' group strongly expressed its desire to increase international cooperation on social policies. The Chilean workers' delegate Luis Solis Solis clearly insisted on the political and technical value of collaborations with the ILO for the labour movement:

> We think that the importance of geographical and historical considerations has been largely over-emphasised. The rapid developments of recent years have abolished many of the differences between the countries. Now that the International Labour Organization has been strengthen by the adherence of the United Sates, and now that it has shown its interest in American problems by calling this Conference, it is surely wisest for us to rally round that Organisation, which has behind it sixteen years of experience and a fine record of scientific and legislative work. The Workers' Group is therefore entirely opposed to the proposal of a separate Pan-American Labour Organisation.[72]

He added: "The workers of Latin America are certainly not prepared to be deprived by a diplomatic manœuvre of the rights they can enjoy within the International Labour Organization".[73] ILO regional conferences were therefore a means of giving an international dimension to their concerns, while at the same time providing leverage to limit governments' influence on trade unions. Luis Solis Solis' statements betray the difficult position of trade unions in Chile, where a 1925 law prohibited the creation of a General Labour Confederation. Moreover, by 1930, Chile was suffering from the effects of the economic crisis, as demand for nitrates and copper, the country's main source of income, had fallen dramatically, along with its prices.[74] The social context became explosive with the railway strike of January 1936, in which Luis Solis Solis took part. Demonstrations multiplied and political tensions soared due to the growing influence of communist-leaning trade unionists.[75] Tension generated by the presence of communists was palpable in the Chilean press which presented the ILO conference as a meeting of communist leaders in Latin America.[76] In response to the

---

72 *Proceedings of the Santiago Regional Conference*, 61. Archives of the League of Nations, United Nations, Geneva. See also D 1086/12 "1st regional conference of American States members of the ILO (Santiago de Chile, Dec.1935) – Notes, Pamphlets and Speech on the Conference", ILOA.
73 *Proceedings of the Santiago Regional Conference*, 61. Archives of the League of Nations, United Nations, Geneva.
74 Cassasus-Montero, C. 1984. *Travail et travailleurs au Chili*. Paris: La Découverte. See in particular Chapter 1 "La formation du prolétariat et du mouvement ouvrier autour de l'enclave (1830–1960)".
75 D 1086/12 "1st regional conference of American States members of the ILO (Santiago de Chile, Dec.1935) – Notes, Pamphlets and Speech on the Conference", ILOA.
76 On the arrest of Luis Solís Solís, see XK 1/12/1 "Arrest of M. Solis (Chilean Workers' delegate. Regional Conference. Santiago, January 1936)", ILOA.

mobilisation of workers, the government made arrests and declared a three-month-long state of emergency. Luis Solis Solis would suffer the direct consequences of this repressive policy as he would be arrested by the end of the Santiago Conference.

Regional cooperation thus seemed to be at the crossroads of a "positioning game" opposing the *national* and the *international*.[77] Both a discourse and a form of action, regional cooperation was in fact a midway compromise between national and international interests, allowing them to come together, not without ambiguities. The experience of the Santiago Conference also showed that the ILO's regional action helped strengthen its position in Latin America, without however completely defusing the demands for a purely regional approach to labour issues. Proposals to create a regional labour office were again taken up by some delegates, such as the Uruguayan government delegate, José Guillermo Antuña.[78] While adopting a position of frank collaboration with the International Labour Office, Antuña stressed the fact that socio-economic problems had become more complex and that their solutions could not, as such, rely solely on the development of social legislation. According to him, they presented an American overtone, which could only be integrated within the framework of regional cooperation, better able to grasp the continent's "social atmosphere", and to defend the national sovereignty of its countries.[79] This discourse clearly held a national, regional and international dimension. While Argentina defended a national and regional policy, which would help reinforce its position in the Cono Sur and in Latin America more broadly, Antuña's speech also echoed the fear of a communist influence in Argentina, as well as the concerns of the Latin American political elite in the context of a possible war in Europe.[80] The declarations made by government representatives then clearly indicated that while they recognised the ILO's capacity to solve labour problems, they also believed that these problems were above all Latin American issues.

---

[77] Revel, J. 1996. *Jeux d'échelles : la micro-analyse à l'expérience*. Paris: Le Seuil.
[78] *Proceedings of the Santiago Regional Conference*, 41. Archives of the League of Nations, United Nations, Geneva.
[79] Antuña referred directly to the Chaco conflict and insisted that this conflict should have been resolved by the American countries and not by the League. *Proceedings of the Santiago Regional Conference*, 141. Archives of the League of Nations, United Nations, Geneva.
[80] Antuña explicitly referred to the communist threat and the need to improve workers' living conditions to counter this influence. *Proceedings of the Santiago Regional Conference*, 1936, 42, ILOA.

3 The Beginnings of the ILO's Regional Programme in Latin America

3.1 Social Insurance: ILO's Key to Latin America

The resolutions adopted at the 1936 and 1939 regional conferences and submitted to the GB formally established the ILO's regional programme in Latin America.[81] One of the major results of the Santiago Conference was the impetus given to the dissemination of the European social insurance model in Latin America.[82] At the 1935 ILC, Latin American delegates presented a wide range of issues that they wished to see addressed, including the living conditions of agricultural workers, the question of wages, housing, leisure, workers' educational development, unemployment from the perspective of international trade restrictions between raw material producing countries and Europe and, finally, emigration.[83] Despite the diversity of these proposals, the Santiago Conference placed social insurance and the working conditions of women and children at the heart of its agenda, under pressure from Adrien Tixier, for whom the conference was primarily intended to position itself in favour of compulsory insurance, an area where the production of international labour conventions was most important, but where the number of ratifications was also the lowest, in Europe and elsewhere.[84] This strategy also stemmed directly from the reports prepared by the ILO during the research missions in Latin America before 1936, whose main objectives were to supplement documentation on existing forms of social insurance, and to better understand its role in economic life by evaluating the "practical functioning as well as the technical and financial organisation of insurance institutions in South American countries".[85]

To guarantee the success of Tixier's strategy, the Office sent its best experts to Santiago. Oswald Stein, Czech by birth, a member of the Social Insurance Sec-

---

[81] Rens, Jef. 1959 "Latin America and the International Labour Organisation. Forty years of collaboration 1919–1959", in International Labour Review 80(1): 1.
[82] Plata-Stenger, V. 2017. "L'OIT et l'internationalisation de l'assurance sociale en Amérique latine dans les années 1930 et 1940 : enjeux et limites", *Revue d'histoire de la protection sociale*, 1(10): 45 and following.
[83] XD 12/1/1 "Regional Conference of American States members of the ILO. Santiago de Chile (December 1935–January 1936)", ILOA.
[84] For a detailed discussion on this point, see Seekings, J. 2008. "The ILO and Social Protection in the Global South, 1919–2005", CSSR Working Paper no. 238, ILO Century project, December, 2–36.
[85] Extract from document GB 68/17/1012, 17. G 900/30/5 "Mr. Tixier's mission to South America, Autumn 1934", ILOA.

tion since 1922 and an actuarial specialist, represented the Office at the Committee on Social Insurance established in Santiago. This committee worked on the basis of the report on social insurance produced by the International Labour Office, which described results achieved since 1919. It is therefore not surprising that the resolutions adopted approved the principle of compulsory and contributory insurance enshrined in ILO conventions, which would be reaffirmed in Havana in 1939. This second conference also adopted the principle of tripartite collaboration in the administration of social insurance and focused on defining the aims and functions of social insurance in terms of prevention, reparation and compensation. However, debates did arise in Havana, in particular concerning the institutions dealing with occupational risk insurance. At that point, the ILO's position had always been to favour institutions exclusively responsible for the prevention and compensation of industrial accidents, or to establish mutual insurance schemes, which, like social insurance, would operate under the financial and administrative supervision of public authorities. To this principle, several employers' delegates, notably Cuban and Mexican, opposed the principle of free choice for employers and freedom of competition among different insurance companies.[86]

Other resolutions show that the Committee on Social Insurance addressed the particular conditions of American countries by proposing adjustments to the rules laid down in the conventions. In 1936, it was decided that special measures should be taken to set up a general health service in sparsely populated areas. On this point, the Santiago Conference marked a further stage in the development of the ILO's reflections, begun in 1927, on the problem of the application of conventions in sparsely populated countries.[87] On the topic of pensions in the event of death, it was decided that when states could not afford the payment of a pension in accordance with the provisions of the insurance system it could be replaced by a lump sum paid to the widow, disabled widower or children.[88] In Havana, the Committee also granted payment in kind and the principle of self-

---

86 Second report of the Social Insurance Committee. *Proceedings of the Santiago Regional Conference.* Archives of the League of Nations, United Nations, Geneva.

87 The issue was raised at the 1927 ILC as part of the discussions on health insurance. Seekings, J. 2008. "The ILO and Social Protection in the Global South, 1919–2005": 19–20. CSSR Working Paper no. 238, ILO Century project, December.

88 This measure was not new to the ILO and reflected the debate that had marked ILCs since the 1920s, between the contributory and non-contributory pension model. On these debates, see Seekings, J. 2008. "The ILO and Social Protection in the Global South, 1919–2005". CSSR Working Paper No. 238. ILO Century Project: 1–50. See also Kott, S. 2008. "De l'assurance à la sécurité sociale (1919–1949): L'OIT comme acteur international": 1–29. Geneva: International Labour Organization, Working paper for the ILO Century Project.

insurance, i.e. coverage by employers for their own risk, whenever a guarantee could be given to comply with their commitments.

Finally, the Santiago and Havana Conferences helped re-launch discussions on the link between social insurance and health policies, which also sparked interest both in the United States and in Latin America, as in Chile, where research and projects for the development of social medicine were encouraged by the state.[89] In 1936, for instance, the Committee on Social Insurance stressed the need to link health insurance to prevention and the education of workers regarding hygiene and nutrition. These facets of health insurance were not necessarily new to the ILO in the 1930s, but reflected the growing influence of American countries, particularly the United States, in guiding the ILO's policy on social insurance.[90]

The interwar regional conferences also spawned the implementation of technical cooperation mechanisms in the field of social insurance. In Geneva, in order to assist national administrators in the financial organisation of their insurance systems, a series of technical conferences on social insurance were organised in 1936, 1937 and 1938, which enabled the ILO to establish the principles of investment policies.[91] Stein admitted that the work of the Social Insurance Correspondence Committee, which met three times between 1937 and 1938, was mainly aimed at monitoring the investment policies of insurance funds rather than providing new knowledge to the Office.[92] The Office was also considering a series of technical publications on statistics and financial forecasts in order, as Tixier pointed out, to provide a basis for action by major trade unions,

---

89 In 1937 the Ministry of Health, Welfare and Social Assistance submitted a draft law on the creation, for all funds, of a preventive and social medicine service for the early detection of tuberculosis. It would be sent to the ILO thanks to Tixier's friendly relations with Eduardo Cruz Coke, Minister of Health starting the same year and main architect of Chile's health system. SI 18/1/12 "Questions médicales de l'assurance sociale, Chile", ILOA.
90 Kott, S. 2008. "De l'assurance à la sécurité sociale (1919–1949)". The definition of social security would be broadened after the adoption of the Atlantic Charter in 1941, which recognises the right to social security as a human right.
91 1st principle: Investments by social insurance institutions must be subject to national regulation. 2nd principle: consultations must be limited to the framework of compulsory insurance. 3rd principle: only long-term investments are considered as part of the investments of social insurance institutions. SI 10/10/9 "Investissement des fonds des institutions d'assurances sociales. Comité d'experts pour les assurances sociales. Genève 8–10 déc. 1937", ILOA.
92 Note from Stein to Tixier, June 27, 1938. SI 10/11/3 "Comité de correspondance pour les assurances sociales. 11e consultation d'experts. Investissement des fonds des institutions d'assurances sociales. Genève, 5 au 9 Décembre 1938. Convocation", ILOA.

which wished to see international conventions reformed, or even ratified.[93] In 1939, these projects were concretised with the publication of a volume on the investment funds of social insurance institutions, followed a year later by the publication of a study on the statistical bases, financial systems and actuarial forecasts of old-age, death and disability insurance, based on the experience of European countries, whose data remained most accessible at this point in time.[94] From 1940 to 1945, important progress was made regarding the adoption of social insurance systems, as well as the extension of social coverage in Latin America. While the ILO had largely inspired this movement, other more regionally specific models were developed, notably in Chile and Peru, where particular attention was paid to health-related issues.[95]

ILO regional conferences could thus be considered as institutions that encouraged a process of "Europeanisation".[96] However, this process was dialectical, insofar as the regionalisation of ILO activities also allowed Latin American elites to internationalise their own social development agenda.[97] The ILO had thereby created an environment conducive to integrating the needs of "peripheral" countries into the international agenda. The development of ILO activities on labour migration also made this clear.

3.2 Migration for Colonisation: Population Redistribution and Development

Social insurance was not the only area of cooperation to be initiated by the regional conferences. For example, the 1936 resolution on indigenous workers gave rise in 1937 to the first publication on indigenous workers in Peru, by Moisés Poblete Troncoso. While the ILO had taken an interest in this issue as early as the

---

[93] Draft programme of work for 1934 and 1935. XO 1/7/1 "Social Insurance Section (1932–1938)", ILOA.
[94] *L'investissement des fonds des assurances sociales*, 1939. Études et documents, Série M, no. 16. Geneva: International Labour Office; *Technique actuarielle et organisation financière des assurances sociales*, 1940. Études et documents, Série M, no. 17. Geneva: International Labour Office. ILOA.
[95] *Proceedings of the Fourth ILO Regional Conference*, Montevideo, 1949, 92 and following, ILOA.
[96] Clavin, P., Patel, K. K. 2010. "The Role of International Organisations in Europeanisation: The Case of the League of Nations and the European Economic Community", in Conway, M., Patel, K. K. eds. *Europeanisation in the Twentieth Century: Historical Approaches*, 110–31. Basingstoke: Palgrave Macmillan.
[97] Two years after Santiago, Antony Alcock noted that the Governing Body had hired 48 American experts in 11 different commissions. This figure also includes experts from the United States. Alcock, A. 1971. 137.

1920s, the practical and technical orientation in this field took place after the Santiago Conference. It became all the more evident after the fourth regional conference in Montevideo in 1949, which recommended that the Governing Body instruct the Office to study and coordinate the organisation of various technical assistance programmes concerning indigenous workers, and the launching of the ILO's Andean Programme in 1952.[98]

However, in the late 1930s, it was in the field of colonial migration that the effects of the ILO's regional action were most acutely felt. The organisation of a research mission to Brazil in 1936, the holding of a conference of experts in Geneva in 1938, which led to the adoption of an international convention on migrant workers in 1939 (No. 66), and the organisation of a mission of technical assistance to Venezuela in 1938 all testify to the central role played by the Santiago Conference in reviving this issue at the end of the 1930s.

Since the 1920s, the issue of migration had been at the heart of the concerns of the Office's social reformers who saw it as a vector for the dissemination of social protection.[99] In a 1925 speech to the Rio de Janeiro Conference of Municipal Employees, Albert Thomas had already stressed the need for a policy ensuring uniform social protection conditions in order to ensure the economic success of immigration policies.[100] In 1925 he had sent Louis Varlez, head of the Office's Migration Service, to Latin America. There he was to study the possibilities of relocating Russian refugees in certain Republics.[101] At the 1927 Geneva Population Congress, Thomas again stressed the need to organise migration internationally and advocated for the creation of what he then called a Supreme Council on Migration, which would allow for a rational distribution of manpower and resour-

---

98 Guthrie, J. 2013. "The ILO and the International Technocratic Class, 1944–1966", in Droux J., Kott, S. eds. *Globalizing Social Rights. The International Labour Organization and Beyond*, 115–136. ILO Centuries Series. Basingstoke: Palgrave Macmillan. For further information on the Andean Programme, see Alcock, A. 1971. *History of the International Labour Organization*, 251–253. London: Macmillan.

99 The First World War had also contributed to making this issue one of the fundamental aspects of reconstruction. Paul-André, R. 2006. "Géopolitique et État-providence. Le BIT et la politique mondiale des migrations dans l'entre–deux–guerres", *Annales. Histoire, Sciences Sociales* 1(61): 99–134.

100 Thomas' speech at the Conference to Employees of the Municipalities of Rio de Janeiro. Thomas, A. 1947. *Politique sociale internationale*, 105. Genève: Bureau international du travail. See also Kévonian, D. 2005. "Enjeux de catégorisations et migrations internationales", *Revue européenne des migrations internationales* 21(3): 95–124.

101 Kévonian, D. 2005: 103. On this mission, see G 900/15/4 "Mission de Varlez en Amérique du Sud, 1925", ILOA.

ces.¹⁰² Despite these initiatives and the creation of an International Commission on Migration in 1921, the ILO failed to develop international cooperation in this field in the 1920s.

It was not until the Santiago Conference that progress was made in this area, when the principles of international coordination and the development of practical strategies for the implementation of migration policies with a colonial lens were first concretised. The economic crisis and the restriction of migration flows meant that the ILO's action favouring organised migration was part of the fight against unemployment in Europe and against the economic imbalances that threatened or delayed social progress in less developed countries. In the international context of the 1930s the question of colonial migration also proved to be urgent, not altogether unrelated to the humanitarian crisis posed by the establishment of the Nazi regime and the proliferation of persecution, particularly targeted at German Jews. For some non-governmental organisations the ILO could play a crucial role in making information on immigration opportunities available to European relief organisations.¹⁰³

In Santiago the resolution on immigration proposed by the Brazilian government directly involved Latin American countries in the international effort for global economic recovery. Since the early 1930s Brazil had sought to mobilise the ILO on this issue. That same year, at the ILC, Bandeira de Mello stressed the importance of migration for colonisation in resolving unemployment in Europe.¹⁰⁴ On the heals of the Santiago Conference, during his stay in Brazil and after meeting its Minister of Foreign Affairs, Macedo Soares, Butler proposed, in connection with the Brazilian draft resolution on immigration, to send an International Labour Office mission to investigate the problem of migration from the perspective of economic and social development.¹⁰⁵ In July 1936 he sent Fernand Maurette and the Argentine Enrique Siewers, a member of the Migration Section, to Brazil, Argentina and Uruguay.¹⁰⁶ For Maurette, the situation in Brazil

---

102 Thomas, A. 1947. *Politique sociale internationale*, 108.
103 Letter from Lord Bearsted, British member of the Governing Body, to Childs, April, 27, 1936. G 900/46/38 "Mr. Maurette's mission to Brazil, Uruguay, Argentina. 1936", ILOA.
104 ILC Record of proceedings, 1930, 172, ILOA.
105 XT 86/1/1 "Director's mission to South ans North America (November 1935–February 1936)". Since the 1920s a movement for the development of industrial social policy had emerged in São Paulo, outside the public sphere, through organisations and institutes created by entrepreneurs, engineers and educators, nurtured by the spirit of rationalisation. Weinstein, B. 1996. *For Social Peace in Brazil Industrialists and the Remaking of the Working Class in Sao Paulo, 1920–1964*, 56. Chapel Hill: University of North Carolina Press.
106 Governing Body, 77ᵗʰ session, 1936, 191, ILOA. G 900/46/38 "Mr. Maurette's mission to Brazil, Uruguay, Argentina. 1936", ILOA.

in the 1930s vividly revealed the need for an organisation of international labour migration for economic development. He was clearly in favour of the government's policy of using still virgin areas for settlements: "The continuity of the occupation and exploitation of the country, both in space and in time, is one of the first conditions for the economic implementation of so many resources".[107] After having visited the Institute of Agriculture located in Campinas thanks to the intervention of Henrique Doria de Vasconcellos, Director of the Institute of Immigration, eager to develop international cooperation with International Labour Office experts, Maurette welcomed the government's agrarian reforms and the development of planning in this sector of activity:

> The era of sole private initiative [...] seems to be over. Although we are not yet speaking of "directed agriculture", we may speak of a controlled, advised, supported and organised agriculture. It is the sign of a State having reached the age of majority. Such a policy of control, advice, concern and organisation is legitimate and must be fruitful in the demographic, social and agricultural sectors.[108]

Both Maurette's report and the Office's comprehensive report on colonial migration were submitted to the ILO's International Committee on Migration which met in November 1936. The Committee decided to include the problem of worker migration in the context of financing difficulties, both from the point of view of their settlement and transportation costs, conclusions which led to the organisation of a conference of experts on migration for colonisation, organised from 28 February to 7 March 1938.[109]

For the first time in its history, the ILO was organising an international technical conference with more representatives from Latin America than from Europe. Argentina, Bolivia, Brazil, Chile, Colombia, Dominican Republic, Ecuador, Peru, Uruguay and Venezuela were represented. However, few of them were

---

[107] Maurette, F. 1937. *Quelques aspects sociaux du développement présent et futur de l'économie brésilienne*, 9. Études et Documents Série B (Conditions économiques), no. 25. Geneva: International Labour Office. Original Quote in French: "La continuité de l'occupation et de l'exploitation du pays, dans l'espace comme dans le temps est une des premières conditions de la mise en œuvre économique de tant de ressources."

[108] *Ibid.*, 29. Original quote in French: "L'époque de l'unique initiative privée [...] semble révolue. On n'en est pas encore à l'agriculture dirigée, [...] mais on en est à l'agriculture contrôlée, conseillée, soutenue, organisée. C'est le fait d'un État arrivé à l'âge de la majorité. Une telle politique de contrôle, de conseil, de sollicitude, d'organisation est légitime et doit être fructueuse dans le domaine démographique et social comme dans celui de l'agriculture."

[109] *La Coopération internationale technique et financière en matière de migrations colonisatrices. Conférence technique d'experts, 1938. Études et documents. Série O (Migrations), no. 7.* Geneva: International Labour Office.

qualified experts, most Latin American governments being represented by consuls, chargés d'affaires or heads of delegations and permanent representatives to the League of Nations. The League of Nations sent several economists, such as the Austrian Richard Schüller, the Italian Pietro Stoppani and the Canadian Louis Rasminsky, the third governor of the Bank of Canada and one of the architects of the future Bretton Woods system implemented in 1944.[110]

The aim of the conference was to define the methods of international technical and financial collaboration, and to make proposals from which emigration and immigration countries could draw inspiration for the conclusion of bilateral agreements. The conference had before it a report from the Office addressing all these points. However, at this point, its work on migrant workers was still at an embryonic stage. To date it had carried out piecemeal studies focusing solely on a description of national experiences and published in the *International Labour Review*.[111] These studies had no practical use for the various emigration and immigration offices.[112] Thus discussions at the Conference reflected the central role played by the experiences of Argentina, Brazil, Chile and Uruguay with the institutional organisation of migration in highlighting a range of issues related to terminology and the international organisation of worker migration.[113] The purely technical nature of this conference made it possible to reach decisions "under conditions of unexpected unanimity", which helped considerably broaden the Office's mandate.[114] It became competent in providing a regular information service on all practical questions raised by the admission of immigrants as settlers.[115] The conference also opened the debate on the financial issues tied to raising capital in third countries, in the cases where neither the country of immigration nor the country of emigration had access to the necessary funds. On this point, it decided to instruct the Office, in consultation with the Economic and

---

110 Clavin, P. 2013. *Securing the World Economy: The Reinvention of the League of Nations, 1920–1946*. Oxford: Oxford University Press. See Chapter 9 in particular.
111 Siewers, E. 1934. "Les possibilités de colonisation en Argentine", *ILR* 30(4): 487–523; Lopes, R. P. 1936. "La colonisation au Brésil", *ILR* 33(2): 164–197; Berenstein, M. 1936. "Les États du Levant sous mandat français et les problèmes d'émigration et d'immigration", *ILR* 33(5): 728–764; Tait, C. 1936. "Migrations et peuplement en Australie, en Nouvelle–Zélande et au Canada", *ILR* 34(1): 37–71, and "La colonisation au Chili. Rapports et enquêtes", *ILR* 34(3): 388–462; Ogishima, T. 1938. "L'émigration japonaise", *ILR* 34(5): 663–698.
112 Governing Gody, 83rd session, April 1938, 24, ILOA
113 Ibid., 56.
114 Ibid., 20.
115 These aspects were present in the ILO report submitted to the Technical Conference and form the basis of the work plan accepted by the Conference. GB, 83rd session, April 1938, 53–63, ILAO.

Financial Sections of the League of Nations, to examine the possibilities of carrying out research on this problem and creating an international lending institution to provide credit for settlement. Lastly, the Conference invited the GB to establish a permanent International Committee on Migration for Colonisation in order to facilitate the coordination of the emigration and immigration countries concerned and study in greater depth the problems of international financing, as well as the means of solving them. As a concrete result of the 1938 conference the Office was able to organise a mission of technical assistance to Venezuela in 1938. The purpose of this mission was to help create an institute for immigration and settlement, a central institution in the government's development strategy.[116] For six weeks, Enrique Siewers, alongside expert Henrique Doria de Vasconcellos, responsible for land settlement policy in Brazil, visited white settlements in Venezuela.[117] They drafted two reports one of which described the situation in the Chirgua settlement where 48 Danish families had settled. The other report presented itself as a general study of the possibilities of immigration and resettlement of Europeans in Venezuela, fruit of a two-week trip in the two most important regions of the country for immigration: the Valencia Lake bassin, and the Andes.[118] If the archives do not specify the Office's role in the organisation of the functioning of the Institute, whose creation was decided by ministerial decree on 15 September 1938,[119] Siewers gave an ideal description, presenting it as "a model for the organisation of settlement and immigration in other Latin American countries".[120]

The Office's activities testify to the central role of Latin American countries in reviving the migration issue at the ILO in the late 1930s. On the one hand, the 1938 conference of experts and the mission of technical assistance to Venezuela illustrate the role of the ILO in the internationalisation of a particular aspect of migration, despite the increasingly nationalistic nature of migration policies in the late 1930s. In 1939 the adoption by the ILC of a Recommendation (No. 61) and the Migrant Workers Convention (No. 66), which concerned the recruitment, placement and working conditions of migrant workers crowned the ILO's efforts.[121] On the other, it exemplifies attempts to link international labour migration to

---

116 Wright, W. R. 2003. *Café Con Leche: Race, Class, and National Image in Venezuela*: 101–102. Ann Arbor: UMI Books.
117 E 22/63/2 "Colonisation and migration. Relations with the Instituto Tecnico de Immigracion y colonizacion, Caracas", ILOA.
118 *Ibid*.
119 *Ibid*.
120 *Ibid*.
121 Alcock, A. 1971. *History of the International Labour Organization*, 136. London: Macmillan.

the problem of economic development in Latin America. This link was reaffirmed at the Havana Conference, where delegates stressed the importance of systematically organising migration for agricultural and industrial development.

Conclusion

As non-binding forums for the exchange of views and experiences on social policies, labour relations and workers' protection, the interwar regional conferences provided an ideal forum for discussing the specific problems of Latin American countries, under the authority of the ILO. The regional conferences in Latin America were not aimed at regionalising international labour standards but reflected a pragmatic approach by the ILO to tackle the practical difficulties preventing less developed countries from adopting and ratifying international labour Conventions. Considered in the interwar period as a means of combating protectionism, the regionalisation of ILO activities was not just a response to the European context, where nationalisms were growing stronger. The ILO's strategy also stemmed from an internal reflection on the need to broaden the modalities of its action (the mere production of international conventions having not succeeded in meeting the needs of the less developed member states), and to extend the scope of possibilities regarding the protection of workers.

The regional conferences also promoted the creation of collaborative networks based on the sharing of technical knowledge. They adopted resolutions that fostered the development of ILO technical studies capable of assisting national administrators in their reform processes, and the establishment of a technical advisory system. This process, which began in the 1930s, undoubtedly explains the survival of the ILO during and after the Second World War. While the Havana Conference did not adopt any resolution promoting the organisation of new regional conferences, their importance for the development of ILO action was highlighted on several occasions. The Havana Conference adopted a resolution, best known today as the "Havana Declaration", drafted by Wilfred Jenks, which incorporated the preamble to the ILO Constitution, the Lima Declaration of 24 December 1938 and the joint Declaration of Continental Solidarity, adopted in Panama on 3 October 1939. It associated the ILO even more clearly with inter-American cooperation, while giving it the mandate of economically and socially preparing the post-war period. Edward Phelan's 1941 annual report confirmed that the ILO was committed to the development of a regional social policy to be included in post-war policy. In Latin America the organisation of regional conferences would continue after the war, in Mexico in 1946, in Montevideo in 1949, in Rio de Janeiro in 1952, and in Havana in 1956. The end of the war and the accompanying wave of decolonisation would also enable the ILO to invest in other continents. In Asia for instance the first ILO regional conference was held in India in 1947 in the wake of the country's declaration of independence.

Chapter III
The Limits of the ILO's Universalist Ambition in Asia and the Problem of Underdevelopment

While the ILO could boast of several achievements in Latin America the diffusion of an international normativity in Asia ran up against a whole series of geographic, political and cultural obstacles during the interwar period.[1] One of the main difficulties stemmed from the domination of a European culture, as mentioned in the previous chapter, which largely contributed to confining the less industrialised Asian countries and colonies to an underdevelopment paradigm. ILO records show the terms used to describe these countries were "less industrialised" or "backward".[2] This differentiated representation of the worlds of labour had direct consequences on the distribution of international standards. Indeed, within Asia, colonial powers and representatives of countries such as India, China and Japan widely used the argument of underdevelopment to stifle the establishment of a universal system of labour market regulation.

In 1919 ILO founding members included a number of Asian countries: China, Japan, India, Iran and Thailand.[3] While there are no studies to date explaining how the participation of Asian countries in the ILO was negotiated there is the exceptional case of India, then a British colony, which participated despite the fact that accession to the ILO was in principle reserved for independent states. Some scholars working on India have focused on Britain's role in supporting India's independent representation in hopes of guaranteeing the presence of an

---

[1] For recent work on the relationship between the ILO and the Asia-Pacific region and its role in disseminating international normativity, see Lichtenstein, N., Jensen, J. M. 2015. *The ILO from Geneva to the Pacific Rim- West meets East*. International Labour Organization, Palgrave Macmillan, ILO Century Series. On Japan, see Thomann, B. ed. 2015. *La naissance de l'État social japonais. Biopolitique, travail et citoyenneté dans le Japon impérial (1868–1945)*, 123–148. Paris: Presses de Sciences Po (P.F.N.S.P.). On China, see Yifeng, C. 2014. "The International Labour Organisation and Labour Governance in China 1919–1949", in Blanpain, R., Liukkunen, U., Yifeng, C. eds. 2014. *China and ILO fundamental principles and rights at work*, 19–54. Netherlands: Wolters Kluwer.
[2] The notion of underdevelopment both describes a country's state of economic and social development and suggests the possibility of changing that state. On the archaeology of the concept of "underdevelopment", see Rist, G. 2007. *Le développement. Histoire d'une croyance occidentale*, 127–145. Paris: Presses de Sciences Po; Sachs, W. ed. 2010. *The development dictionary: a guide to knowledge as power*, London: Zed Books.
[3] Aamir, A. 1969. "Fifty Years of the ILO and Asia", *International Labour Review* 99(3): 347–361.

ally in negotiations at the ILO.[4] However, India's situation must also be understood as a manifestation of the changes that took place in international relations after the First World War. The country's participation in the war effort on the side of Britain, which certainly served as an argument for the Indian representatives at the 1919 Paris negotiations, must undoubtedly be taken into account. India also benefited from the benevolent attitude of the United States.[5] Granting independent representation to India was also a consequence of the growing importance of emerging Asian economies after the First World War. In India textile and coal industries expanded at an unprecedented rate during the war while the "fragmented nature" of the industrialisation process remained unchanged.[6] Japan also saw its silk and cotton production increase considerably in that time.[7] The economic importance of India and Japan was reaffirmed by the fact that the ILO granted them permanent representation on the Governing Body, this status being granted to eight countries of "considerable industrial importance".[8] As early as 1919 Japan enjoyed such status and, in 1922, following repeated requests India was also granted permanent representation on the GB.[9]

In order to create a steady flow of information with Asia, the International Labour Office developed a network of correspondents. In 1924 the first correspondence office was opened in Tokyo, headed by Junshiro Asari of the Ministry of Agriculture and Trade. A second office was established in New Delhi in 1929, and a third in Nanking in 1930. The correspondents, who were paid by the ILO, played an important role as information relays, particularly concerning the ILO's activities and the development of national social legislation. The voluminous correspondence between the International Labour Office and Purushottama Padmanabha Pillai, director of the New Delhi office, allows us to follow precisely the evolution of labour legislation in this country. These correspondents also facilitated the development of contact networks useful for the constitution of international conference delegations. The question of representation of Asian delegates

---

[4] On the relations between the ILO and Great Britain, see Hidalgo-Weber, O. 2017. *La Grande-Bretagne et l'Organisation internationale du travail (1919–1946). Une nouvelle forme d'internationalisme*. Paris: l'Harmattan.

[5] Aamir, A. 1969. "Fifty Years of the ILO and Asia", 347.

[6] Rothermund, D. 1993. *An Economic History of India from PreeColonial Times to 1991*, 66. London; New York: Routledge.

[7] Burkman, T. W. 2008. *Japan and the League of Nations: Empire and World Order, 1914–1938*, 18. Honolulu: University of Hawaii Press.

[8] "Member states of Chief Industrial Importance". ILC, First session, Washington, 29 octobre–29 novembre 1919, ILOA.

[9] Between 1923 and 1935 the permanent members of the Governing Body were France, Great Britain, Italy, Germany, Belgium, Japan, Canada and India.

to the ILC was in fact a regularly raised issue. That of the Japanese worker delegates to the ILC was, for instance, frequently addressed in correspondence between the Office and the Tokyo office. It was not until the 1924 ILC that the first workers' delegate was selected, Mr Bunji Suzuki, President of the General Confederation of Labour of Japan, in accordance with ILO rules and regulations. During the 1920s some countries such as China only sent government representatives.[10]

Despite the presence of institutional relays and Asian representatives within the organisation, these actors regularly criticised the ILO's poor evaluation of their social experience and that of the colonies. That said, as early as the 1920s, under Albert Thomas' leadership, the Office sought to give international visibility to working conditions in Asian colonies and countries. During this decade its action consisted of producing documentation on working conditions and encouraging the ratification of international labour Conventions. In this chapter I will focus on the evolution of ILO activities in the 1930s marked as it was by an increased mobilisation on the issue of Asian trade competition. This theme provides an opportunity to analyse the ILO's role in building a differentiated representation of labour-related issues in Asia. This "comparison game" ("*jeu de la comparaison*", in the words of Professor Gilbert Rist),[11] to whom the ILO gave international legitimacy, invites us to reflect on the role this organisation played in the construction of the problem of underdevelopment, understood in its descriptive and performative dimensions. In particular, the disorganisation of the international economy as a result of the global economic crisis led to an evolution in the ILO's development discourse which revolved around the imperative of production modernisation, industrialisation and planning in order to raise workers' living standards and redress deep social inequalities. I will first consider the ILO as a space for dialogue and the articulation of demands in order to analyse the factors that led to the construction of a differentiated representation of labour-related issues in Asia. From a labour standpoint I will then probe the ILO's attempts to regulate trade relations between Western powers and emerging Asian economies. I will also study the ILO's contribution to a growing discourse on colonial development in the 1930s, emphasising the particular conception of development it articulated during this period. Finally, I will analyse the first missions of technical assistance in China, the organisation of which stemmed directly from the ILO's desire to encourage the adoption of new social laws and to

---

10 Hu, A. 2015. "China's Early Labor (Social Insurance) Legislation: The Role of the International Labor Organization, 1910s–1928", in Hu, A. ed. *China's Social Insurance in the Twentieth Century: A Global Historical Perspective*, 51–75. Leyde: The Brill Academic Press.
11 Rist, G. 2007. *Le développement. Histoire d'une croyance occidentale*, 136.

strengthen its presence in the region, by disseminating its know-how and standards.

1 Two-tier Social Justice: Imperial Domination and "Special Regimes"

1.1 Exporting the "Civilising Mission"

While the ILO was not intended as a tool to promote colonial policies, the discourse that prevailed at its inception indisputably borrowed certain notions, such as moral responsibility, from colonial rhetoric. The ILO's creation, much like that of the League of Nations, infused the notion of a "civilising mission" with international legitimacy, both in its descriptive and prescriptive dimensions. Indeed, for social reformers tasked with the creation of the ILO, the diffusion of high social standards in the colonies guaranteed a step forward in economic prosperity and the social progress of civilisation. This idea also appears clearly in Article 22 of the Covenant of the League of Nations, referring to the future Permanent Mandates Commission (PMC), to which the ILO directly participated. According to this article, "the well-being and development of such peoples form a sacred trust of civilisation [...]."[12] This discourse crystallised a representation of international organisations as epicentres of modernity, capable of both producing the most advanced knowledge and exporting it. However, the cultural presuppositions imposed on indigenous workers, considered undisciplined and incapable of adapting to modern working conditions, largely served the representatives of colonial powers in maintaining the notion of a "civilising mission" in the strictest colonial framework. The absence of representatives from the colonies, with the already noted exception of India, rendered changes to representation in the interwar period all the more unlikely.[13] Moreover, Indian government delegates were often linked to the Colonial Office.[14] This phenomenon was

---

[12] Article 22 of the Covenant of the League of Nations: June 28, 1919.
[13] This problem had also been raised at the 1921 conference by Archibald Crawford, South African Workers' Delegate, who wanted to have an amendment adopted on the reform of the Governing Body which affirmed the principles of equity and uniformity in favour of dependent territories. ILC, *Record of proceedings*, 1921, 554, ILOA.
[14] Rodgers, G.; Bhattacharya, S., Krishnamurty, J. 2011. "India and the ILO in Historical Perspective", *Economic and Political Weekly* 46(10): 47.

not unique to India, the British having also sought to control its dominions' delegations at the ILO.[15]

1.2 Putting in Place "Special Regimes"

Western powers were therefore entirely free to ensure that international conventions would not apply within their empires. Indeed, Article 421 of the Treaty of Versailles gave them considerable leeway in this regard.[16] The ILO also created a special social protection regime in the colonies, whose conventions and recommendations coalesced as the Indigenous Labour Code.[17] Some scholars have seen the adoption of these standards as a positive sign of a change in colonial rule.[18] That being said, neither the ILO's power structure, nor the way colonial issues were understood allowed for what Luis Rodrìguez Piñero called the "erosion of the colonial norm".[19] In his research, Daniel Maul also concludes that the colonial metropole ensured that "all initiatives aimed at achieving more rapid social progress in the colonies, or at securing the large-scale implementation of ILO norms, came to nothing".[20]

Pushing past this colonial framework, the scope of international labour Conventions was therefore probed as early as the 1919 Paris Peace Conference. In Paris, the delegates acknowledged the difficulty of applying labour standards uniformly, considering that the economic and social conditions in less industrialised countries did not allow the adoption of the highest standards. In concrete

---

15 Hidalgo-Weber, O. 2017. *La Grande-Bretagne et l'Organisation internationale du travail (1919–1946). Une nouvelle forme d'internationalisme*, 193–234.
16 Article 421 states that "[t]he Members engage to apply conventions which they have ratified in accordance with the provisions of this Part of the present Treaty to their colonies, protectorates and possessions which are not fully self-governing: (1) Except where owing to the local conditions the convention is inapplicable, or (2) Subject to such modifications as may be necessary to adapt the convention to local conditions. And each of the Members shall notify to the International Labour Office the action taken in respect of each of its colonies, protectorates and possessions which are not fully self-governing."
17 Rodgers, G., Lee, E., Swepston, L., Van Daele, J. 2009. *The International Labour Organization and the Quest for Social Justice 1919–2009*, 41 and following. Geneva-Ithaca: ILO-Cornell University Press.
18 Bonvin, J.-M. 1998. *L'Organisation internationale du travail. Étude sur une agence productrice de normes*, 187–188. PUF: Paris.
19 Rodríguez–Piñero, L. 2005. *Indigenous Peoples, Postcolonialism, and International Law. The ILO Regime (1919–1989)*, 37. Oxford: Oxford University Press.
20 Maul, D. 2012. *Human Rights, Development and Decolonization. The International Labour Organization, 1940–70*, 19. UK: Palgrave Macmillan.

terms, Article 405 of the Treaty recognised the possibility of exempting the countries presenting "special" conditions from full or partial application of international labour Conventions:

> In framing any recommendation or draft convention of general application, the Conference will have due regard to those countries in which climatic conditions, the imperfect development of industrial organisation or other special circumstances make the industrial conditions substantially different and will suggest the modifications, if any, which it considers may be required to meet the case of such countries.

This clause was introduced at the insistence of the Chinese, Japanese and Indian delegations, which were anxious to preserve the international competitiveness of their industries.[21] The ILO quickly sought to define the "special" clauses to be included in the draft conventions. During the 1919 ILC in Washington, D.C., a committee was thus created to assess the possibilities of applying the convention on hours of work in industry to "special" countries, in accordance with Article 405. This committee, which never met again during the interwar period, adopted recommendations allowing amendments to the provisions of the convention with a view to its application in Japan and India.[22] The committee also recognised that major problems prevented the application of the convention in China, such as the sheer extent of its territory, the absence of a customs policy and the existence of foreign concessions.[23] Similarly, India and Siam (Thailand) obtained the right to apply lower standards concerning the Night Work Conventions (1919), partly under the influence of Great Britain, which was anxious to protect the interests of its companies there. Japan and India were also authorised amendments on the application of the Minimum Age (Industry) and Night Work of Young Persons (Industry) Conventions in 1919.

The limitations imposed on raising labour standards did not just stem from particular economic and environmental conditions. Several studies have since revealed that the imperial and racial assumptions on which the superiority of European powers was built marked the debates at the ILO and seriously limited the possibility of raising labour standards in Asia.[24] Leon Fink's analysis of the de-

---

[21] Javillier, J.-C., Gernignon, B., Politakis, G. eds. *Les Normes internationales du travail : un patrimoine pour l'avenir. Mélanges en l'honneur de Nicolas Valticos*, 466. Genève: Bureau international du Travail.
[22] Ibid.
[23] Chen, Y. 2016. "ILO, Extraterritoriality and Labour Protection in Republican Shanghai", in Liukkunen, U., Chen, Y. eds. *Fundamental Labour Rights in China. Legal Implementation and Cultural Logic*, 83–116. Cham: Springer International Publishing.
[24] Lichtenstein, N., Jensen, J. M. 2015. *The ILO from Geneva to the Pacific Rim*, 7.

bates at the 1920 Genoa Maritime Conference demonstrates that imperial powers used racial arguments to justify the impossibility of uniformly applying the 1919 Convention on the eight-hour day in the field of maritime labour. Asian and African sailors were not considered to have the same capacity for work as their white counterparts.[25] The debates on the Convention on Forced Labour adopted in 1930 by the ILC also vividly reveal the racial discrimination to which colonial workers were subjected.[26] We can thus clearly see the limits of the ILO's universalist discourse and, through them, the different visions of the labour world that influenced discussions on the application of international labour Conventions from the outset.

1.3 Loosening the Colonial Grip: Indian Workers' Delegations to the ILO

However, the tripartite representation system at the ILO meant that delegations' discourse was never monolithic. It revealed sometimes violent oppositions which reflected social tensions within nations.[27] In general, during the interwar period, Asian workers' representatives opposed what they perceived as two-tier international cooperation. They thus tended to reject the international competitiveness argument and to use the ILO as an arena to demand higher labour standards. Indian workers' delegates were particularly active in defending the adoption of high standards of social protection, as they did not see India as an underdeveloped country. This sentiment would come to play a leading role in the late 1930s' demands for independence within national trade union organisations.[28]

---

25 Fink, L. 2015. "A Sea of Difference: The ILO and the Search for Common Standards, 1919–45", in Lichtenstein, N., Jensen, J. M. *The ILO from Geneva to the Pacific Rim*, 15–32.
26 Daughton, J. P. 2013. "ILO Expertise and Colonial Violence", in Droux, J., Kott, S. eds. *Globalizing Social Rights: The International Labour Organization and Beyond*, 85–97. Basingstoke: Palgrave Macmillan, ILO; Maul, D. 2007. "The International Labour Organization and the Struggle against Forced Labour", *Labour History* 48(4): 477–500.
27 Cobble, D. S. 2015. "Japan and the 1919 ILO Debates over Rights, Representation and Global Labour Standards", in Lichtenstein, N., Jensen, J. M. *The ILO from Geneva to the Pacific Rim*, 55–79. On the development of the Japanese welfare state, see Thomann, B. ed. 2015. *La naissance de l'État social japonais*.
28 Sugata Bose, questioning the origins of the concepts of colonial development and national development in India, notes: "the institutional expression on the concept of national development predated that of colonial development". Bose, S. 1998. "Instruments and Idioms of Colonial and National Development. India's Historical Experience in Comparative Perspective", in Cooper, F., Packard, R. eds. *International Development and the Social Sciences: Essays on the History and Politics of Knowledge*, 45–63. Berkeley, Los Angeles [etc.]: University of California.

India's presence at the ILO encouraged the creation of national trade union organisations, promoted by metropolitan trade union federations, who wished to allow trade unions from the colonies to express themselves at international conferences.[29] In 1920, the creation of the All-India Trade Union Congress (AITUC) ensured the representation of Indian workers at the ILO. One of the prominent figures of the time was delegate Narayan Malhar Joshi, Secretary General of the IATUC. At the ILO, he regularly defended Indian workers' interests (who were undoubtedly a minority, Bombay being the only major industrial province in the country at the time). In 1931 for instance, Joshi intervened directly with Albert Thomas to seek advice concerning minimum workers' rights and their integration into the Indian constitution, then in the process of being reformed. Among union demands, several were ILO priorities, in particular: decent pay, healthy working conditions, protection against the economic consequences of old age, sickness and unemployment, the prohibition of child labour and the right to form trade unions.[30] At the 1932 ILC, Indian workers' delegate Diwan Chaman Lall of the All India Trade Union Federation (founded by Joshi in 1931 in response to the growing Communist influence within AITUC) insisted once again that the provisions of the Convention fixing the minimum age for admission of children to industrial employment be applied to Indian children.[31] He stated: "Do the children of India not deserve full and effective protection, like those in all other countries of the world?"[32] Sir Bhupendra Nath Mitra, delegate of the British Government of India, opposed the implementation of a special regime in India based on the country's economic situation and India's delay regarding protective legislation.[33] In 1937 the Indian employers' delegate, Sir Hormusji Mody, declared that India's industrialisation should not be impeded by the adoption of regulations based on the experiences of European countries, the country's economic competitors.[34] Indian workers' delegates also mobilised for a minimum wage in India, particularly as of 1934, with the imposition of quotas

---

[29] Bureau international du Travail. 1945. *La Politique sociale dans les territoires dependants*, 61. Genève: Bureau international du travail.
[30] Rodgers, G., Bhattacharya, S., Krishnamurty, J. 2011. "India and the ILO in Historical Perspective", *Economic and Political Weekly* 46(10): 47.
[31] In the Washington Convention on the age of admission of children to industrial work, a special derogation was granted for India. Not only was the age of admission lowered, but the provisions of the Convention were to apply only to certain industrial establishments.
[32] ILC, *Record of proceedings*, 1932, 410, ILOA.
[33] *Ibid.*, 413.
[34] ILC, *Record of proceedings*, 1937, 91 and following, ILOA. Rodgers, G., Lee, E., Swepston, L., Van Daele, J. 2009. *The International Labour Organization and the Quest for Social Justice 1919–2009*, 70.

by Britain on Japanese textile imports into the Empire, which restricted Indians' access to affordable products.³⁵ They also used institutional mechanisms to denounce British colonial rule, as evidenced by the repeated use of the sanction procedure provided for in the ILO constitution. In 1934, they denounced the non-application of the convention on working hours in industry, on weekly rest and on unemployment.³⁶ Their influential work at the ILO played a central role in the government's ratification of 11 international labour conventions in 1930.³⁷The discourse on competitiveness was nevertheless a powerful argument enabling employers to justify the maintenance of minimum social standards and guaranteeing the persistence of practices condemned by the ILO throughout the interwar period.

In addition to the economic and social stakes, the appeal of communism in Asia was also one of the key issues around which Indian unions were mobilising at the ILO.³⁸ In 1929 Joshi was already insisting on the attractiveness of communist ideas among Indian workers.³⁹ That same year this concern regarding communism's influence in Asia led the Indian workers' delegates to propose that an Asian conference be organised by the ILO.⁴⁰ Thomas supported this idea as a means for the Office to provide assistance to the moderate trade union forces led by Joshi.⁴¹ His recent mission to the Far East had made him aware of the need to spread reformist morality to Asia and to curb the development of communism.⁴² Discussions about the possibility of organising an ILO conference in Asia more broadly reflected the ILO's willingness to pay greater attention to the colonies. In 1928, R. K. Shanmukham Chetty, then the employers' delegate, also openly threatened the ILO with systematic opposition by Indian employers to the ratification of international conventions should it not guarantee a better integra-

---

35 Constantine, S. 1984. *The Making of British Colonial Development Policy, 1914–1940*, 229. London: Routledge.
36 See the intervention of Jamnadas Mehta, Indian Workers' Delegate at the 1934 International Conference. ILC, *Record of proceedings*, 1934, 158 and following, ILOA.
37 Das, R. K. 1930. "La législation du travail de l'Inde", *ILR* 22(5): 625–650.
38 On the ILO's historical relationship with communism, see Kott, S. 2018. "OIT, justice sociale et mondes communistes. Concurrences, émulations, convergences", *Le Mouvement Social* 263(2): 139–151.
39 ILC, *Record of proceedings*, 1929, 109, ILOA.
40 The Japanese workers' delegates also proposed this project twice, to the 1927 and 1928 ILCs.
41 Letter from Atul Chatterjee to Butler, December 18, 1929. XD 6/1/1 "Asiatic Conference", ILOA.
42 Thomas, A. 1959. *À la rencontre de l'Orient. Notes de voyage, 1928–1929*. Genève: la Société des amis d'Albert Thomas. See also Letter from Albert Thomas to Condliffe, September 1ˢᵗ, 1930. CAT 5/19/1/9 "Relations et informations. Chine"; D 600/1000/30/3 "Institute of Pacific Relations. Conference. China 1931. Shanghai and Hangchow Oct-Nov. 1931", ILOA.

tion of the colonies into discussions on international labour standards.⁴³ A resolution for an Asian conference was therefore put to the vote by the ILC in 1931.⁴⁴ However, in October 1931 the GB decided to postpone the organisation of the conference, which would not take place until 1947.⁴⁵ British delegates did not support this project apparently because of the lack of studies on working conditions in Asia, as well as the tense political relations between India, China, Japan and Europe, a position shared by Asian delegates.⁴⁶ The failure of the Asian conference project under the aegis of the ILO, far from putting an end to the initiatives of trade union representatives, led them to seek to better organise on a regional scale. In 1933, under the impetus of the Indian Trade Union Federation, a project for an Asian social congress was born.⁴⁷ The same year, the General Confederation of Labour of Japan and the Indian Federation announced to ILO members the adoption of a resolution to hold this regional meeting, which took place in 1934. However, the project was not intended to oppose the ILO.⁴⁸ Moderate Asian trade union leaders were in fact seeking to use the ILO to define a social development agenda for Asia as a bulwark for the development of communism.

Although the ILO was far from grasping the complexity of the economic, political and social problems at play in Asian countries, it nevertheless opened a space for discussion between the industrial powers and Asian countries on the difficulties of diffusing social progress in Asia – amidst a logic of economic competition – without developing an approach that would be more respectful of the economic interests of countries in this region. The possibility of partially applying international labour Conventions bears witness to this phenomenon. These special regimes were regularly criticised by Western powers, which did not hesitate to accuse Asian countries of "unfair competition". This matter was to become a central concern at the ILO in the 1930s.

---

43 ILC, *Record of proceedings*, 1931, 316, ILOA.
44 XD 6/1/1 "Asiatic Conference", ILOA.
45 "Preparatory Asian Regional Conference of the International Labour Organisation, New Delhi, 27 October–8 November 1947", *ILR* 57(5): 425–437.
46 The British government also opposed the organisation of a regional conference in Sydney, proposed by the Australian Association for the League of Nations in 1936. D 1004/3 "Proposed Regional ILO Conference. Sydney. Australia" and XR 33/1/2 "Relations with India: Notes on the political, economic and social situation, 1932–1939" ILOA.
47 Stolte, C. 2012. "Bringing Asia to the world: Indian trade unionism and the *long road* towards the Labour Congress, 1919–37", *Journal of Global History* 7(2): 257–278.
48 *Ibid.*, 259.

2 The ILO's Attempts to Regulate Economic Competition

2.1 Combating Social Dumping

In addition to the obvious exceptions and limitations they had imposed on the principles of equality and universality, European countries grounded their discourse regarding the adoption (or not) of international standards according to their own economic interests. In this context, the ILO may have appeared to those more "advanced" countries as an instrument to show the "backward" countries the way to social progress. During ILCs, representatives of European countries regularly criticised, but only when it served them, the incapacity of Asian countries, and more generally less industrialised countries, to ratify international conventions. Their objective was to eliminate what was then perceived as unfair competition based on a policy of low wages and long working hours in order to preserve the working and living conditions of European workers while protecting the profit share of European employers.[49] In 1925, in response to that, the ILC asked the Office to produce a study of the working conditions in China, India and Japan, with the aim of encouraging them to reduce working hours in industry and intensify the modernisation of industrial production techniques.

In the early 1930s, the most frequently raised issue by European industrialists was the question of wage cost discrepancy. Meanwhile, the degradation of global commercial relations engendered by the economic crisis greatly preoccupied Harold Butler. Japan, which had not ratified any of Washington's international conventions, was suffering the effects of the tariff-raising trade policies of Britain, the United States and Germany. Rivalries were also particularly fierce between the Asia-Pacific countries, faced with Japan's aggressive economic policies, anxious to pursue its industrial expansion.[50] In India, competition imposed by Japanese products had caused a widespread reduction in staff num-

---

[49] Seekings, J. 2010. "The ILO and Welfare Reform, in South Africa, Latin America, and the Carribbean, 1919–1950", in Van Daele, J. et al. eds. 2010. *ILO Histories. Essays on the International Labour Organization and Its Impact on the World During the Twentieth Century*, 145–172. Bern: Peter Lang.

[50] Between 1919 and 1929, Japan adopted conventions covering, *inter alia*, the minimum working age, compensation for occupational diseases and the inspection of emigrants. See the complete list of conventions adopted by Japan at:

http://www.ilo.org/dyn/normlex/en/f?p=NORMLEXPUB:11200:0::NO::P11200_COUNTRY_ID:102729 [last accessed 17.09.2019].

bers, closing factories and aggravated social tensions in the textile industry.[51] In the broader context of nationalising economies, the emergence of new revolutionary aspirations and the rise of totalitarian states, the ILO's mobilisation around the issue of commercial competition in Asia also had a broader objective, that of ensuring legitimacy for democratic powers in promoting a liberal discourse on the improvement of people's working and living conditions.

The Office's missions in Asia testify to the fact that trade competition and social dumping in less developed countries became central concerns for the ILO. It should be noted that in the 1930s few economic experts took problems posed by the world's production conditions seriously, in particular the spread of industrialisation in less developed countries.[52] The ILO therefore offers important insight in understanding the way in which the economic competition of less developed countries was analysed. On the trade front, Japan was the most problematic and, for ILO civil servants, solving the issues posed by Japanese competition was an important key to pacifying international economic relations. In 1934 the Frenchman Fernand Maurette travelled to China and Japan, the latter having notified its withdrawal from the League of Nations the year before.[53] Through the organisation of this mission Butler wished to better understand the conditions of Japanese economic competition, and to limit the negative effects on the ILO of the League of Nations' policy in Asia, having failed to settle the Sino-Japanese conflict. Maurette, who joined the Office in 1924 as the head of the Scientific Division and who was promoted to Deputy Director of the Office in 1933, was a geographer but not a specialist of Asia. During his international career he became increasingly interested in the social and economic geographies of less developed countries. He had travelled to the Near East, China, Japan, Brazil and Argentina and had conducted major economic surveys.[54] Officially, the 1934

---

51 Extract from the report of the Tokyo office correspondent, March 23, 1934. XT 13/1/1 "Maurette's mission to China and Japan, February-April 1934", ILOA; XE 6/2/1 "Japanese competition in World Markets", ILOA.
52 James, H. 2001. *The End of Globalizazion. Lessons from the Great Depression*, 120. Harvard: Havard University Press.
53 Plata, V. 2014. "Le Bureau international du travail et la coopération technique dans l'entre-deux-guerres", *Relations internationales* 157(1): 55–69.
54 These trips are summarised in a book entitled *Tour du Pacifique*, which led to new economic geography studies. Maurette, F. 1934. *Tour du Pacifique*. Paris: Librairie Hachette. Dupuy, P., Gallois, L. 1938. "Fernand Maurette (1879–1937)", *Annales de Géographie* 47(266): 199–202. A PhD dissertation on Fernand Maurette is currently being prepared at the University of Geneva. Carrupt, R. *Un processus d'internationalisation entre la rue d'Ulm et les bords du Léman : Fernand (1878–1937) et Marie-Thérèse Maurette (1890–1989)*. PhD thesis in progress, University of Geneva.

mission was to supplement the Office's information on the development of labour legislation in Asia.[55] This interest in the region, particularly Japan, was strategic on several levels. According to Percival Martin, member of the Office's Economic Section, Japan was a tangible example of the success of state-driven economic planning in a liberal regime where private property and initiative were preserved.[56] Japan also boasted the best economic recovery record in the context of the crisis, while becoming a key player in the international economy. Moreover, according to Martin, the effect of industrialisation on the Japanese social system could indicate the likely evolution of the industrial evolution in other Asian countries, thereby justifying an interest in its economic and social development. Lastly, in addition to flattering Japan, an international survey proved without a doubt the Office's interest in countries outside of Europe, at a time when regional logics were gaining in strength. The production of economic and social expertise on Japan would also potentially make it easier for Western governments to understand the conditions of Japanese competition, and help the diffusion of higher social standards there.[57] Maurette's mission to Japan therefore took on the appearance of a Trojan horse. In his report, however, he painted a somewhat different picture of Japanese competition than that which dominated American and European industry at the time, where the general impression was that Japanese commercial advantage resided solely in low wages and dumping. Maurette thus explained that the low wages of the workers in Japan were due to an overall low standard of living in the country.[58] However, he also insisted on the fact that, in export sectors, social standards were higher. This social progress had been made possible by the rationalisation of production and technological development, two processes which beckoned encouragement.[59]

---

[55] The ILO published several papers on the subject from the late 1920s. Ayusawa, I. 1926. *Industrial Conditions and Labour Legislation in Japan*. Genève, Bureau international du travail; Idei, S. 1930. "Japan's Migration Problem", *ILR* 22(6): 773–789 and "The Unemployment Problem in Japan", *ILR* 22(4): 503–523.
[56] G 900/101/4 "Proposed mission of Mr. P.W. Martin to Japan and China. (Preparation of a report on recent measures of economic organisation in Japan and their consequences)", ILOA.
[57] Letter from Butler to Sir Ralph Glyn, Bt., M.C., M.P., London, January 29, 1934. XR 25/1/18 "Relations with the Rt. Hon. J. Ramsay MacDonald, Prime Minister, and with Major R. Glyn, Parliamentary Private Secretary to the Prime Minister, 1922–1937", ILOA.
[58] Maurette, F. 1934. *Aspects sociaux du développement industriel au Japon*, 57. Études et documents, Série B, no. 21, Genève: Bureau international du travail.
[59] *Ibid.*, 59. Between 1934 and 1935 Maurette gave several conferences in France and Switzerland on the subject. G 900/46/30 "Comité national des Conseillers du Commerce Extérieur de la France. Requesting Mr. Maurette to give a lecture on Japanese labour at their assembly, 21 Feb.1935. Paris", ILOA; G 900/46/35 "*Syndicat* de l'Union sociale *d'Ingénieurs Catholiques*,

2.2 Breaking Down the Walls of Protectionism: the ILO as an Instrument of US Economic Diplomacy in Asia

Maurette's mission in Asia was above all perceived as an act of diplomacy. The 1934 ILC pointed to the "spirit of openness and impartiality" that prevailed in organising this mission and commended the ILO's efforts towards a rapprochement with non-European countries. Maurette's mission, however, did not stop at that. It demonstrated the Office's ambition to link the regulation of international trade to the improvement of working conditions and, if possible, to achieve the adoption of an international convention in this field. For Butler this was a crucial issue. Indeed, he saw Asian competition as an opportunity for the ILO to engage in concrete actions to combat the economic protectionism that had led to overproduction, declining consumption and a deterioration in workers' living standards.[60] To emerge from the crisis, Butler advocated adjusting production to an adequate standard of living, "an ever-increasing volume of employment" and, above all, "an equitable distribution of benefits" between workers and employers. All this would lead to a general policy of raising workers' living standards, stimulating consumption and making the symptomatic overproduction of the Great Depression disappear.[61]

The Office's economic research programme was clearly oriented in this direction. Formulated by the American economist Lewis Lorwin, it defended the idea that protectionist policies and the multiplication of customs barriers were factors in the decline of world prosperity, particularly in less developed countries.[62] The Office's research aimed at elaborating solutions for the international regulation of business practices following the guidelines laid down by the United States' National Relief Administration. Created in 1933 by the National Industrial Recovery Act, it authorised industries to draft codes on fair competition, with the overall objective of regulating wages, working hours and prices.[63] Butler therefore hoped that Americans would be receptive to a form of international trade regulation that considered working conditions. The presence of the United States at the ILO would indeed provide new opportunities to promote the international

---

Paris (André Pairault). Requesting Mr. Maurette to give a lecture on the industrial equipment of Japan and Turkey and its effect on unemployment. Winter 1935–1936", ILOA.
60 Dierctor's Report, ILC, *Record of proceedings*, 1935, 395, ILOA.
61 "Provisional socio-economic research programme", by Lewis Lorwin, July 5, 1935. XO 1/9/1 "International Labour Office: Economic Section", ILOA.
62 *Ibid.*
63 "Economic research program", by Lewis Lorwin. XO 1/9/1 "International Labour Office: Economic Section", ILOA.

regulation of economic competition between Asian and industrialised countries. The United States would prove to be a powerful player in the ILO's discussions and proposals for an international convention on the reduction of working hours in the textile industry, which, if adopted by all the countries concerned, would contribute, according to its promoters, to combating one of the main causes of protectionism.[64]

While proposals to reduce working hours were made as early as the 1930s under pressure from workers' representatives, European government and employers' representatives were systematically opposed to them as they felt this measure disproportionately favoured emerging industries.[65] However at the 1935 ILC, two conventions were adopted: the Forty-Hour Week Convention (1935, No. 47) and the Reduction of Hours of Work (Glass-Bottle Works) Convention (1935, No. 49). Governments that ratified Convention No. 47 committed to reducing working hours without reducing workers' wages. The workers' representatives therefore supported this convention insofar as they saw it as a means of achieving reduced work time in industry more broadly. Under the leadership of the US labour delegate Martin Tracy, the ILC also adopted a recommendation that encouraged the Office to study "ways to provide social guidance for industrial development".[66] In particular, the US government delegate and economist Walton H. Hamilton proposed that the ILO examine the economic and social conditions of the textile industry.[67] This proposal was a product of American concerns regarding industrial competition. [68] Union pressure for a 40-hour work week in certain export sectors such as automobiles and textiles was particularly strong. In the spring of 1935, members of Congress from textile-producing states had asked President Roosevelt to take concrete steps to save the textile industry "from a repetition of the tremendous fluctuations that characterised the industry

---

64 Box 45: Conferences. 174.3.1 "Records of Secretaries". Office of the Secretary Frances Perkins. General Subject File, 1933–1941, RG 174 "General Records of the Department of Labor", National Archives and Records Administration, Washington (hereafter NARA)
65 Maurette, F. 1933. "La conférence préparatoire pour la semaine de quarante heure", *ILR* 27(3): 315–343, ILOA. Feiertag, O. 2011. "Humaniser la crise économique (1929–1934): l'expertise du BIT dans la crise de mondialisation des années 1930", in Aglan, A., Olivier F., Dzovinar K. *Humaniser le travail. Régimes économiques, régimes politiques et Organisation internationale du travail (1929–1969)*, 19–38. Bruxelles: Peter Lang.
66 ILC, *Record of proceedings*, 1935, 294, ILOA.
67 *Ibid.*, 353, ILOA.
68 Lorenz, E. C. 2001. *Defining Global Justice. The History of U.S. International Labor Standards Policy*, 81–84. Notre Dame: University of Notre Dame Press.

during the past twenty years".[69] Later that year, faced with this pressure, the President's Administration established a subcommittee to report on the causes of instability in the textile industry. This report, entitled *Cotton Textile Industry* and submitted to the President and Congress, recommending that the United States cooperate with the ILO to develop studies on the problems affecting the textile industry on a global scale, testifies to the international dimension of American concerns.[70]

At the 1936 ILC the American delegation was instructed by the government to advance the idea of the 40-hour week in several important industries, such as textiles and mining.[71] The delegation was composed of John G. Winant, appointed Deputy Director of the ILO in 1935 and again from 1937 to 1939[72]; Frieda Miller, an expert on labour statistics who had played a central role alongside Winant in the 1930s in the debate on the minimum wage in the United States; and Emil Rieve, one of the architects of the Social Security Act of 1935 as well as Winant's adviser to the SSB.[73] At the 1936 ILC, Winant and government delegate Justin Godart, an ardent defender of the eight-hour workday in France,[74] tabled a draft resolution calling for the establishment of a committee to study the application terms of the 40-hour week in the textile industry.[75] It was then decided that an international conference on textile would be organised, despite Great Britain's vivid opposition,[76] alongside employers' delegates such as Frenchman Pierre Waline, who denounced what he considered the "dangerous illusion of the forty-hour week".[77]

Following the 1936 ILC, Frances Perkins, Arthur Wubnig, temporarily hired at the Office's Economic Section, American economics professor Ellison Chalmers, Edward Phelan and Ronald James Patrick Mortished, trade unionist and

---

[69] Letter from Isador Lubin to Frances Perkins, March 1st, 1937. Box 45: Conferences. 174.3.1 "Records of Secretaries". Office of the Secretary Frances Perkins. General Subject File, 1933–1941, RG 174 "General Records of the Department of labor", NARA.
[70] Ibid.
[71] Box no. 46: Conferences. 174.3.1 "Records of Secretaries". Office of the Secretary Frances Perkins. General Subject File, 1933–1941, RG 174 "General Records of the Department of Labor", NARA.
[72] John G. Winant would become the third Director of the Office from 1939 to 1941.
[73] Lorenz, E. C. 2001. *Defining Global Justice. The History of U.S. International Labor Standards Policy*, 111.
[74] Lespinet-Moret, I. 2004. "Justin Godart et le Bureau international du travail", in Wieviorka, A. ed. *Justin Godart: Un homme dans son siècle (1871–1956)*, 81–86. Paris: CNRS Ed.
[75] ILC, *Record of proceedings*, 1936, 669, ILOA.
[76] Ibid., 59.
[77] Ibid., 69.

technical adviser to the Irish workers' delegation, met in Geneva to articulate a strategy for the international conference on textiles scheduled for 1937. The Office wanted to propose a vast social policy programme, a project considered too ambitious and too vague by the Americans.[78] The idea was therefore limited to producing a general study on the problems affecting the textile industry. Given the convergence of US interests with the recommendations adopted at the ILO, President Roosevelt suggested that the conference be held in the United States. It opened in Washington on 2 April, nearly 20 years after the United States entered the First World War. While this was a mere coincidence it was clear that the United States was seeking to position itself at the centre of the regulation of international economic cooperation.

At the conference, which for the first time brought together textile industry experts from around the world (with the exception of Italy), the American delegation, numbered at around 50, was by far the most impressive. On Perkins' initiative, the members of the former subcommittee that had prepared the report submitted to the President on 21 August 1935 were reconvened to act as advisers.[79] The conference based its work on Lorwin's report, *The World Textile Industry: Economic and Social Problems*. It was the Office's first report summarising information on production, world trade and working conditions in the textile industry, which at the time affected some 14 million workers worldwide.[80]

The report clearly posed the problem of competition between the West and Asia. Competition in emerging textile industry markets such as India and Japan was presented as one of the most important structural changes. What these countries had in common were lower labour standards than those of Western Europe or the northern United States. This added competition resulted in a general tendency to reduce wages, particularly in the textile industries of the United States and Great Britain, and to increase import quotas. According to a British study by the Joint Committee of Cotton Trade Organisations in June 1936 cited in the Office's report, Japan's textile exports had thus been restricted on 56 of the 106 markets in which it was dumping its products.[81] The conference recog-

---

[78] Letter from Chalmers to Lubin, August 17, 1936. Box no. 46: Conferences. 174.3.1 "Records of Secretaries". Office of the Secretary Frances Perkins. General Subject File, 1933–1941, RG 174 "General Records of the Department of labor", NARA.
[79] Letter from Perkins to the Secretary of Agriculture Henry A. Wallace, February 9, 1937. Box no. 46: Conferences. 174.3.1 "Records of Secretaries". Office of the Secretary Frances Perkins. General Subject File, 1933–1941, RG 174 "General Records of the Department of Labor", NARA.
[80] Lorwin, L. L. 1937. *The World Textile Conference*, 18. National Peace Conference, New York. Arch. L.L.
[81] Lorwin, L. L. 1937. *The World Textile Conference*, 29.

nised that the global spread of the textile industry was inevitable and that it represented an opportunity for less developed countries to increase their national income. However, the organisation of industrial development in these countries was seen as an essential factor in achieving balanced global economic growth. In particular, the conference insisted that the restoration of the textile industry in Europe was linked to economic development and rising living standards in Asia, and that the development of international trade between industrialised and Asian countries could mitigate the risk of mass unemployment in Europe.[82] The report also stressed that the increase in world production did not fully explain the problems affecting the textile industry. It highlighted the fact that consumption levels had remained mostly stable since 1909 to 1913 and pointed to people's low purchasing power as an aggravating factor. In particular, the conference recognised the need to involve the agricultural sector in the economic growth of less developed countries, without specifying how investment should be distributed between this sector and the more dynamic industrial sectors. It nonetheless stressed the need to improve the consumption capacity of agricultural populations in Asian countries in order to absorb national textile production. However, differences of opinion emerged as to what means might strengthen their purchasing power. The workers' delegates defended wage increases, while the European employers' delegates argued in favour of reducing production costs. The economic underdevelopment of countries such as India and Japan served as an argument against reducing working hours and increasing wages in the textile industry. Only the American representatives were in favour of reducing working hours. European and Asian employers' representatives, who felt it would hinder their economic development, refused to follow the American model.

Still, the results of the conference were significant in many regards. For the first time, the ILO had become a forum for discussion on the regulation of international trade from a labour perspective in an important industrial sector. The conference also led to proposals for ways of regulating international trade, in particular the adoption of international agreements as a means of adjusting the production and consumption of the various textile products. This was clearly a US inspired measure.[83] The conference also opted to establish a Standing Tex-

---

82 *Tripartite Technical Conference on The Textile Industry.* Washington, 2–17 avril 1937. *Record of proceedings*, Geneva, ILOA.

83 For instance, as early as 1933 James T. Shotwell had indeed proposed to Cordell Hull that new trade agreements include as a condition for the lowering of tariffs the attainment of core labour standards. Charnovitz, S. 2014. *The Path of World Trade Law in the 21st Century*, 35, footnote 143. New Jersey: World Scientific.

tile Committee, which predated the establishment of the ILO Industrial Committees by nearly a decade.[84] Finally, at the 1937 ILC, an international convention on the reduction of working hours in the textile industry (No. 61) was adopted, despite strong opposition from representatives of Asian and European employers, particularly those from Britain.[85] Hormusji Mody, an Indian employer delegate who became president of the Textile Millowners' Association in 1927, clearly expressed his disagreement.[86] Finally, not a single government ratified this convention, "child of the crisis, born prematurely."[87] Despite this failure, the ILO was undoubtedly an important forum for debates on how to combat unfair competition, expand the global consumer market and integrate all territories into the international economy. However, Japan's withdrawal from the ILO in 1938 and its decision to expand its economic and military presence in the Pacific highlighted the limits of the ILO's influence in the region and especially its inability to pacify economic relations.

2.3 The Office's Economic Research Missions

An analysis of the Office's daily activities also reveals the efforts made by international civil servants to give international visibility to the economic development of the colonies. While in the 1930s the ILO attempted to "modernise" practices without questioning colonial exploitation – a phenomenon already perceived by other colonial historians[88] – its reflections were part of an ambiguous context, marked by European imperialism and its "civilising mission" on the one hand, and the desire to liberalise trade (a central aspect of US internationalism) and to integrate the colonies into the international economy on the other. These issues were at the origin of an evolution of ILO's discourse towards modernising production, industrialisation and planning. These measures were aimed at raising workers' standards of living and alleviating the profound economic and social inequalities plaguing the colonies, aggravated by the collapse of in-

---

84 In 1945 the ILO decided to create an industrial committee on coal mining and land transport.
85 It should be noted that no state ratified this Convention. In 2000, the ILC decided to remove it from the list of Conventions.
86 ILC, *Record of proceedings*, 1937, 391, ILOA.
87 *Ibid.*
88 Cooper, F. 1997. "Modernizing Bureaucrats, Backward Africans, and the Development Concept", in Cooper, F., Randall P. eds. *International Development and the Social Sciences*, 64–92. University of California Press.

ternational trade. This sheds light on the specificity with which the discourse on colonial development was emerging at the ILO.

As seen in Chapter 1, the economic crisis was at the heart of a shift in the way social policy was perceived. Office civil servants were now seeking to integrate labour issues into a strategy for the recovery of national economies, conceptualised first on a European scale and then globally. The Office also tried to link its reflection on the reconstruction of Europe and the role of public investment with resource development in less developed regions, particularly in the colonies. In 1932 Thomas thus evoked the idea of international collaboration for the exploitation of global resources. Indeed, according to him, Europe could not emerge from the crisis without a global movement for economic development.[89] For civil servants at the Office, public works programmes had to be established in collaboration with indigenous peoples to foster the colonies' development.[90] However, in the interwar period, while the urgency of improving living conditions in the colonies was gaining ground, the implementation of certain Keynesian formulae in these territories remained above all motivated by the desire to boost Europe's industrialised economies.[91] In particular, the regulation of production costs was perceived as an important factor in solving unemployment in Europe.[92]

As such, the economic crisis had revealed the weakness of the colonies' economies, along with their vulnerability.[93] Improving living standards had become a major concern in the minds of policy makers, economists, administrators and experts when thinking of ways to increase industrial production, lower trade barriers and strike a balance between production and consumption.[94] The idea was that with modern production methods, access to raw materials and the development of a consumer market, it would be possible to lift the most disadvantaged populations out of poverty. Until the 1930s, although the metropoles took some administrative measures, social policies were nevertheless largely inspired by the laissez-faire principle. For this reason, the improvement of the colonies'

---

89 Director's Report, ILC, *Record of proceedings*, 1932, 917.
90 EP 1000/5 "Economic problems: Congrès des économistes de langue française – Congrès international des sciences économiques et sociales. 01/1937–12/1937", ILOA.
91 Cooper, F. 2008. *Decolonization and African Society: The Labor Question in French and British Africa*, 68. Cambridge: Cambridge University Press.
92 Constantine, S. 1984. *The Making of British Colonial Development Policy, 1914–1940*, 102. London: Routledge.
93 Bureau international du Travail. 1945. *La Politique sociale dans les territoires dépendants*, 51. Etudes et Documents, Série B. n°38 (Montreal).
94 Clavin, P. 2013. *Securing the World Economy: The Reinvention of the League of Nations, 1920–1946*. Oxford: Oxford University Press.

social conditions only truly began gaining momentum after the Second World War.⁹⁵

In the context of criticism of the deteriorating social conditions of the colonies, which generated a renewed need for expertise on the economic and social problems facing them, the Office sought to better understand the factors preventing the economic development of the colonies by organising research missions. For Butler the organisation of these missions reflected the changes that had taken place in public opinion, then increasingly aware of the problems of nutrition, public health, industrialisation and the role of the latter in alleviating the economic pressure on farmers. The internationalisation of colonial expertise also reflected the changes that took place in the 1930s in the administrative management of the colonies, and was part of a broader "scientification" of colonial policies.⁹⁶ Still rather infrequent in the 1930s, economic research missions are interesting to observe for more than one reason. On the one hand, they provide an opportunity to discuss the Office's role in distributing information on the economic and social problems affecting the colonies and in integrating the colonies into international and transnational networks of social expertise.⁹⁷ On the other hand, these studies highlight the emergence of a discourse on colonial development, which, according to civil servants at the Office, relied on industrialisation and modernisation. However, the industrialisation of the colonies was perceived as a serious problem. Indeed, opposition among colonial authorities was substantial, some seeing it more as a danger than a solution.⁹⁸ This particular issue would remain the subject of heated debates among politicians, colonial administrators and economic experts well into the 1940s.

2.3.1 John Riches' Mission to Samoa

In 1935 and 1936, the New Zealand civil servant John Riches, a member of the Office's Economic Section, travelled to Western Samoa, then a territory under

---

95 Thurston, A. 2008. *Sources for Colonial Studies in the Public Record Office*, 320. London: HMSO. Cooper, F. 2008. *Decolonization and African Society: The Labor Question in French and British Africa*, 60; Singaravélou, P. 2009. "Le moment 'impérial' de l'histoire des sciences sociales (1880–1910)", *Mil neuf cent. Revue d'histoire intellectuelle* 1(27): 87–102.
96 Amrith, S. 2006. *Decolonizing International Health India and Southeast Asia, 1930–65*, 12. UK: Palgrave Macmillan.
97 See Clavin, P., Sunil, A. 2013. "Feeding the world: Connecting Europe and Asia, 1930–1945", *Past and Present* 218 (suppl. 8): 29–50.
98 Havinden, M. A., Meredith, D. 1993. *Colonialism and Development: Britain and its Tropical Colonies, 1850–1960*, 173. London and New York: Routledge.

the League of Nations' mandate, entrusted to New Zealand after the First World War.[99] Few investigations had been carried out on the island. Indeed, New Zealand's administration mistrusted international experts greatly, in particular those of the PMC. The fact is that New Zealand had, on several occasions, been accused by the PMC of not respecting the mandate's provisions, in particular those pertaining to the use of forced labour, as well as purposefully not seeking solutions to the social conflicts that were then shaking Western Samoa.[100] This dominion, ruled until 1935 by a Conservative government, had remained mostly absent from the ILO. The Office's economic research missions had two objectives: to establish diplomatic relations and to enrich documentation on economic and social conditions in dependent territories.[101]

Riches travelled to New Zealand twice, in 1933 and 1935.[102] The technical documentation he obtained, in addition to the contacts he established as early as 1933, informed the Office of the country's social landscape, in a context not otherwise conducive to reforms. Riches noted in one of his reports that "the main body of opinion in the country is still conservative, and there is an almost hysterical fear of Communist ideas".[103] This first mission, confined to an exchange of information, had relatively little impact in terms of governance. The second mission, in 1935, took place in a very different context, with reformist and liberal members of the Labour Party coming to power that same year. Opportunities to improve living and working conditions in New Zealand and Samoa were the subject of a series of reports written by Riches and commissioned by the new Minister of Labour, H. Timothy Armstrong, who was seeking to strengthen relations between New Zealand and the ILO. The first report was however devoted to sending delegations and experts to the ILO and to possibly ratifying certain international conventions.[104] Another report was devoted to the study of the tools implemented or envisaged in the new government's social policy. This report attested to the importance placed on housing problems, reduced working hours and working conditions in the agricultural industry.[105] Despite the lauda-

---

99 Chaudron, G. 2012. *New Zealand in the League of Nations: The Beginnings of an Independent Foreign Policy, 1919–1939*. Jefferson, NC: McFarland & Company.
100 *Ibid.*, 189–193.
101 In the ILO, the notion of dependent territory includes colonies, mandated territories, overseas territories and dominions.
102 G 900/82/2 "Mr. Riches mission to New Zealand 1933", ILOA. See also John Riches. 1937. "Le planisme et les salaires dans l'agriculture en Nouvelle-Zélande", *ILR* 35(3): 309–349.
103 Report of Mr. Riches mission to New Zealand, 27. G 900/82/2, ILOA.
104 From 1936 onwards, New Zealand sent a full delegation to the ILC every year. Chaudron, Gerald. 2012. *New Zealand in the League of Nations*, 27.
105 H. Belshaw. 1933. "La main-d'œuvre agricole en Nouvelle-Zélande", *ILR* 28(1): 27–50.

ble intentions of the new Labour government, Riches expressed serious doubts regarding New Zealand's capacity to undertake far-reaching reforms.[106] New Zealand industry had been hard hit by the economic crisis, as Riches had already noted in 1933. The fall in the prices of products intended for export – a direct consequence of the restrictive measures adopted by European countries – in particular, wool, cheese, butter and mutton, coupled with the deflationary effect of the cessation of all foreign borrowing had "reduced New Zealand to a state of economic depression quite without parallel in living memory".[107] Interestingly enough Riches' report reflected a desire to better understand the relationship between foreign capital and its consequences on the standard of living of indigenous workers. For example, in his 1933 report, he estimated that total output had fallen by one-third since 1929, and that the nominal rates of wages had fallen, in particular after the abolition of compulsory arbitration in 1932, exposing the workforce to forced labour in some industries.[108] The abolition of compulsory arbitration had resulted in New Zealand workers, including unskilled agricultural workers, being deprived of any protection against wage cuts in the export sectors. According to Riches: "The result has been a definite stiffening of the unions, a stimulus to the fighting spirit and a tendency on the part of union leaders to explore every possible line of action".[109]

The new Labour government also wished to embark on a reform programme in Samoa and had suggested that Riches join a research mission in December 1935. The situation in Samoa had deteriorated significantly since the end of the First World War.[110] This situation had degenerated into social conflict, aggravated by acts of repression, leading to a weakening of the Mau movement.[111] The new government, having decided to break with the previous policy, abolished anti-Mau legislation.[112] Riches had also recommended these measures. In one of his reports he insisted on the need to establish greater collaboration between indigenous leaders and the New Zealand administration in order to lift the island out of its social crisis. This discourse on the need to integrate indigenous peoples into economic development and to set in motion a process of democratisation in Samoa portended the Office's proposals on colonial social policy developed from

---

[106] Report of Mr. Riches mission to New Zealand, 10. G 900/82/2, ILOA.
[107] Ibid.
[108] Ibid., 19.
[109] Ibid., 4.
[110] Pedersen, S. 2006. "The Meaning of the Mandates System: An Argument", *Geschichte und Gesellschaft* 32(4): 569.
[111] Report of Mr. Riches mission to New Zealand, 21. G 900/82/2, ILOA.
[112] Chaudron, G. 2012. *New Zealand in the League of Nations*, 195.

1943 onwards.[113] On the social front Riches called for urgent action to improve housing and working conditions on banana, cocoa and copra plantations, where the workforce had no social protection and trade unionism was very weak. Riches' proposals were based on the Office's classic triptych: production increase – capital accumulation – wealth redistribution.[114] Riches' model of economic development for Samoa was based on the belief, widely held at the Office, that cultural change was made possible by the expansion of the market economy. His rhetoric, however, remained anchored in a paternalistic view of modernisation in Samoa, which he said was prevented by the conservative attitude of the Mau leaders. Riches' reports thus allowed for the emergence of a series of ideas on colonial development oriented towards improving living conditions, in collaboration with metropoles, local governments and international organisations, towards the progressive democratisation of the colonial system. However, this discourse had not yet been articulated into a body of doctrines that could be generalised to all colonial contexts.

There is no record of the various exchanges that took place in Samoa between Riches and colonial administrators, or even with members of government, much less with indigenous leaders. However, the ratification in 1938 of 20 international labour Conventions, in particular on forced labour, hours of work in industry, unemployment, compensation for agricultural accidents and occupational diseases suggests that international research missions such as Riches' had a positive impact on the distribution of international standards.[115] This said, the ratification of these conventions was primarily intended to support Labour Party policy in New Zealand. As such, it is highly likely that few of them were actually implemented, particularly in Samoa.

2.3.2 Harold Butler's Mission to India

In the context of discussions at the ILO on the regulation of international trade between Western industrial powers and Asia's emerging economies, Butler's 1937 mission to India, Ceylon and Malaysia offered an additional opportunity to dis-

---

[113] Wilfred Benson, an ILO civil servant specialising in colonial issues, was the main architect of the ILO's colonial programme after the Second World War. For a detailed analysis of his proposals, see Maul, D. 2012. *Human Rights, Development and Decolonization. The International Labour Organization, 1940–70*, 64–69.
[114] Report of Mr. Riches mission to New Zealand, 25. G 900/82/2, ILOA.
[115] The complete list of conventions ratified by New Zealand can be found at the following address: http ://www.ilo.org/dyn/normlex/fr/f?p=1000 :11200 :0 : :NO :11200 :P11200_COUNTRY_ID :102775 [last accessed 12.09.2019].

cuss these ideas with representatives of employers' and trade union organisations as well as political authorities.[116] Archival records show that the primary objective of this mission was to study the economic and social consequences of industrialisation in Asia and the possibilities of elaborating legislation adapted to less developed countries.[117] It was also meant to measure the extent to which the standards of protection provided by ILO conventions were likely to encourage social progress and economic development in the colonies.

In India one of the central problems that mobilised discussions with Indian textile employers was the recent adoption of the International Labour Convention on the 40-hour week following the April 1937 World Textile Conference. There was strong opposition to this convention, particularly from the highly influential Millowners' Association, or the South Indian Millowners' Association. Although it provided for a longer workweek in less developed countries, this convention, according to Hormusji Mody, did not realistically take into account the production conditions in India, where poverty was a central economic problem. Butler was well aware of the problems posed by the application of the 40-hour workweek in less developed countries.[118] But while Bombay textile employers insisted on the need to reduce production costs, Butler insisted on the need to raise living conditions, in line with the conclusions reached by the World Textile Conference.[119]

Discussions between Butler and the Bombay unions reflected workers' concerns with wage cuts and their willingness to involve the ILO in their struggle for a minimum wage. In 1937 numerous strikes were organised in the textile sector.[120] The increase in tariffs had strongly mobilised the textile unions, which

---

[116] Butler also wanted to go to China and Japan, but the war prevented him from making this part of the trip.
[117] This was the case in particular in Pondicherry, where between 1936 and 1937 measures were taken by decree to regulate working conditions. During a mission, between January and March 1937, the Frenchman Justin Godart, a former parliamentarian and minister, representative of France at the 1930 ILC, and in charge of an investigation into the Pondicherry mills, concluded that it was necessary to promulgate a Labour Code, largely inspired by international labour Conventions. The Code was established by decree on 15 May 1937. However, Butler's visit demonstrated the lack of effective enforcement of these laws. G 900/3/54/1 "Director's visit to Pondicherry. December 1937", ILOA.
[118] Meeting with The Millowners' Association of Bombay, January 7, 1938. G 900/3/54, ILOA.
[119] Butler, H. 1938. *Problème de travail en Orient*, 85. Études et documents, Série B (Conditions économiques), no. 29, Genève, Bureau international du travail.
[120] See Weaver's 1933 mission report; head of the Indigenous Labour Section, to India, Persia, Iraq and Turkey. The purpose of the mission to India was to get in touch with workplaces in India and with some employers' and trade union organisations. Weaver, C.W.H. 1933. "Notes sur un voyage en Inde, en Irak, en Perse et en Turquie", *ILR* 28(4): 491–527.

saw it as an attempt by employers to pursue a wage reduction policy.[121] This was one of the main fault lines between textile workers and employers, who were sticking to their policy of reducing production costs while showing no intention of investing in technological modernisation whatsoever.[122] The Office ultimately felt that "India [could not] afford to lag much behind [...] when the rest of the world [was] advancing".[123]

For Butler, however, the question of a minimum wage in India could not be considered solely from the point of view of a legitimate social right to be achieved. He felt it had to be integrated into broader economic concerns. In fact, Butler made economic development an essential condition for the acquisition of new social rights.[124] He identified a considerable number of obstacles to India's economic development. The imbalance between production and consumption was compounded by low labour productivity. Butler also stressed the issues of population growth, poverty and illiteracy.[125] In his report, he called for "energetic measures to improve agricultural yields, colonise virgin lands, develop latent resources and intensify industrial production".[126] Butler's mission thus helped disseminate Western conceptions of economic development. He concluded that social progress in Asia could not take place without the organised development of trade relations, a better control of economic cycles and the opening of economic markets to the colonies, a process which, in his view, was the collective responsibility of all states.[127]

The findings of Butler's report were well received by Indian industrial employers, as evidenced by comments made at the 1938 ILC. Sir Hormusji Mody even wrote an enthusiastic letter to Stephen Lawford Childs, a member of the Of-

---

121 Letter from Pillai to Butler, May 11, 1933. XC 33/1/1 "India. Correspondence Office. Delhi", ILOA.
122 Chandavarkar, R. 1994. *The origins of Industrial Capitalism in India: Business Strategies and the Working Classes in Bombay, 1900–1940*, 342. Cambridge [England]: Cambridge University Press.
123 Report of discussions held at the Southern India Chamber between members of the South Indian Millowners' Association, Percival Martin and P. P. Pillai, December 15, 1937. G 900/3/54, ILOA.
124 Butler, H. 1938. *Problème de travail en Orient*, 82–83. It should be noted that the conception of the minimum wage as a measure for improving productive efficiency would not be achieved until 1944, when the Philadelphia Declaration was adopted.
125 Butler, H. 1938. *Problème de travail en Orient*. 63.
126 *Ibid.*, 67. Original quote in French: "des mesures énergiques tendant à améliorer le rendement agricole, à coloniser les terres encore vierges, à mettre en valeur les ressources latentes et à intensifier la production industrielle".
127 *Ibid.*, 86.

fice's Director's cabinet, which reads: "I thought Geneva was becoming a threat to industrialists in countries like India. Now that Congress Governments are in power in the various Provinces, I feel like complimenting the ILO on its moderation and its sense of realism!"[128] The report was also published the same year in the Office's economic studies series. Butler had also produced a second confidential report which he had sent to Lord Linlithgow, viceroy and Governor General of India between 1936 and 1943, and to R. A. Butler, of the Department of Labour in London, who at that time was collaborating with the Colonial Office on social matters in the colonies. In this report Butler called on the British colonial administration to strengthen its action, particularly in the field of housing.[129] He also highlighted the need to train colonial administrators, who lacked general knowledge of industrial development in the various provinces of India.[130] While the Office was aware of the problem posed by the colonies' dependence on the metropoles' market, its thinking was not geared towards the colonies' independence but towards strengthening relations within the framework of the empire with the participation of experts from international organisations. The civilising mission had thus found in the development discourse produced by the Office a new paradigm in which to flourish at a time when new ideas on colonial reform were emerging. Butler would continue to push for the reform of colonial policies and a more active involvement of the metropoles in the development of social progress during the war but this time as the minister responsible for British information services in the United States.[131]

3 Early Technical Assistance in Asia: The Case of China

In the 1930s, ILO action was not limited to producing knowledge on working conditions in Asia, organising international conferences and encouraging countries to ratify international labour Conventions. Civil servants at the Office, increasingly aware of the inability of less industrialised countries to ratify ILO conventions,

---

[128] Letter from Sir Hormusji P. Mody K.B.E, Employers Federation of India from Bombay to Stephen L. Childs, June 1, 1938. XR 33/2/1 "Relations with Sir Hormusji P. Mody K.B.E Employers Federation of India, Bombay. 1938", ILOA.
[129] Butler's confidential report, February 16, 1938, 5. XT 33/2/1, ILOA.
[130] Ibid., 3.
[131] He was appointed to this position in 1942. Lee, J. M., Petter, M. 1982. *The Colonial Office, War, and Development Policy: Organisation and the Planning of a Metropolitan Initiative, 1939– 1945*, 123. University of London, Institute of Commonwealth Studies, Commonwealth Papers, number 22. London: Maurice Temple Smith, for the Institute.

began developing new international practices and engaging in technical assistance projects to help member countries implement social reforms directly on the ground. Between 1931 and 1934, the Office organised two missions of technical assistance in China, the only Asian country to have made such a request through the Office.[132]

3.1 Labour Inspection Reform

As soon as it came to power in 1927 the Chinese national government based in Nanjing embarked on a vast economic and social reconstruction programme. This programme was based on Sun Yatsen's principles and policies, which he had formulated in a 1922 plan for China's industrial development. The great dream envisioned by the leader of the nationalist party to make China not only a "dumping ground" for foreign goods but also an "economic ocean" was achieved with the help of foreign experts.[133] In 1931, amidst a major reform of the labour code, the Office was called upon to assist the Chinese nationalist government in setting up a labour inspection system.[134] This request was part of a broader programme of economic and social cooperation between China and the League of Nations.[135] The Office's commitment met several needs. On the one hand, it was an opportunity for the Office to give social reform a good reputation in the region. On the other hand, this mission provided concrete proof of the ILO's usefulness in less developed countries, which often lacked experience in social reform and suffered a general shortage of experts. As the establishment of labour inspection in China met with opposition from the concessionary powers, the Governing Body also felt that the ILO could play an important diplomatic role in facilitating negotiations between foreign powers and the Chinese government.[136] Chinese local authorities had no administrative power over foreign concessions, while foreign companies enjoyed extraterritorial rights and were not re-

---

[132] G 900/95/1/1 "Proposed visit of Mr. Pône to China. Administrative and Financial arrangements", ILOA.
[133] Yat-sen, S. 1922. *The International Development of China*, 1–10. New York: G.P. Putnam's Sons.
[134] LE 211 "Projet de la loi chinoise des fabriques", ILOA.
[135] Margherita, Z. 2007. "Exporting Development: The League of Nations and Republican China", *Comparative Studies in Society and History* 49(1):143–169.
[136] GB, *Minutes*, April 1931, 233–237, ILOA.

quired to comply with Chinese laws.[137] However, the application of the Labour Inspection Act was intended to put an end to some of these companies' exploitative labour practices. Christian non-governmental organisations, such as the Young Women's Christian Association (YWCA) in Shanghai, had also attracted the ILO's attention through information campaigns on the exploitation of child labour in Chinese factories run by industrial powers.[138] These denunciation campaigns had been organised by a network of English-speaking reformist women who played a central role in improving the working conditions of Chinese factories in Shanghai. Some of them, such as Adelaide Anderson, worked closely with the Office.

Of British origin, Anderson carried out several research missions for the Office between 1923 and 1926. She soon came to be considered by the Chinese authorities and the Office as an expert on working conditions.[139] Anderson had worked as senior inspector of factories in Britain for over 20 years and had extensive experience assessing working conditions in China having served on the Commission on Child Labour established by the Municipal Council of the International Settlement of Shanghai and on a committee on labour issues established by the National Christian Council of China.[140] From 1929 onwards she took a keen interest in the new Labour Inspection Act and contacted the Office for assistance to implement it.[141] Albert Thomas was very familiar with this Act. During his 1928 mission, he received a copy from Thomas Tchou, a member of Nanjing's Ministry of Industry and Commerce and an important figure of Chinese social reformism. In 1921, after studying naval architecture and mechanical and civil engineering in Glasgow, Tchou became Executive Secretary of the Industrial Testing Department of the Young Men's Christian Association (YMCA) in Shanghai.[142] There he began to take an interest in working conditions in

---

[137] Chen, Y. 2016. "ILO, Extraterritoriality and Labour Protection in Republican Shanghai", in Liukkunen, U., Chen, Y. eds. *Fundamental Labour Rights in China. Legal Implementation and Cultural Logic*, 99 and following. Cham: Springer International Publishing.
[138] Lake, M. 2016. "The ILO, Australia and the Asia–Pacific Region: New Solidarities or Internationalism in the National Interest?", in Lichtenstein, N., Jensen, J. M. *The ILO from Geneva to the Pacific Rim*, 42.
[139] CAT 5–19–2 "Relations Chine, folder 5–19–2–7: Travail des enfants", ILOA.
[140] Paddle, S. 2001. "For the China of the Future': Western Feminists, Colonization and International Citizenship in China in the Inter-War Years", *Australian Feminist Studies* 16(36): 325–329.
[141] Letter from Anderson to Butler, January 8, 1929. CAT 5–19–1 "Relations et informations. Chine", ILOA.
[142] Sun, Y., Hein, C., Song, K. 2017. "Planning of public housing in modern Tianjin (1928–1945). Planning Perspectives" 34(3): 442. https://www.tandfonline.com/doi/full/10.1080/02665433.2017.1408487 [last accessed 17.09.2019].

China. In April 1931 the Governing Body unanimously agreed to send two experts to China. Thomas had supported the Chinese government's request for technical assistance as an instrument of economic stabilisation and a means of limiting the influence of communist forces. To John Bell Condliffe, he wrote: "In China, I believe we could carry out some experiments in economic stabilisation that could succeed in channeling the healthy forces of this country around a civilising project."[143] The responsibility of carrying out this "civilising project" fell to Adelaide Anderson, recruited as an external expert, alongside the civil servant and French national Camille Pône.[144] The choice of Pône for this mission reveals the primarily diplomatic role of the ILO. Pône was not in fact an expert on working conditions in Asia and his presence was above all meant to encourage the Chinese government and foreign companies to reach a compromise.[145] While in principle all parties finally agreed to the establishment of a labour inspection system in foreign concessions, Japan's invasion of Manchuria in September 1931 halted its implementation.[146]

3.2 Vocational Training and Economic Reconstruction

A second mission of technical assistance was organised in 1934 by the League of Nations' International Institute of Intellectual Cooperation (IIIC). In order to continue the reforms undertaken in the field of education, the Chinese Ministry of Education had asked the League of Nations to send a qualified person with extensive experience in adapting educational methods to a general policy of industrial reconstruction. The IIIC chose Fernand Maurette. His hiring was explained by the fact that as early as 1924 he represented the Office at the IIIC. Maurette also had a good experience of the problems of higher, secondary and primary education which he acquired in the course of his career, before joining the International Labour Office. During his mission in 1934, Maurette gathered informa-

---

143 Letter from Albert Thomas to John Bell Condliffe, September 1st, 1930. D 600/1000/30/3 "Institute of Pacific Relations. Conference. China 1931. Shanghai and Hangchow Oct-Nov.1931", ILOA. Original quote in French: "Je ne crois pas qu'il serait impossible de faire, en Chine, quelques expériences de stabilisation économique qui pourraient réussir à coordonner les forces saines de ce pays autour d'une œuvre de civilisation."
144 G 900/95/1/1 "Proposed visit of Mr. Pône to China. Administrative and Financial arrangements", ILOA.
145 Camille Pône's personal file, P 9, ILOA. Pône, C. 1932. "Vers l'établissement d'une inspection du travail en Chine", *ILR* 25(5): 621–635.
146 Letter from the Minister of Industry to Albert Thomas, February 23, 1931. G 900/95/1/1 "Proposed visit of Mr. Pône to China. Administrative and Financial arrangements", ILOA.

tion on the education system reform and visited several companies.[147] From his investigations he concluded that the reform of Chinese education should take into account the needs of agriculture and rural life.[148] His report portrayed an "underdeveloped" China, where the living and working conditions of workers were miserable. Beyond this economic and social diagnosis his expert's role was also to facilitate the government's decisions regarding economic development. Maurette thus advocated the creation of a Chinese employment agency that would enable the government to carry out intellectual and technical labour market studies and thus lay the foundations for the organisation of a nationwide network of vocational training. According to Maurette this agency needed to establish contacts with other foreign associations seeking to train Chinese students, as well as with international organisations in Geneva. For Maurette the Office had a central role to play, insofar as the professional training of workers fell within its competence. He thus proposed that the Office organise courses in specialised institutes and internship placements in the public administration sector or in companies, in order to enable Chinese students to become "good professionals".The ILO archives, however, did not allow us to identify the projects that may have been set up before the Second World War.

For the Office, vocational training was not a new concern. It appears in the preamble to the ILO Constitution of 1919 as one of the reforms to be undertaken to improve working conditions. In the 1930s the crisis had renewed interest in this question, first and foremost in connection with the issue of unemployment. The work of the International Congress of Technical Education in Paris in 1931 – at the origin of the creation of the International Bureau of Technical Education (IBE), legally attached to the Office – in Brussels in 1932, and in Barcelona in 1934, contributed to deepening the general understanding of vocational training, in particular its economic relevance.[149] At the 1935 ILC the problem was analysed as part of the economic measures for reconstruction. The ILO thus played a role in the establishment of vocational training as a means of adjusting the structure of the labour market to economic needs. The 1939 Vocational Training Recommendation (No. 57) enshrined this trend and marked a new international recognition of the role of vocational training in economic development.

---

[147] Extract from the report of the Tokyo office correspondent, March 23, 1934. XT 13/1/1 "Maurette's mission to China and Japan, February-April 1934", ILOA.
[148] Fernand Maurette's report to ICIC, June 27, 1934. 5B 11685.1226, ASDN.
[149] 1938. "La formation professionnelle: Problèmes et tendances", *ILR* 37(2): 145–174. Hofstetter, R., Schneuwly, B. 2013. "The International Bureau of Education (1925–1968): a platform for designing a 'chart of world aspirations for education'", *European Education Research Journal* 12(2): 215–230.

Conclusion

Since its inception the ILO sought to adapt its action to the economic and social conditions of less developed countries. However, in Asia the regulation of labour markets through the adoption of universal standards ran up against a series of difficulties linked to Asian elites' perception of the policies formulated by the ILO, the state of their economic and social development, the policies of the imperial powers as well as the tensions that animated the debates at the ILO concerning the reform of working conditions in the colonies. Above all, I have stressed the problem posed by underdevelopment in the distribution and application of international labour standards. This problem was clearly identified as early as the 1920s as a limit to the ILO's universalist ambition. However, this analysis highlights the complex realities of underdevelopment. Invoked to describe a state of weak industrialisation it served opposing objectives: to fight against unfair competition by encouraging the adoption of labour standards on the part of Western powers while preventing the imposition of these same standards in the interest of economic development on the Asian side. However, the line between these contradictory ambitions was blurred. As we have seen, Western powers had no problem adapting their discourse to their economic interests. Moreover, various actors at the ILO defended different points of view. In particular, I have highlighted the workers' representatives' use of the ILO to demand the adoption of high social standards in direct opposition to employers' representatives. At the same time, the international diffusion of social reform was encouraged and supported by individual actors and non-governmental associations who used the ILO to promote the diffusion of high social standards in Asia. Thus, the ILO did not stop at simply acknowledging the limits of its action. It also sought, through the organisation of research missions, international conferences, the production of technical reports and technical assistance, to guide the development of Asian countries, like it did in Latin America, by identifying problems in the functioning of the labour market and by formulating reform proposals compatible with the principles of international labour Conventions.

**Second Part
Development Tools and Practices:
Between Knowledge Building, Expertise
and Diplomacy**

Chapter IV
The ILO's Contribution to the Internationalisation of the Standard of Living

As we have seen in previous chapters, in the 1930s the ILO was emerging as an organisation that wished to act in less developed countries to raise the standard of living of workers. But how exactly did the ILO define the concept of "standard of living", and what was its knowledge of income and its role in economic development? What was the progress of its statistical work on housing, nutrition and income? What methods had it developed to make international comparisons? The ILO was in fact very little advanced on these issues, as its research activities, particularly on wages, focused mainly on European countries. The 1930s were nevertheless an important moment in the ILO's mobilisation on how to raise the standard of living of workers in less developed countries. The ILO had become a forum for the growing protests of trade unions, particularly in Asia, against low living standards. Besides, the Santiago Conference of 1936 adopted a resolution specifically calling upon the ILO to institute cost of living and family budget enquiries in American countries covering food, clothing, housing conditions, health and education. Other resolutions dealt with nutrition, and one urged that the International Labour Conference consider the question of the minimum wage and that of family allowances from the point of view of their adequacy to meet the essential needs of workers and their families. These new demands engaged the ILO towards a new horizon, as stated by Harold Butler in his 1938 annual report:

> Its purview is no longer confined to the technical problems of industrial regulation, which it inherited from the International Association for Labour Legislation (IALL). Its horizon embraces all those wider questions which are inherent in the vast problems of stabilising employment and lifting the standard of life to more civilised levels everywhere.[1]

The topic of raising the standard of living was not a novel one. Since the 1920s it had been discussed in tandem with the regulation of wages and working hours. From a statistical point of view, the Office had from the beginning tried to produce data on the standard of living across countries, but mainly in Europe. In the 1930s it sought to integrate less developed countries in its scientific work and to expand the defining factors of the standard of living, without, however, man-

---

1 Director's Report, ILC, 1938, 82. ILOA.

aging to clearly define what "standard of living" meant.² Despite its claim to scientificity, the Office's discourse was marked by great fragility.³ Statistical and scientific production of comparative studies on living standards would prove to be, as they had been in the 1920s, very difficult to carry out. Difficulties abounded tied to collecting national statistical data, as well as competition from the League of Nations, itself engaged in this type of action.

I will start by highlighting the Office's approach to the issue of living standards since the 1920s. The first international statistics produced were primarily concerned with workers' wages in industrial cities and were in keeping with the tradition of socio-economic surveys on family budgets dating back to the nineteenth century.⁴ Since its creation the Office looked to European and American social sciences in developing its methods to gather international statistics intended to support the development of social policies.⁵ This scientific production empowered discussions led by trade union organisations calling for increased wages and reduced working hours. In the second half of the 1930s, in a context of increased economic competition between states and the growing importance of extra-European countries, the Office developed wage and cost of living studies, in particular in some Asian countries. Lastly, I will focus on one of these studies, entitled *Le Standard de vie des travailleurs*, and analyse the conditions of its production. Published in 1938 this study highlights the fragility of the expert discourse when it comes to producing statistical data. This fragility will be further analysed through the institutional competition that arose surrounding international comparison and the selection of the defining attributes

---

2 Today the concept of standard of living is part of everyday language. It is the ultimate measure of economic growth and its rise the main target of international development policies. The term is also used to describe the state of so-called underdeveloped countries and is often used in the official reports of international organisations. Both a more or less clear and distant horizon of expectation, legitimising the most diverse development policies, and an instrument for measuring economic and social progress, standard of living is considered by some development specialists to be one of the main inventions of the post-World War Two era. Sachs, W. ed. 2010. *The Development dictionary. A Guide to Knowledge as Power*, 279–294. London and New York: Zed Books.
3 Bonnecase, V. 2008. *Pauvreté au Sahel. La construction des savoirs sur les niveaux de vie au Burkina Faso, au Mali et au Niger (1945–1974)*. Phd diss., University of Paris 1, École doctorale d'histoire, Centre d'études des mondes africains.
4 Cohen, Y., Baudouï, R. eds. 1995. *Les Chantiers de la paix sociale (1900–1940)*. Fontenay/Saint-Cloud: ENS.
5 Kevonian, D. 2008. "La légitimation par l'expertise: le Bureau international du travail et la statistique internationale", *Les Cahiers Irice* 2(2): 81–106.

of standard of living, not only between the League of Nations and the Office, but also between statisticians and economists at the Office.

1 Raising the Standard of Living in Industrialised Countries

In the 1920s and 1930s the notion of standard of living made its way into the activities of international organisations, accompanied by intense efforts to define its attributes. From this point of view, the Office is a privileged observatory of the scientific and statistical evolution of the concept, given that since 1920 it has produced consistent studies on the subject.

1.1 Wages and Minimum Wage

A decent wage, reduced working hours and the development of social insurance were the three pillars of the ILO's action to raise workers' living standards in the 1920s. This was not a new conception of the standard of living, embedded as it was in a tradition of struggles led by social reformers since the 1850s, in particular within international congresses of social reform.[6] For social reformers, improvements to the standard of living was perceived mainly through the lens of social protection, while in their eyes its maintenance and elevation justified the adoption of international standards.[7] These questions continued to mobilise experts at the beginning of the twentieth century, notably within the IALL, created in 1900 during the Paris Universal Exhibition, which functioned as a sort of "proto-ILO".[8] From 1919 onwards the battles of social reformers to improve living conditions were fought within the ILO. The social reformers who were members of the Commission on International Labour Legislation, which met in Paris in 1919 and elaborated the first ILO Constitution, placed the improvement of workers' living standards at the top of the ILO's priorities. They adopted a social def-

---

[6] For a study of the French reformist networks, see Topalov, C. ed. 2009. *Laboratoires du nouveau siècle: la nébuleuse réformatrice et ses réseaux en France, 1880–1914*. Paris: Éditions de l'EHESS; Rasmussen, A. 2001. "Tournant, inflexions, ruptures: le moment internationaliste", *Mil neuf cent. Revue d'histoire intellectuelle* 1(19): 27–41.

[7] Scelle, G. 1930. *L'Organisation internationale du travail et le BIT*, 239. Paris: M. Rivière.

[8] Kott, S. 2014. "From Transnational Reformist Network to International Organization: The International Association for Labour Legislation and the International Labour Organization (1900–1930s)", in Rodogno, D., Struck, B., Vogel, J. eds. *Shaping the Transnational Sphere: Experts, Networks and Issues from the 1840s to the 1930s*, 239–258. New York: Berghahn Books.

inition of standard of living, linking its increase to access to "an adequate living wage",[9] a series of insurance benefits, and the regulation of working hours. In particular, the eight-hour day was considered as a measure to promote the well-being of workers and improve their quality of life, thanks in part to the share of time it freed up for leisure. The ethically minded, social reformers in general, and Albert Thomas in particular, saw it as guaranteeing the independence of the working-class world and the safeguarding "of its civilisation".[10] The regulation of working hours and wages were also the main demands of the international trade union movement, formulated over many years, and stemming from the desire to discourage economic competition between countries and companies. Trade unions also consistently expressed concern that reduced working hours might be accompanied by reduced wages. They were particularly concerned about the economic situation in some European countries after the First World War, which had led to a reduction of wages. In 1922, Mr. Kupers, delegate for Netherlands' workers, declared the following in front of ILC representatives:

> Attempts are being made to lower the standard of living of the workers to the pre-war level. It should not be forgotten, however, that the workers are no longer what they used to be fifty years ago. They have made progress, and they have learned what can be done by means of their organisations [...] They want at least to retain the position which they enjoyed during the war.[11]

Having Part XIII of the Treaty of Versailles in mind, in particular the responsibility of the ILO to encourage "the provision of an adequate living wage", the Commission of Selection adopted a resolution in 1922 which instructed the Office to develop studies on the standard of living of the working class in countries with depreciated exchanges, especially in Germany, in order to identify the means for "securing the workers an adequate living wage".[12] Trade unions' delegates had regularly mobilised the ILO on the issue of wage regulation and, since the late

---

9 The "living wage" is mentioned in Article 427 of the Treaty of Versailles: "Third. – The payment to the employed of a wage adequate to maintain a reasonable standard of life as this is understood in their time and country." Reynaud, E. 2017. "The International Labour Organization and the Living Wage: A Historical Perspective", 3. International Labour Office, Inclusive Labour Markets, Labour Relations and Working Conditions Branch. – Geneva: ILO.
10 Director's Report, ILC, 1924, 829. ILOA. On the issue of leisure at the ILO, see Grandjean-Jornod, C. 2015. *Entre organisation et liberté: politiques de loisirs dans l'entre-deux-guerres au Bureau international du travail et en Suisse*. Master dissert., University of Geneva.
11 ILC, *Record of Proceedings*, 85, ILOA.
12 Ibid., 487.

1920s, on how to set a minimum wage that would guarantee workers' ability to support themselves and their families. There were, however, two opposing trends regarding wages and their role in development. The first, supported in particular by employers in the industrialised countries of Europe, was to lower wages to reduce production costs and increase consumption. The second, supported by workers and some governments such as the United States, was to increase wages to increase consumption capacity.

In response to worker mobilisation on wage regulation, the Office had considerably expanded its statistical research on wages during the interwar period. Albert Thomas gave statistics a central importance in the Office's research activities. This was reflected in his choice, in 1920, to entrust the direction of the Scientific Division of the Office to the American, Royal Meeker, an expert statistician. Originally from Pennsylvania, Meeker had a university education in political science, history and economics.[13] Following the election of President Wilson in 1912, he had worked with the government to reform the banking sector. In 1913 he was appointed by Wilson to be commissioner of the Bureau of Labor Statistics. Meeker was in favour of government action to protect workers, women and children. On the side of statistics, he was involved in the origin of a series of important reforms.[14] During the war, for instance, he collaborated with the government in its attempts to adjust wages to the rising cost of living. In this context he had conducted an extensive consumer survey. This statistical work focused primarily on families in shipbuilding and the data was used to set uniform national wage rates for workers. Between 1918 and 1919 the Bureau of Labor Statistics also conducted a national cost of living survey involving some 12,000 families in 92 cities and 42 states. As of 1920, and in collaboration with the Austrian Karl Pribram and the British James Nixon, Meeker worked to support and validate the Office's activities with accurate numbers.

In the 1920s the Office's statistical research on standard of living was limited to the production of data on the situation of industrial workers. This statistical work is historically linked to the development of welfare states and the sociological studies on workers' consumption that developed in the nineteenth century, when the first attempts to determine the attributes defining a standard of living were made. At this time the standard of living was presented "as an empirical,

---

13 Royal Meeker, personal file, P 192. ILOA.
14 See also his complete biography on the official website of the Bureau of Labor Statistics of the US Department of Labor: http://www.bls.gov/bls/history/commissioners/meeker.htm [last accessed 17.09.2019].

action-oriented science of happiness or improvement".[15] The absence of a standardised method led to selection work largely based on the investigators' individual points of view.[16] In the words of the British liberal Seebohm Rowntree, one of the leaders in consumer research and among the first to define poverty: "We are forced to rely heavily on our own judgment to determine what to include."[17]

Since 1924 the Office had published statistics on family budgets, which contributed to "the internationalisation of this social technique".[18] The collected data made it possible to highlight the significant differences that existed at the time between the purchasing power of workers in different European cities. Other studies also sought to demonstrate the relationship between the cost of living, currency depreciation and workers' standard of living. In 1925, for instance, the Office published *The Workers' Standard of Life in Countries with Depreciated Currency*, addressing the problem of a comparison between real and nominal wages, the cost of living and price control in Germany.[19] The Office's early statistical surveys indicate that it sought to produce scientific data on the social consequences of economic change in industrial cities. After the First World War, the economic and social problems posed by the restructuring of economic activity in peacetime, in particular the significant reduction in wages which limited workers' ability to consume, had led the Office to reflect on the relationship between high wage policies, production and economic development. This action programme or, in the words of Albert Thomas, this "classification of our issues", was intended to support the trade union organisations in their wage demands. The Office took the opportunity of the international economic conference that was to take place in Geneva in 1927 to prepare a report on the standard of living of workers.[20] The ILO Section of Statistics elaborated the report, which, using the

---

15 Yeo, E. J. 2003. "Les enquêtes sociales aux 18ᵉ et 19ᵉ siècles", in Porter, T. M., Ross, D. eds. *The Cambridge History of Science*, Volume 7. *The Modern Social Sciences*, 83–99. Cambridge: Cambridge University Press.
16 Desrosières, A. 2005. "Décrire l'État ou explorer la société: les deux sources de la statistique publique", *Genèses 1(58)*: 4–27; Desrosières, A. 2000. *La Politique des grands nombres. Histoire de la raison statistique*. Paris: La Découverte; Desrosières, A. 1989. "Comment faire des choses qui tiennent: histoire sociale et statistique", *Histoire & Mesure* 4(3–4): 225–242.
17 Rowntree, B. S. 1942. *Poverty and Progress. A Second social survey of York*, 102. London: Longman; Rowntree, B. S., Lavers, G. R. 1951. *Poverty and the Welfare State: A Third Social Survey of York Dealing only with Economic Questions*, 22. London: Longmans.
18 Cohen, Y., Baudouï, R. eds. 1995. *Les Chantiers de la paix sociale (1900–1940)*, 64.
19 1925. *The Workers's Standard of Life in Countries with Depreciated Currency*, Studies and Reports, Series D (Wages and Working hours), no. 15. Geneva, International Labour Office.
20 Personal note from Albert Thomas, May 11, 1927. CAT 6B-3 "Questions économiques, monétaires financières. Oct. 1925-Mai 1927". ILOA.

wages and budgets of workers' households since 1914 as data, mapped the evolution of workers' living standards in various countries.[21] Based on data collected by the Office and the British Department of Labour between 1914 and 1923, the report analysed the wages of a range of industrial occupations in key European capitals, as well as in Ottawa, Sydney and Philadelphia. The report was not limited to Europe, as also shown by the data provided on the distribution of workers' household expenditure in Argentina, India and Japan.

The fact that London was designated as the standard suggests that the report was primarily aimed at mobilising European countries on the issue of workers' wages. Indeed, the objective of this report was to show that, in Europe, after the war, wages for a 48 hour workweek were relatively lower than pre-war wages. Each type of consumption was represented by a basket of selected goods, the price of which was determined by the market value in a given city.[22] The total price of this basket represented the unit of measurement from which the purchasing power of nominal wages was assessed, following the method established by the Office in its 1926 study on household budget survey methods, *Les Méthodes d'enquête des budgets familiaux*. This study, which was largely inspired by sociological research on the consumption habits of the working class, in particular that of Maurice Halbwachs in France,[23] nevertheless insisted on the diversity of methods applied nationally. The 1926 report also stressed the technical limitations of comparing real wages internationally (available data covered only a few labour categories, real wages only determined purchasing power in relation to foodstuffs, while the types of consumption analysed did not necessarily correspond to the average consumption in each country).[24] While the lack of methodological precision could be criticised, this production of statistical data proved to be very useful after all. By focusing on wage gaps, their use was aimed at "raising awareness on the international character of so-

---

21 "Report on the Standard of Living of the Workers in Various Countries". Preparatory Committee for the International Economic Conference. Documentation for the Second Session (November 1926). International Labour Office and League of Nations. Conférence économique internationale, Geneva, May 4, 1927. Documentation... [Vol. II]. ILOA.
22 "Report on the Standard of Living of the Workers in Various Countries", 18. ILOA.
23 1926. *Les Méthodes d'enquête sur les budgets familiaux*. Studies and Reports, Series N (Statistics), no. 9. Geneva, International Labour Office.
24 "Report on the Standard of Living of the Workers in Various Countries", 10 and following. For a more detailed analysis of the development of statistical techniques at the national level from a nutritional science perspective, see Vernon, J. 2007. *Hunger: A Modern History*, 81–117. Cambridge Mass.: The Belknap Press of Harvard University Press.

cial justice values".[25] Besides, labour statistics remained scarce at that time, despite the strong impetus generated by the gradual establishment of "engineer states"[26] and the development of national censuses.

Since 1919 the ILO had also addressed the issue of minimum wages in trade sectors, where workers' living conditions were particularly difficult. Minimum wage was seen by the member states as a way to limit exploitation and unfair competition.[27] This being said, in the 1920s minimum wage policies were applied in only a handful of countries. In Australia and New Zealand, industry and regional districts had set minimum wages.[28] The United States had minimum wage legislation in six states and Canada in four provinces. In France and Norway, only the textile industry had some form of wage regulation. In Uruguay the principle of minimum wages was applied in state industries.[29] The issue was therefore far from reaching international consensus. As evidence of this, at its second session held in Paris in January 1920, the Governing Body refused to follow a proposal by the Paraguayan delegation to establish a commission on minimum wages.[30] However, the idea continued to develop among trade union representatives that a kind of government intervention was necessary to ensure a decent standard of living for workers. It was only in 1925, following a proposal by the British Government delegate, Humbert Wolfe, that the ILO began to study the methods by which wage rates could be fixed in certain trade industries. Workers in sweated industries were particularly targeted.[31] For the British government the ILO's role was to identify means for minimum wage fixing machinery, and fixing an international minimum wage was out of the question.[32] The member states then agreed to instruct the ILO with the preparation of a draft convention. The proposed convention led to the elaboration of a questionnaire, which was sent to governments. For many of them, in particular in Europe, it did not seem necessary to involve the state on this issue, especially when col-

---

25 Kevonian, D. 2008. "La légitimation par l'expertise: le Bureau international du travail et la statistique internationale", 86.
26 "États ingénieurs". Desrosières, A. 2003. "Historiciser l'action publique: l'État, le marché et les statistiques", in Trom, D., Laborier, P. eds. *Historicités de l'action publique*, 209. Paris: PUF.
27 Marinakis, A. 2008. "The role of the ILO in the development of minimum wages", ILO Century Project Paper. https://www.ilo.org/global/topics/wages/minimum-wages/definition/WCMS_180793/lang-en/index.htm[last accessed 12.09.2019].
28 *Ibid.*, 3.
29 ILC, *Record of Proceedings*, 1927, 399. ILOA.
30 Reynaud, E. 2017. "The International Labour Organization and the Living Wage: A Historical Perspective", 11.
31 *Ibid.*, 13–15.
32 Marinakis, A. 2008. "The role of the ILO in the development of minimum wages", 7.

lective bargaining mechanisms existed.[33] In 1928 a Minimum Wage-Fixing Machinery Convention (No. 26) was nevertheless adopted, which limited the ILO's responsibility to the study of the various national methods in minimum-wage fixing machinery.[34]

1.2 From Detroit to Europe: International Comparison of Purchasing Power

ILO statistical studies had raised important discussions on the possibilities for international comparisons, particularly in the context of the work of the International Conferences of Labour Statisticians (ICLS).[35] The Office's Section of Statistics had repeatedly stressed the need to establish methods for the standardisation of statistics.[36] It looked to improve comparability, particularly on the side of the United States. Collaborations developed for instance between the Office, the Industrial Relations of the SSRC and the American Statistical Association (ASA). Statisticians were generally very cautious about the conclusions that could be drawn from international comparisons. I will focus here on the Ford-Filene survey, which was one of the ILO's first attempts to compare workers' living standards between the United States and Europe.

The Ford-Filene enquiry, published with the support of the Twentieth Century Fund, marked a new, albeit controversial, incarnation of the role played by the Office in comparing data on living standards in the industrial societies of Europe and the United States, in a context of increased economic competition. Some aspects of the history of this survey have already been well studied. In her trans-Atlantic history of consumerism, Victoria De Grazia situates it in the broader context of a stimulating reflection on the impact of American mass consumer culture

---

[33] For an analysis of the different responses to the questionnaire, see Marinakis, A. 2008. "The role of the ILO in the development of minimum wages".

[34] "Minimum wage-fixing machinery". Interim report and questionnaire, ILC, *Record of Proceedings*. 10th session, Geneva, 1927. Quoted in Rodgers, G. et al. 2009. *The International Labour Organization and The Quest for Social Justice, 1919–2009*, 128. Ithaca: ILR Press.

[35] 1934. *The International Standardisation of Labour Statistics, A Review of the Statistical Work of the International Labour Office and of Various International Statistical Conferences*. Studies and Reports, Series N (Statistics) No. 19. Geneva: ILO.

[36] The ILO published several studies on the subject. 1932. *Contribution à l'étude de la comparaison internationale du coût de la vie*, Études et Documents, série N, no. 17. Genève, Bureau international du travail; Staehle, H. 1934. *International Comparison of Food Costs*, Studies and Reports, Series N, no. 19. Geneva, International Labour Office; Staehle, H. 1934. "The Reaction of Consumers to Changes in Prices and Income: A Quantitative Study in Immigrants' Behavior", *Econometrica* 2(1): 59–72.

in Europe.³⁷ Devoting an entire chapter to the question of living standards, she shows that the adopted definitions reveal profound differences between Europe and the United States regarding the nature of work, productivity and leisure.³⁸ During the interwar period the Fordist model was indeed more successful in the United States, while in Europe this mode of corporate organisation provoked hostility from conservative employers. For de Grazia, the Ford-Filene enquiry thus had the objective of spreading the American consumption lifestyle and production organisation to Europe, with a clear imposition of what Americans at the time considered to be a "decent" standard of living.³⁹

The ILO's involvement in this survey is best described in Thomas Cayet's study on the International Management Institute (IMI). He places the enquiry within the framework of strategies developed by the Institute to acquire economic expertise outside the League of Nations.⁴⁰ He also situates it in the broader context of efforts undertaken in the late 1920s to develop market research in Europe, in order to better understand the relationship between production and consumption.⁴¹ One of Albert Thomas' main concerns was the role of rationalisation, and in particular the means of articulating a policy of high wages with a policy of rationalisation.⁴² These two aspects fascinated him, but his ideas on these two points were still unclear. Following a diplomatic mission to the United States from December 1922 to January 1923 during which he was in contact with several industrialists who convinced him of Europe's backwardness in rationalising labour, Thomas decided to encourage American collaboration in the development of the Office's scientific research on rationalisation. In particular, he developed a relationship with entrepreneur Edward Albert Filene, founder of the Twentieth Century Fund. Filene was an important figure in New England's pro-

---

37 De Grazia, V. 2005. *Irresistible Empire: America's Advance Through Twentieth-Century Europe*. Cambridge, MA [etc.]: Belknap Press of Harvard University Press.
38 *Ibid*. See Chapter 2 "A Decent Standard of Living. How Europeans Were Measured by the American Way of Life", 75–129.
39 *Ibid.*, 78.
40 Cayet, T. 2010. *Rationaliser le travail, organiser la production: le Bureau international du travail et la modernisation économique durant l'entre-deux-guerres*. Rennes: PUR; Cayet, T. 2007. "Le Bureau International du travail et la modernisation économique dans les années 20: esquisse d'une dynamique institutionnelle", in "Centenaire du ministère du Travail. Première partie," special issue, *Travail et Emploi* 110, April-June: 15–27.
41 For a stimulating analysis of market research in Europe, especially in Germany, see also Conrad, C. 2004. "Observer les consommateurs. Études de marché et histoire de la consommation en Allemagne, de 1930 aux années 1960", *Le Mouvement social* 1(206): 17–39.
42 Letter from Albert Thomas to Edgard Milhaud, July 25, 1929. "CAT 6b–6–2–1 Questions économiques, monétaires et financières. Mai 1921 Oct.1929." ILOA.

gressive movement, and one of the architects behind the creation of the IMI. Like Henry Ford he was convinced that a reorganised European industry, lower cost prices and a higher standard of living would help expand the economic market for American industries. This convergence of ideas, alive on both sides of the Atlantic, could in turn lead to a convergence of interests. As Ford sought to expand into Europe, Percival Perry, the London-based head of Ford in Europe, became aware of the difficulties related to accurately setting wages and tried to develop a method for making comparisons. A first contact was established with the Office, from which he requested an extension of comparative statistics on wages in European cities.[43] In June 1929 Filene spoke directly with Thomas about raising living standards in Europe and offered the sum of $25,000 for an international enquiry on purchasing power, which was to serve the interests of the Ford Company. In a telegram sent to Éric Drummond, the League's first General Secretary, Filene explained the reasons behind his financial commitment: "I make this offer because American business as a whole will benefit from such an initiative by Mr. Ford and because it is in the interest of other American industrialists with factories abroad that the purchasing power of the peoples of Europe be increased."[44]

Thomas saw in the Office's participation in the Ford-Filene enquiry the opportunity to take a first step towards a much broader wage survey that would not be confined to a single type of company and was therefore in line with the international wage regulation policy trade unions wished to develop. Edgard Milhaud, economist at the Office and close friend of Thomas, was himself very optimistic at the idea of a co-production between the United States and the Office, but he had also warned Thomas against the American commercial credit policy, which generated much opposition in European employer circles:

> The idea that Mr Filene should attempt to bring into American circles is that – as it is well understood that Europe's economic recovery is of international interest and also important to the USA – these must support it not by a sort of eviction policy that eliminates the European direction in favour of the American direction, but by granting credits which can include a share of control, while leaving industrialists themselves with the upper hand.[45]

---

43 Guérin, D. 1996. *Albert Thomas au BIT, 1920–1932. De l'internationalisme à l'Europe*, 68. Genève: Euryopa.
44 Métral, A. 1931. *Deux conceptions économiques: Europe ou États-Unis?*, 401. Paris: Nouvelles Editions Latines.
45 Note from Edgard Milhaud to Albert Thomas, June 26, 1929. CAT 6b–6–2–1 "Questions économiques, monétaires et financières. Mai 1921-Oct. 1929". ILOA. Original quote in French: "L'idée que M. Filene devrait s'attacher à faire pénétrer dans les milieux américains, c'est que, s'il est bien entendu que le relèvement économique de l'Europe est d'intérêt international et importe

American industrialists, capitalists and financiers had in fact long been engaged in a subsidising relationship with Europe. This aggressive trade policy was a central element in the opposition of ILO employer delegates to collaborating on wages with the United States. In 1929, the GB decided to appoint a committee to discuss the study project. It was composed by the Canadian government delegate Walter Riddell, the French employer delegate Alfred Lambert-Ribot of the Union of Metal and Mining Industries, the socialist Léon Jouhaux, whose presence attested to the interest of French workers in this enquiry, Lyndall Urwick, Director of the IMI since 1928, Filene himself, Albert Thomas, Fernand Maurette, James Nixon, who became Head of the Office's Section of Statistics in 1929, and J. H. Richardson, also a statistician. While employers and workers' representatives generally doubted the scientific results of the study, the strongest opposition came from Lambert-Ribot.[46] He reiterated his criticisms before the GB in October 1929, where he attacked the project using political arguments. Questioning Henry Ford's real intentions, he feared that this enquiry, by serving American interests, would lead to unfair competition between American and French companies.[47] His fears were not entirely unjustified. Lambert-Ribot also saw it as an attempt to force European countries to raise workers' living standards before allowing them access to the American market. From the employers' point of view, the promotion of high wages was rather difficult to accept. The ensuing debate that occured between Urwick and Lambert-Ribot in the *Journée industrielle* journal betrayed the fear of European employers' circles with regard to the economic power of the United States. Urwick saw Lambert-Ribot's opposition as a more systematic dynamic of mistrust that "consists of making a mountain out of a molehill when it comes to the United States".[48] This attitude also revealed to a large extent the hostility of conservative European employers in face of wage raising policies. Léon Blum, a prominent member of the French Socialist Party, reportedly declared in the *Populaire* that French employers "were too petty and too mun-

---

aussi aux USA, ceux-ci doivent le seconder non pas par une sorte de politique d'éviction qui élimine la direction européenne au profit de la direction américaine, mais par des octrois de crédits pouvant comporter une part de contrôle, mais laissant la haute main aux industriels eux-mêmes."

46 De Grazia, V. 2005. *Irresistible Empire*, 82 and following.
47 *Minutes of the Governing Body*, 46th session, October 1929, 14–15. ILOA.
48 Urwick, L. "L'enquête Ford-Filene au sujet des salaires et le BIT". T 101/0/3 "Labour statistics: Ford Filene enquiry on cost of living – press clippings–1929, 1931". ILOA.

dane to consider the employee as a consumer, and to seek the development of consumption through the rise of wages".[49]

While the Ford-Filene enquiry was limited to the description of purchasing power in industrial societies, the prevailing technical discourse did not entirely mask the political issues that overlapped with the production of expertise. The opposition of European industrialists highlighted contrasting positions on the economic development model to be promoted, in particular on the role of wages. Despite the opposition of employers and after some hesitation, particularly with regard to the technical obstacles posed by the lack of data on purchasing power in Europe, i.e. the goods and services that a worker could obtain with his salary, the GB accepted Filene's offer, but decided to entrust the IMI with this investigation, rather than the Office. The Office's Section of Statistics, which was nevertheless mobilised, enlisted the help of an external expert, Hans Staehle, to process statistical data.[50] Another manifestation of the controversial nature of this investigation was Thomas' decision, in 1931, to publish the report without referring to the GB. By 1932, in reaction to this initiative, employers and government representatives had managed to ensure that there would be no reprint of the study's English and French version, which had greatly irritated employers, in Paris and London.[51]

The objective of the Ford-Filene investigation was to determine the salary a European worker would need to earn to be ensured the same standard of living

---

[49] Métral, A. 1931. *Deux conceptions économiques*, 402. Original quote in French: Le patronat français "était trop mesquin, trop routinier, pour envisager le salarié en tant que consommateur et pour rechercher le développement de la consommation dans la hausse des salaires".

[50] Born in Germany, Staehle had studied at the Universities of Tübingen, Munich and Hamburg and had obtained a doctorate in social sciences in 1924. He was assistant to Herbert von Beckerath, professor of economics at the University of Bonn, where he had also worked with the economist Joseph Schumpeter between 1925 and 1927. In 1928, he was awarded a scholarship under a German-American exchange programme and went to Chicago for a year to study economic theory and statistics under economics professors Jacob Viner and Paul H. Douglas. Between 1928 and 1930, he was a Rockefeller scholar and continued his research in New York City. He became a member of the ILO's Statistical Section in 1931 and then a member of its Economic Section. He left the ILO in 1939 and went to the United States, as a guest lecturer at Harvard University. Between 1946 and 1947, he worked for the International Monetary Fund (IMF) before becoming head of the Statistical Section of the Research Division of the UN Economic Commission for Europe (UNECE). In 1953 he joined the Permanent Secretariat of the General Agreement on Tariffs and Trade (GATT) and served as Director of the Trade Information Division until his death in 1961. Hans Hermann Ludwig Staehle, personal file, P 2446. ILOA.

[51] Letter from Lyndall Urwick to Evans Clark, first executive director of the Twentieth Century Fund, January 21, 1932. T 101/0/3. ILOA. The study was not published in German.

as a worker in a Detroit Ford factory, who at the time was earning $6 a day.[52] The report showed, with figures to support it, that the standard of living of an American worker in the car industry was higher than that of a European worker, with the exception of workers in the city of Stockholm.[53] This survey made it possible to demonstrate to European trade unions and employers' organisations that rationalising production would ultimately lead to an increase in wages, seen from the Office's point of view and in accordance with Fordist ideas, as a means of absorbing ever-increasing production, with the aim of generally improving living standards. This survey reflected the American atmosphere at the time, namely that "high wages and high productivity should go hand in hand with high employment and high output levels".[54] For Thomas, all these questions were, however, crucial in formulating ideas on economic and social development in Europe, and in initiating collaboration between trade unions and employers' organisations:

> With increased production comes the search for an increased share of wages. It is on this precise point that employers and workers could collaborate. Workers with an interest in the development of their wages would be encouraged to participate in a more rational organisation of the industry, they too would seek to reduce the share of overheads, the share of waste, [etc.], in order to increase the remuneration of the workforce.[55]

Trade unions had consistently expressed concern that reduced working hours, justified by the development of rationalisation, could be accompanied by reduced wages. The Office's objective was to provide European trade union organisations with a scientific survey, which could encourage them to become more involved in the rationalisation process and which they could use as leverage in their demands for increased wages.[56]

---

52 XI 1/6/61 "Ford-Filene enquiry into cost of living + wages Statistics". ILOA.
53 1931. *An international enquiry into costs of living. A comparative study of workers' living costs in Detroit (USA) and fourteen European cities*, Studies and Reports, Series N (Statistics), no. 17. Geneva, International Labour Office.
54 Rodgers, G. et al. 2009. *The International Labour Organization*, 130.
55 Note from Albert Thomas, May 11, 1927. "CAT 6B-3 Questions économiques, monétaires financières. Oct. 1925-Mai 1927". ILOA. Original quote in French: "Dans cette production accrue, la recherche d'une part accrue des salaires. C'est sur ce point précis que pourrait s'exercer la collaboration patronale et ouvrière. Les ouvriers ayant intérêt au développement de leurs salaires seraient incités à participer à une organisation plus rationnelle de l'industrie, ils chercheraient, eux aussi, à diminuer la part de frais généraux, la part de gaspillage, etc., pour augmenter la rétribution de la main-d'œuvre."
56 Note from Edgard Milhaud. "Projet économique de la FSI". CAT 6b-6-2-1 "Questions économiques, monétaires et financières. Mai 1921-Oct. 1929". ILOA. Edgard Milhaud and Albert Tho-

IV The ILO's Contribution to the Internationalisation of the Standard of Living — 139

For the first time, the Ford-Filene enquiry had established an international comparison of purchasing power for several European and American cities. Apart from the statistical data collected by national statistical offices and centralised at the Office, the survey had also produced its own figures. Henry Ford had sent the Office a box of articles containing the regular clothes worn by Ford factory workers and their wives in England, France, Belgium, Germany and Denmark. The price of the items sent had made it possible to establish the share of the family budget dedicated to clothing, with Detroit as a standard. Similar comparisons were made for food, electricity and rent, showing the diversity of factors taken into account in establishing consumption patterns. Interestingly, the survey showed that the European worker spent more on food than the American worker who consumed a greater diversity of material goods (cars, household appliances). However, the value of this survey had suffered from significant technical limitations. The choice of attributes, which were not mathematically comparable, was problematic when assessing the level of well-being of industrial workers, whose lifestyle varied from one environment to another. Some other key factors, which directly impact living standards, such as social benefits, were not taken into account. The Detroit worker had the highest standard of living and yet had no social insurance except accident benefits. Despite its limitations the Ford-Filene enquiry marked an important step. Among other things, it established a hierarchy of industrial societies in the collective imagination, reinforcing the notion that the rational and Taylorist organisational model of the American economy was what European societies should strive towards. As Serge Latouche, one of the proponents of postmodern criticism of development, notes: "Living standards could at last be quantified and thus compared. The global ideal of a uniform standard of living ceased to be a futile concept; it now came to be represented by a specific quantum of dollars which could at least be referred to, even if not realised."[57]

---

mas also saw this as an opportunity to get closer to the American Federation of Labor (AFL), which was not a member of the International Federation of Trade Unions (IFTU). Note from Edgard Milhaud to Albert Thomas, January 12, 1928. CAT 6b–6–21 "Questions économiques, monétaires et financières. Mai 1921-Oct. 1929". ILOA.

57 Latouche, S. 2010. "Standard of Living", in Sachs, W. ed. 2010. *The Development Dictionary. A Guide to Knowledge as Power*, 281. London and New York: Zed Books.

2 Extending Research Towards Less Developed Countries

In the 1930s, growing political tensions and the general disorganisation of the global economy reinforced the need for concerted international efforts to raise living standards worldwide. The world was being slowly choked by an enormous capacity to produce goods and an abnormal inability to allow those in need to secure and consume them. The standard of living of workers was particularly affected by the aftermath of the Great Depression. The dumping of "starvation wages" and long days imposed by employers undermined the progress of the working class.[58] Workers representatives, who saw international capitalism as "exploiting these rivalries to the benefit of its policy of social regression", demanded that the ILO focus on the improvement of working and living conditions in countries where workers were still living in miserable situations.

The development of fascisms in Europe lent a particular tone to the discourse on raising the standard of living, which also comes through in Patricia Clavin's study on the activities of the Economic and Financial Committees of the League of Nations.[59] The danger posed by these models was reinforced by intense Italian and German propaganda in less developed countries, in Eastern and Southern Europe, the Middle East and Latin America.[60] Meanwhile, communist movements were gaining strength in South and Southeast Asia.[61] The second half of the 1930s thus constituted a change in the meaning of the standard of living, shifting from the minimum for living to a desired way of living. International cooperation to raise living standards became a bulwark against political radicalisation, as evidenced by the tripartite agreement between the United States, France and Great Britain signed in September 1936, which attested to the commitment of Western powers to regulate international trade through a policy of currency stabilisation, associated to the rise in living standards. The American internationalists involved in the New Deal programme, led by Secretary of State Cordell Hull, had in fact been involved in the liberalisation of international

---

[58] Note by Edgrad Milhaud entitled "Projet économique de la FSI". CAT 6b–6–2–1 Questions économiques, monétaires et financières. Mai 1921 Oct.1929. ILOA

[59] Clavin, P. 2013. *Securing the World Economy: The Reinvention of the League of Nations, 1920–1946*. Oxford: Oxford University Press.

[60] Williams, M. 2005. *Mussolini's Propaganda Abroad: Subversion in the Mediterranean and the Middle East, 1935–1940*. London: Routledge; Blancpain, J.-P. 1994. *Migrations et mémoire germaniques en Amérique latine*. Strasbourg: Presses universitaires de Strasbourg; Bessis, J. 1981. *La Méditerranée fasciste: l'Italie mussolinienne et la Tunisie*. Paris: Ed. Karthala.

[61] Rodan, G. ed. 1996. *Political Oppositions in Industrialising Asia*, 41. London, New York: Routledge.

trade since 1933, in reaction to the protectionist policy developed under Herbert Hoover, whose administration instigated the Hawley-Smoot Act (1930).[62] In France the commitment to raising living standards further betrayed the Popular Front's fear that the coalition of left-wing parties would collapse, particularly under pressure from trade unions engaged in the fight to reduce working hours and in favour of a public works policy.[63] In Britain the renewed interest in the question of living standards was driven by a desire to determine the scale of the economic problems posed by the global economic crisis, but also, and more importantly, to encourage the development of trade within the empire.

2.1 The Impetus Given by the Santiago Conference

Thus, while it had been the subject of targeted studies, the question of raising the standard of living became one of the central issues in the reflections of politicians, economists, administrators and experts looking to increase industrial production, lower trade barriers and balance production and consumption. The ILO wanted to make its contribution to the study of all these problems. Already in his 1933 annual report, Butler had paid particular attention to the problem of global disparities in development, which, according to him, was the cause of increased economic competition between countries. Raising the standard of living in less developed countries was seen as a means to counter the influence of non-democratic powers, to combat labour exploitation and to revive trade. The 1935 ILC staged consensus on standard of living as an international issue that must be studied by the ILO. This paved the way for the development of the Office's studies in this area, without defining how the notion would be framed. The discussions in 1935 highlighted a wide diversity of possible indicators making the standard of living a "catch-all" notion: access to employment, adequate wages, nutrition, hygiene, housing, clothing, migration and modernisation where generally evoked. Less developed countries, in particular, were interested in the ILO's new focus. The ILO received strong support from Latin America. The 1936 Santiago Conference adopted resolutions specifically calling upon the ILO to institute cost of living and family budget enquiries:

> [The Conference] requests the Governing Body of the International Labour Office to place on the Agenda of an early Session of the International Labour Conference the question

---

[62] Scott, M. N. 2010 *Free Trade and the New Deal: The United States and the International Economy of the 1930s.* Phd diss., Graduate College, Iowa State University.
[63] Clavin, P. 2013. *Securing the World Economy*, 172–173.

of the minimum wage and that of family allowances, to be considered primarily from the point of view of their adequacy to meet the essential needs of the worker and his family, these being taken to include food, clothing, housing and general and vocational education, rest and cultural recreation.[64]

As for the question of wages, the international Convention on minimum wage was ratified in 1936 by Cuba, followed by Chile, Colombia, Mexico, Nicaragua and Uruguay. At the national level many Latin American countries adopted minimum wage fixing systems, which applied in almost every case to men and women.[65] The Santiago Conference also called for an extension of the scope of the minimum wage study to include the working conditions of agricultural workers. Particular attention was also paid to the problem of low wages for female labour. The ILO's 1928 Recommendation (No. 30) already stated that particular attention should be paid to women's work in trades.[66] The Santiago Conference highlighted the need to give more attention to home industries, in which large amounts of female labour was engaged. It drew the ILO's attention to the special case of domestic labour, owing to one inevitable effect of low wages in this type of work, namely the almost unlimited extension of working hours. In order to protect women's wages, research on this issue was to be developed, through the application of statutory minimum wage rates.[67] It was incorporated in the ILO's research programme in 1939.

2.2 Collaborations with the Institute of Pacific Relations

The growing international interest in the issue of living standards from the point of view of trade competition also led the Office to produce a number of studies on living standards in Asian countries, particularly Japan and India. For instance, in 1933, it published a study on industrial labour in Japan; in 1937 a study on labour conditions in Indochina, written by the French expert Jean Gou-

---

[64] See also Resolution concerning minimum wages. *Proceedings*, 1936, 168 and Appendix II. ILOA.
[65] Report on the action taken to bring the resolutions adopted by the Santiago Conference into effect. Second Conference of American States Members of the International Labour Organisation, 1939. Havana (Geneva): 96–98. ILOA
[66] Minimum Wage-Fixing Machinery Recommendation, 1928 (No. 30).
[67] Report on the action taken to bring the resolutions adopted by the Santiago Conference into effect, 106–107. ILOA.

IV The ILO's Contribution to the Internationalisation of the Standard of Living — 143

dal; and in 1939, another study on India.[68] These studies reflected the ILO's growing interest in living and working conditions in Asian countries. They also reflected the diversity of factors that were taken into account in determining the living standards of industrial workers in these countries. However, the available information was still not sufficient to give any indication of the real wages of workers. In the case of India, the information was limited to the results of the family budget surveys conducted in the 1920s by the Bombay Labour Office and the Burma Bureau of Labour Statistics. The study was also based on the surveys of industrial workers' living standards conducted for the Royal Labour Commission in 1930.[69] This study did not allow for a comparison of living standards, as the data were compiled at different times and covered different categories of workers. However, it did provide interesting information on the composition of families in different urban centres in India, family income, expenditure on food, clothing and alcohol consumption. It also provided data on fluctuations in living costs.

The Office also collaborated with other extra-European research networks active in Asia, where it diffused its statistical knowledge and production. A particularly interesting collaboration was with the Institute of Pacific Relations (IPR).[70] In 1933 the latter contacted the ILO to develop research on living standards in Asia and the Pacific. The ILO saw an opportunity to diffuse and expand its statistical knowledge of wages, family budgets, national income, consumption and all other indicators of living standards in the region.

The Office's first contact with the IPR dates back to the late 1920s. During his trip to Asia, Thomas first came into contact with some of its members and, despite his rather negative initial impression of the institution, convinced the Office to pay greater attention to its activities: "From a distance, it's something. But up close, it's nothing [...]. It is obviously a movement to watch out for (like a League of Nations of the Pacific). But if it presents a very YMCA image, as we say – very American and very superficial – the only drawback is that it has funds and is

---

[68] 1933. *Le travail industriel au Japon*. Études et Documents. Série A, n°37. Geneva: International Labour Organisation; 1937. *Problèmes de travail en Indochine*. Études et Documents. Série B, n° 26. Geneva: International Labour Organisation; 1939. *Le travail industriel dans l'Inde*. Études et Documents. Série A, n°41, 316 and following. Geneva: International Labour Organisation. ILOA.
[69] 1939. *Le travail industriel dans l'Inde*. Études et Documents. Série A, n°41, 316 and following. Geneva: International Labour Organisation. ILOA
[70] On the history of this Institute, see Akami, T. 2002. *Internationalizing the Pacific: The United States, Japan and the Institute of Pacific Relations, 1919–1945*. London: Routledge Studies in Asia's Transformations.

strong at bluff." [71] In the 1930s, cooperation between these two organisations rested on a handful of American reform-minded internationalists active at the IPR, who were in regular contact with the Office. Lewis Lorwin and James T. Shotwell, a member of the IPR Programme Committee, were the driving forces behind cooperation with the Office. In 1930, the IPR secured the Office's involvement in the 1931 conference, which was to address the question of statistical comparisons on living standards. In order to organize this participation, a meeting was held in Geneva between the Office and the economist John Bell Condliffe, a member of the economic committee of the League of Nations, who had attended the Institute's first conference in Honolulu in 1925 as a member of the New Zealand delegation and former Secretary of the IPR.[72] Condliffe's visit to the Office followed criticism by some members of the Social Research Council (SSRC) of the IPR's work, particularly regarding the lack of methods for collecting statistical data. One of the most critical reports was that of Lewis Lorwin, who stressed the need to collaborate with the Office, especially since the Director's 1929 annual report had mentioned issues specific to Asian countries.[73] The Office was also present at the Banff conference in 1933, where the question of expansionist policies – their economic justification, the benefits they generated for European industrial powers as well as for the United States and Japan, even the question of their impact on the economic status of underdeveloped regions – were at the heart of the discussions.[74] The conference stressed the need for Pacific nations to stimulate their economic development through planning, the development of tariff control policy, the adoption of immigration restrictions and the development of raw material export. The sub-committee on living standards, of which Lewis Lorwin was a member, stressed the need for statistical comparisons among Pacific countries. It suggested the development of a series of studies on the living standards of workers in certain export industries.[75] One of the objectives of the IPR was "to devise a satisfactory way

---

[71] Thomas, A. 1959. À la rencontre de l'Orient, 165. Original quote in French: "De loin, c'est quelque chose et de près ce n'est rien [...]. C'est évidemment un mouvement à surveiller (sorte de SDN du Pacifique). Mais s'il est, pour reprendre notre formule accoutumée, très *YMCA*, très américain et très superficiel, le seul inconvénient est qu'il dispose de fonds et qu'il s'entend au bluff."

[72] D 600/1000/30/3 "Institute of Pacific Relations. Conference. China 1931. Shanghai and Hangchow Oct-Nov.1931", ILOA.

[73] "Social Research council committee – memorandum de Lewis Lorwin", March 14, 1930. Archives Lewis Lorwin, Columbia University, New York. (hereafter Arch. ALL).

[74] D 600/1000/30/4, ILOA.

[75] Report of the Sub-committee on Living Standards, Banff. T 110/3 "Labour Statistics: Standard of living inquiry- Institute of Pacific Relations-Collaboration. 03/1934 – 07/1938", ILOA.

of determining how far standards or planes of living enter as a factor in aggravating international trade competition".[76]

The proposed research programme at Banff was extremely ambitious. Among the points of interest it should be noted that these studies were meant to assess the extent to which differences in living standards between East and West had been a factor in the dynamics of recent international competition, particularly in the textile, sugar and rubber industries. Studies had to analyse to which extent the paucity of natural resources or raw materials in combination with increasing population numbers influenced the development of international competition. The members of the subcommittee on living standards were also particularly interested in certain trading systems such as the *comprador* system in China, where indigenous people played an intermediary role in financial and trade transactions between Europeans and indigenous Asians, particularly from Portuguese trading posts such as Macao and Guangzhou (Canton) in China.[77] Following the adoption of this research programme, in 1934, William L. Holland, Secretary of the IPR, asked the Office's Section of Statistics to put together a report on various methods for collecting and comparing statistical data. The Office sent a report to the 1935 conference in Tokyo on the data needed to compare living costs and standards of living but provided no information on the issue of workers' wages or incomes. ILO assistance helped the IPR to carry out various statistical analyses on wages in Canada, Britain, Japan, Australia and Hawaii. However, by 1936, only a few studies had been completed, notably on the living conditions of Filipino workers, in sugar plantations in Hawaii and Chinese tobacco farms.[78] The war prevented further collaborative projects.[79] Such collaborations were nonetheless important for the Office as they contributed to the progressive standardisation of statistical data collection methods. This standardisation would become an issue of power for Office statisticians who were trying to define an international methodological framework for collecting and processing data. During the Second World War the ILO would continue its work on statistical standardisation, at first by providing technical assistance to national administrators in Latin America. Between 1940 and 1944, the French statistician Robert Guye travelled to several Latin American countries to assist the various statistical services in order to improve their methods of collecting

---

76 Letter from Holland to Faith Williams, November 27, 1935. T 110/3, ILOA.
77 Sub-Committee report, 1933. T 110/3 "Labour statistics: Standard of living inquiry – Institute of pacific relations – Collaboration. 03/1934 – 07/1938", ILOA.
78 Letter from Holland to Nixon, January 4, 1936. T 110/3, ILOA.
79 Letter from Holland to Winant, May 9, 1939. RL 01/4/37 "Relations with Institute of Pacific Relations", ILOA.

and processing data.⁸⁰ In 1943 the ILO also published a study on the international standardisation of labour statistics, which summarised its pre-war activities in this field, while being presented by ILO experts as a practical tool for national statisticians.⁸¹

2.3 The ILO's 1938 Study on the Workers' Living Standard

Despite its claim to scientificity, the ILO's discourse was, however, marked by great fragility. The work of collecting data was hampered by the inability of national bodies to provide information and sometimes even, as we have seen, by the hostility of social actors, in particular some employer representatives. Increased competition between the League of Nations and the ILO and the lack of consistency in their scientific production further contributed to the ILO's difficulties, as evidenced by the completion of the study on workers' living standards published by the Office in 1938.

The concentration of the economic activities of the League of Nations and the Office regarding the means of raising the standard of living led to an increase in collaborations within the framework of expert committees.⁸² These collaborations, however, highlight the institutional competition between the two organisations, in a context where the redefinition of the competencies of one butted against the defence of the prerogatives of the other.

In 1937 the General Assembly of the League of Nations adopted a resolution to study national and international measures to raise living standards in collaboration with the ILO.⁸³ The creation of the Sub-Committee on the Standard of Living within the League's Economic and Financial Organisation (EFO), as well as the backgrounds of the experts who participated in its works, are well known to us thanks to Patricia Clavin's research.⁸⁴ However, the Office's participation has yet to be analysed. In December 1937 a first meeting of the Sub-Committee was held in the office of Pietro Stoppani, director of the Economic Section of the League of Nations, where the orientation of the report on living standards was dis-

---

80 MI 11 "Missions – Robert Guy, Jacket 1, 07/1940–12/1944", ILOA.
81 1943. *La normalisation internationale des statistiques du travail.* Études et Documents, série N. Genève: Bureau international du travail. ILOA.
82 *Minutes of the Governing Body*, 79th session, 1937, 52. ILOA.
83 Appendix VIII: Report of the Office on economic issues of interest to the International Labour Organisation. *Minutes of the Governing Body*, 1938, 138–141, ILOA.
84 Clavin, P. 2013. *Securing the World Economy*, 172–179.

cussed.⁸⁵ The Sub-Committee on the Standard of Living was composed of F.L. McDougall, Australian Representative at League of Nations Assembly, the French radical socialist Paul Elbel (also government delegate to the League's Economic Committee), Stoppani, Alexander Loveday, Director of the Finance Committee, Frenchman René Charron, Noel Hall, British economics professor at the University of London, Hans Staehle, the Office statistician who had collaborated in the Ford-Filene enquiry, and Lewis Lorwin.⁸⁶

This was not the first time that the League and the Office had collaborated on the production of technical studies, but it often gave rise to opposition, leading to a kind of "clandestine competition"⁸⁷ between the two organisations.⁸⁸ At the Sub-Committee on the Standard of Living meeting, Lorwin therefore lobbied for a single report to be published based on the information gathered by the Office. McDougall supported this division of labour. The experts then agreed on the report's general structure, which aimed to show that relatively low living standards existed in some countries and that action to raise them was possible. At the Office, this discourse aimed to orient economic policies towards improving wages, housing, nutrition, and hygiene conditions. However, Hans Staehle noted several objections were raised on the subjects to be covered. Stoppani proposed that the study be based on a comparison between industrial countries, agricultural countries in Eastern Europe and Asian countries. Loveday, on the other hand, did not wish to engage in an analysis of the situation of industrial workers. He proposed limiting the study to a few concrete questions concerning agricultural workers in Eastern Europe. René Charron also urged that the study be limited to Eastern Europe. His 1926 mission to Bulgaria as Special Commissioner for

---

85 For information on Pietro Angelo Stoppani, see the Lonsea database: http://lonsea.de/pub/person/5203 [last accessed 12.09.2019].
86 EP 200/01/1 "Economic problems – Collaboration of the ILO with the economic committee and section. 12/1937–08/1939". ILOA.
87 Report prepared by Hans Staehle, August 30, 1938. Personal file, P 2446. ILOA.
88 Pernet, C. 2013. "Developing Nutritional Standards and Food Policy: Latin American Reformers Between the ILO, the League of Nations Health Organization, and the Pan-American Sanitary Bureau", in Droux, J., Kott, S. eds. *Globalizing Social Rights. The International Labour Organization and Beyond*, 249–261. Basingstoke: Palgrave Macmillan; Pernet, C. 2011. "L'OIT et la question de l'alimentation en Amérique latine (1930–1950): Les problèmes posés par la définition internationale des normes de niveau de vie", in Lespinet-Moret, I., Viet, V. eds. *L'Organisation internationale du travail*, 167–178. Rennes: PUR; Barona, J. L. 2008. "Nutrition and Health. The International Context during the Inter-War crisis", *Social History of Medicine* 21(1): 87–105; Saunier, P.-Y. 2010 "Borderline Work: ILO Explorations onto the Housing Scene until 1940", in Van Daele, J., Rodríguez García, M., Van Goethem, G., Van der Linden, M. *ILO Histories. Essays on the International Labour Organization and its Impact on the World during the Twentieth Century*, 197–221. Bern: Peter Lang.

Refugees familiarised him with the economic problems of that region, which at the time was also the site of the financial stabilisation plans of the League of Nations.[89] McDougall, on the other hand, looked at the problem of consumption solely from the perspective of nutrition.[90] Finally, the League's representatives on the Sub-Committee decided to task Noel Hall, an external expert, with writing the report despite Lorwin's opposition. The decision to commission this study by an independent expert suggests that the EFO did not actually wish to take responsibility for the study. For the Office's civil servants, the EFO's commitment was definitely unclear. At the meeting of the Sub-Committee, Loveday had moreover declared that the Secretariat should not produce a technical and scientific report, but should instead limit itself to establishing a list of studies to be undertaken.[91] The EFO's ambivalent attitude towards its own responsibilities was confirmed in September 1938 when the General Assembly decided to adopt a resolution following the reading of Hall's study, which was limited to inviting the EFO to continue research in collaboration with the ILO. The members of the Sub-Committee had certainly felt overwhelmed by the scope and complexity of the aspects to be covered in determining the attributes of the standard of living, but also in formulating the guidelines to be given to economic policies.[92] It also seems, however, that the League's experts did not in fact intend to study these questions, but above all wished to use the League's EFO as a centralising body for expertise produced by other international organisations and by independent experts. At least that was Nixon's opinion, as expressed in an internal note of 15 December 1938:

> It seemed evident from the outset that the League's Economic Section did not intend, if possible, to do much itself, on these questions, but hoped to rely on outside experts and on the Health and Transit Organisations and on the ILO [...]. The Sub-Committee seemed to arrogate to itself the right to review the work of all other Sections and Organisations dealing with problems connected with Standard of Living. Thus, members of the Health Organisation (HO), the Transit Organisation and the Economic Relations Section were questioned as to when various reports which they had in hand would be ready: even the representatives of the ILO were cross-examined as to when the contributions it was making for the Conference

---

89 Beyersdorf, F. 2011. "Credit or Chaos"? The Austrian Stabilisation Programme of 1923 and the League of Nations", in Laqua, D. ed. *Internationalism Reconfigured. Transnational Ideas and Movements Between the World Wars*, 134–158. London: I.B. Tauris.
90 Notes on the meeting of the Sub-Committee on Living Standards, December 1–3, 1938. EP 200/01/1. ILOA.
91 Economic Committee of the League of Nations. 1938. *Preliminary survey on national and international measures to raise the standard of living*. Memorandum prepared by M.N.F. Hall., Geneva. ILOA.
92 Report by Hans Staehle, December 1–3, 1938. EP 200/01/1. ILOA.

IV The ILO's Contribution to the Internationalisation of the Standard of Living — 149

on Rural Life would be available for examination by the Sub-Committee! The contributions by the staff of the Economic and Financial Organisation EFO were hardly mentioned and it does not seem that it intends to give much time to this subject, if it can get other people to do the work. [...] We are in danger of finding this small (and not very efficient) Sub-Committee discussing or reviewing nearly all the main activities of the two organisations.[93]

This situation led to a rapid evolution of the Office's position, as it vowed in February 1938 to carry out and publish its own study.[94] The completion of the Office's study on the standard of living of workers, entitled *Le Standard de vie des travailleurs*[95] and published in 1938, clearly highlights the difficulty experts have in exactly determining the attributes of the standard of living. The tense relations that developed between Lewis Lorwin, Hans Staehle and James Nixon underline the interest of carrying out an almost biographical analysis of the technical studies of international organisations, insofar as their elaboration reveals how difficult it was, not only to produce a scientific discourse, but also for the experts themselves to contest it. These tensions are visible through the discourse of Office statisticians, who expressed important reservations regarding the possibility of establishing "minimum social standards". These reservations can be summarised in two points.

The first refers to the very definition of socially desirable standards. James Nixon and Hans Staehle were extremely critical on this point. In their internal notes they both insisted that it was impossible to establish a working definition of the standard of living or to set standard attributes. Staehle wrote that "the standard of living is a strictly individual and not a collective notion".[96] Besides, in their view, to make comparisons of living standards across countries was impossible, since an individual's needs, which vary in time and space, could not be accurately determined. Many years later in 1949, while working for the International Monetary Fund (IMF), Staehle would write in a report: "Any attempt to apply the theory [of identical needs] in international comparisons of real in-

---

[93] Nixon internal report on the December 1 meeting of the League's Sub-Committee on Living Standards, December 15, 1938. EP 200/01/1. ILOA.
[94] Lorwin wrote to John Winant, keeping him informed of the progress of this case, that the ILO must take prompt action to publish its own study. Correspondence between Lorwin and Winant, February 14, 1938. EP 200/01/1. ILOA.
[95] 1938. *Le Standard de vie des travailleurs*. Études et Documents, Série B (Conditions économiques), no. 30. Genève: Bureau international du travail.
[96] He also used this argument in his 1934 study on the comparison of living costs. Other statisticians shared his opinion. Allen, R. D. G. 1933. "On the Marginal Utility of Money and Its Application", *Economica* 40: 201.

comes should therefore be ruled out."[97] His position must have had some value in the scientific world, since he himself was an expert statistician who had worked extensively on wage statistics. Some civil servants at the Office saw in him "unusual statistical abilities".[98] As of 1935 Staehle was intensively involved in the statistical study of wages, but also of international trade and employment, and his expertise extended to the United States, Great Britain, Germany, Italy and Japan.[99] He embodied the mathematical shift that statistical science was then taking.[100] In 1931, his entry into the prestigious Econometric Society, founded in the United States in 1930 with the objective of developing international statistical science, testified to this. For Staehle the living standards research project deviated too far from his scientific standards. He rejected what he considered to be "reasonings which have as their most solid, and often as their only, foundation the eloquence of their authors".[101] Nixon, who shared Staehle's scepticism about the possibilities of defining the concept of standard of living, also insisted on the controversies that would arise from "an average standard of living". This problem had already been raised in the summer of 1937 when Duncan Sandys, a British conservative member of the International Association for Labour Legislation (IALL), sought to associate the Office with a national campaign to promote minimum social standards, the aim of which, according to Sandys, was "to form a social conscience in the country and to mold public opinion in favour of social reform". However, M.R.K. Burge of the London Correspondence Office warned Camille Pône against this project: "I myself see some danger in attempting to establish a 'Minimum British Standard'. Suppose it turned out to be far higher than what other countries would regard as the minimum?"[102]

The second problem statisticians underscored was the measurement of consumption levels. Nixon had pointed out that years would be needed to obtain comparable statistical data. This problem betrayed the sheer multiplicity of definitions adopted at the national level and the absence of a "conventional equiv-

---

97 Staehle, H. 1949. "International Comparison of Real National Income: A Note on Methods", in National Bureau of Economic Research, *Studies in Income and Wealth*, Conference on Research in Income and Wealth, 221–272 (224).
98 Annual Report by Lewis Lorwin, 1936. Hans Staehle's personal file, P 2446, ILOA.
99 See the different working reports in Staehle's personal file, P 2446, ILOA.
100 Desrosières, A 1989. "Comment faire des choses qui tiennent", 228.
101 Staehle, H. 1934. *International Comparison of Food Costs*, Studies and Reports, Series N. Geneva: International Labour Office. Staehle, H. 1934. "The Reaction of Consumers to Changes in Prices and Income: A Quantitative Study in Immigrants' Behavior", *Econometrica* 2(1): 59–72.
102 Correspondence from Burge to Camille Pône, September 21, 1937. XE 1/9/1 "Measures for raising the standard of living (Minimum standards), 1937–1938". ILOA.

alence space", a prerequisite for statistical comparison.[103] As such, in 1935, Hans Staehle published an article in *Econometrica*, the journal of the Econometric Society, which showed the important national differences in methods applied to family budget surveys.[104] In 1937, John Lindberg, another statistician at the Office, also recalled the lack of information on family budgets and the distribution of family income, both of which became insurmountable problems the moment less developed countries were considered:

> It appears that one of the objects of this inquiry is to suggest measures for raising standards of living among backward countries, e. g. India, China, Japan, countries of Africa, etc., but it is precisely for these countries that no, or very little, information is available as to wages, family budgets, national income, consumption or any other indicators of the standard of living.[105]

In the absence of comparable national wage and expenditure data, Nixon concluded that there was no way to compare the living standard of a worker in a less developed country with that of a European worker. In keeping with the statistical compilation work done by the Office on wages and living costs since the 1920s, Nixon indicated that the only possible measure was to observe changes in living standards over time.[106] Generally speaking, national statisticians also agreed that statistical science was not sufficiently developed and that national data was lacking. Following the resolution of the General Assembly of the League of Nations in October 1937, Butler had sent Lorwin to London and France to seek the opinion of several experts. Their position was unanimous. The sociologist Maurice Halbwachs, the British Edward Max Nicholson of the PEP, the economist and statistician Roy George Douglas Allen of the London School of Economics had all expressed their doubts given the scarcity of available statistical data.[107]

Nixon and Staehle thus had many objections to the publication of a study by the Office on living standards. Its production must therefore be considered as a forceful move on the part of the Economic Section of the Office. In an internal note, Percival Martin insisted: "the raising of the standard of life is the outstand-

---

103 Desrosières, A. Kott, S. 2005. "Quantifier", *Genèses* 1(58): 2–3.
104 Staehle, H. 1935. "Family Budgets", *Econometrica* 3(1): 106–118.
105 "The ILO and the problem of the Standard of Living". Internal report by John Lindberg. EP 200/01. ILOA.
106 "Notes concerning report on Measures to improve standards of living". Internal report by James Nixon. EP 200/01. ILOA.
107 EP 200/1/25 "Economic Problems – Standard of living enquiry – UK. 10/1937–01/1938". ILOA.

ing practical activity of the International Labour Organisation".[108] Economists at the Office assumed much better than statisticians the fact of having "an imperfect tool rather than having nothing at all". Faced with Nixon and Stahele's reluctance, Lorwin decided to control the realisation of the study as much as possible by excluding the Section of Statistics from the flow of communications, as evidenced by this internal note by Nixon dated 30 March 1939, on the absence of certain documents from the Office's file on the standard of living:

> I am surprised to see that the top-copy is not in this file. Will you please add the original copy, and return copy of my minute of 15/12 which I should like to keep in view of the difficulty of obtaining this file? (I have been trying to get this file every (sic) since January!) Collaboration should be reciprocal: at present it is rather one-way only.[109]

Staehle's doubts regarding the living standards study and the possibility of setting minimum social standards also led to strong criticism from Lorwin. According to him, Staehle was not fulfilling his professional obligations to the Office. Staehle responded to this attack in an internal four-page document, which in the Office's personal files is quite rare, invoking the scientific precision required to produce technical studies.[110] In 1939, because of these tensions, the American John G. Winant, newly appointed as Director of the Office, pressured Staehle to resign and leave for the United States. The problem posed by Staehle vanished with his departure on 28 February 1939.

While Lorwin finally did succeed in having Staehle entirely removed from participating in the study, the latter had nevertheless written the first theoretical section. This includes references to American economists, such as Jacob Viner and Paul H. Douglas, who had had a strong influence on him. While recognising the legacy of early work by economists and statisticians on living standards, Staehle extended its definition, which was then almost systematically reduced to a "sum", "set", "quantity" or "supply" of goods and services,[111] integrating social benefits and working conditions, in line with ILO policy. The second part of the study presented statistical data from the United States, Poland, Japan and India. An analysis of correspondence highlights the important involvement of

---

[108] "The international Labour Organisation and the Standard of Life". Report by William Percival Martin (undated but probably from 1939). EP 200/01/1. ILOA.
[109] Note from Nixon, March 30, 1939. EP 200/01. ILOA.
[110] Hans Staehle's Personal file, P 2446. ILOA.
[111] Douglas, P. H., Wolff Douglas, D., Smith Joslyn, C. 2009 [1921]. *What Can a Man Afford*, 50. Kessinger Publishing; Lyon-Bowley, A. 1923 [1915]. The Nature and Purpose of the Measurement of Social Phenomena, 164. London: P.S. King.

the following American national institutions, then engaged in the production of national studies on the comparison of living standards between the North and the South of the country: the SSRC, the National Resources Committee, the Bureau of Home Economics of the Department of Agriculture. Lorwin had also secured the collaboration of the U.S. Department of Labor, which had seconded a member of the Cost of Living Division of the Bureau of Labor Statistics, Alice Hanson, in assistsing the Office. Not without difficulties, the Office had obtained statistical data on Poland, via the Institute for the Study of Social Problems and the Public Institute of Hygiene in Warsaw – whose creation and studies had developed under the influence of Ludwik Rajchman[112] – as well as on India, via the collaboration of the Coonoor nutrition research laboratories financed by the Rockefeller Foundation. All the consumption data reproduced in the study showed the extent of poverty and low living standards, both in relation to national minimum standards and international standards. While the study was limited to "highlighting methods for using available data",[113] it concluded that low standards of living varied not only according to habits, traditions and customs, but also according to the state of economic development of countries. In particular, the statistical factors taken into account suggested that inequalities in living standards were mainly due to low purchasing power.

Among the measures envisaged, the survey stressed the need to develop social services and, in line with the work of the American economist Frank Knight, encouraged a policy of creating and developing new needs.[114] Less developed countries were particularly targeted.[115] The originality of the study, however, lay in the definition of the attributes of the standard of living it adopted, which integrated working conditions and social benefits. Thus, this study reflected the ILO's particular approach to raising living standards, which was gaining ground. While the standard of living of workers was influenced primarily by cash income amount or wage levels, as well as by the relationship between that income and the price of commodities, it was also influenced by the way in which income was acquired and by social provisions "which provide the worker

---

112 EP 200/1/50 "Economic problems – Standard of living – Poland". ILOA.
113 1938. *Le Standard de vie des travailleurs*, Études et Documents, séries B (Conditions éciomiques) no. 30, 115. Geneva: International Labour Office.
114 Knight, F. 1923. *The Ethics of Competition and Other Essays*. New York and London: Harper & Bros.
115 1938. *Le Standard de vie des travailleurs*, Études et Documents, séries B (Conditions éciomiques) no. 30, 71.

with protection against risks, or a free income, and which have a direct effect on his health and material well-being".[116]

Conclusion

The interwar period marked thus a turning point in the history of the standardisation and universalisation of measures of consumption. The ILO clearly stated its ambition to build statistics at the global level. While the statistical data centralised and disseminated by the Office in the interwar period had the general objective of better understanding the relationship between production and consumption, it also aimed to encourage the improvement of workers' living conditions, in particular by promoting a policy of raising wages. After the 1929 economic crisis, the raising of living standards became closely linked to the problem of regulating international trade and workers' demands to maintain their wage levels. In the context of the rise of totalitarian states, studies on living standards also served to maintain the legitimacy of democratic powers in promoting a liberal discourse on improving people's living conditions.

The Office is therefore a particularly compelling site from which to observe the historical process that led to the internationalisation of the notion of raising the standard of living from a labour perspective. The compilation of wage data, family budget surveys, international comparisons of the cost of living and the living standards of special categories of workers, as well as early attempts to define the notion of standard of living itself, demonstrate how tools to promote a specific model of economic and social development were gradually elaborated at the international level. Today, these indicators have multiplied, and more qualitative attributes are taken into account, in line with Amartya Sen's work on capability.[117] This multiplication of poverty measures shows the constant scientific challenge of assessing living standards and the central place, that it still holds today, in the development programmes of international organisations.

---

[116] 1938. *Le Standard de vie des travailleurs*, Études et Documents, séries B (Conditions éciomiques) no. 30, 20.

[117] Capability refers to political, philosophical, social and anthropological indicators that aim to explain the state of poverty not by lack of resources but by inability to obtain the means necessary to well-being. This incapacity is linked to personal data, but also to the social opportunities of the individual. See Sen, A. 1985. *Commodities and Capabilities*. Amsterdam and New York: North-Holland; Sen, A. 1987. *The Standard of Living. The Tanner Lectures*, Clare Hall, Cambridge: Cambridge University Press.

Chapter V
Technical Assistance "Experts": ILO Brokers Around The World

The intensification of ILO activities towards non-European countries has not only led ILO officials to broaden the spectrum of their research and scientific production. It was also accompanied by a reflection on the need to develop forms of action that were better adapted to the conditions specific to these countries, with particular attention to their need for expertise. The ILO's first experiences in the field of technical assistance were rooted in this reflection. While it is true that in the 1930s and 1940s, technical assistance was implicitly conceived as a means to overcome the gap between the norms developed by the ILO and the economic and social realities of less industrialised countries, until the end of the Second World War, technical assistance was not explicitly perceived as a tool for economic development, but rather as a means to help governments reform their labour legislations according to the principles of international labour Conventions. Missions were not only meant to help governments, but also, and above all, to raise awareness of the usefulness of the ILO. Thus, originally, the ILO conceived technical assistance primarily as a kind of technical diplomacy. The way technical assistance was conceived of and practised at the time is therefore not comparable to what occurred in the 1950s and 1960s, with the institutionalisation of international development within the UN. In order to better understand how the International Labour Office used technical assistance during these first trial years, I begin by looking at the profile of the actors involved, their backgrounds and the rationale behind their respective selection to technical assistance. It is through the study of the often-ignored biographical backgrounds of its actors that we can understand the specificity of technical assistance. This analysis is also fruitful in questioning the very notion of "expert".

Within historical literature on international organisations, experts have recently received increasing attention.[1] Some research has led to a better under-

---

[1] For studies on the ILO, see Kott, S. 2014. "From Transnational Reformist Network to International Organization: The International Association for Labour Legislation and the International Labour Organization (1900–1930s)", in Rodogno, D., Struck, B., Vogel J. eds. *Shaping the Transnational Sphere: Experts, Networks and Issues from the 1840s to the 1930s*. New York: Berghahn Books; Kott, S. 2011. "Les organisations internationales, terrains d'étude de la globalisation. Jalons pour une approche socio-historique", *Critique internationale* 3(52): 9–16; Van Daele, J. 2005. "Engineering Social Peace: Networks, Ideas, and the Founding of the International Labour Organization", *International Review of Social History* 50(3): 435–466. For studies on development

standing of the recruitment logic of these experts, often aggregated into "epistemic communities".² By specifying the use made of expertise, particularly in the development of new international standards,³ and by broadening the discussion on the correlation between the rise of experts and the development of international cooperation,⁴ these studies have opened up the field of analysis, where international organisations become spaces for reconfiguring economic, social and technical expertise. Some studies also highlight the diverse logic that prevailed in their selection, the social resources that allowed these actors to position themselves as experts.⁵ Others have also highlighted the professional and national rivalries that shaped the experts' positions in international commissions, committees, conferences and congresses.⁶

This quasi-ethnographic way of questioning notions of "expert" and "expertise" has led to a better understanding of how international organisations struc-

---

issues, see in particular Webster, D. 2011. "Development Advisors in a Time of Cold War and Decolonization: The United Nations Technical Assistance Administration, 1950–1959", *Journal of Global History* 6(2): 249–272; Hodge, J. M. 2010. "British Colonial Expertise, Post-Colonial Carreering and the Early History of International Development", *Journal of Modern European History* 8(1): 24–46; Zanasi, M. 2007. "Exporting Development: The League of Nations and Republican China", *Comparative Studies in Society and History* 49(1): 143–169. Mitchell, T. 2002. *Rule of Experts: Egypt, Techno-politics, Modernity.* Berkeley and Los Angeles: University of California Press.
2 Adler, E., Haas, P. M. 1992. "Conclusion: Epistemic Communities, World Order, and the Creation of a Reflective Research Program", *International Organization* 46(1): 367–390.
3 See the special issue edited by Sandrine Kott in *Critique internationale,* "Une autre approche de la globalisation: socio-histoire des organisations internationales (1900–1940)" 3(52).
4 Haas, P. M. 1992. "Introduction: Epistemic Communities and International Policy Coordination", *International Organization* 46(1): 1–35; Barnett M. N., Finnemore, M. 1999. "The Politics, Power, and Pathologies of International Organizations", *International Organization* 53(4): 699–732; Barnett, M. N., Finnemore, M. 2004. *Rules for the World: International Organizations in Global Politics.* Ithaca: Cornell University Press; Dard, O. 2003. "Technocrates et architectures européennes durant les années Trente", in Schirmann, Sylvain ed. *Organisations internationales et architectures européennes, 1929–1939: actes du colloque de Metz, 31 mai–1er juin 2001,* 269–284. Metz: Centre de recherche Histoire et civilisation de l'Europe occidentale de l'Université de Metz.
5 Kott, S. 2008. "Une "communauté épistémique" du social? Experts de l'OIT et internationalisation des politiques sociales dans l'entre-deux-guerres", *Genèses* 2(71): 26–46. For sociological analyses, see Trépos, J.-Y. 1996. *La Sociologie de l'expertise.* Paris: PUF. See the two special issues of the journal *Genèses* edited by Bakouche, I. 2006. "Expertise" 4(65), and Bakouche, I. 2008. "Devenir expert" 1(70). See also Bérard, Y., Crespin, R. eds. 2010. *Aux frontières de l'expertise, dialogues entre savoirs et pouvoirs.* Rennes: PUR; Dubois, V., Dulong, D. eds. 1999. *De l'invention d'une figure aux transformations de l'action publique.* Strasbourg: Presses Universitaires de Strasbourg.
6 Droux, J. 2011. "L'internationalisation de la protection de l'enfance: acteurs, concurrences et projets transnationaux (1900–1925)", *Critique internationale* 3(52): 17–33.

tured networks of technical knowledge.[7] However, in my analysis, we are not dealing with experts recruited from outside the ILO (with rare exceptions), but with civil servants at the Office who adopted a very specific career path. Within technical assistance, the status of expert therefore tends to be confused with that of international civil servant. I intend to nuance this implicit definition of the civil servant as an expert, through an analysis of the identities, motivations, and resources that enabled these individuals to position themselves as such.[8] The analysis of personal trajectories, quite traditional in sociology and anthropology of expertise, will be supplemented by a three-fold questioning based on the links between the mastery of scientific knowledge, a deep understanding of international cooperation, and the ability to transmit this knowledge.[9] First, I will analyse the selection processes for civil servants at the Office, as well as the expectations placed on them in their recruitment for technical assistance.[10] Access to an expert position depended on the ability of these civil servants to mobilise technical knowledge. This will lead me to study their career path before they entered the Office. Thirdly and finally, I will study the daily activities of civil servants in order to reconstruct the logic of their professional careers, which helps us better understand their role in the context of technical assistance and, by extension, to define the meaning and scope of this practice for the Office.

---

7 Sacriste G., Vauchez, A. 2005. "Les " bons offices " du droit international: la constitution d'une autorité non politique dans le concert diplomatique des années 1920", *Critique internationale* 1(26): 101–117.
8 Studies on the actors of the European integration, which have shown, in particular, the emergence of a transnational identity among civil servants, were inspiring. See Robert, C. 2010. "Les groupes d'experts dans le gouvernement de l'Union européenne. Bilans et perspectives de recherche", *Politique européenne* 3(32): 7–38; Georgakakis, D., de Lassalle, M. 2007. "Genèse et structure d'un capital institutionnel européen. Les très hauts fonctionnaires de la Commission européenne", *Actes de la Recherche en Sciences Sociales*, 39–53. Paris: Editions du Seuil.
9 2012. "L'anthropologie des organisations internationales", *Critique internationale*, Special Issue: 54(1); Abélès M., Bellier, I. 1996. "La Commission européenne. Du compromis culturel à la culture politique du compromis", *Revue française de science politique* 46(3): 431–456.
10 Research perspectives borrowed to Cécile Robert. Robert, C. 2010. "Les groupes d'experts dans le gouvernement de l'Union européenne. Bilans et perspectives de recherche", *Politique européenne* 3(32): 7–38.

1 Socialisation at the Office and the Emergence of a Sense of Belonging

1.1 ILO Civil Servants Engaged in Technical Assistance

Based on the archives available at the Office, it was possible to isolate, among all international civil servants, those selected to provide technical assistance between 1930 and 1939, and thereby determine the number and geography of the missions undertaken between the two world wars.[11] Information on the identity of civil servants has been supplemented by data on their nationality, year of birth, the date of their entry to the Office and the positions they held, as shown in the table below.

Tab. 1: Civil Servants Hired for Missions of Technical Assistance (1930–1939)

Name	Nationality	Year of Birth	Date of Entry at the Office	Missions of Technical Assistance	Positions held at the ILO
Adrien Tixier	French	1893	12.04.1920	Romania and Greece (1930) Brazil (1934) United States (1935)	1920: Service for war veterans and victims of war 1922: Chief of Section 1923: Chief of the Social Insurance and Disabled Persons Service, then of the Section of Social Insurance 1936: Deputy Director of the Office
Camille Pône	French	1884	07.01.1920	China (1931)	1920: Chief of Section, Diplomatic Division 1932: Member of the Director's Office
Harold Butler	British	1883	01.02.1920	Egypt (1932, 1938)	Deputy Director of the Office 1932: Director of the Office
Fernand Maurette	French	1878	07.10.1924	China (1934)	Chief of the Research Division 1933: Deputy Director of the Office
Cyrille Dechamp	French	1894	04.12.1924	Cuba (1934) Venezuela (1938)	Intern, Social Insurance and Disabled Persons Service 1926: Member of Section

---

11 The missions selected are those that were the subject of a government request.

Tab. 1: Civil Servants Hired for Missions of Technical Assistance (1930–1939) *(Continued)*

Name	Nationality	Year of Birth	Date of Entry at the Office	Missions of Technical Assistance	Positions held at the ILO
Moisés Poblete Troncoso	Chilean	1893	01.05.1927	Cuba (1934)	Temporary Editor, Information and Relations Section 1929: Member of Section 1934: Extra-European Countries Section
Maurice Thudichum	Swiss	1890	01.03.1920	Chile (1936)	Member of the central services: archives 1931: Office Chief for the Secretariat of the Administrative Section 1933: Deputy Chief of the Administrative Section
David Blelloch	British	1896	18.07.1921	Venezuela (1936)	Intern, Relations Division 1922: Member of Section 1924: Service Head 1926: Diplomatic Division 1937: Labour Law and Inspection Section
Roger Plissard	French	1894	26.02.1920	Tunisia (1936–1937)	Editor, Diplomatic Division 1922: Member of Section 1927: Member of Section, Indigenous Labour, 3rd Section, Diplomatic Division
Christie Tait	British	1886	30.03.1921	Canada (1937)	Emigration Service, Diplomatic Division 1929: Unemployment and Migration Section, 5th Section, Research Division
Wilfred Jenks	British	1909	1931	Venezuela (1938)	Legal adviser to the Office
Enrique Siewers	Argentinian	1900	01.12.1927	Venezuela (1938)	Member of the Auxiliary Section Migration Service, Diplomatic Division 1928: Member of Section
Luigi Carozzi	Italian	1880	20.09.1920	Egypt (1938)	Chief of Section and Technical Adviser, Industrial Hygiene Section
Oswald Stein	Czecho-Slovak	1895	1922	Turkey (1939)	1922: Member of Section, Social Insurance

Tab. 1: Civil Servants Hired for Missions of Technical Assistance (1930–1939) *(Continued)*

Name	Nationality	Year of Birth	Date of Entry at the Office	Missions of Technical Assistance	Positions held at the ILO
					1937: Chief of the Social Insurance Section
Maurice Stack	British	1895	1922	Turkey (1939)	1922: Research Division, Publishing Section 1923: Social Insurance and Disabled Persons Service

The relatively small number of civil servants engaged in technical assistance illustrates the still marginal place this practice occupied in the Office's overall activities during the interwar period. Moreover, technical assistance did not constitute a separate category in the general economy of the Office's activities. From an institutional point of view, there was no distinction between technical assistance and diplomatic, research or information missions. Indeed, the term "technical assistance" rarely appears. The term used at the time was "mission" or sometimes "Government invitation" and "technical collaboration".[12] Finally, these missions were not subject to a specific budget,[13] nor even to a formal decision by the Governing Body. However, they were distinguished by a government request, addressed to the Office directly or in its name. This is worthy of note as this practice did not reflect the tripartite nature of the ILO.

The deployment of technical assistance over a relatively short period of time, concentrated in the 1930s, suggests an intensification of the Office's expertise activities, at a time when international cooperation was being affected by the rise of nationalism in Europe and the global economic crisis. Far from being confined to the colonies or dependent territories, Office expertise spread to Central and Eastern Europe, Asia, the Maghreb and Latin America, where the Office concentrated its action during the Second World War. Even then, international technical assistance, although carried out on an ad hoc basis, was already being organised

---

[12] I only saw the term "technical assistance" once, in a 1938 mission report, written by the Britain, Wilfred Jenks, while he was in Venezuela.

[13] According to Albert Thomas' wish, the financial treatment of these missions was to be assessed "on a case-by-case basis". Until the end of the Second World War, there was no budget specifically dedicated to technical assistance activities. Some missions were partly funded by the requesting government and the ILO, such as the missions in Latin America. Others were financed entirely by the ILO, partly with the budget dedicated to representation expenses.

on a global scale. The above table shows that most missions took place in Latin America, confirming its central role in the development of international technical cooperation in the 1930s. However, the table shows that technical assistance was also deployed in Europe. After the Second World War, the Office would reiterate the fact that technical assistance was never conceived by the ILO as a specifically non-European activity, and even less as one limited to underdeveloped countries.[14] This said, during the interwar period, technical assistance to Western industrial countries remained uncommon. As the table shows, only the United States' government in 1935, and Canada in 1937, requested such assistance from the Office.[15]

1.2 International Civil Servants: A Homogeneous Social Group?

Not all civil servants were required to act as experts in the context of technical assistance. The group I identified, consisting of 14 people and the Director of the Office, forms the core of the civil servants who first acted in that capacity. The Office's selection process highlights some of this group's common characteristics.[16] Indeed, most of them were young when they embarked on an international career. Wilfred Jenks was only 22 years old and David Blelloch, 26. Fernand Maurette, then aged 46, is an exceptional case considering the profile of civil servants hired at the Office in 1920, the majority of whom were in their 20s and 30s.[17] Six

---

14 In 1949, on presenting to the United Nations General Assembly the report drafted by David Morse (Director-General of the International Labour Office between 1948 and 1970) on the Office's technical assistance activities, Wilfred Jenks, then in charge of the Office's liaison with the United Nations, insisted on this point. Z 1/1/1/13 (J.2) "Correspondence between the Director-General and Mr. Jenks 1948–1955", ILOA. I would like to thank Sandrine Kott for providing me with the excerpt from this letter.
15 On Tait's mission to Canada, see the file G 900/55/11 "Mr. Tait's mission to Canada. 1937", ILOA. The government requested Tait's assistance in drafting a law on unemployment insurance, based on the principles of voluntary and compulsory coverage. He collaborated with the Ministry of Labour. The German model largely inspired Tait's expertise.
16 The data were collected from the information provided by the Curriculum Vitae. It includes ten entries, where personal data (surname, first name, marital status, number of children, address in Geneva) are supplemented by information on the applicants' training, professional background and language skills. It is interesting to note that ILO applicants did not systematically send their CVs when they offered their services. The first contact with the ILO, or rather with its Director, was more often in the form of private correspondence, the formality of which varies considerably.
17 Published studies on the recruitment of staff at the ILO in the interwar period do not exist. Part of the results of the study of the rationale behind their recruitment is based on my Masters

civil servants sent on missions of technical assistance held management positions within the Office. Some, such as Christie Tait, Moisés Poblete Troncoso, Cyrille Dechamp, Maurice Stack,[18] or Roger Plissard, while they did not hold official management positions, effectively directed much of the research work done in their Section. In 1933 for example, the head of the Unemployment Section, Henri Fuss, wrote that Tait was "the most solid pillar" in his Section.[19] Similarly, from 1932 onwards, Stack led research work on social insurance in several European and Latin American countries, as well as in Egypt, Japan and India.[20] The civil servants selected for technical assistance thus represented the vanguard of international cooperation, having devoted at least ten years to the Office – with the exception of Poblete Troncoso – and having attained a relatively privileged position there. This suggests that they had acquired a deep understanding of the mechanisms of international cooperation in social policy, as well as a relatively strong sense of belonging to the institution.[21] While measuring their degree of acculturation to international cooperation is no simple task, it is worth analysing the modalities of the socialisation fostered by the Office.[22]

---

degree research, carried out in 2009–2010. Plata, V. 2010. *Le Recrutement des fonctionnaires du Bureau international du travail en 1920: une approche prosopographique*. Master thesis, University of Geneva.

18 He became head of the Social Insurance section in 1943. Personal file, P 1188, ILOA.

19 Christie Tait's working report, written by Henri Fuss, December 12, 1933. Christie Tait, personal file P 752, ILOA.

20 See his CV. P 1188, ILOA.

21 Marc Abélès uses the term *homo communautarius* in the case of the European Commission. Abélès, M. 1998. "Homo coconmmunautarius", in Kastoryano, R. ed. *Quelle identité pour l'Europe? Le multiculturalisme à l'épreuve*, 43–63. Paris: Presses de Sciences Po.

22 Georgakakis, D., de Lassalle, M. 2007. "Genèse et structure d'un capital institutionnel européen. Les très hauts fonctionnaires de la Commission européenne", *Actes de la Recherche en Sciences Sociales*, 39–53. Paris: Editions du Seuil; Buchet de Neuilly, Y. 2009. "Devenir diplomate multilatéral", *Cutltures & Conflits* 75(3): 75–98; Checkel, J. T. 2005. "International Institutions and Socialization in Europe: Introduction and Framework", *International Organization* 59(4): 801–826; Lewis, J. 2005. "The Janus Face of Brussels: Socialization and Everyday Decision Making in the European Union", *International Organization* 59(4): 937–971; Georgakakis, D. 2010. "Comment les institutions (européennes) socialisent", in Michel, H., Robert, C. *La Fabrique des Européens : Processus de socialisation et construction européenne (Sociologie politique européenne)*, 129–167. Strasbourg: Presses universitaires de Strasbourg. Some researchers consider that the acculturation of experts to international cooperation and the production of international standards is first and foremost the product of previous national socialisation. See Hooghe, L. 2005. "Several Roads Lead to International Norms, but few via International Socialization. A case study of the European Commission", *International Organization* 59(4): 861–898.

1.3 Institutional Arrangements for International Socialisation

Joining an international organisation implied gaining access to a new status, that of international civil servant, which distinguished these actors from their national counterparts. Belonging to this "specific social class"[23] implied enjoying a certain status and sharing values that strengthen group cohesion. As Jan Beyers noted regarding the impact of this shared European experience: "This not only has consequences for individual actor opportunities; it also leads to an *esprit de corps* and mutual understanding."[24] In the particular case of the Office, what institutional measures promoted this esprit de corps?

The status of international civil servant came with an obligation to represent the institution that, without causing a complete rupture with it, contributed in detaching civil servants from their national space. Civil servants also benefited from union representation and advocacy at the Office. As was the case with David Blelloch, membership to an organisation involved in staff policy certainly enhanced their identification with the position. The salary policy and internal competitions, awarding civil servants with improved positions within the Office, were two other instruments of institutional policy that fostered a sense of belonging. Indeed, in this environment characterised by internal promotion, civil servants more readily internalised their loyalty to it.

When entering the Office, international civil servants also entered into a system of international representations and values. This became apparent when a civil servant transgressed the model. In a book about the early years of the Office, Phelan tells the story of a Chinese civil servant who, convinced that the Office was neglecting the Far East, established official relations with a minister in China without talking to his superiors.[25] This event, presented as an "incident" by Phelan, testifies to the complex situation facing international civil servants, whose identities were inexorably linked to their membership in other national, professional, or militant groups. However, the ability to transcend these interests was required to define compromises at the ILO that might bring together member states, employers and workers. International civil servants were therefore under the permanent control of the rigid centralised internal functioning of the Office under the direction of Albert Thomas. In concrete terms this permanent control

---

[23] Georgakakis, D. 2010. "Comment les institutions (européennes) socialisent", in Michel, H., Robert, C. eds. *La Fabrique des Européens: Processus de socialisation et construction européenne (Sociologie politique européenne)*, 137–138. Strasbourg: Presses universitaires de Strasbourg.
[24] Beyers, J. 2005. "Multiple Embeddedness and Socialization in Europe: The Case of Council Officials", *International Organization* 59(4): 908.
[25] Phelan, E. J. 1936. *Albert Thomas et la création du BIT*, 95. Paris: Grasset.

over the inner workings of the Office was embodied in the director's signature, which was found on every single letter that left the Office. "By signing, Thomas would say, I know what's going on in the house."[26] That Thomas considered the Office his "home" also demonstrates his full identification with the institution. This directly impacted relations between civil servants and their director – imbued with respect and loyalty. Thomas had had a profound impact on the Office and 1932 marked an important date in its history. That year, exhausted by 12 years of relentless work to ensure the development of the Office's activities, Thomas died. After his death in Paris, he lived on in the institution as well as in the memory of his collaborators. Although no longer physically present, he remained very much alive in the minds of those he left behind at the Office.

Albert Thomas' reign was a particular, if not unique, period in the ILO's history. He truly embodied internationalism by profession and ensured its strength by surrounding himself with civil servants who had demonstrated a strong institutional commitment. "Zeal", "dedication", investment and initiative were important qualities that appear systematically in positive personnel assessments. Civil servants exhibiting these qualities were granted salary increases. The staff working reports also show that civil servants were regularly called upon outside working hours, contrary to the 1923 Staff Regulations, which limited the working day to seven hours and "exceptionally to a longer daily working period, if the service so requires".[27] In the 1935 Statute, however, civil servants could be required to work longer hours whenever the Director requested it. The Office had thus quickly acquired the reputation of being a demanding institution, where one only remained if one was truly "committed", as Albert Cohen, himself a former civil servant of the Office, evoked in *Belle du Seigneur*, in which he described work at the League of Nations and the Office at length.[28]

Adherence to a value system and membership of an international institution with an internal control undoubtedly led to a process of denationalisation. Among the Office's civil servants, many did not return to their country in 1939. Adrien Tixier (who was recalled by General de Gaulle in 1941), Wilfred Jenks, Maurice Stack, Christie Tait and Oswald Stein had fled Geneva for Montreal in 1940, along with the limited staff the Office had decided to keep under contract during the war. Beyond a career strategy, some had come to consider the interests of the Office above those of their home nation state. In 1940 Jenks wrote a personal note that testifies to this phenomenon: "For almost a decade I had been

---

26 *Ibid.*, 161.
27 See the 1923 Staff Regulations, Article 78, ILOA.
28 Cohen, A. 1968. *Belle du Seigneur*, 98, 105 et 123. Paris: Gallimard.

an international and although I had always the closest touch with my native land my attitude had long ceased to be a national center one. I was accustomed to attempting to see every problem from a variety of contrasted standpoints."[29]

For others, the fear of Nazi expansion had strengthened their internationalist commitment. As Blelloch noted in 1978, he had joined the ILO struggle at the outbreak of the Second World War, "not for king and country", "not for nation against nation", but against the horrors of Nazionalsozialismus".[30] Marked by a socialisation that led to a more or less strong identification with the interests of international cooperation and the adoption of its practices and values, this transition to the international level undeniably constituted a singular social reconversion.

2 The Professionalisation of Civil Servants Before their Entry to the Office

Assessment of the civil servants' capacity to satisfy the Office's requirements was made on the basis of criteria that highlighted the skills sought by the institution. They acquired most of these skills during their training and professional careers at the national level. Considering socialisation in the national space allows us to better identify the types of actors who were likely to become international civil servants and to act as experts. Besides, as Cécile Robert notes in the case of the European Union, this perspective "also questions political representations and practices, ways of thinking and making Europe, which European experts and civil servants are likely to have in common".[31]

2.1 Professional Trajectories in National Spaces

Members of universities or research institutes, former civil servants serving in national administrations, the Office's civil servants belonged to an intellectual elite. Based on a qualitative analysis of the group of civil servants engaged in technical assistance, it is possible to highlight the knowledge and practices acquired in

---

[29] Note written at the Canadian Pacific Hotel, Montreal, 1940. Wilfred Jenks Private Archives, VII–XII, ILOA.
[30] Private Archives of David Blelloch. Library of the University of Leeds, Great Britain.
[31] Robert, C. 2010. "Être socialisé à ou par " l'Europe "? Dispositions sociales et sens du jeu institutionnel des experts de la Commission européenne", in Michel, H., Robert, C. eds. La fabrique des " Européens " : processus de socialisation et construction européenne, 318.

national spaces and valued at the international level, and which defined the profile of civil servants who would act as experts. The table below gives an overview of the group's academic and professional background before joining the Office, as well as their language skills.

Tab. 2: Civil Servants Profiles

Name	Languages	Credentials	Professional Experience
Adrien Tixier	French English	- Châteauroux Normal School Teachers' College. - Higher education teaching certificate - Normal school certificate.	- Teacher, Higher Vocational School of Albi (Tarn). - Secretary General, Office départemental des Pupilles de la nation for wards of the state. - Vice-President, Union fédérale des associations françaises de mutilés de guerre et anciens combattants for war veterans and victims of war.
Camille Pône	French German English Extensive knowledge of Italian, Spanish and Russian.	Degree in Literature: German, English.	- 1908: Editor at the Ministry of Labour. - 1916: Deputy Head of Office, Ministry of Labour. - 1919: Secretariat for the French delegation. Commission on International Labour Legislation at the Paris Conference. - 1919: Secretariat of the French delegation to the Washington ILC.
Harold Butler	English German French	- Eton College. - Literae Humaniores. - Scholar at the All Souls College (1905).	- 1907: Local Government Board. - 1908: Home Office. - 1910: Secretary of the British delegation to the International Air Navigation Conference. - Captain at the Inns of Court Officers' Training Corps. - 1916: Secretary of the Foreign Trade Department, Foreign Office. - 1917: Ministry of Labour. - 1918: Drafted the work programme of the Commission on

Tab. 2: Civil Servants Profiles *(Continued)*

Name	Languages	Credentials	Professional Experience
			International Labour Legislation. - 1919: Secretary of the organising committee, General Secretary of the first ILC.
Fernand Maurette	French nglish Italian German (written) Spanish (written)	- Graduate of the University of France. - Former student of the École normale supérieure.	- 1903–1924: Professor of economic geography at the École de hautes études commerciales de Paris. - Attached to the secretariat and administration of the ENS.
Cyrille Dechamp	French English German	- Secondary school.	- 1918–1922: Head of the Documentation Department of the Allied Standing Committee. - 1922–1923: Comité départemental des Mutilés de la guerre for war veterans and victims of war. - 1924: Director of Administrative Services for the Association nationale des officiers mutilés for disabled officers.
Moisés Poblete Troncoso	Spanish French	- Studies at the University of Chile and the Sorbonne, Paris. - Law and Political Science Graduate. - Doctor of Law.	- Lawyer. - Under-Secretary of State at the Ministry of Hygiene, Assistance, Social Security and Labour. - Former Director General of Labour, Chile. - Vice-President of the Social Hygiene League. - Ex-Counsellor of the health insurance fund. - Member of the Social Legislation Committee, National Congress. - Since 1922: Professor of Social Economy at the University of Chile. - Secretary of the Faculty of Law of the University of Chile.

Tab. 2: Civil Servants Profiles *(Continued)*

Name	Languages	Credentials	Professional Experience
			- Professor at the School of Social Service in Santiago. - 1923: Delegate of the Chilean government to the Congress of Social Security in Rio de Janeiro. - Delegate of the Chilean Government to the Congress of Social Economy of Buenos Aires. - 1925: Technical Adviser, ILC.
Maurice Thudichum	French English Spanish Italian Portuguese German	- Collège de Genève classical section. - 1914: Doctor of Philosophy (Literature and Pedagogy) from the University of Munich.	- 1914: War mobilisation: 18 months of service as first Lieutenant of mountain artillery. - 1914–1917: Three years of teaching at the Collège. - 1918: Preceptorship in Fribourg. –1919: Interpreter at the Washington Conference.
David Blelloch	English French	- Bachelor, Oxford University.	- 1916–1919: Friends' Ambulance Unit.
Christie Tait	English French German	- Bachelor of Economics.	- 1911–1912: English teacher in Germany. - 1912–1913: Associate Editor of English publications in Germany. - 1914–1917: Assistant in an English secondary school. - 1917–1919: Service in the army. - 1919–1921: Assistant Master.
Roger Plissard	French English Spanish Basic knowledge of Italian and German	- Brevet supérieur, Certificate of Pedagogical Aptitude. - Certificate of proficiency in teaching English in teachers' colleges and upper primary schools. - Bachelor's degree in litera-	- Delegate for the teaching of Literature and English at the upper primary school of Viré, Calvados. - Editor at the Office national des Mutilés et Réformés for disabled and veteran workers,

Tab. 2: Civil Servants Profiles *(Continued)*

Name	Languages	Credentials	Professional Experience
		ture and law from the University of Paris. - Graduate degree in political economy and public law from the Faculty of Law of Paris.	attached to the Ministry of Labour.
Wilfred Jenks	English French	- Cambridge University (law and history), 1927 - Winner of the Cecile Prize, 1928. - International School of Geneva, under the direction of Alfred Zimmern, 1929–1930. - Bachelor's degree, Cambridge University, 1931.	- Gray's Inn. November 1930. - President of the Cambridge Union Society, 1930. - Treasurer of the British Universities League of nations Society.
Enrique Siewers	Spanish German French English Italian Portuguese (written)	- Doctor of Economics, University of Buenos Aires.	- Journalist. - Project Manager at the Institute of Economic and Financial Research of the University of Buenos Aires. - Former lecturer of Spanish and Argentinian Economics, Haut Institut de Sciences Commerciales, Manheim.
Luigi Carozzi	Italian French English German	- Doctorate in occupational medicine.	- 1906: International Congress on Occupational Diseases, Milan. - Head of Services at the Milan Labour Clinic. - 1910: Municipal Deputy, Milan. - 1914: Inspector, occupational physician, Ministry of Labour.
Oswald Stein	German Czech Russian Polish French (written) English (written)	- Graduated from the Classical College in Valasske Mezirici (1913). - Doctor of Law in Vienna.	- Social Insurance Division, under Director F. Kaan, former Austrian Ministry of Social Protection. - 1920: Social attaché in Prague.

Tab. 2: Civil Servants Profiles *(Continued)*

Name	Languages	Credentials	Professional Experience
Maurice Stack	English French Spanish German	- Graduate of the Faculty of Arts of the Sorbonne. - Spanish studies at the University of Madrid. - German Studies at Kings College.	- British Air Force. - Indian Trade Commissioner's Office (six months).

All Office civil servants engaged in technical assistance, except for Harold Butler and Cyrille Dechamp, held university degrees. While the training of some had been interrupted by the war, they were nevertheless part of the Western intellectual elite. As university or college professors, their social capital was often combined with a technical professionalisation in the social field. Such participation in a national professional environment, whether in ministries or professional associations, was often a first step for these future civil servants in acquiring technical and even practical knowledge of labour issues.

However, international civil servants held a wide variety of responsibilities which require clarification.[32] Some professional trajectories testify, in particular, to the close ties that tied them to the political world. The case of Moisés Poblete Troncoso is illustrative here. On several occasions, he was appointed government delegate to national and international congresses and became Under-Secretary of Social Welfare and Labour at the Ministry of Hygiene, Assistance, Social Security and Labour in Chile. Cabinet shuffles had halted his national career and he saw the Office in Geneva as a desirable outcome. Some historians have indeed pointed to the kind of resource an international transition could represent for national experts seeking legitimacy, or simply new professional opportunities, as well as the fact that experience acquired in international organisations constituted a significant qualitative gain in their careers.[33] In turn, the functions of Vice-President of the Social Hygiene League and expert on behalf of the National Health Insurance Fund, which could be added to Poblete Troncoso's curriculum, met the Office's need to tap into national professional networks. In a 1934 working report, Mack Eastman highlighted the extent to which Poblete

---

[32] Bérard, Y., Crespin R. eds. 2010. *Aux frontières de l'expertise. Dialogues entre savoirs et pouvoirs*, 22. Rennes: Presses universitaires de Rennes, coll. "Res Publica".

[33] This is the thesis defended by Godard, S. 2014. "Construire le " bloc " par l'économie. Configuration des territoires et des identités socialistes au Conseil d'Aide Économique Mutuelle (CAEM), 1949–1989". PhD diss., University of Geneva.

Troncoso had leveraged his political and professional networks in developing the Office's relations with Latin American countries: "His academic standing and his wide acquaintance with men of learning, coupled with his knowledge of social movements throughout that vast continent and friendship with many political leaders of different countries, – all redound to the advantage of the ILO."[34]

This role of "sensor and diffuser" invites us to consider the international civil servant as a "Janus with two faces",[35] both a national representative and representative of the Office. Representation at the national level allowed civil servants to gain recognition from the Office and gave them authority when establishing relations with certain member states. For instance, in 1934 Poblete Troncoso was promoted to head the Latin American group, responsible for developing relations with these countries. He was also the instigator of the first ad hoc meeting of Latin American delegates held on the margins of the 1934 ILC, which sought to intensify relations with the continent.

2.2 The Importance of Administrative Careers

While experts could be useful in developing the Office's activities, they were not necessarily popular. The Office had in fact mainly encouraged the recruitment of people with administrative experience. This can be explained by the fact that international organisations are immense machines that require staff with a high capacity for management, methodology and control. Professional background and theoretical knowledge were thus carefully measured for recruitment. In 1919, when he was Secretary General of the Governing Body, Butler had insisted on the importance of administrative experience.[36] In 1927 Albert Thomas also noted: "In our international organisation, we needed civil servants who were already experienced, with a sense and taste for administration."[37] Moreover, in its early days, the role of the Office as a centre of expertise was neither recognised nor promoted. The Office civil servants who held managerial positions were re-

---

34 Report of work, August 6, 1934. Moisés Poblete Troncoso, personal file, P 2037, ILOA.
35 Lespinet-Moret, I., Viet, V. eds. 2011. *L'Organisation internationale du travail : origine, développement, avenir*, 21. Rennes: PUR.
36 Minutes of the 2nd session of the Governing Body, Annex II, Washington, D.C., November 28, 1919, ILOA.
37 Working Report, January 5, 1927. Camille Pône, personal file, P 9, ILOA.

cruited among national ministries.³⁸ Fernand Maurette, Roger Plissard, Camille Pône, and Adrien Tixier were civil servants seconded from the Ministry of Education and the Ministry of Labour. If the emphasis on administrative experience seems obvious, given the prevalence of this criterion in the recruitment of international civil servants, it goes beyond the simple issue of professional selection, insofar as it resulted in the majority of international civil servants in management positions at the Office being from European industrialised countries. Finally, several civil servants had also distinguished themselves by their involvement in the "construction" of the first iteration of the Office. Fernand Maurette had organised and headed the Research Division since 1924. Adrien Tixier had given life to the Social Insurance Section, which he took over the management of in 1923. In 1937 David Blelloch oversaw the organisation of the Labour Inspection Section, created the same year. This position of administrative leadership was important because it placed them at the centre of the internal flow of information. They managed an extraordinary number of documents and correspondence that allowed them to have an overview of the operations system at the Office.

2.3 The Experience of War and the Networks of Social Reform

The emergence of an esprit de corps stemmed in part from the fact that most civil servants had shared the experience of war. Some had joined the military service, while others had worked in sectors directly affected by the war and its aftermath. This was the case for Roger Plissard. Tasked with teaching literature and English at the upper primary school in Viré, Calvados, he had been hired as editor of the Ministry of Labour's *Office national des mutilés et réformés* for war veterans and victims of war, created in 1916.

Albert Thomas had entrusted the Social Insurance Section to three maimed war veterans: Adrien Tixier, Cyrille Dechamp, and Oswald Stein. Dechamp was born in Paris in 1894 into a modest family. Shortly after completing high school he was mobilised before being demobilised due to injuries that left him severely mutilated.³⁹ Between 1918 and 1922, he worked as Head of the Documentation Department of the Allied Standing Committee. From 1922 onwards he collaborated with the *Union fédérale des associations françaises de mutilés de guerre et an-*

---

38 For a study of the representation of the French Ministry of Labour at the ILO, see Lespinet-Moret, I. 2007. "Le vivier de la Direction du travail et du ministère du Travail au sein de l'Organisation internationale du travail, 1919–1932", in Chatriot, A., Join-Lambert, O., Viet, V. eds. *Les Politiques du Travail (1906–2006). Acteurs, institutions, réseaux:* 241–257. Rennes: PUR.
39 Cyrille Dechamp, personal file, P 1729, ILOA.

ciens combattants as deputy head of the services of the Seine departmental committee. By 1924 he was Director of Administrative Services for the Federal Union. The second was Oswald Stein. Born in Litomysl in Bohemia in 1895, Stein graduated from the classical college of Valasske Mezirici in 1913.[40] An active member of the student movement led by Masaryk, he studied law, economics, and mathematics in Prague and Vienna, where he obtained a doctorate in law. He was also secretary of the insurance commission at the International Law Association, founded in 1873 in Brussels. During the First World War, he was 60 per cent mutilated and taken as a prisoner of war in Russia. After his release in October 1918, he passed the admission examination at the Ministry of Social Security in Vienna, where he worked under the Victims of War Section, gathering official information. In 1919 he negotiated the first arrangement on unemployment insurance and war victims between Czechoslovakia and Austria and in 1920, was hired as a social attaché in Prague. Between the wars, Stein continued to participate in the socialist mutuality network. He was honorary secretary with Adrien Tixier at the *Association des unions nationales de sociétés de secours mutuels et de caisses d'assurances maladie*, an association of national unions of mutual benefit societies and health insurance funds (1928–1938),[41] which they had created together.

Adrien Tixier's commitment in 1920 also highlights the importance of the socialist networks and militants of the French reformist movement, widely represented in the Office. Born on 31 January 1893 in Folles (Haute-Vienne), Tixier first turned towards a career in teaching.[42] He was then mobilised in August 1914 as a reserve officer. Because of injuries sustained during fighting in the Ardennes, his left arm was amputated. In 1915 he resumed his teaching activities in Buzançais, in the Indre region. He also taught at the Albi Higher Professional School. Founder in 1917 of the Federal Union of Veterans, he left the school institution and became Secretary General of the *Office départemental des pupilles de la nation* for wards of the state; and Vice-President of the *Union fédérale des associations françaises de mutilés de guerre et anciens combattants* for war veterans and victims of war. As an activist in the French Section of the Workers' International (SFIO), he established close relations with Albert Thomas.

---

[40] Oswald Stein, personal file, P 1289, ILOA. See also his obituary of 1944. In the *International Labour Review* 49(2): 157–162.

[41] This association became the International Social Security Association in 1947. For more information, see Kott, S. 2008. "Une " communauté épistémique " du social? Experts de l'OIT et internationalisation des politiques sociales dans l'entre-deux-guerres": 38–40.

[42] Adrien Tixier, personal file, P 217, ILOA.

British social reformist networks were also well represented at the Office. Reader of the *Clarion*, a weekly left-wing political journal founded by the socialist Robert Blatchford in 1891, David Blelloch was trained in reformist socialist ideas at Oxford University, which then had some ties to the Fabian Society.[43] In 1916 he became secretary of the No-Conscription Fellowship (NCF), a political association dedicated to fighting conscription and informing conscientious objectors of their rights. Blelloch had indeed opposed the war and, without claiming to be part of them, had integrated pacifist networks.[44] His refusal to join the army led him to spend some time in London's Wandsworth prison. There he met Albert Victor Murray, future secretary of the Student Christian Movement of Great Britain.[45] His activities with the NCF had also put Blelloch in contact with several Quakers. In 1916 these relationships had in turn enabled him to join the Friends' Ambulance Unit; a Quaker organisation created in 1914 and led by George Newman, a British doctor. The task of this unit was to provide emergency medical assistance to the British and French armies in conflict areas. Time spent in this organisation undeniably opened up new horizons for him. A devoted socialist, having been involved in British reformist networks and experienced in humanitarian assistance during the war, Blelloch joined the Office in 1921.

Beyond the wide array of trajectories taken by the civil servants of the Office during the war, the common experience of conflict was a central element in building the cohesion of this group. The careers of many of them were directly linked to the social problems generated by the war. Whether in governments, national administrations or professional social utility organisations, some of these civil servants had not only been trained in social policy but had also participated in the movement to extend the social prerogatives of the state. In a way, their entry into the Office, whose activities were based on the principle of increased and negotiated state interventionism in the field of social policies, was in line with these initial experiences.

3 Professionalisation Within the Office

Unlike their fellow countrymen, those involved in the Office had a common desire to act at the international level. Probing the Office allows us to observe the training mechanisms that could lead civil servants to act as experts. By studying

---

43 David Blelloch, "What Did I do in the Great War", private archives, Universiy of Leeds.
44 *Ibid.*
45 Letter from Victor Murray to David Blelloch, May 3, 1916, private archives, Universiy of Leeds.

the learning process of civil servants and the nature of the knowledge acquired, it becomes possible to specify the skills valued by the Office.

3.1 A Predisposition to International Openness

The acquisition of international life skills was the first sign of successful socialisation in international organisations, although it was not without limits.[46] There is no criteria to guide the evaluation of this know-how, made all the more difficult by the fact that civil servants at the Office did not necessarily share a common vision of social policy, nor of the means to implement it. However, they had to operate in a variety of national spaces, which meant mastering several languages.[47] The acquisition of international languages generally took place before entering the Office, through trips abroad, at university, in professional trainings, or during military service.

However, the importance of the language requirement decreased in selecting civil servants for the missions of technical assistance. In fact, few of them spoke the language of the countries they were sent to. Cyrille Dechamp, Wilfred Jenks, David Blelloch and Oswald Stein did not speak Spanish, but this did not prevent them from acting as experts in Latin America. Camille Pône and Fernand Maurette, who had no knowledge of Mandarin, went to China.[48] This clearly indicates that for the ILO, which counted among its ranks very few non-Europeans, these countries and their concerns were not high priorities. It also illustrates a common thread among international civil servants who, unlike their colonial coun-

---

[46] Robert, C. 2010. "Être socialisé à ou par " l'Europe "? Dispositions sociales et sens du jeu institutionnel des experts de la Commission européenne", in Michel, H., Robert, C. eds. *La fabrique des " Européens " : processus de socialisation et construction européenne:* 320.

[47] On the impact of multilingualism, see Bellier, I. 1995. "Une culture de la Commission européenne? De la rencontre des cultures et du multilinguisme des fonctionnaires", in Mény, Y., Muller, P., Quermonne, J.-L. eds. *Politiques publiques en Europe*, 49–60. Paris: L'Harmattan.

[48] On the mission of Jules Pône in China in 1931, see the files G 900/95/1/1 "Proposed visit of Mr. Pône to China. Administrative and Financial arrangements"; CAT 5–19–1 "Relations et informations. China"; LE 211 "Projet de la loi chinoise des fabriques"; LE 211/1 "Draft Labour Code China", ILOA. On Maurette's 1934 mission in China, see the files G 900/46/23/1 "Mr. Maurette's mission to China and Japan, 1934"; G 900/46/23/3 "Mr. Maurette's mission to Japan and China. 1934. Financial and administrative arrangements"; XT 13/1/1 "Maurettes's mission to China and Japan, February–April 1934", ILOA. A.III.55 "China. Commission nationale chinoise de coopération intellectuelle", in UNESCO Archives, Paris. A.I.135 "Réorganisation de l'enseignement en China, 1932–1936", in UNESCO Archives, Paris. AG 1 "International Institute of Intellectual Co-operation–IIIC", in UNESCO Archives, Paris.

terparts, did not possess geographical specialisation. In her study of the League's missions of technical assistance to China, Margherita Zanasi writes that the feature of experts at the League of Nations was nevertheless their knowledge of underdeveloped economies.[49] As far as the Office was concerned, with the exception of Fernand Maurette, few civil servants had such expertise. While some had indeed carried out missions in less developed countries, such as Tixier and Stein in Latin America, and Plissard in North Africa, these missions were few and brief, raising doubts about the depth of understanding these civil servants could have obtained in the field. It also seems difficult to conceive of an expertise on underdeveloped economies that discounts social, cultural, geographical or demographic conditions. This lack of knowledge of local conditions was thus the most characteristic feature of the civil servants of international organisations, a feature also found among experts involved in international technical cooperation programmes conducted within the framework of the International Monetary Fund (IMF) and the World Bank after the Second World War.[50] Finally, in and of itself, the experience of travelling abroad did not awaken in civil servants the desire to acquire geographical specialisation. They remained committed to their universalist conception of social reform, as evidenced by Jenks' statement written towards the end of his mission in Venezuela: "I have no special desire to become a Latin-American specialist and would prefer to have a peep at Asia or Africa for a change."[51] This way of looking at things was the direct consequence of the process of international acculturation and professionalisation within the Office, whose technical discourse worked to homogenise social problems as a prerequisite for its universalisation.[52]

3.2 In-Depth Knowledge of National and International Social Legislation

As shown in the table below, the kind of expertise required by governments in the context of technical assistance essentially covered two fields of competence: social legislation, and administrative organisation. The table shows that it is in the field of social insurance that the need for expertise was most strongly felt by governments. The Office's expertise was drawn upon undoubtedly because it had

---

[49] Zanasi, M. 2007. "Exporting Development: The League of Nations and Republican China", *Comparative Studies in Society and History* 1(49): 144.
[50] Mitchell, T. 2002. *Rule of Experts: Egypt, Techno-politics, Modernity*, Berkeley and Los Angeles: University of California Press.
[51] Letter from Jenks to his mother, June 5, 1938. Wilfred Jenks private archives, ILOA.
[52] Mitchell, T. 2002. *Rule of Experts: Egypt, Techno-politics, Modernity*: 54.

acquired legitimacy and experience in the field of international social insurance regulation, which the number of conventions drafted between the two world wars indicates.[53] In turn, social insurance had generated an intense body of scientific work and the mobilisation of many European experts at the ILO, in particular through the activities of the Office's Correspondence Committee for social insurance. The Social Insurance Section was also one of the most important Sections of the Office and had been the focal point of its activity in the field of international legislation since the organisation's inception in 1919.[54] It was not until after the Second World War, when productivity began dominating the ILO's concerns, that this trend was reversed.[55] Finally, ILO regional conferences in Latin America had stimulated technical cooperation in this area.

Tab. 3: ILO Missions of Technical Assistance in the Interwar Period

	Year	Country Request	Field of Expertise 1	Field of Expertise 2
1	1930	Greece	Social Insurance	
2	1930	Romania	Social Insurance	
3	1931	China	Labour Inspection	Labour legislation
4	1932	Egypt	Administrative organisation of the labour department	Labour legislation
5	1934	China	Reform of the education system	
6	1934	Cuba[56]	Administrative organisation of the labour department	
7	1934	Brazil	Social Insurance	
8	1935	United States	Social Insurance	
9	1936	Chile	Organisation of the Archives Service, Ministry of Foreign Affairs	
10	1936	Venezuela	Labour legislation	Creation of a labour office

---

53 Of the 68 conventions adopted between the wars 15 concern social insurance.
54 In 1923 the service consisted of only five members. In 1936, the section had ten members, including two actuaries and a doctor. Kott, S. 2008: 30.
55 In 1954, according to the ILC report, almost 50 per cent of the ILO's assistance activity targeted vocational training, compared to less than six per cent for social security. Activity Report, *ILC record of proceedings*, 1954: 63, ILOA.
56 The archives concerning this mission have been deleted. The reason is not known.

Tab. 3: ILO Missions of Technical Assistance in the Interwar Period *(Continued)*

	Year	Country Request	Field of Expertise 1	Field of Expertise 2
11	1936	Tunisia	Labour relations in the mines	
12	1937	Canada	Social Insurance	
13	1938	Venezuela	Labour legislation	
14	1938	Venezuela	Social Insurance	
15	1938	Venezuela	Workers' Immigration	Creation of a technical institute for immigration and colonisation
16	1938	Egypt	Labour legislation	
17	1938	Egypt	Industrial hygiene	
18	1939	Turkey[57]	Social Insurance	
19	1939	Ecuador	Social Insurance	

The primary objective of technical assistance was to encourage the development of social legislation. Civil servants had in fact a dual task, which was to guide governments in their reform process, while ensuring that national laws complied with the principles enshrined in international conventions or adopted by international commissions of experts. By and large, civil servants who had a solid grasp of social legislation and international labour Conventions therefore carried out technical assistance. While some civil servants had acquired legal knowledge in their home country, the international dimension of this expertise stemmed from their career within the Office. It should be stressed that – with the exception of Oswald Stein, Moisés Poblete Troncoso, and Luigi Carozzi – upon joining the Office, civil servants did not have expertise in the technical fields to which they would be assigned. Adrien Tixier, now widely recognised, by ILO and social insurance scholars alike, as an expert of social insurance, only became a specialist in this field through contact with the Office. In a 1924 labour report, one year after taking over the management of the newly created social insurance department, it states: "Although Mr Tixier did not systematically deal with the problem of social security, through diligent studies, he soon managed to obtain the necessary knowledge for the management of his Department."[58] In a 1932 report on Fernand Maurette's work, Albert Thomas stated that:

---

[57] Missing file.
[58] Work report, January 4, 1924. Adrien Tixier, personal file P 217, ILOA.

[i]n the immense body of scientific work produced here, he is the Direction's safeguard. The impeccable care with which he oversees his collaborators' work, the intelligence he has demonstrated in matters whose technical complexity was, until recently, unknown to him, and his great administrative competence make him a perfect head of division.[59]

Roger Plissard, who joined the Office as an editor at the age of 26, had no particular expertise in indigenous labour issues. It was not until 1927 that he began to learn about the problems of long-term employment contracts and forced labour.[60] The data he collected was used to prepare official reports and notices for *Informations sociales*. He also gradually became specialised in labour regulation and employment contracts in Muslim regions, a completely new field of research for the ILO. Harold Grimshaw noted that Plissard "[broke] new ground and [dealt] with a problem hitherto little touched upon either inside or outside the Office in any scientific way".[61] At the Office, research activity was rarely limited to a single national space. While civil servants were geographically distributed according to their nationality and mastery of a particular language, this logic was far from being the rule. Cyrille Dechamp, who did not speak Spanish, was responsible for collecting information on social insurance for Cuba and Uruguay, for instance.[62] This knowledge was used to produce international studies. The studies, not limited to the reproduction of national knowledge, engaged civil servants in a more global analysis and reflection. Civil servants had to be able not only to master the literature on national experiences, but also to "find the methods, principles and criteria that [thus] make an original work".[63] Knowledge on national legislation met with thorough knowledge of international labour Conventions and their content. Civil servants sent on missions of technical assistance had participated directly or indirectly in the formulation of international labour Conventions. The case of Wilfred Jenks is emblematic here. He was the legal adviser to the Office, which placed him in an ideal position to benefit from a thorough understanding of international law, ILO standards and procedures, along with the theory and practice of international organisations, which he himself had helped shape.[64]

---

59 Annual Report, 1932. Fernand Maurette, personal file P 1720, ILOA.
60 Work report, 1927. Roger Plissard, personal file, P 82, ILOA.
61 Work Report, December 21, 1927. Roger Plissard, personal file, P 82, ILOA.
62 Cyrille Dechamp, personal file, P 1729, ILOA.
63 Work Report, May 30, 1931, signed by Tixier. Cyrille Dechamp, personal file, P 1729, ILOA.
64 Co-author with Edward Phelan of the 1944 Philadelphia Declaration, he played a central role in the ILO's positioning in the system of international organisations after 1945. Gopinath, P. 1998. "Wilfred Jenks", *Bulletin des anciens* 25, 11. Geneva, International Labour Office.

The research work of civil servants, coupled with analytical skills, enabled them to acquire solid and varied technical knowledge, which they used in turn to strengthen their position within the Office. This affirmation of their authority took a variety of forms, from publications in specialised journals, particularly the *International Labour Review*, to participation in technical conferences. To illustrate the international scientific production of the Office's civil servants and the way in which it enabled them to gradually build a reputation as international experts, I would like to cite the working reports of Enrique Siewers, an Argentine national and member of the Employment and Migration Section.[65] Upon joining the Office, Siewers was entrusted with auxiliary work such as the publication of *La Réglementation des Migrations* and the Office's annual statistical report.[66] From 1930 onwards he was relieved from his previous tasks, as his work grew more scientific in nature. In 1933 he participated in the work of the Committee for Labour Migration. Siewers then played an important role at the Santiago Conference in 1936. He was responsible for the resolutions passed on unemployment and migration. This moment represents a highlight in his career. Indeed, from then on, he was granted stronger authority within the Office, responsible among other things for organising the 1938 conference of experts on migration and colonisation. That same year, Butler selected him to lead a mission of technical assistance to Venezuela. Siewers' activities within the Office thus testify to the importance of scientific production in the evolution of civil servants' tasks and responsibilities.

This scientific work also enabled civil servants to position themselves within transnational networks of expertise. This was the case with Cyrille Dechamp of the Social Insurance Section, who had made considerable progress in the Office's work on the financial aspects of social insurance. He authored several international studies on social insurance benefit systems, pension techniques, as well as methods for assessing social security contributions. Between 1936 and 1937 he also conducted an international study on the investment policies of social insurance institutions, while drafting the Office's preliminary report, which served as a basis for the expert consultation, held concurrently.[67] The Dechamp report was the first comprehensive international study of the issues tied to investing social insurance institution funds. In 1938 he put forward his expertise on these issues during a mission of technical assistance to Venezuela. In itself the mobilisation of scientific or technical knowledge in the context of technical assistance was

---

[65] Enrique Siewers, personal file, P 2122, ILOA.
[66] Work Report, May 17, 1928. Personal file, P 2122, ILOA.
[67] Annual report 1936–1937. Cyrille Dechamp, personal file, P 1729, ILOA.

not surprising. However, its implementation testifies to the importance of these missions in projecting the Office's scientific and technical apparatus at the national level. Civil servants never left empty-handed: suitcases or even crates filled with ILO-stamped documents accompanied them on their journeys. Technical assistance was therefore not politically neutral, as it served to disseminate and promote ILO knowledge, principles and methods.

It is also interesting to note that technical assistance itself contributed to "making the expert", especially when technical knowledge was lacking. They were a means for the civil servants to increase their technical knowledge, as shown by Tixier's 1934 mission to Latin America, where he advised governments, particularly Brazil's. This mission was presented as a scientific mission, which was intended, on the one hand, to study the organisation of the ministerial services responsible for drafting and monitoring the application of social insurance laws, and on the other hand, to observe the administrative, technical and financial functioning of insurance institutions themselves.[68] This information, gathered directly from the field, contributed to the formulation of a more detailed analysis of the social problems. "Two weeks in a country taught me more than ten years studying laws and documents," noted Tixier in his 1935 mission report.[69] This knowledge was in turn mobilised to produce scientific documentation, in particular articles published in the *International Labour Review*, and technical studies published by the Office.[70] It also allowed civil servants to contribute to the work of experts committees.[71]

3.3 A Sense of Diplomacy

It is well known that the ILO's multilateral cooperation model rests on renewed and negotiated agreements between governments, employers and workers.[72] The

---

[68] Working report, 17. G 900/30/5 "Mr. Tixier's mission to South America, autumn 1934", ILOA.
[69] Mission Report, January 22, 1935. RL 86/0 "Relation of the ILO with central and south America. General", ILOA.
[70] Back from his mission, Adrien Tixier published a report on the development of social insurance in the countries he visited. Tixier, A. 1935. "Le développement des Social Insurance en Argentine, au Brazil, au Chile et en Uruguay" I et II, *International Labour Review* 32(5): 646–673 and (6): 797–827.
[71] For example, in 1938, following his 1937 mission of technical assistance to Canada on unemployment legislation, Tait took part as an expert in the first meeting of the International Commission on Public Works. Report of January 4, 1939. Christie Tait, personal file, P 752, ILOA.
[72] Some authors who have worked on the European Commission have also stressed the importance of the meaning of the political compromise that prevails in the profile of experts. Robert,

efforts of Office civil servants thus aimed at the slow and arduous construction of reciprocity in economic and social relations between the member states. For the Office, strong negotiation capacities were crucial in obtaining the support of tripartite delegations for the ratification of international conventions. Civil servants had to successfully identify various political strategies, overcome potential conflicts and defuse opposition towards international normativity. The logic was the same during the missions of technical assistance, with an additional difficulty: the actors with whom civil servants collaborated were sometimes totally unaware of the nature and scope of the ILO's work. Acting as a catalyst for international cooperation, the missions were an opportunity to connect with national administrators and civil servants, trade union leaders and influential representatives of industry, who then might represent their respective countries and sectors at international conferences, committees or commissions.[73] The table below highlights the individual actors who negotiated the organisation of technical assistance, as well as the Office's previous international missions, where specific requests for assistance were first made.

Tab. 4: National and International Actors Involved in the Organisation of ILO Missions of Technical Assistance

Requesting Country	International Setting for Technical Assistance Request	National Organisational Network
1930 Greece	Adrien Tixier's 1929 mission in collaboration with the League of Nations.	Andreas Zakkas, Director of the Labour Department, Delegate to the ILC.
1930 Romania	Albert Thomas' 1930 diplomatic mission in the Balkans.	Ion Răducanu, Minister of Labour.
1931 China	Albert Thomas' 1928–1929 diplomatic mission to Asia.	Mr Kung, Minister of Industry. Thomas Tchou, Director of the Labour Department of the Ministry of Industry, Trade and Labour.
1932 Egypt	Albert Thomas' 1929 diplomatic mission. Mission of Mr Graves in 1931, Director of the British Department of Labour and government representative.	Isma'il Sidqi, President of the Council of Ministers.

C. 2010. "Être socialisé à ou par " l'Europe "? Dispositions sociales et sens du jeu institutionnel des experts de la Commission européenne", 337 and following.
73 Director Report, *ILC record of proceedings*, 1936, 66, ILOA.

Tab. 4: National and International Actors Involved in the Organisation of ILO Missions of Technical Assistance *(Continued)*

Requesting Country	International Setting for Technical Assistance Request	National Organisational Network
1934 China	Missions of the Commission on Intellectual Cooperation, League of Nations, 1931–1932.	Ministry of Public Education.
1934 Cuba	Missing file.	
1934 Brazil	Discussions with several delegates to the 1934 ILC.	Affonso Bandeira de Mello, Director of Labour.
1935 United States	Harold Butler's 1934 diplomatic mission.	John G. Winant, Director of the Social Security Board.
1936 Chile	First ILO regional conference.	Miguel Cruchaga Tocornal, Minister of Foreign Affairs.
1936 Venezuela	Discussions with Manuel Arocha in 1936, delegate to the League of Nations.	Manuel Arocha, Permanent Delegate, and International Officer to the League of Nations. Esteban Gil Borges, Director at the Ministry of Foreign Affairs.
1936–1938 Tunisia	Roger Plissard's mission of technical assistance in 1931 and 1935.	French Ministry of Foreign Affairs, Department of Political and Commercial Affairs. Africa-Levant.
1937 Canada	Social Insurance Section of the Office.	Department of Labour.
1938 Venezuela	David Blelloch's 1936 mission of technical assistance.	Tito Gutiérrez Alfaro, Director of the National Labour Office.
1938 Venezuela	David Blelloch's 1936 mission of technical assistance.	Manuel Arocha, Permanent Delegate and international civil servant to the League of Nations.
1938 Venezuela	David Blelloch's 1936 mission of technical assistance.	Caracciolo Parra Pérez, Government Delegate to the ILC.
1938 Egypt	Harold Butler's 1932 mission of technical assistance.	Department of Labour, Ministry of the Interior.
1938 Egypt	Harold Butler's 1932 and 1938 missions of technical assistance.	Mohamed Kamel El-Bindari, Minister of Public Health. Ali al-Shamsi Pasha, permanent Government Delegate to the League of Nations and the Office.
1939 Turkey	Missing file.	

Tab. 4: National and International Actors Involved in the Organisation of ILO Missions of Technical Assistance *(Continued)*

Requesting Country	International Setting for Technical Assistance Request	National Organisational Network
1939 Ecuador	Social Insurance Section of the Office.	National Social Welfare Institute, Quito.

Technical assistance helped develop official relations with government, employers' and trade union organisations and had huge potential for disseminating information on the nature, functioning and activities of the Office, as noted by Butler in his 1938 annual report:

> They represent one of the most useful forms of service which the Office is called upon to perform, as they may be expected not only to provide assistance to the countries in question, but also to create a better understanding of the work and usefulness of the Office.[74]

Technical assistance was thus a particularly important diplomatic tool. Butler's first mission of technical assistance to Egypt in 1932 was a striking example of the blurred boundaries between science and politics. Officially, Butler was mandated by the Egyptian government to prepare a report on the administrative restructuring needed to carry out a broad social policy programme applicable to Egyptian industry "at its current stage of development" and to provide his opinion on a series of possible social reforms before a government legislative commission. However, his mission also had an obvious diplomatic function, as Egypt was not yet a member of the ILO.[75] The second mission in 1938, two years after Egypt's entry into the ILO, was furthermore devoted to questions of Egypt's representation in ILCs and ratification of conventions than to social reforms.[76] The discussion regarding possible new ratifications was in fact very common during ILO missions of technical assistance. The Office also used the context provided by technical assistance to insist on the development of certain social rights, in particular freedom of association and the right to unionise. While they were regularly discussed between Office civil servants and national administrators, these issues were never tackled head-on. It remains difficult to measure the impact of technical assistance in this area between the wars. The practice of observation missions to monitor freedom of association did not develop until the

---

[74] Report of the Director, *ILC record of proceedings*, 1938, 64, ILOA.
[75] XT 69/3/1 "Mr. Butler's visit to Egypt, February 1932", ILOA.
[76] XT 69/2/2 "Director's visit to Egypt, April 1938", ILOA.

late 1940s.⁷⁷ In the interwar period, although such measures were not yet in place, and no missions aimed specifically at monitoring fundamental rights were conducted, Office archives highlight civil servants' attempts to mobilise national actors on this issue. However, in countries without a legacy of state dialogue, trade union participation remained relatively low. Moreover, and despite what might have been expected, technical assistance did not constitute a resource for workers' organisations in less developed countries, as they were contending with increased state intervention in social and economic relations.⁷⁸ The missions actually played a very limited role in the development of trade unionism. Regarding Butler's 1938 mission to Egypt for instance, Zachary Lockman and Joel Beinin note that he had neither stimulated the trade union movement nor produced labour legislation that would have increased workers' bargaining power.⁷⁹ The question of the relations among the various actors of the economic market and the role of technical assistance in the development of social dialogue was nevertheless a concern for the civil servants of the Office.

3.4 Professional Trajectories and Continuity After the Second World War

The biographical approach emphasises the continuity that marked the 1930s through the Second World War and into the 1950s; while highlighting the ties between international technical assistance, humanitarian assistance, reconstruction and development, all forged during this period. The acquisition of an international body of expertise in the interwar period allowed some civil servants to find themselves at the heart of the first technical cooperation programmes after the Second World War. Cyrille Dechamp, who had not been reinstated by the Of-

---

77 See, in particular, Jef Rens' 1949 mission to Venezuela. MI 321 "Missions. Missions to Venezuela-Freedom of associations (July 1949). 06/1949–05/1958", ILOA. As for the Office's role as critical observer, the Committee of Experts on the Application of Conventions and Recommendations only institutionalised it in 1968. Gernignon, B. 2004. "La liberté syndicale et les missions sur place de l'OIT", in Javillier, J.-C., Gernignon, B. eds. *Les Normes internationales du travail : un patrimoine pour l'avenir. Mélanges en l'honneur de Nicolas Valticos*, 108. Geneva: International Labour Office.
78 The post-war years and the conferences of 1947, 1948 and 1949 on freedom of association, the right to organise and collective bargaining provided important instruments for trade union organisations seeking recognition of their right to participate in economic and social development, while proviing a basis for the ILO to develop projects to assist workers' organisations and then employers' organisations.
79 Lockman, Z., Beinin, J. 1987. *Workers of the Nile: Nationalism, Communism, Islam and the Egyptian Working Class (1882–1954)*, 205. Princeton: Princeton University Press.

fice after the war, was hired in 1947 by the French Ministry of Foreign Affairs as deputy director of the Labour Division of the French section of the Control Council in Berlin. He was one of the first French experts in charge of drawing up reconstruction plans for Germany after the war.

The professional experience acquired during the Second World War also contributed directly to the hiring of some civil servants in international technical cooperation programmes after 1945. Maurice Thudichum's career is significant in this respect. On 1 March 1941, he left the Office. He then headed the technical service of the British Service at the Central Prisoners of War Agency of the Red Cross. From 1944 onwards he carried out missions for the International Committee of the Red Cross (ICRC). In Italy, and with the collaboration of the Secretary General of the Italian Red Cross, Thudichum dealt with the issue of relief for the more than 600,000 Italians deported to Germany. In 1947 he became Director of the International Research Service in Arolsen, Germany. His relief experience during the Second World War, which had enabled him to develop many contacts in Germany, Central Europe and Yugoslavia, convinced American David Morse, Director-General of the Office from 1948 to 1970, to hire him to oversee the 1953 implementation of the ILO's Manpower Programme in Yugoslavia.[80]

Morse's career during the Second World War also highlights the intertwining of military careers, reconstruction and international development. Morse's biographical study highlights these entanglements, as well as the different institutional settings that participated in the emergence of a development discourse in his country.[81] His social reconstruction activities in Italy and Germany had directly contributed to reflections on the challenges of post-war economic and social development, in particular the need for states to establish a labour bureaucracy and develop a consumer policy.[82] While his task of organising the workforce and employment services were, at that time, an integral part of reconstruction activities in Europe, his duties as Director-General of the Office from 1948 onwards enabled him to give a global dimension to the concerns and solutions he had ex-

---

[80] The aim was to find industrialists in Germany and Austria who agreed to provide the services of foreman-instructors in Yugoslavia. For a description of the Manpower Programme, see Roberts, R. S. 1962. *Economic Development, Human Skills and Technical Assistance: A Study of I.L.O. Technical Assistance in the Field of Productivity and Management Development*. Geneva: Droz.

[81] Maul, D. 2012. *Human Rights, Development and Decolonization: The International Labour Organization, 1940–70*. Basingstoke, Palgrave Macmillan; Geneva: International Labour Organization.

[82] Folder 7 "Sicily and Italy", 1943, Box 67 and folder 4 "Germany", Box 67, 1944–1945. David A. Morse Papers. Seeley G. Mudd Rare Books and Manuscript Library, Princeton.

perienced during the war. Finally, for other civil servants engaged in technical assistance in the interwar period, commitment to the Office was enduring. Wilfred Jenks devoted his entire career to the Office and became its sixth Director-General from 1970 to 1973. David Blelloch also had a long career at the Office, which found a second wind within the UN's development programmes.[83]

Conclusion

The deployment of ILO technical assistance suggests an intensification of exchanges of expertise with extra-European countries at a time when international cooperation was suffering from the effects of the Great Depression and the rise of nationalism in Europe. In the 1930s, technical assistance concerned mainly social protection, especially the adoption of new legislation on social insurance. Here lies the specificity of the ILO's technical assistance, what the historian Daniel Maul has called the ILO's "integrated approach" to development, were the provision of technical assistance and expertise was linked to the legislative work of the ILO[84].

The missions of technical assistance testify to the growing importance of the Office's professional knowledge in the elaboration of national social reforms as well as the empowerment of the Office vis-à-vis member states, which never intervened in the organisation of technical assistance, the modalities of its implementation, the objectives of the missions or the selection of civil servants. All these issues were negotiated exclusively among the heads of division, Chiefs of Section, Director of the Office and representatives of the requesting government.

The Office's new purpose attests to the presence of specialists with internationally recognised professional skills within it. The biographical approach I developed shows that technical assistance was essentially based on European experiences, on the skills of actors from Europe having undergone a process of professionalisation in the European networks of the social reform. This being said, upon joining the Office, their technical skills and scientific knowledge were often lacking in the field of expertise assigned to them. My analysis thus highlights the importance of the Office as a space for the acquisition of social expertise. The technical legitimacy of the expertise offered by the Office was

---

[83] David Blelloch, personal file, P 760, ILOA.
[84] Maul D. 2009. "Help Them Move the ILO Way": *The International Labor Organization and the Modernization Discourse in the Era of Decolonization and the Cold War. Diplomatic History* (33)3: 387–404.

however based on a complex set of skills required of civil servants at the time of their recruitment, well beyond the mere possession of technical expertise. I underscored other essential factors in civil servants gaining access to expert status. Learning international cooperation and developing a strong institutional culture are two key elements.

As an instrument of international technical diplomacy, however, technical assistance was not limited to the transmission of expert knowledge. In this respect, the analysis of the profiles of experts sent on mission confirms the fundamental role of this practice in exporting and strengthening the ILO's position in the world. Carrying out social modernisation actions in national spaces, the selected civil servants were also pillars of the institution that employed them and to which they felt strongly committed. From this point of view, the technical assistance experts, who defined themselves above all as International Labour Office experts, acted as international brokers, working to promote the institution worldwide, its knowledge, its methods, and its values. This posture had a direct impact on the progress of technical assistance. The ILO was not always successful in stimulating the modernising process of national social policies. While it is true that the adoption of new laws always remained in the hands of nation-states and their political class, the various correspondences highlight the difficulties experienced by international civil servants during their missions. Relations with national elites were often difficult and the social interactions that took place bear witness to the equally important weight of actors' strategies for individual advancement, competition between international organisations, or the economic interests of foreign companies. The challenges of technical assistance, the contested nature of the exchange of technical knowledge, the daily work of ILO civil servants on the ground, and their perception of their role as experts will be addressed in the following two chapters.

Chapter VI
The Social Reconstruction of Europe's Periphery: Technical Assistance to Greece and Romania

Between April and June 1930, Adrien Tixier, head of the International Labour Office's Social Insurance Section, went on various missions of technical assistance to Central and Eastern Europe. After Greece, he travelled to Bulgaria on a mission to study social insurance institutions. He then went to Romania.[1] The missions to Greece and Romania were intended to assist governments in the drafting of social legislation and the administrative organisation of social security. On the one hand, taking a closer look at these missions offers insight into the role of international social protection standards in the modernisation of social policy in Central and Eastern Europe in the 1930s. On the other hand, it allows us to question the ILO's responsibility in the social reconstruction and development of this part of Europe. Although states played a central role in the implementation of public policies, interventions made by Office civil servants emphasise the transnational nature of the political arena, and the relative permeability of governments to the discourse of foreign experts.[2]

The Romanian and Greek governments were undertaking large-scale reforms in a context of profound economic and social upheavals spawned by decisions made at Versailles in 1919. Chief among them were the new borders established following the disintegration of the central empires. The newly created or reconstituted states faced many challenges: economic disorganisation, powerful nationalisms, political tensions between states, ethnic divisions, social tensions, all leading to movements of revolt, particularly in defeated countries.[3] Many authors have pointed out that by the end of the First World War these countries' state of development resembled those of societies in the contemporary Third World: dualism, monoculture, inequality and dependence on foreign capital, not to mention authoritarianism, political instability and clientelism. Located

---

[1] Kott, S. 2010. "Constructing a European Social Model: The Fight for Social Insurance in the Interwar Period", in Van Daele, J. et al. eds. *ILO Histories. Essays on the International Labour Organization and Its Impact on the World During the Twentieth Century*, 193. Bern: Peter Lang.
[2] Kettunen, P., Petersen K. eds. 2011. *Beyond Welfare State Models: Transnational Historical Perspectives on Social Policy*. Cheltenham: Edward Elgar Publishing; Albert, M., Bluhm, G., Helmig, J., Leutzsch, A., and Walter, J. eds. 2009. *Transnational Political Spaces. Agents-Structures-Encounters*, 7–31. Frankfurt, New York: Campus Verlag.
[3] Evans, R. 2007. "The Successor States", in Gerwarth, R. ed. *Twisted Paths: Europe 1914–1945*, 214. Oxford: Oxford University Press.

on the periphery of Europe, they formed its "underdeveloped" part.[4] In particular, countries whose borders had been altered needed to adapt to territorial remodelling, state reorganisation and power redistribution, by merging economic systems and putting in place new administrations and legal systems. Economic and social development was therefore inseparable from the process of nation-state building.[5] However, development projects were limited by the lack of resources associated with these countries' circumstances (weak government, incomplete bureaucratic apparatus, impoverished rural population). For these countries, social progress was less a priority than maintaining the power of local elites and fighting communism.[6] European aid for reconstruction was also limited. This situation remained more or less unchanged during the interwar period; European economic and financial aid programmes after the First World War never reached the scale of those hatched after the Second World War. In this context, international organisations tried to address the issue of Europe's reconstruction and foster international cooperation in economic matters. Several studies describe the role played by the League of Nations, for instance, in the field of hygiene and agriculture.[7] Others stress the role of the League's Finance Committee in the economic and financial stabilisation of Eastern Europe, particularly in Austria and Romania[8]. Regarding social reconstruction, some research has high-

---

4 Aldcroft, D. H. 2006. *Europe's Third World: the European Periphery in the Interwar Years*, 42. Aldershot, Hants, England; Burlington, Vt.: Ashgate; Batou, J., David, T. eds. 1998. *Le Développement inégal de l'Europe (1918–1939). L'essor contrarié des pays agricoles*. Genève: Droz; Halperin, S. 1996. *In the Mirror of the Third World: Capitalist Development in Modern Europe*, Ithaca and London: Cornell University Press; Berend, I. T. 1982. *The European Periphery and Industrialization, 1780–1914*. Cambridge: Cambridge University Press; Berend, I. T. and Ranki, G. eds. 1974. *Economic Development of East-Central Europe in the 19th and 20th Centuries*. New York: Columbia University Press.
5 David, T. 2009. *Nationalisme économique et industrialisation: l'expérience des pays d'Europe de l'Est (1789–1939)*. Genève: Droz.
6 Steffen, K. and Kohlrausch, M. 2009. "The Limits and Merits of Internationalism: Experts, the State and the International Community in Poland in the First Half of the Twentieth Century", *Revue européenne d'histoire* 41, EUI Working Paper RSCAS: 715–737; Wonik, K. 2007. "Social Insurance Expansion and Political Regime Dynamics in Europe, 1880–1945", *Social Science Quarterly* 88(2): 494–514.
7 Borowy, I. 2009. *Coming to Terms with World Health: The League of Nations Health Organisation, 1921–1946*. Frankfurt a.M., Bern [etc.]: Peter Lang.
8 Racianu, I. 2012. "La mission de Charles Rist en Roumanie (1929–1932)", in Feiertag, O., Margairaz, M. eds. *Les Banques centrales à l'échelle du monde. L'internationalisation des banques centrales des débuts du xxe siècle à nos jours*, 59–78. Paris: Presses de Sciences Po; Beyersdorf, F. 2011. "'Credit or Chaos'? The Austrian Stabilisation Programme of 1923 and the League of Nations", in Laqua, D. ed. *Internationalism Reconfigured. Transnational Ideas and Movements be-*

lighted the circulation of social insurance models as promoted by the ILO in Central and Eastern Europe.[9] Other research has provided an understanding of the ILO's participation in the reconstruction of agricultural economies, focusing on attempts to link international labour legislation to the problems of agricultural workers.[10] However, the ILO's activities in this area did not lead to an international coordination of agrarian reforms. In Chapter 1, I analysed Thomas' proposals for the international coordination of public works, recommended as early as 1931 to boost the economy and employment in Europe. The driving force behind his proposals was the belief that developing economic exchange within Europe would help restore economies affected by the economic crisis and pacify social relations. In the 1930s, this idea took hold and came to be widely shared by European planists, of which Thomas was one of the main proponents. Technical assistance was another aspect of this economic diplomacy, which the ILO was seeking to build in Europe. The analysis of the missions in Romania and Greece aims to highlight the importance of Central and Eastern Europe as a field for the application of international technical assistance practices. While it is true that technical assistance practitioners did not tend to consider their work in terms of development, the principles that guided their action were not entirely foreign to this idea. By studying technical assistance to Romania and Greece, some of the central characteristics of the development practices are revealed: the rationalisation and organisation of economic and social life, the institutionalisation of social policy, and the need for direct contact with reality.

First, I will present an overview of the development of social protection policies in Central and Eastern Europe in order to assess the scope of the ILO's influence in this region. Second, closely observing how the missions of technical assistance unfolded will underscore the potential, and limits, of Office action when it came to disseminating technical expertise, which was an important source of institutional competition, particularly with the League of Nations. I will focus on the ways in which Office civil servants operated and the extent to which they succeeded in encouraging a process of social development focused on the social protection of industrial workers.

---

tween the World Wars, 135–157. London: I. B. Tauris; Flandreau, M. ed. 2003. *Money Doctors: The Experience of International Financial Advising, 1850–2000*. London: Routledge.
9 Kott, S. 2010. "Constructing a European Social Model".
10 Forclaz, A. R. 2011. "A New Target for International Social Reform: The International Labour Organisation and Working and Living Conditions in Agriculture in the Interwar Years", *Journal of Contemporary European History* 20(3): 307–329.

1 European Modernity and the Development of Social Policy

Since the 1920s, Albert Thomas had pushed for international research on the economic and social problems in Central and Eastern Europe. These attempts to map the economy of the region were, according to the Office Director, a prerequisite for the construction of a genuine pan-European economic and social development policy. For Thomas this dream of constructing an economically and politically integrated Europe required the development of social protection and the modernisation of industrial production. However, the instability in this region at the time, one also largely dominated by agriculture, limited the participation of Central and Eastern European countries in Office activities, as well as in the construction of the social Europe Thomas envisioned. Social policies were thus developed extremely slowly, attesting to the hypothesised presence of a centre and a periphery in the movement towards social progress.[11]

1.1 The Difficult Reconstruction of Central and Eastern Europe

Historian and geographer by training, Albert Thomas had travelled all over Europe to better understand the world of labour.[12] Before all else, these were diplomatic missions. They were peppered with official meetings, political discussions on current national and international situations, meetings with employers and workers and, of course, negotiations on the ratification of ILO conventions. Thomas was also interested in the economic and social conditions of the countries he visited. The notes he took during these trips provide a rich, complex and contrasting picture of the social reform movement in Europe in the 1920s and 1930s.[13] Thomas' travels enabled him to take stock of the repercussions of the First World War, and contributed to forging in him the image, albeit somewhat romantic, of an economically and socially divided Europe. The 1921 to 1931 missions, in particular, testify to the relative stagnation of social policy development in this region, as well as to the ILO's limited influence. In 1927, as he

---

[11] Francis Delaisi saw this as an opposition between Europe A (of the steam horse) and Europe B (of the draught horse). Delaisi, F. 1929. *Les Deux Europes : Europe industrielle et Europe agricole*. Paris: Payot. Thomas uses this terminology. "Speech to the Alliance Française in Sofia", February 26, 1930. CAT 1/30/1/3, ILOA.

[12] Aglan, A. 2008. "Albert Thomas, historien du temps présent", *Les Cahiers Irice* 2(2): 23–38.

[13] Hoehtker, D., Kott, S. eds. 2015. *À la rencontre de l'Europe au travail. Récits de voyages d'Albert Thomas (1920–1932)*. Paris, Genève: Publications de la Sorbonne, Bureau international du travail.

visited the Agricultural Museum in Budapest, Thomas wrote: "Truly, this museum blatantly exposes Europe's need for an economic and administrative reorganisation. But the impression we are left with here is, still and always, of a kind of intellectual and social stagnation, remnant of the war."[14] Thomas' observations highlight the area's state of underdevelopment compared to Western Europe. In Lithuania, in Kovno, for instance, the low urbanisation levels driven by the influence of the Russian empire struck him: "Kaunas (Kovno) looks and feels quite provincial. Small horse-drawn trams run through the uneven streets. There are one or two boulevards, with a pedestrian walkway through the middle, under the trees. Two poorly paved roads flank each side, and the line of alternating wooden houses and stone buildings are reminiscent of Russian cities."[15] Regarding industrialisation and workers' living conditions, his overall impression remained that low-productivity activity still dominated the economy. While in Hungary, where the government had embarked on an industrialisation programme in hopes to off-set the effects of its atrophied economic market following the tightening of its borders, Thomas noted: "The war, due to its difficulties, intensified this effort towards Hungarian industry. Large textile factories, in particular, have been created. There are 35,000 workers in the textile industry. But this industry imposes quite heavy burdens. In addition, it has difficulty training its workforce, as the country is almost entirely an agricultural nation to this day."[16] This region's economic development was also hampered by the international economic context. The fall of the Austro-Hungarian Empire led to the disintegration of the economic market. Growing agricultural production overseas and reduced prices competed with the sale of agricultural products from Central Europe. Czechoslovakia and Austria had erected customs barriers. Western Europe had also made it more difficult for Central and Eastern European industries to compete in interna-

---

14 *Ibid.*, 169. Original quote in French: "Vraiment, la nécessité d'une réorganisation économique et administrative de l'Europe éclate aux yeux, dans ce musée. Mais l'impression qu'on y éprouve, c'est encore et toujours cette espèce de stagnation de la vie intellectuelle et sociale depuis la guerre".
15 *Ibid.*, 100. Original quote in French: "Kaunas (Kovno) a tout à fait l'air provincial. Par les rues inégales courent de petits tramways trainés par des chevaux. Il y a un ou deux boulevards, avec une promenade pour les piétons, sous les arbres, au milieu. Deux chaussées mal pavées de chaque côté et la ligne des maisons de bois alternant avec quelques bâtiments de pierre qui rappellent tout à fait les villes russes".
16 *Ibid.*, 150. Original quote in French: "La guerre, en raison de ses difficultés, a accentué cet effort vers une industrie hongroise. De grandes usines de textile, en particulier, ont été créées. Il y a 35 000 ouvriers dans le textile. Mais cette industrie impose d'assez lourdes charges. De plus, elle a de la peine à former sa main-d'œuvre, le pays étant presque tout entier, jusqu'à ce jour, un pays agricole".

tional markets. At a reception in Riga, Thomas met the owner of a spinning company, who reportedly declared: "The Latvian industry is sick, morally and physically ill. Europe is abandoning it, funds are insufficient".[17] Despite promises made in Paris in 1919, loans from Western European governments had been limited to say the least, and by the end of the economic crisis, had almost entirely dried up. Western Europe quickly lost interest in the industrial development of Central and Eastern Europe.[18] The economies of Central and Eastern Europe were, after all, largely dominated by the agricultural sector. The ILO was thus not seen as a very helpful organisation. In Lithuania, the Prime Minister, Augustinas Voldemaras, said the following to Thomas:

> While your trip has been successful, and many results came of it, don't fool yourself into thinking that many more will come[...]. What is applicable to others and what is applicable to us is terribly different. Above all else, it is agricultural work that interests us. In total, in Lithuania, there are 20,000 industrial workers. Legislation is rudimentary at best. International conventions could not be implemented without significant changes. However, in agricultural matters, your main thesis is to demand equal rights for agricultural workers and industrial workers. But since industrial workers have no rights here, since there is no industrial law either, you can see that nothing is possible[...]. The truth, you see, is that you can't expect big results here.[19]

Thomas understood the situation, but he was above all preoccupied by the social consequences of poverty and the tensions it generated between peasants and workers. What Thomas feared was the social revolt movement that was brewing all over Europe. He was particularly concerned about the influence of communism within workers' organisations and sought to promote the idea of strong

---

17 *Ibid.*, 87. Original quote in French: "L'industrie lettone est malade, malade moralement et physiquement. L'Europe l'abandonne, les crédits sont insuffisants".
18 Evans, R. 2007. "The Successor States", in Gerwarth, R. ed. *Twisted Paths: Europe 1914–1945*, 225. Oxford: Oxford University Press.
19 Hoehtker, D. and Kott, S. eds. 2015. *À la rencontre de l'Europe au travail*, 95. Original quote in French: "Si votre voyage a été fructueux, si vous avez eu beaucoup de résultats, ne vous dissimulez cependant pas que vous n'en aurez pas beaucoup ici. [...] Ce qui est applicable chez les autres et ce qui est applicable chez nous est terriblement différent. C'est le travail agricole surtout qui nous intéresse. En tout, dans la Lituanie, il y a 20 000 ouvriers industriels. Il y a une législation rudimentaire. Les conventions internationales ne pourraient pas être appliquées sans des modifications sensibles. Or, en matière agricole, votre grande thèse est de demander des droits égaux pour les ouvriers agricoles à ceux des ouvriers industriels. Mais comme il n'y a pas de droits chez nous pour les ouvriers industriels, puisqu'aussi bien il n'y a pas de droit industriel, vous voyez bien que rien n'est possible. [...] La vérité, voyez-vous, c'est que vous ne pouvez pas attendre ici de gros résultats".

trade unionism everywhere.[20] He saw the adoption of a genuine social policy as the best way to meet workers' demands, while acting as an effective bulwark against political radicalisation.

1.2 The Pursuit of a European Social Model and its Limits

Despite many obstacles, as early as the 1920s, the ILO became involved in the process of defining Europe's social model, as evidence by its attempts to influence the development of social insurance in Central and Eastern Europe.[21] The interwar development of social insurance systems in this region is part of a broader history of welfare state building, which began at the end of the nineteenth century.[22] These "emergency welfare states", as they came to be called by Tomasz Inglot, were essentially modelled after the principles of social insurance embodied in the Habsburg (1906) and German (1911) imperial laws, considered as templates for economic and social development.[23] After the First World War, the social protection movement took a variety of different trajectories when it came to social spending, the relative importance of social institutions and social rights. Tomasz Inglot notes that social protection policies in Hungary, Poland and Czechoslovakia were limited to three key elements: a social insurance programme for workers, a benefit delivery system for public employees, and programmes to assist the poor.

Regarding social insurance, fear of social unrest caused by war and poverty helped to build a consensus around its development. The growing popularity of communist ideology among workers after 1917 also became a factor.[24] However, in several countries, the shadow of the Bolshevik revolution – which by the late 1920s was still looming – led some governments to adopt more conservative policies in the face of social demands. Hungary, then under an authoritarian regime dominated by political elites from the conservative aristocracy, pursued a policy of repression. The country's communist movement was vilified, its ruling party

---

20 *Ibid.*, 82.
21 Kott, S. 2010. "Constructing a European Social Model", 180.
22 Szikra D., Tomka, B. 2009. "Social Policy in East Central Europe: Major Trends in the Twentieth Century", in Cerami, A. and Vanhuysse, P. eds. *Post-Communist Welfare Pathways. Theorizing Social Policy Transformations in Central and Eastern Europe*, 17–34. Basingstoke: Palgrave Macmillan; Inglot, T. 2008. *Welfare States in East Central Europe, 1919–2004*. Cambridge: Cambridge University Press.
23 Inglot, T. 2008. *Welfare States in East Central Europe, 1919–2004*, 24.
24 *Ibid.*, 58.

altogether hostile to the idea of addressing social issues, in particular those relating to social protection. This was made clear in Thomas' 1927 interview with Regent Miklós Horthy, which he summarised as follows: "First, I go over the International Labour Office basics. I explain what we are doing, why I came to Hungary. The Regent tries to appear interested. But his capacity to listen is evidently clouded by all his obsessive prejudices about workers, about socialists, etc."[25]

Overall, the movement for social insurance remained very limited, as did the ILO's influence on its development. By the late 1920s only Poland, Czechoslovakia, Slovenia and Hungary had compulsory insurance schemes covering unemployment, illness, accidents and old age.[26] In Romania, legislation on old age and health insurance was adopted in 1912, under pressure from the urban political elite.[27] At the end of the war, administrative disorganisation resulting from border changes complicated matters. Transylvania, Bessarabia, Bukovina and parts of the Banat were added to the new kingdom's territory, doubling its size and increasing its population considerably, from seven and a half million inhabitants to over 17 million.[28] With regard to social insurance, in the early 1920s, the government developed a strategy to limit the autonomy of social insurance funds and strengthen state control over their management.[29] Harold Butler, who went on a mission to Bucharest in 1922, noted that "[t]here is no real interest in social questions in Rumania."[30] Bulgaria also underwent a process of economic and social transformation, driven by the democratically inclined, revolutionary peasant

---

[25] Hoehtker, D., Kott, S. eds. 2015. À la rencontre de l'Europe au travail, 158. Original quote in French: "Je reprends d'abord le BA BA du BIT. J'explique ce que nous faisons, la raison de ma venue en Hongrie. Le Régent s'efforce de paraître intéressé. Mais il a évidemment en m'écoutant l'obsession de tous ses préjugés sur les ouvriers, sur les socialistes, etc".
[26] In 1926, Czechoslovakia acquired invalidity, old age and life insurance. Kott, S. 2010. "Constructing a European Social Model", 184.
[27] Cerami, A., Stanescu, S. 2009. "Welfare State Transformations in Bulgaria and Romania". In Cerami, A. and Vanhuysse, P. eds. *Post-Communist Welfare Pathways. Theorizing Social Policy Transformations in Central and Eastern Europe*, 114. Basingstoke: Palgrave Macmillan; G 900/127/4 "Mission of Stein to Bulgaria. April 1939", ILOA.
[28] Berend, I. T. 2006. *An Economic History of Twentieth-Century Europe*, 54. Cambridge: Cambridge University Press.
[29] Workers' demands for freedom of union in Romania, documents, reports of Albert Thomas' trip, 1924. Speech signed by the President and the Secretary of the General Council of the Trade Unions of Workers of Romania, November 28, 1924. CAT 5–63–2–1 "Relations et informations. Roumanie", ILOA.
[30] Harold Butler's report, July 11, 1922. CAT 5–63–2–2 "Relations et informations. Roumanie, 1921–1930", ILOA.

movement.³¹ Led by Alexander Stamboliyski, the Bulgarian Agrarian National Union won the 1919 elections and launched a democratic programme, focusing on social equality and land redistribution.³² In 1920, as part of the government's policy of economic reconstruction, a new law on compulsory labour was adopted. It should be noted that the Office acted as guarantor of its legitimacy against international criticism, for this law was perceived abroad as a communist measure. In 1922 the government thus invited the Office to conduct an international inquiry on the topic. Stamboliyski felt the Office's presence might help "spread among the public opinion of other peoples a more accurate impression of the principles currently guiding the Bulgarian government".³³ Thomas entrusted this mission to an external expert, Max Lazard, a French economist and sociologist, member of the *Association internationale pour la lutte contre le chômage involontaire*, founded in 1910 by himself and Louis Varlez.³⁴ Lazard had established close ties with Thomas during the war while employed in his cabinet. After the war Lazard also participated in the creation of the ILO at the Paris Conference, and chaired the Unemployment Commission at the first ILC in Washington, in 1919. Lazard's report, which was published in the Office's *Studies and Reports* series, and provided information to Western Europe on government measures taken in the East, clearly aimed to demonstrate that the communist principle of compulsory labour could be applied to capitalist economies.³⁵ In the late 1920s, Bulgaria also sought to develop its social insurance system, hampered by a chronic deficit in capitalisation funds, caused in part by the policy of limiting state budget deficit recommended by the Finance Committee of the League of Nations. In addition, the new Statute of the Bank of Bulgaria, drafted by the League's Finance Committee, provided that the funds deposited by the state would not generate interest. This same Committee then, "considering insurance funds as state property rather than funds belonging to the community of insured

---

31 Berend, I. T. 1986. *The Crisis Zone of Europe. An Interpretation of East-Central European History in the First Half of the Twentieth Century*, 50. Cambridge: Cambridge University Press.
32 Evans, R. 2007. "The Successor States", in Gerwarth, R. ed. *Twisted Paths: Europe 1914–1945*, 55. Oxford: Oxford University Press.
33 Letter from Albert Thomas to Stamboliyski, President of the Council of Ministers of Bulgaria, 30 April 1922. G 900/4/1 "Max Lazard's mission to Bulgaria", ILOA. Original quote in French: "répandre dans l'opinion publique des autres peuples une impression exacte sur les principes qui guident à l'heure actuelle le gouvernement bulgare".
34 Lespinet-Moret, I., Liebeskind, I. 2008. "Albert Thomas, le BIT et le chômage : expertise, catégorisation et action politique internationale", *Les Cahiers Irice* 2(2): 162.
35 1929. *La Loi bulgare sur le travail obligatoire*, 4. Études et Documents, série C (Chômage), no. 3. Genève: International Labour Office, ILOA.

persons", absorbed insurance funds into state funds.[36] Contribution arrears were considerable, and a tendency to withhold the state's contribution to meet Treasury needs effectively reduced the insurance's autonomy. In 1929, Stoitcho Mochanoff, then member of the Standing Committee of the Higher Labour Council, asked the Office and the League to help resolve the problem, without success. Finally, in Greece, social insurance remained limited to government employees, as well as to certain categories of workers, such as seamen and miners.[37] In 1922, despite the adoption of several legislative measures in the 1910s by the Greek liberals led by Elefthérios Venizélos, the first ever to use state-driven economic intervention, social insurance covered only some 10,000 workers. Venizélos social policy, as Lito Apostolakou pointed out, engaged the emerging workers' movement "in a peculiar mixture of legislative novelties, political manipulation and repression – a rather imaginative set of policies combining the 'stick and the carrot' with far-sighted political planning".[38] In 1922 and 1923, the radicalisation of the workers' movement, along with the humanitarian issues tied to the arrival of refugees from Asia Minor after the signing of the Treaty of Lausanne in 1923 and the disintegration of the Ottoman Empire, pushed the government to adopt new social security legislation.[39]

This brief overview of social protection policy development in Central and Eastern Europe aims to highlight the relatively recent existence of the social reform movement in the region, with the notable exception of Czechoslovakia, where a movement had been developing since the late nineteenth century, along with industrialisation. It also shows that leaders had limited knowledge of work done by the ILO, to which they participated only anecdotally. Thomas' criticism of the Lithuanian Prime Minister, Augustinas Voldemaras, leader of the nationalist party, further substantiates this point:

---

36 Note from Tixier to the Director, 16 October 1929. SI 2/10/1 "Social insurance, General Questions, Bulgaria", ILOA. Original quote in French: Le Comité financier de la SDN "considérant que les fonds de l'assurance sont la propriété de l'État et non de la collectivité des assurés, a assimilé les fonds des assurances à des fonds de l'État."
37 Matsaganis, M. 2005. "Greece-Fighting with Hands Tied behind the Back. Anti-Poverty Policy without Minimum Income", in Ferrera, M. ed. *Welfare State Reform in Southern Europe: Fighting Poverty and Social Exclusion in Italy, Spain, Portugal and Greece*, 25. Routledge: EUI Studies in the Political Economy of the Welfare State
38 Apostolakou, L. 1997. "'Greek' Workers or Communist 'Others': The Contending Identities of Organized Labour in Greece", *Journal of Contemporary History* 32(3): 410.
39 Compulsory old-age insurance was introduced in 1922. Petmesidou, M. 2006. "Tracking Social Protection: Origins, Path Peculiarity, Impasses and Prospects", in Petmesidou, M., Mossialos E. eds. *Social Policy Developments in Greece*, 26 and following. Burlington: Ashgate.

And, Mr President, I would even go so far as to add that most people, when they find themselves in such a situation, wish to inform us, I would not say so much as to apologise, but at least to explain themselves. However, since then, since Lithuania has been part of our organisation, it has been poorly and very irregularly represented at the Conference, and it has not even bothered to respond to our correspondence. I do not need to know how your services are run, but I certainly do have the right to say that these services have considerably neglected us.[40]

On his way back to Geneva, Thomas, not without sarcasm, still noted: "Jewel of modern Europe, having failed to reconcile the triumph of nationalities with an expanded notion of nationhood itself, incapable of economic organising beyond national borders!"[41] While the Office sought to develop its relations and disseminate information, particularly through international missions, in Central and Eastern Europe, its activity was limited to building a kind of "social diplomacy".[42]

However, looking at the ILO's influence through the lens of expertise reveals a transnational circulation of knowledge and experts, one that proves the ILO's activities were not completely ignored. This was the case in Czechoslovakia and Poland in particular. Sandrine Kott, for instance, has highlighted the role played by Czechoslovakia in the ILO's Commission of Social Insurance Experts. Within the framework of this commission, the ILO received the expert input of influential Czech personalities in the field of social insurance.[43] Collaboration between the ILO and Czech experts within the Association of National Unions of Mutual Benefit Societies and Health Insurance Funds reflects in particular the existence of a movement towards public, autonomous and democratic social insurance institutions in the country.[44] According to Tomasz Inglot, in Czechoslovakia, as

---

40 Hoehtker, D., Kott, S. eds. 2015. *À la rencontre de l'Europe au travail*, 96. Original quote in French: "Et, Monsieur le Président, je me permettrai même d'ajouter que la plupart des peuples, lorsqu'ils sont dans une telle situation, tiennent à nous informer, je ne dirais pas à s'excuser, mais au moins, à s'expliquer. Or, depuis lors, depuis que la Lituanie fait partie de notre organisation, elle a été peu et très irrégulièrement représentée à la Conférence et elle ne daigne même pas répondre à notre correspondance. Je n'ai pas à savoir comment vos services sont organisés, mais j'ai bien le droit de dire que ces services nous ont considérablement négligés".
41 *Ibid.*, 103. Original quote in French: "Beauté de l'Europe moderne qui n'a pas su concilier le triomphe des nationalités avec un élargissement de l'idée nationale elle-même, qui n'a pas su s'organiser économiquement au-dessus des frontières nationales !"
42 Kott, S. 2010. "Constructing a European Social Model", 180.
43 *Ibid.*, 184.
44 On the ILO's attempts to counter the influence of private insurance in the 1930s, see the files SI 26/02/3/10 "X^e congrès international d'actuaires. May 1934. Rome"; SI 26/02/3/11 "XIe congrès

well as in Poland and Hungary, the movement for this kind of institution was particularly strong in the early 1920s, providing the ILO with a pool of experts through which it could build, defend and disseminate its social insurance model.[45] It was also within national social reform institutions that the Office recruited its members. This was the case of Oswald Stein, a member of the Office's Social Insurance Section since 1922. It was also true of Emil Schoenbaum, a social insurance expert who worked closely with the Office to export the notion of compulsory social insurance, first to Greece from the late 1920s on and then to Latin America during the Second World War. Nevertheless, despite a strong social insurance tradition and ILO-favourable relays, the adoption of international labour Conventions was not guaranteed. Neither Poland nor Czechoslovakia adopted the conventions on sickness, old age and disability insurance adopted by the 1933 ILC, which were based on the principle of social institution autonomy and democratic management.[46] Resistance to the spreading of ILO social protection models did not come solely from governments. In countries with economies dominated by agriculture, economic and political elites tended to develop modernisation policies based on agrarian reform. Fear of the spread of communism among rural populations led most governments to make land reform a priority after the First World War. In Romania the National Peasants' Party, while theorising this new, peasant-centred society, never proposed extending social insurance to peasants.[47] The success of these sweeping projects, launched by national elites between 1919 and 1921, rested on the expropriation of large landowners of Magyar origin in Transylvania, where opting for Hungarian nationality meant forfeiting their right to property. These policies testify to the central role the threat of communism played in the country's economic policy, and more broadly, across Central and Eastern Europe.[48]

---

international des actuaires. Paris, June 17–24 1937"; SI 26/02/2 "Comité permanent des congrès internationaux d'actuaires. Conseil de direction", ILOA.

45 Kott, S. 2010. "Constructing a European Social Model", 195.

46 Old Age (Industry, etc.) Convention, 1933 (No. 35); Old Age (Agriculture) Insurance Convention, 1933 (No. 36); Disability Insurance (Industry, etc.) Convention, 1933 (No. 37); Disability Insurance (Agriculture) Convention, 1933 (No. 38); Death Insurance (Industry, etc.) Convention, 1933 (No. 39); Death Insurance (Agriculture) Convention, 1933 (No. 40).

47 Roger, A. 2002. *Fascistes, communistes et paysans. Sociologie des mobilisations identitaires roumaines (1921–1989)*, 108–110. Bruxelles: éditions de l'Université de Bruxelles.

48 Van Meurs, W. 1999. "Land Reform in Romania – A Never-Ending Story", *South-East Europe Review for Labour and Social Affairs* 2(2): 109–122; Micu, C. 2012. *From Peasants to Farmers? Agrarian Reforms and Modernisation in Twentieth Century Romania*. Frankfurt am Main: Peter Lang.

2 The Challenges of Technical Assistance

2.1 Legitimising State Action and Building Territorial Unity in Romania

To combat underdevelopment, the Romanian ruling National Peasants' Party was mainly interested in carrying out agrarian reform. However, with the onset of the 1929 economic crisis, many members of the National Peasants' Party advocated for accelerated industrialisation as a way to preserve Romania's independence and support farmers by providing them with employment and capital.[49] The year 1929 was also marked by vivid social tensions in industrial areas, culminating in the Lupeni strike, which mobilised several thousand miners from the Jiu Valley in Transylvania.[50] Workers' unions were mobilising to demand more protection. However, in Romania, employers were opposed to reforms, while trade unions were disunited. Some industrialists accused the Office of feeding the rebellious spirit of the workers. In a conference given in Bucharest by engineer Sylvio Marino, director of the *Lemaître* factories, under the auspices of the Romanian General Union of Industrialists, the latter accused Adrien Tixier, who headed the mission of technical assistance, of being a true disciple of Marx.[51] The reports of the ILO mission of technical assistance testify to the high political tensions generated by the social insurance reform projects.

The Office mission was organised at the instigation of Ion Răducanu, a left-leaning member of the National Peasants' Party, Minister of Labour in 1929.[52] The same year, he sent the Office a request for technical assistance, through the Romanian workers' representative at the ILC, with a project he devised himself to unify the social insurance system.[53] Tixier had expressed serious doubts regarding this invitation. According to him the reform project submitted by Răducanu was above all a political coup aimed at "tearing social insurance management

---

[49] Sergiu, D. 2014. "The welfare-state as a means of nation-building in interwar Romania, 1930–1938", 46. Master of Arts. Budapest: Hungary.
[50] Kideckel, D. 2004. "Miners and Wives in Romania's Jiu Valley: Perspectives on Postsocialist Class, Gender, and Social Change", *Identities* 11(1): 44.
[51] "Première lecture critique concernant les principes directeurs de la loi". SI 2/52/2 "Social Insurance. Roumanie: Projet de loi tendant à la création d'une législation unitaire d'assurances sociales obligatoires", ILOA.
[52] Madgearu, sociologist and economist, close to Romanian left-wing activists in the 1920s, was Minister of Industry and Trade between 1928 and 1932. He devoted a large part of his life to developing an alternative theory to both economic liberalism and Marxism. Love, J. L. 1996. *Crafting the Third World: Theorizing Underdevelopment in Rumania and Brazil*, 66–67. Palo Alto, California: Stanford University Press.
[53] CAT 1–30–1–6 "Relations. Roumanie", ILOA.

away from the Liberals". If successful, the project was in any case meant to strengthen the state's prerogatives in a politically fragmented territory. Centralising the administration of social insurance came in response to the broader project of strengthening ties between peripheral regions, in particular Transylvania, and the capital. Some political elites were ready to use the ILO to redistribute power in the management of social security, in order to consolidate Bucharest's power on Romanian territory.

The call for ILO assistance also came at a time when Romania's presence on the international scene was increasingly felt. Under the leadership of Prime Minister Iuliu Maniu, co-founder of the National Peasants' Party, the country had opened up to foreign capital and moved closer to international organisations. In 1929 the ILO received approval to open a correspondence office in Bucharest, and succeeded in getting the government to ratify the 1927 Convention on Health Insurance (Industry) (No. 24).[54] The financial stabilisation missions organised by the League of Nations between 1929 and 1932 also speak to this rapprochement. Ion Răducanu was also active in international networks of expertise, in particular in the Economic and Financial Committee of the League of Nations, where he sought to draw experts' attention to the agrarian problems of Central and Eastern Europe. In January 1930 he called on the League to coordinate measures to rationalise agriculture.[55] He then defended the interests of the agrarian bloc at the 1932 conference in Stresa. It was essentially he who worked alongside Tixier on designing the social insurance legislation project.

2.2 Social Insurance Reform in Greece: A Point of Contention Between the Office and the League of Nations

As in Romania, the Office's assistance in Greece was useful insofar as it helped the government circumvent political and social opposition, and legitimise public action. The Office's mission took place against the backdrop of an economic and social crisis. Between 1922 and 1932 the cost of living tripled, while between 1928

---

54 CAT 5–63–1 "Relations et informations. Roumanie, Correspondance, 1921–1932", ILOA.
55 Gilbert, N. 2004. "La solidarité agricole européenne: des congrès d'agriculture à la politique agricole commune", in Canal, J., Pécout, G., Ridolfi, M. eds. *Sociétés rurales du XXᵉ siècle: France, Italie et Espagne*, Collection de l'École française de Rome 331, 310–326. Rome: École française de Rome; David, T. 2009. *Nationalisme économique et industrialisation: L'expérience des pays d'Europe de l'Est (1789–1939)*, 180. Genève: Droz.

and 1931 the daily wage of workers fell by 11 per cent.⁵⁶ By 1932, 40 per cent of the working population in Greece was unemployed. Social forces were mobilising, demanding job creation and the establishment of a social insurance system.⁵⁷ The movement for the adoption of new social legislation began in 1928 with the return to power of Eleftherios Venizélos. The government's plans were driven above all by the desire to reduce the pressure exerted by Greek workers' organisations on the government,⁵⁸ and to integrate the working classes, considered as potential sources of resistance, into the national reconstruction project. In early 1930 a government project for social reform was submitted to and approved by employers' and workers' organisations, with the exception of socialist trade unionists who found the insurance benefits to be insufficient.⁵⁹ According to a report by the Social Insurance Section of the Office, some Greek industrialists were however mobilising with "extreme violence" against the reform projec.⁶⁰ The Office's intervention in Greece cannot, however, be understood solely as an action of social mediation. Competition between the ILO and the League over the development of social and health policies in Greece was also a driving force.

Since 1925 the Hygiene Section of the League, then headed by the Polish Ludwik Rajchman, had been working with the Greek government to develop a public health policy that would address the settlement of refugees from Asia Minor in the country.⁶¹ The lack of health institutions and the shortage of experts in the face of such a monumental task explain the need to call on the League's advice. During Rajchman's visit to Athens in February 1929, important discussions on social insurance took place with representatives of workers' organisations. Through the press, the ILO learned that the government had committed

---

56 Nikolaidis, G., Sakellaropoulos, S. 2012. "Social Policy in Greece in the Interwar Period Events. Conflicts, and Conceptual Transformations", SAGE Open 2(4): 9. http://sgo.sagepub.com [last accessed 17.09.2019].
57 Petmesidou, M. 2006. "Tracking Social Protection: Origins, Path Peculiarity, Impasses and Prospects", in Petmesidou, M., Mossialos E. eds. *Social Policy Developments in Greece*, 27. Burlington: Ashgate.
58 SI 2/26/3 "Social Insurance Greece. Projet de loi tendant à l'institution d'un système général d'assurances sociales obligatoires", ILOA.
59 Note from Tixier to Albert Thomas, February 6, 1931. SI 2/26/3, ILOA.
60 Report on the social insurance situation in Greece, 10 February 1930. SI 2/26/1 "Social Insurance. General questions. Greece", ILOA.
61 Theodorou, V., Karakatsani, D. 2008. "Health Policy in Interwar Greece: The Intervention by the League of Nations Health Organisation", *Dynamis* 28: 53–75; Weindling, P. ed. 2007. *International Health Organisations and Movements, 1918–1939*, 301–305. Cambridge: Cambridge University Press.

to drafting a bill on compulsory insurance covering accidents and occupational diseases, as well as to organising a comprehensive system of compulsory social insurance covering illness, disability, old age and death, with the support of the League of Nations' Hygiene Section. The details of the Greek reform programme were then discussed on 22 February 1929 in Geneva, within the framework of the League's Joint Commission on Hygiene and Health Insurance. Tixier and Oswald Stein, who attended this meeting, reported to Albert Thomas with some concern regarding the influence of the League on the development of social insurance in Greece. The recommendations made by the Joint Commission put the Office in a difficult position, despite Rajchman's proposal to consult the Social Insurance Section of the Office. Besides, Tixier insisted on the international imbroglio that would result from the Office's involvement in a collaboration between the Greek government and the League of Nations, resulting in the publication of a report outside the ILO's authority![62] He asked Thomas to take action directly with the Greek government, as well as to intervene with Rajchman, whose action in Greece, he believed, threatened the future position of the ILO: "Dr. Rajchman has it easy, because, while claiming that he limits his work and interventions to aspects of insurance concerning health, with some skill manages to pull everything into it and all regulation on the delimitation of attributions remains and will remain powerless."[63] The real problem was that hygienists at the League and the Office were increasingly opposed, particularly on the question of the organisation of the Medical Service. The position of the ILO, as defined in the 1927 Sickness Insurance Convention, was to defend the autonomy of health insurance. For Rajchman, on the other hand, the development of social insurance was linked to improving hygiene conditions. For him, at least a portion of health insurance benefits therefore had to be administered by public health services. The opposition between Tixier and Rajchman was therefore not so much political as opinion-based, born of the diverging perspectives on social insurance that prevailed at the ILO and the League of Nations at the time.

Cooperation between the League of Nations and the Greek government forced the Office out of its shell, and to move beyond its policy of "passive resistance". Following discussions with Tixier, Thomas sent a letter to Andreas Zak-

---

[62] Tixier Report, February 22, 1929. SI 2/26/2 "Greece. Reorganisation of sanitary administration and social insurance. Draft of the commission of Enquiry of the Health Section of the League of Nations", ILOA.

[63] Tixier's note, February 25, 1929. SI 2/26/2. Original quote in French: "Le Dr. Rajchman a le jeu facile, car, tout en affirmant qu'il limite ses travaux et ses interventions aux aspects de l'assurance qui ont un intérêt sanitaire, avec un peu d'adresse il arrive à y faire tout entrer et tous les règlements sur la délimitation des attributions demeurent et demeureront impuissants".

kas, Director of Labour and Social Welfare at the National Labour Office, in hopes of convincing him of working with the Office rather than with the League's hygiene department. Thomas insisted on the need to avoid imposing "on the working class alone the financial burden necessary for the functioning of a public health service benefitting the entire population."[64] At the same time, and following an interview with Rajchman, Thomas succeeded in having Tixier admitted onto the League's Hygiene Commission, which was to go to Athens in March 1929 to launch an inquiry and give recommendations on the hygiene policy. Tixier's presence on this commission allowed the ILO to defend its point of view and to participate in the drafting of the expert report, later presented to the International Health Committee. Tixier also managed to arrange with Prime Minister Venizélos that he send to the Office the draft bill on compulsory insurance covering occupational accidents, occupational diseases, maternity, disability, old age and death; which was to include a detailed request for recommendations. This in turn led to the Office sending a mission of technical assistance.

3 The Effects of Technical Assistance

The first stage of technical assistance consisted in Office civil servants analysing draft bills drawn up by government. Regardless of the national context, working methods and solutions recommended by Office civil servants remained more or less the same. They drew heavily on international labour Conventions, recommendations and technical studies produced by the Office to assess national reform projects. In addition, Office civil servants always put forward solutions that would ultimately abet the application of international conventions. These instruments constituted a kind of "technical boundary" that Office civil servants could not transgress, which in return limited the scope of the expertise they were entitled to provide.[65]

3.1 The Limits of the Unification of Social Insurance Law (1933) in Romania

Tixier's analysis of the Romanian project submitted to him highlights the way in which expertise came to turn economic and societal concerns into objects of knowledge and intervention. He began by making a series of observations on

---

64 Letter from Thomas to Andreas Zakkas, March 7, 1929. SI 2/26/2.
65 Report by Adrien Tixier, 1929. Geneva, SI 2/52/2, ILOA.

the guiding principles, the provisions relating to social insurance, "the legal and administrative structure and the social orientation of the project".⁶⁶ He noted some technical shortcomings, such as the absence of provisions on the unification of the contributions and benefits system.⁶⁷ While Tixier, like most civil servants at the Office, felt his activities were above all aimed at helping the government develop social policies, his efforts inevitably ended up guiding its choices. Office civil servants passed judgement on how public authorities should formulate and elaborate reforms. In doing so they proposed recommendations on legislative provisions. These recommendations were focused on the nature and scope of social insurance benefits, or on administrative aspects. Tixier's preliminary evaluation of the bill, in which he simply "noted key points", was followed by a mission to study the inner workings of the National Social Insurance Fund in Bucharest and new large-scale insurance funds, particularly in Transylvania.⁶⁸ Arriving in Bucharest on 20 May 1930, Tixier had ten days or so to visit the social insurance institutions of Bucharest, the local insurance funds of Timisoara, Resita, Anina and Transylvania, as well as to study the project of unifying social insurance in relation to existing legislation. Tixier's expertise served to further streamline the government's reform project and reduce its cost. Regarding the financial aspects of social insurance, however, Tixier's expertise was highly incomplete and in the end the Office could not provide a detailed opinion on the economic viability of Romanian social insurance. Tixier found himself in the same situation as three years prior, when the Romanian government had asked him for information on the methods used to determine the financial balance of social insurance.⁶⁹ This was due to the absence of actuaries at the Office. Moreover, Tixier was unable to address the question of the free choice of doctors or the question of the recruitment of social insurance administrative staff, since his expertise had to be confined to problems which had given rise to the adoption of international labour conventions or recommendations, or which had been the subject of official consultations by the International Committee of Experts on Social Insurance.⁷⁰

Following Tixier's mission and subsequent technical reports on the provisions of the draft bill, the new Minister of Labour, Emil Hațieganu, a member

---

66 Letter from Tixier to Albert Thomas, March 22, 1930. SI 2/26/3, "Social Insurance Greece. Projet de loi tendant à l'institution d'un système général d'assurances sociales obligatoires", ILOA.
67 Note from Tixier to Albert Thomas, February 6, 1930. CAT 5–63–2–2 "Relations et informations. Roumanie. Informations diverses. 1921–1930", ILOA.
68 Letter from Tixier to Racoassa, 17 April 1930. SI 2/52/2, ILOA.
69 Minute Sheet, March 4, 1933. SI 2/52/2, ILOA.
70 Report by Adrien Tixier, 1929. Geneva, SI 2/52/2. ILOA.

of the former Romanian National Party in Transylvania and Banat, then member of the National Peasants' Party, indicated to Albert Thomas that the Office's opinion would be taken into account. He spoke of drafting a new bill, in consultation with Romanian trade unions grouped under the General Confederation of Labour (GCL), which had not been done during the collaboration between Tixier and Răducanu.[71] On 4 and 6 April 1933 the Romanian Chamber and Senate adopted a law for the unification of social insurance, the main lines of which, according to Tixier, met international standards and rationalisation requirements: "I only did a quick review of the new law, but my first impression is excellent."[72] The new legislation unified and coordinated coverage for work accidents, sickness, maternity, disability and death.[73] The organisation of insurance was essentially territorial in nature. The management of occupational risks was entrusted to the National Social Security Fund, which could draw on territorial funds or mutual societies for this purpose. Territorial social insurance funds formed autonomous mutual societies, each of which had about 10,000 employees. They were administered by a Board of 12 to 18 members, composed in equal parts of representatives of employers and employees, the Director and Chief Medical Officer of the Fund, as well as the Chief Medical Officer of Health Services for the territorial district or city in which the Fund was located.

In accordance with the principles of ILO international conventions, the legislation aimed for social insurance funds to remain autonomous and to be managed democratically. The resources for social insurance consisted of contributions payable by insured persons and their employers, an additional contribution for accident insurance, a government contribution and miscellaneous income. All these resources formed the "Social Insurance Mutual Fund", which was responsible for covering the various risks included in the new legislation, as well as old age.[74] However, according to Tixier, the financial bases established by the national administrators did not guarantee the economic viability of Romanian social insurance. The law provided for an overall contribution of only six per cent from the insured worker and the employer, which made it impossible to pay all of this legislation's proposed benefits.[75] Despite the shortcom-

---

71 Report of the Romanian correspondent, 1930. SI 2/52/2, ILOA.
72 Letter from Tixier to Vladesco-Racoassa, May 18, 1933. SI 2/52/4 "Rumania. New insurance legislation. April 1933", ILOA. Original quote in French: "Je n'ai fait qu'un examen rapide de la nouvelle loi, mais ma première impression est excellente. C'est un progrès considérable et les lignes générales de l'organisation administrative me paraissent très rationnelles."
73 *Informations Sociales*, volume XLIII, no. 5, 1.08.1932, ILOA.
74 Tixier's report. SI 2/52/4. ILOA.
75 Note from Tixier to Cyrille Dechamp, June 12, 1933. SI 2/52/4, ILOA.

ings of the new Unification Social Insurance Law, it clearly bears the stamp of the ILO's influence.

3.2 Czech Experts to Support the Development of Social Insurance in Greece

Concerning the Greek social insurance project, while Tixier generally found the draft bill to comply with Office recommendations,[76] he criticised its administrative organisation. This is evidenced in a letter sent to Georges Cahen-Salvador,[77] member of the French Legation in Athens, State Councillor, Secretary General of the National Economic Council and close friend of Albert Thomas, in which he wrote: "I find the construction too bold, too complicated, heavy and expensive, for a total number of insured persons that does not exceed 250 000."[78] This figure is difficult to ascertain, since no employee statistics existed at the time in Greece. Moreover, in the decade leading up to this project, not a single financial forecast was made for social insurance legislation, which had remained largely unimplemented. Tixier felt it was precisely the absence of national actuaries that explained this omission. In the preliminary report he sent to the Greek Government, he insisted on the need to collect statistical data to establish the financial and administrative organisation of the reform project.[79] Seeking government agreement on this point, Tixier asked Cahen-Salvador to intervene with Venizélos and Zakkas. Tixier feared that the need to carry out in-depth financial studies would delay the bill's submission to the legislature until the end of 1930, or even early 1931. He worried that employers, or even the government itself, would reject the project as too costly. He also feared that Zakkas would take these matters "too lightly and [appear] to want to engage in a kind of technical camouflage rather than serious studies".[80] Albert Thomas shared Tixier's apprehensions and believed that Minister Vourloumis seemed more concerned with "safeguarding the competence of the Ministry of National Economy and the au-

---

[76] Note from Tixier, July 10, 1929. SI 2/26/3 "Social Insurance Greece. Projet de loi tendant à l'institution d'un système général d'assurances sociales obligatoires", ILOA.
[77] CAT 7–225 "Dossiers nominaux de correspondance. M. Cahen-Salvador", ILOA.
[78] Letter from Tixier to Cahen-Salvador, November 4, 1929. SI 2/26/3, ILOA. Original quote in French: "Je trouve la construction trop osée, trop compliquée, lourde et coûteuse, pour un effectif d'assurés qui ne dépasse pas 250 000".
[79] Work programme drawn up by Adrien Tixier. SI 2/26/3, ILOA.
[80] *Ibid.* Original quote in French: "les choses trop à la légère et [paraisse] vouloir se livrer plutôt à une sorte de camouflage technique qu'à des études sérieuses".

tonomy of social insurance".[81] As a condition of the Office's mission, Tixier required the prior approval by the Greek Government of his work plan. On 7 April 1930, Tixier's mission order was issued.

From the moment Tixier arrived in Athens, the reform project was the subject of correspondence and discussions between the administrators of the National Labour Office and the ILO. Regular contact between Tixier and Zakkas resulted in the formulation of a completely revised draft bill, which was made possible by an atmosphere of open collaboration. Between 1930 and 1931 the two men met regularly within transnational networks of social insurance experts, setting the stage for the revision of the Greek project. They met in Geneva on 20 February 1931 alongside the Committee of the International Federation of Health Insurance Funds in which Zakkas participated.[82] During this meeting Tixier pressed upon Zakkas the need to set up a tripartite commission when drafting the bill. They discussed this project at a second meeting in April 1931 during the International Congress of Health Insurance Funds, held in Dresden.[83]

At the same time, Tixier managed to obtain the agreement of the Greek Prime Minister to set up a commission composed of "a small number of specialists in insurance, actuarial and statistical matters",[84] whose task was to determine the method to be followed for the statistical census of salaried workers and to establish the preparatory calculations necessary to determine disability and old-age insurance benefits and contributions.[85] The purpose of this commission was to distribute responsibilities between the Greek administrations and the Office. However, the absence of Greek actuarial experts led Tixier to propose the hiring of foreign experts. As previously mentioned in the Romanian case, the Social Insurance Section of the Office did not have sufficient competent staff to both ensure the Section's actuarial work and to satisfy requests for assistance abroad. In fact, in the 1920s, the Office only had one actuarial expert, the Czechoslovakian Oswald Stein, hired in 1922. The Office's work therefore suffered a technical deficit in the economic and financial aspects of social insurance, which Office civil servants would never overcome fully in the interwar period.

---

[81] Letter from Albert Thomas to the Minister of National Economy Vourloumis, May 11, 1929. CAT 5–37–1 "Grèce. Correspondance", ILOA. Original quote in French: "sauvegarder la compétence du ministère de l'Économie nationale et l'autonomie de l'assurance sociale".
[82] Letter from Tixier to Emil Schoenbaum, February 24, 1931. SI 2/26/3, ILOA.
[83] Letter from Andreas Zakkas to Tixier, February 30, 1931. SI 2/26/3, ILOA.
[84] Correspondence with Venizélos, undated. SI 2/26/3, ILOA. Original quote in French: "un petit nombre de spécialistes des questions d'assurance, d'actuariat et de statistiques".
[85] Correspondence between Schoenbaum and Tixier, June 18, 1931. SI 2/26/3, ILOA.

The external experts recruited for the mission in Greece, paid directly by the Greek government, were of Czech origin. The importance of this nationality is explained by the emergence of a process of professionalisation of social insurance actuaries at the beginning of the twentieth century. The experts chosen by the Office were members of the Society of Czechoslovakian Insurance Technicians, founded in 1919 by academics from Vienna and Prague. One of the leading figures in this professional field was Professor Emil Schoenbaum, born in Bohemia in 1882. Between the wars he worked on the development of social insurance and, in particular, drew up the amendment to the 1922 Pension Act. He was a member of Czechoslovakia's Higher Council of Social Insurance, as well as the author of the financial forecasts for most major bills in the context of the complete reorganisation of social insurance in Czechoslovakia between 1920 and 1927. Until 1939, while teaching at the Charles University in Prague, he worked as an administrator at the General Institute of Pensions. Having adopted the most developed social insurance system at the time, Czechoslovakia served as a model for the development of social insurance in the region. His collaboration with the ILO was not only due to the technical knowledge he possessed, but also to the fact that he shared Tixier's vision of what a "good" social insurance system was. While his social origin played a decisive role in his involvement, it also directly influenced the drafting of the Greek social insurance legislation, carried out in Prague. In 1931, in agreement with Tixier and Zakkas, Schoenbaum formed an office in the Czech capital city, composed of a Greek administrator and three Czech actuaries, including Anton Zelenka of the Social Institute in Prague.[86] Unfortunately, we don't have much information on the discussions between these experts. It is worth noting though that Greek national administrators participating in the work of the Social Welfare Institute in Prague played a role in their government's commitment to the creation of a similar institute in Athens. Indeed, Labour Department administrators had directly witnessed the benefits of such institutions in the administration of social security, which they then con-

---

86 Anton Zelenka's personal file, P 3611, ILOA. Born in 23 November 1903, Zelenka studied at Charles University in Prague. In 1926 he passed the university examinations in insurance mathematics, mathematical statistics and actuarial sciences. In 1927 he received his doctorate, with a dissertation in mathematics. From 1927 to 1935 he was employed as an insurance mathematician at the Social Insurance Institute in Prague, where he became director in 1935. During this period, he took part in all legislative work relating to social insurance in Czechoslovakia and collaborated with Schoenbaum. In 1938 he also made his expertise available to the Office as part of a mission of technical assistance to Venezuela. He joined the Office in 1946 as Schoenbaum's successor and, in 1953, became Deputy Head of the Social Security Division of the Office, where he remained until 1967. He then continued to work for the Office as an external collaborator until 1979, as an actuarial expert on technical assistance assignments.

veyed to the Ministry of Labour. The Social Insurance Institute of Athens was established in 1935. Under the Chairman of the Board of Directors, Panajotis Kanellopoulos, it maintained contact with the Office until the outbreak of the war.[87]

The Greek Parliament eventually adopted the bill on 10 October 1932.[88] It established compulsory insurance for occupational diseases, the list of which corresponds to that of the ILO Workmen's Compensation (Occupational Diseases) Convention adopted in 1925 (No. 18). However, occupational disease insurance and accident insurance were not autonomous branches. The Greek government's choice therefore seems to have been based on the solution recommended by League of Nations hygienists. In a correspondence with Zakkas in 1933, Tixier also criticised some of the provisions that did not comply with the Workmen's Compensation (Accidents) Convention, 1925 (No. 17).[89] According to Tixier, despite the law's limitations, it constituted one of the "rare advances in social insurance legislation we have to report".[90]

The law would, however, never be implemented. The 1933 election of the extreme right-wing Tsaldaris government led to its suspension. On 8 April 1933, the government submitted a request to the Chamber of Deputies to postpone the implementation of social security for six months. This delay would allow the government to draft a new, less costly project. The Chamber of Deputies passed the revised bill on 24 July 1934. In November 1934, the House and Senate did the same. The law enacted on 10 October 1934 bore no resemblance to the project developed in collaboration with the ILO Social Insurance Section. According to a letter sent by the Social Insurance Institute of Athens, the law enshrined compulsory insurance for all employees and workers, regardless of their wage. It covered illness, old age, disability and death risks.[91] The insurance funds were funded by employer and employee contributions and the law did not provide for state participation in insurance costs. Internal political unrest further delayed its implementation and it was not until 1 December 1937 that it entered into force in Greece's main cities.

---

87 SI 2/26/1, SI 2/26/5, ILOA.
88 Letter from the Minister of National Economy of Costa Rica to Albert Thomas, October 17, 1932. SI 2/26/5 "Greece. New legislation on social insurance. October 1932", ILOA.
89 Correspondence between Tixier and Andreas Zakkas, January 17, 1933. SI 2/26/5, ILOA.
90 Note from Tixier, 16 January 1933. SI 2/26/5, ILOA. Original quote in French: l'un "des rarissimes progrès des législations d'assurance sociales que nous ayons à signaler".
91 Only the risk of unemployment remained outside its scope. Note sent by the Social Insurance Institute of Greece, 11 February 1938. SI 2/26/5.

Conclusion

Attempts to build an economic and social Europe during the 1920s and 1930s were foundational for Europe,[92] and in many ways for international organisations. In this respect, the Office's technical assistance to Greece and Romania were rare attempts to carry out direct social reform work in collaboration with governments.[93] From 1933 onwards Nazi Germany started to dominate the Balkans politically and economically, putting an end to ILO initiatives in the region.[94] The ILO Social Insurance Section maintained relations with Central and Eastern Europe as best it could, as evidenced by Stein's missions to Austria, Hungary, Czechoslovakia and Poland in 1935, and Bulgaria in 1939.[95] However, for the Office, there remained little to do in the region except to provide information on migrant workers' rights and on the social clauses contained in trade treaties between Germany and the countries of South-East Europe.[96]

ILO Technical assistance reflected the Office' ambition to build a socially integrated Europe. In particular, the Office's efforts were directly aimed at helping to create democratic social institutions. However, at the beginning of the 1930s the increasing popularity of corporatist and fascist regimes encroached to varying degrees on the democratic nature of welfare state building, and in particular on the autonomy of social institutions. This phenomenon extended to the entire region. Czechoslovakia alone remained firmly committed to the principle of insurance autonomy until 1938.[97]

Technical assistance to Romania and Greece also reflected a shift in civil servants' perception of the role of social policy, in particular protective legislation. In the 1920s the development of social insurance policies was born of a reformist tradition, aimed above all at ensuring the protection of workers. Howev-

---

92 Bussière, E. 2005. "Premiers schémas européens et économie internationale durant l'entre-deux-guerres", *Relations internationales* 123(3): 51–68.
93 Skocpol, T. 1985. "Bringing the State Back In: Strategies of Analysis in Current Research", in Evans, P., Rueschemeyer, D., Skocpol, T. eds. *Bringing the State Back In*, 3–43. New York: Cambridge University Press. She highlights the role of the state in social change and its ability to implement economic objectives, despite the opposition of powerful social groups and the existence of unfavourable socio-economic environments.
94 Gerwarth, R. ed. 2007. *Twisted Paths. Europe 1914–1945*, 247.
95 G 900/127/1 "Mr. Stein's Mission to Austria, Hungary Czechoslovakia and Poland. April-May 1935". G 900/127/4 "Mission of Stein to Bulgaria. April 1939". The objective of these missions was to collect information on the functioning of social insurance institutions and to make useful contacts.
96 Mission Report, April 17, 1939. G 900/127/4.
97 Inglot, T. 2008. *Welfare States in East Central Europe, 1919–2004*, 61.

er, Tixier's missions testify to the role that the Office sought to play in establishing economically viable insurance systems. In this context the development of social insurance in the early 1930s was at the crossroads between worker protection and economic rationalisation under governmental leadership. This is evidenced by the creation of the Social Insurance Institute in Greece, as well as by the establishment of the Social Insurance Fund in Romania. This extension of the bureaucratic system was one of the mainsprings of the Office's technical assistance work.

Chapter VII
On the Roads of Venezuela: Experiences and Representations of International Expertise

When it comes to technical assistance, Europe was not the only field of experience for the ILO. In fact the majority of such missions were organised outside Europe. Not only did these official trips promote a new kind of world knowledge, they also bridged the ILO and the rest of the world. While these were ephemeral ties, dissolved after each mission, they nevertheless represented a major challenge for international institutions whose legitimacy depended above all on public opinion. This was something Albert Thomas had perceived very early on. In 1925, during a mission in Latin America, he wrote: "Our organisations are young. Are they still sometimes being discussed? How will we be able to highlight their usefulness? How will we gain the full and unreserved support of all the peoples of the universe?"[1]

Thus, travel appears essential in understanding the ways in which the ILO built the legitimacy of its action. ILO historians who have studied international missions have stressed their role in the development of official relations and the exchange of information, which helped facilitate the dissemination of international labour standards. From this point of view the intellectual and social resources of civil servants who went on missions, their ability to understand the economic and social conditions of the countries they visited, to enter into dialogue with social actors and to convince political elites – all these were essential conditions for the success of these missions. Drawing on the analysis framework provided by the missions of technical assistance organised in Venezuela, I have therefore tried to develop a social and cultural history of the construction and dissemination of expert knowledge.

Venezuela was a particularly important area of application for the International Labour Office's technical assistance, having received the greatest number of missions: one in 1936 and three in 1938. The first mission was led by the British David Blelloch and concerned the drafting of a new labour code. In 1938 his compatriot Wilfred Jenks joined the mission, alongside French civil servant Cyrille Dechamp and the Czechoslovak expert Anton Zelenka, who had left for Ca-

---

[1] CAT 1-25-2 "Organisation voyage Amérique latine, juillet–août 1925", ILOA. Original quote in French: "Nos organisations sont jeunes. Ne sont-elles pas encore parfois discutées? Comment réussirons-nous à mettre en évidence leur utilité? Comment gagnerons-nous l'adhésion complète et sans réserve de tous les peuples de l'univers?"

racas in February 1938, where they were to set up a social insurance system. Finally, as previously mentioned in Chapter 4, in 1938, in collaboration with Henrique Doria de Vasconcellos, Director of Immigration and Settlement Services of the Brazilian State of São Paulo, and the Venezuelan Ministry of Agriculture, the Argentinian civil servant Enrique Siewers went to Caracas to study a plan to establish an Institute of Immigration and Settlement.

In this chapter, through the study of technical assistance, I insist first on the need to take the mental framework of civil servants into account, in order to understand the type of discourse and practices they developed in this context.[2] Among other things, these trips abroad were important vectors in the construction and dissemination of a discourse and representation of "underdevelopment". The civil servants' correspondence during their missions is a precious source from which to access a constellation of representations and personal experiences, which the civil servants drew upon in various ways. Secondly, through the study of spaces of negotiation and observation, through meetings and exchanges that took place between Office civil servants and local experts, this chapter probes the social, material and psychological conditions that underpin the production of expertise.[3] In particular, correspondence provides compelling insight into the day-to-day running of these missions, such as the difficulties Office's civil servants encountered in collaborating with local experts. These exchanges also raise questions regarding the significance, scope and limits of technical assistance and international expertise, the latter often appearing inadequate. The internal tensions generated by relocating overseas reveal the cognitive dimension of expertise. The Venezuelan missions highlight the fragility of the experts' discourse and the strategies they deployed to safeguard the ILO's interests.[4] From this point of view the study of these missions unveils the extent to which international civil servants succeeded in influencing reform processes undertaken by government actors, along with the degree of understanding

---

2 Veynare, S. 2012. *Panorama du voyage (1780–1920). Mots, figures, pratiques*. Paris: Les Belles Lettres.
3 Pestre, D. 1995. "Pour une histoire sociale et culturelle des sciences. Nouvelles définitions, nouveaux objets, nouvelles pratiques", *Annales. Histoire, Sciences Sociales*, 50(3): 487–522.
4 Krieg-Planque, A., Oger, C. 2010. "Discours institutionnels. Perspectives pour les sciences de la communication", Mots. Les langages du politique [Online], 94 | 2010, online since 06 November 2012. http://journals.openedition.org/mots/19804 [last accessed 17.09.2019]; Duchêne, A. 2004. "Construction institutionnelle des discours. Idéologies et pratiques dans une organisation supranationale", *TRANEL (Travaux neuchâtelois de linguistique)* 40: 93–115. For a critical analysis, see Rist, G. 2002. *Les Mots du pouvoir. Sens et non-sens de la rhétorique international*. Genève: Nouveaux Cahiers de l'IUED.

they had of the role they were called upon to play in the development of international cooperation between ILO member states.

After highlighting the national and international contexts as well as the issues behind technical assistance in Venezuela, I will analyse the daily progress of the missions. I will focus, in particular, on the practices that made it possible to characterise the work of experts in the field. A closer look at the collaborations between international civil servants and certain local and transnational actors will underscore the dynamics of international expertise dissemination. Finally, I will examine the various constraints that affected the work of the Office in Venezuela, highlighting the fragility of international civil servants' expert status.

1 Contexts and Challenges of Technical Assistance in Venezuela

1.1 Caracas: A Breeding Ground for Social Reformers

The end of the dictatorship of General Juan Vicente Gómez in 1935 launched a period in Venezuelan politics dominated by liberals and social democrats with reformist tendencies, some of whom would help found the Venezuelan Democratic Party (VDP) in 1941.[5] The reformist political elite that came to power in Venezuela marked a change of regime that enabled the organisation of the Office's technical assistance. Ministries run by reformers tend to be conducive to the

---

[5] While a genealogy of social rights can be traced back to the early nineteenth century and the adoption of Venezuelan constitutional rights enshrined in the "Declaración de Derechos del Pueblo", drafted in 1811 following the country's independence, the influence of reformism in the interwar period is indissociable from the construction of Venezuelan nationalism, of which Simon Bolivar was a central figure. Venezuelan political elites were also influenced by liberal ideas of European tradition, which led to the first economic development policies, supported by the "Order and Progress" movement. However, government methods inspired by positivist ideas varied significantly, ranging from the enlightened authoritarianism of Porfirio Díaz in Mexico to the violent dictatorship of Estrada Cabrera in Guatemala. García Belaunde, D., & Antillón Montealegre, W. (1992). Los sistemas constitucionales iberoamericanos, 780–783. Madrid: Dykinson; González Oquendo, L. J. 2008. "Bolívar y la constitución del discurso nacionalista en Venezuela", *Amérique Latine. Histoire et Mémoire. Les Cahiers ALHIM* [On line], 16 | 2008, online on 04 November 2009. URL: http://journals.openedition.org/alhim/3060 [last accessed 17.09.2019]; Dabène, O. 2003. *L'Amérique latine à l'époque contemporaine*. Paris: Armand Colin. For a discussion on Bolivarian heritage and its influence on the discourse of Latin American delegates to the League, see Wehrli, Y. 2010. "L'Amérique latine à la Société des Nations : le rêve de Bolívar réalisé?", paper presented at the conference "Les Amériques latines : héritages et mirages des indépendances (1810–2010)", IHEID, Geneva, 18–19 March 2010.

development of social policies. The Ministry of the Interior, headed since 1936 by Diogenes Escalante, a member of the Venezuelan Liberal Party and future member of the VDP, gave a strong impetus to the reform of the labour law. In Caracas, ILO civil servants found significant support in Escalante. Close to the liberal ideas developed by Espíritu Santo Morales, a great figure of the Venezuelan revolutions of the late nineteenth century, Escalante embarked very early on a diplomatic career and left for Europe as an ambassador. During the First World War, he lived in Paris, then London. He played a central role in Venezuela's accession to the League and was a member of the national delegation from 1920 to 1936.[6] In 1934, General Gómez entrusted him with the task of defending Venezuela's interests in the border dispute with Colombia to the League of Nations. He came into contact with international civil servants during these travels to Geneva. David Blelloch also wrote that Escalante was a former student of the Thudichum International School in Geneva.[7] ILO civil servants also found valuable political support in Luis Pietri, appointed Minister of Labour and Communications in 1937. Pietri supported the introduction of a social insurance system in Venezuela until the end of his ministerial term in August 1938.[8] The Ministry of Foreign Affairs, headed from February 1936 by Esteban Gil Borges, also played an important role in establishing technical cooperation with the Office. Born in Caracas in 1879, he obtained a law degree and a doctorate in political science from the Central University of Venezuela in 1898.[9] He then embarked on a political career and joined Foreign Affairs. He was appointed Legation adviser for several years in Europe and the United States before becoming Minister of Foreign Affairs in 1919. In 1921 he moved to New York City where he worked for the Pan-American Union (PAU) and became its deputy director. He held that position until 1936, when he returned to Caracas as Minister, before being appointed Chancellor. Esteban Gil Borges, who was trained in multilateral diplomacy at an early age, played an important role at the 1936 Santiago Conference by publicly confirming Venezuela's support for the ILO.[10]

During their mission, international civil servants also relied on the help of Dr. Félix Soublette, son of the playwright of the same name and labour inspector

---

6 Ewell, J. 1996. *Venezuela and the United States: From Monroe's Hemisphere to Petroleum's Empire*, 127. Athens, GA [etc.]: University of Georgia Press.
7 Letter from Blelloch to Butler, March 22, 1936. XT 63/1/1 "Invitation from Venezuelan Government to send Ilo expert in labour legislation. (Blelloch's mission, 1936)", ILOA.
8 SI 2/63/1 "Social Insurance. General questions. Venezuela", ILOA.
9 See his complete biography in Picón, D. 1999. *Historia de la Diplomacia Venezolana 1811–1985*, 147–148. Caracas: Universidad Catolica Andres Bello.
10 In 1941, he served as an international law adviser to the Colombia Boundary Commission.

for the Federal District of Venezuela; Vicente Millan Delpretti, Labour Law Specialist and Head of the Agriculture and Cost of Living Department of the National Labour Office; Rafael Caldera, deputy director of the National Labour Office,[11] ILO correspondent from 1937 and future President of Venezuela in 1969. In the 1930s, however, Caldera was a young law student and represented the interests of the Catholic youths, which he succeeded in uniting in 1936 within the *Unión Nacional Estudiantil* (UNE).[12] Finally, international civil servants could also look to a handful of legal specialists for advice. Many of these specialists would come to found the *Escuela Libre de Ciencias Económicas y Sociales* in 1938, enabling the emergence of an academic space where experts capable of taking charge of the country's modernisation would be trained.[13] International civil servants had the opportunity to collaborate with some of them, such as Tito Gutiérrez Alfaro, a specialist in labour law, who was appointed Director of the National Labour Office in 1936. Government delegate to the ILC in 1937,[14] he was also the instigator of Wilfred Jenks' mission of 1938.[15] These elites were directly involved in the reforms of the labour code. Orchestrated by a group of professionally homogeneous civil servants, these reforms attest to the consolidation of a socially coherent elite, formed around the draft labour code and capable of using state power to advance its own vision of economic development, based on a nationalist and reformist ideology. This vision was not, however, shared by all political actors.[16]

---

11 Alvarez García, M. 2007. *Líderes Políticos del Siglo XX en América Latina*, 296. Santiago, Chili: Lom Ediciones.
12 *Ibid.*
13 Plata, V. "La difusión de las normas internacionales del trabajo en Venezuela, 1936–1939: una práctica de cooperación técnica internacional en la OIT", in Herrera León, F., Herrera González, P., & Wehrli, Y. (2013). *América Latina y la Organización Internacional del Trabajo: Redes, cooperación técnica e institucionalidad social (1919–1950)*, 127–160. (Colección encuentros. UMSNH 14). Morelia: Universidad Michoacana de San Nicolás de Hidalgo – Instituto de Investigaciones Históricas.
14 SI 2/63/2 "Technical collaboration with Venezuelan Government concerning social insurance. Jacket I, 1937–1938", ILOA.
15 XT 63/2/1 "Invitation from Venezuelan Government to send ILO expert in labour legislation (Mr. Jenks' Mission, 1938)", ILOA.
16 On the decisive role of elites in state-building, see Stepan, A. C. 1978. *The State and Society: Peru in Comparative Perspective*, 73–116. Princeton: Princeton University Press; Centeno, M. A., Silva, P. 1998. "The Politics of Expertise in Latin America: Introduction", in Centeno, M. A., Silva, P. (eds.), *The Politics of Expertise in Latin America*, 1–12. Basingstoke: Macmillan Press.

1.2 Contact Point: Venezuelan Internationalists in Geneva

The presence of a reformist breeding ground does not fully explain the Office's intervention in Venezuela. Technical assistance could not have been carried out without the intervention of a few Venezuelan personalities, located in Switzerland or Geneva. The organisation of technical assistance was the result of a certain degree of international mobility among Venezuelan elites that facilitated the use of the Office's expertise. These national actors played a central role in the internationalisation of the social problems facing Venezuela at that time.

In 1936, contact with the Office occurred through delegates to the League or at ILCs. The first was Manuel Juan Arocha, Ambassador to Bern and delegate to the most important international technical conferences on intellectual cooperation, disarmament, labour and international migration. Born on 17 June 1892 in Valencia, Venezuela, Arocha studied literature, philosophy and law at the University of Caracas between 1909 and 1912.[17] In 1916 he left for New York City to study. His linguistic knowledge – he spoke French, English, Spanish, with a good knowledge of Italian and Portuguese – led him to take up the position of consul in Geneva in 1921. He quickly became familiar with the activities of the League, where he became the first member of the Latin American Office, created in 1923. Manuel Arocha was not the only Venezuelan to have made an international commitment. Caracciolo Parra Pérez,[18] diplomat, chargé d'affaires in Bern, represented Venezuela at the League of Nations and acted as government delegate to the 1923 ILC. Historian and jurist José Gil Fortoul, a specialist in social legislation and former magistrate at the National Congress, was also a delegate to the League of Nations and the ILC between 1923 and 1935. Finally, the intellectual César Zumeta[19] was several times delegate to the ILC. These personalities, thanks to whom contact with international organisations in Geneva was made and maintained, formed the group of Venezuelan internationalists, whose profile was at the crossroads between diplomatic and academic careers.[20] While none of them were directly involved during the Office's technical assistance missions, the links they established with the Office nevertheless contributed to the preparation of requests for technical assistance. It was they who, in Geneva, at

---

17 Wehrli, Y. 2003. *Créer et maintenir l'intérêt : la liaison entre le Secrétariat de la SDN et l'Amérique latine (1919–1929)*, Master diss. University of Geneva, 93–94.
18 Picón, D. 1999. *Historia de la Diplomacia Venezolana 1811–1985*, 149.
19 *Ibid.*, 149–150.
20 On the mechanisms of the internationalisation of lawyers, see Sacriste, G., Vauchez, A. 2005. "Les " bons offices " du droit international : la constitution d'une autorité non politique dans le concert diplomatique des années 1920", *Critique internationale* 1(26): 101–117.

the very heart of international life and far from Venezuelan realities, organised technical assistance, in collaboration with the Office.

1.3 In Search of International Support

While the social consequences of the global economic crisis gave a new impetus to the adoption of measures to protect workers in Venezuela, requests addressed to the Office reflected more than the government's growing involvement in economic and social affairs and increased need for expertise. The reform of the labour code also came in response to the social demands made by Venezuelan workers, supported by a portion of the political elite, who wanted to counter the influence of the oil companies. International technical expertise was therefore mobilised as an instrument of "social regulation",[21] in a context of growing opposition between workers, oil companies and the government. The civil servants' interventions also took place amid great political instability characterised by the growing influence of Venezuelan communist leaders, who returned to the country after General Juan Vicente Gomez's death in 1935.

On 1 February 1936, Manuel Arocha contacted Frank Walters, Assistant Secretary General of the League, asking him to send a labour legislation expert.[22] The government's official request was sent on 3 February to Joseph Avenol, Secretary General of the League, who forwarded the message to the Office.[23] Interestingly, perhaps unaware of the institution's mission, the Venezuelan government did not pass directly through the Office. [24] On 6 February Manuel Arocha presented, in a telegram addressed to the League, the mission's objectives very succinctly:

> Experts to work on labour legislation preparation and help with general study of social laws. They should have no political affiliation to the left. Preferably – but not necessarily – speak Spanish. Duration and contract conditions to be suggested by you.[25]

---

[21] Backouche, I. 2006. "Expertise", *Genèses* 65(4): 2–3.
[22] XT 63/1/1 "Invitation from Venezuelan Government to send ILO expert in labour legislation (Blelloch's mission, 1936)", ILOA.
[23] LE 229, "Labour legislation: invitation from Venezuela for an ILO Expert to cooperate in the preparation of draft legislation": 02.1936–12.1936" Jacket 1, ILOA.
[24] Only on 17 February the Office received a first telegram from the Minister of Foreign Affairs, Pedro Itriago Chacín, soon to be replaced by Esteban Gil Borges.
[25] See telegram from Manuel Arocha dated 6 February 1936 to Frank Walters of the League. XT 63/1/1 "Invitation from Venezuelan Government to send ILO expert in labour legislation. (Blelloch's mission, 1936)", ILOA.

This request for assistance was clearly linked to the government's anti-communist campaign, aimed at undermining an unprecedented communist mobilisation, especially in the oil-rich region of Maracaibo. During his mission, Jenks also received about 100 pages of anti-communist propaganda from Arocha, along with "misleading" pictures of life in the Soviet Union.[26] Worried the mission might be co-opted for political purposes, Jenks sent the folder to Butler, who discarded it to avoid a diplomatic incident.

A short-lived period of political transition followed the end of General Gómez's dictatorship. Having returned from exile, communists and anarcho-syndicalists encouraged the creation of communist organisations.[27] One of the central figures of this movement was Juan B. Fuenmayor, former Secretary General of the Communist Party of Venezuela (CPV), founded in 1931. The same year, Romulo Bétancourt founded the *Asociación Revolucionaria de Izquierda* (ARDI), a left-wing front that brought together communist exiles and students. As a result of the government's anti-communist policy, the CPV was dissolved in 1935 and transformed into the Progressive Republican Party (PRP), unifying most trade union leaders. ARDI became the *Movimiento Organización Venezolana* (ORVE). In 1937 the *Partido Democrático Nacional* (PDN) was created, assembling members of ORVE, the PRP, the National Democratic Party and the left-wing national bloc in Zulia State. However, the PDN did not receive legal status. The government soon launched a campaign of repression against the movement, culminating on 13 March 1937, when President Contreras sentenced 47 ARDI and other communist organisation leaders to exile. Internal ideological oppositions also weakened this coalition. Non-communist factions and communists split, leading to the re-founding of the CPV and the creation of the *Acción Democrática* (AD) party in 1941.

The arrival of new communist leaders coincided with a series of strikes that shook the country. In fact, since the 1920s, the country had been plagued by major strikes in the oil sector, which, until then, had been central to the Venezue-

---

26 Letter from Jenks to Butler, February 22, 1938. FWJ private archives, ILOA.
27 For a history of the workers' movement in Venezuela, see Urquijo, J. I. 2000. *El Movimiento Obrero de Venezuela*. Caracas: Universidad Catolica Andres; Ellner, S. 1979. "The Venezuelan Left in the Era of the Popular Front, 1936–1945", *Journal of Latin American Studies* 11(1): 169–184; Alexander, R. J. 1982. *Rómulo Betancourt and the Transformation of Venezuela*, 92–117. New Brunswick and London: Transaction Books. For a general history of trade union organisations in Latin America, see Alexander, R. J., Parker, E. M. 2009. *International Labor Organizations and Organized Labor in Latin America and the Caribbean: A History*. Santa Barbara, Denver, Oxford: ABC-CLIO; Berquist, C. 1986. *Labor in Latin America. Comparative Essays on Chile, Argentina, Venezuela and Columbia*. Stanford: Stanford University Press.

lan working class. Strikes took place in 1924 in Zulia. They also occurred in the east of the country, particularly in the state of Portuguesa. To these strikes, General Gómez – who was a long-time defender of foreign interests, in particular the Standard Oil Company of New Jersey and the Royal Dutch Shell – responded with repression and a few concessions. In 1928 the adoption of the first Labour Code made way for the first social laws on occupational safety, the eight-hour workday and Sunday rest. However, the provisions of this code were never applied. Foreign companies, firmly opposed to reforms, could count on their financial power and political influence, along with the steady support of General Gómez and the conservatives, who were well represented in the army as well as in Congress.

In the 1930s, particularly in the Zulia region, an increase in violations of the 1928 Labour Code by oil companies, responsible for organising work in the *campamentos*, caused major popular uprisings.[28] By 1936, inspired by nineteenth-century corporatist organisations, workers were organised in trade unions. They demanded better working conditions, higher wages and better sanitary conditions in the oil-producing sector.[29] The Contreras government also weathered increasingly virulent political clashes led by nationalist elites and directly targeting oil companies, whose existence and privileges were closely associated with the Gómez regime.[30] Faced with mounting criticism, Contreras decided to carry out a series of reforms. First, he approved a law increasing taxes on oil companies. On 14 February 1936, he also established the "February Programme", a reform plan committing to several economic development actions and mobilising a large number of national and foreign experts.[31] However, opposition between supporters of the former dictator and his opponents resulted in a political cleavage that rendered the desired political changes almost impossible. This was the backdrop to the first ILO mission of technical assistance in 1936. As a result of

---

[28] The oil sector was not the only one affected by strike action. The National Labour Office, created in 1936 by the new President Eleazar López Contreras, with the aim of expanding the government's economic and social function, would identify 31 labour disputes in the second quarter of that year affecting all export sectors. Pla, A. J., 1985. *Syndicats et Politique au Venezuela, 1924 – 1950*, PhD diss., University of Paris, 253 – 254.

[29] Croes González, H. 2011. *Transformations économiques et formes d'État au Venezuela : un siècle de "capitalisme pétrolier" (1908 – 2008)*, PhD dissert., University Paris I, 140 – 146.

[30] On the personal links between Gómez and the oil companies, see, in particular, McBeth, B. S. 2002. *Juan Vicente Gómez and the oil companies in Venezuela, 1908 – 1935*. Cambridge [etc.]: Cambridge University Press.

[31] For an analysis of the growing involvement of experts in Venezuela in the field of environment and agriculture, see McCook, S. G. 2000. *States of Nature: Science, Agriculture, and Environment in the Spanish Caribbean, 1760 – 1940*. Austin: University of Texas Press.

this mission, opposition to the new labour code David Blelloch helped elaborate crystallised around a series of judgments handed down by the Federal Court, which had become the focal point of the struggles being waged by oil companies and the state. On 13 April 1937, the Standard Oil Company brought a lawsuit before the Court, with the objective of restricting the provisions of the Labour Code. On 19 April, the Court rendered its decision in favour of Standard Oil.[32] The American oil companies' categorical refusal to negotiate with trade unions was also due to the fact that their CEOs were generally against Roosevelt's new policy. William T. Doyle of Shell and Leon C. Booker, representative of the Standard Oil Company, for instance, openly supported old imperialist policy.[33] Tensions generated by American companies' oppositions represented however an obstacle to the development of trade relations between Venezuela and the United States.[34] It is in this context that the 1938 missions of Dechamp, Zelenka and Jenks were organised. In early 1938 Rafael Caldera, former member of the National Labour Office, wrote to the Office: "Someone is needed, provided with competence and authority to save the social progress of our legislation without private interest."[35]

As mentioned in Chapter 2, the ILO had little to no influence in Latin America before the Santiago Conference. Blelloch confirmed this shortly after his arrival in Caracas in March 1936. The ILO was little known in the country. According to Blelloch, the press release announcing his arrival did "not even mention the Office because they were not sure what its name was or in just what way I was connected with it".[36] The absence of a correspondence office in Caracas deprived the Office of an important institutional relay.[37] Although missions had been organised by the Office in 1934 and 1936, Venezuela was not a high priority

---

[32] Singh, K. 1989 "Oil Politics in Venezuela During the Lopez Contreras Administration (1936–1941)", 95–96.
[33] Singh, K. 1989. "Oil Politics in Venezuela During the Lopez Contreras Administration (1936–1941)", in Journal of Latin American Studies, 21(1–2): 95.
[34] Venezuela. Preliminary discussions respecting a trade agreement between the United States and Venezuela, Foreign Relations of the United States (FRUS), 1936, 955–977; Rivas, R. 1995. "Venezuela, petróleo y la Segunda Guerra Mundial (1939–1945): Un ejemplo histórico para las nuevas generaciones", *Economía* 10: 163–179.
[35] Undated letter from Caldera. LE 229/3 "Invitation from the Government of Venezuela for the collaboration of Blelloch in view of the preparation of a New Labour Code, 1938", ILOA.
[36] Letter to Harold Butler, March 22, 1936. XT 63/1/1 "Invitation from Venezuelan Government to send ILO expert in labour legislation. (Blelloch's mission, 1936)", ILOA.
[37] In 1936, Butler began discussions with Manuel Arocha about the possibility of opening an office in Caracas. XC 63/1/1 "Proposed appointment of Correspondent in Venezuela, 1936–1938", ILOA.

for the ILO, as were Brazil and Chile. The absence of Venezuelan nationals hired at the Office parallels the organisation's lack of knowledge on Venezuela.[38] Lastly, government reports sent under Article 408 of the ILO Constitution did not provide useful information. Regarding these reports, Blelloch mentioned that the one sent "by the previous government" in the autumn of 1935 "was absurd".[39] During his mission to Caracas, he thus suggested strengthening the authority of the National Labour Office by proposing to give it a right of scrutiny over correspondence with the ILO. During their mission in Venezuela, Blelloch and Jenks were also instructed to negotiate the opening of an office in Caracas, which would secure information exchange.

The Office wished to secure Venezuela's participation in the ILO, particularly since several European powers had withdrawn from it in the 1930s. Other Latin American countries, which were not very active in Geneva, soon left the League of Nations and the ILO despite the presence of the United States and the 1936 Santiago Conference.[40] Whereas Brazil and Chile decided to stay in the ILO, Venezuela withdrew from the League in 1938, hesitating about its ILO membership.[41] According to some sources, the organisation of a mission of technical assistance to Caracas was *sine qua non* for Venezuela to remain in the ILO.[42] Given this tenuous diplomatic balance, technical assistance became a means of developing political alliances based on the exchange of expertise. This explains why the Office responded keenly to the Venezuelan government's requests, sending several civil servants. Technical assistance was indeed successful in preventing Venezuela from withdrawing from the ILO.[43] Technical assistance to Venezuela was also part of the Office's policy of geographical conquest envisioned by Butler, who greatly encouraged the strengthening of its activities outside Europe. He had not only perceived this strategy's political potential, but also the possibilities it provided for developing scientific research, exchanging social information and ratifying international conventions. Just as the Santiago Conference, a concrete expression of the ILO's global perspectives, had made it possible to raise

---

[38] XO 4/63 "National representation on Staff. Venezuela", ILOA.
[39] Letter to Butler, March 31, 1936. XT 63/1/1 "Invitation from Venezuelan Government to send ILO expert in labour legislation. (Blelloch's mission, 1936)", ILOA.
[40] After Costa Rica in 1927, El Salvador notified its withdrawal in 1937, one year after Guatemala and Nicaragua.
[41] Letter to his mother, May 12, 1938. FWJ, ILOA.
[42] This is suggested in Butler's note of 29 April 1936. XT 63/1/1 "Invitation from Venezuelan Government to send ILO expert in labour legislation. (Blelloch's mission, 1936)"; XH 7/63/1 "Attitude of Venezuela towards the League of Nations", ILOA.
[43] Telegram from Jenks, May 14, 1938. XH 7/63/1 "Attitude of Venezuela towards the League of Nations", ILOA.

the ILO's flag all over the Latin American continent, technical assistance encouraged a better dissemination of the Office's expertise in this region. According to Jenks, technical assistance helped shape a favourable opinion regarding the Office's usefulness, particularly in areas of concern to Latin American countries.[44] Missions of technical assistance thus contributed directly to the ILO being recognised worldwide as a global institution.

2 The Day-to-Day Running of the Missions

2.1 A Universalist Approach to Reform Projects

Before international civil servants left for Venezuela, the Office crafted an action programme in Geneva, outlining the missions' objectives. These objectives were born of a universalist approach, which did not take into consideration local conditions. Moreover, the Office's limited knowledge on the country suggests that it was proceeding blindly in agreeing to provide Venezuela with technical assistance. The mission that sent Cyrille Dechamp and the Czech actuary Anton Zelenka, recruited to draw up social insurance financial plans, bears witness to this.

In April 1936, through a request for information sent by Manuel Arocha, Venezuela informed the Office of its intention to introduce a social insurance system.[45] The Social Insurance Section responded immediately by sending its monographs on Brazil and Mexico. Then, with little knowledge on the state of social insurance in Venezuela or its feasibility, Office civil servants determined the objectives of technical assistance on the basis of other national experiences, the principles enshrined in international labour Conventions and the resolutions of the Santiago Conference. In April 1936, when Arocha had just been appointed permanent delegate in Geneva, he spoke with Butler about the Office's technical collaboration with Venezuela. On 26 October a new meeting took place between Arocha, Butler and Adrien Tixier, who personally provided some observations on the possible collaboration of European experts. In order to support Arocha's action with the government, Tixier sent him a report in November 1936, in which he insisted on the need to start reform projects with health and maternity insurance. At the time, since Blelloch, who was in Caracas, had already received approval

---

[44] "Some aspects of ILO relations with Latin-American countries", Caracas, 3 May 1938". XT/63/2/1 "Invitation from Venezuelan Government to send ILO expert in Labour legislation (Mr. Jenk's Mission, 1938)", ILOA.
[45] SI 2/63/1 "Social Insurance. General questions. Venezuela", ILOA.

from the Office Director to encourage the government to draft a social insurance bill based on the compulsory insurance model, the Office was acting on two fronts. In March 1937 the Office pursued its work of influence, sending a brief on the possibilities of introducing compulsory health and maternity insurance. In the absence of quantitative data on Venezuela, however, the memorandum merely recalled the general principles, highlighting the technical, administrative and financial issues involved in introducing this insurance model.

By the close of the 1937 ILC, Oswald Stein and Tito Gutiérrez Alfaro had jointly developed a work plan. Alfaro was not a social insurance technician, but he had become acquainted with Venezuelan social legislation, particularly through his 1928 doctoral thesis, *Concepto General sobre la Condición de los Asalariados en el Derecho Venezolano*.[46] Stein, on the other hand, had no local knowledge. He had acquired his theoretical and practical experience of social insurance systems in Europe. The Dechamp and Zelenka mission work plan thus integrated special considerations to general principles. Among these principles the Office upheld the mandatory nature of social insurance, along with the participation of workers in its management. Drawing on international labour Conventions and Resolutions adopted at the Santiago Conference, Stein advocated for a vast administrative organisation programme. An autonomous central federal body, operating on the tripartite model – with representatives of insured persons, employers and public authorities jointly managing the central fund – would carry it out. He also insisted that reforms should start with health insurance. Stein saw compulsory health insurance as the best way to protect Latin American workers, who were more exposed to diseases. For him, the mission should "emphasise that all diseases, whatever their origin, must be covered"[47] by a form of compulsory insurance: "Clearly, in a country severely affected by all kinds of social diseases (tuberculosis, syphilis, cancer), it is necessary to begin with health insurance and to postpone the introduction of old age and death insurance."[48]

The regional context of social insurance development further explains this position. Indeed, the development of health insurance in Latin America remained limited, particularly in Chile, Peru and Colombia. However, this particular aspect of social insurance neither appeared in the government's initial draft, nor was it provided for in the 1936 Labour Code. These discussions testify to the

---

46 Report by Wilfred Jenks, 1938. FWJ, ILOA.
47 Note from Stein to Tixier and Butler, June 21, 1937. SI 2/63/3, "Invitation by the Government of Venezuela for technical collaboration in matters of social insurance", ILOA.
48 *Ibid.*

evolution of the mission's objectives over time.⁴⁹ In Geneva, Alfaro also pressed for social insurance to be given first and foremost to farmers, who were severely affected by the economy's shift towards oil production and the 1929 economic crisis.⁵⁰ On this point Stein expressed strong reservations, which were confirmed by Dechamp in 1937. During his mission the latter insisted on the impossibility of extending insurance coverage to agricultural workers. In his report dated 23 May 1938, he went so far as to conclude that Venezuela lacked the social and administrative structures as well as the psychological outlook necessary for the introduction of a general social insurance system. However, Dechamp also wrote that "[t]he mechanism according to which insurance organisations must operate in principle may be freely determined, without taking into account the current state of affairs, except to establish the most simple system possible."⁵¹ Similarly, in July 1936, Blelloch wrote Butler about accident insurance: "The soil is virgin – there are not any companies in the field doing accident insurance business – and I think that it ought to be possible to draft and enforce a satisfactory scheme."⁵² This perceived opportunity to "create" directly informed international civil servants' awareness of the role they were called to play in social transformation and economic development.

In concrete terms, the modalities of Office civil servants action were essentially based on translating the ILO's international standards into national social law. As previously mentioned, they were not assigned the piloting of national social policies based on their thorough knowledge of local realities. Rather, they were given these responsibilities in great part thanks to an argumentation system developed by the Office, the codes and language of which international civil servants had perfect command. For instance, the way Jenks described his work in drafting the Labour Code and more specifically in formulating hygiene and housing standards in oil enclaves is very indicative of this phenomenon:

Do you know when an electricity plant should have stand-by lighting, whether open air boilers should be bricked in, what is a reasonable size of house to ask an oil co. to build for its workmen, what are the best methods of

---

49 Meyer, J.-B., 1997. *Experts en mission : les coulisses d'un transfert de technologie*, 79. Paris: Karthala-ORSTOM.
50 Croes González, H. 2011. *Transformations économiques et formes d'État au Venezuela : un siècle de "capitalisme pétrolier" (1908–2008)*, PhD dissert., University Paris I, 106–139.
51 Report by Cyrille Dechamp on the possibilities of introducing social insurance in Venezuela, 23 May 1938. XT 63/2/2 "Invitation from Venezuelan Government to ILO to send insurance experts to Venezuela. Mission Dechamp", ILOA.
52 Excerpt from a letter from Blelloch to the Director, Caracas 17 July 1936, SI 2/63/1 "Social Insurance. General questions. Venezuela", ILOA.

purifying undrinkable water under oilfields conditions? Nor I, but to give up the ghost is impossible [...] so I just lay awake at nights and bite my nails in a sort of vain hope that inspiration will appear below the bedstead in a halo of light.[53]

This assertion clearly shows that the Office's expertise, while intended to be scientific, was in fact constructed "through action".[54] The work of Office civil servants also aimed to promote the opening of Venezuelan social law to the influence of international conventions, with a view to obtaining the ratification of international labour Conventions. This process was based on a series of attempts at knowledge grafting but also on discursive strategies to remove from Venezuelan law what was perceived as being in violation of international standards. For instance, David Blelloch underlined the positive role he played in preventing the adoption of legislation that contradicted the letter or the spirit of international conventions.[55]

Careful work was involved in translating laws into universal language, which in fact consisted of standardising the law using international terminology, with each word, title and comma treated as the guarantor of its conformity. This phenomenon is revealed in this passage, where Jenks describes his work on the code's text:

> We have taken a great deal of trouble to maintain uniformity hitherto. We have done it with success over the best part of thirty conventions which contain official short titles. And I think a slip up now would be most unfortunate. I apologise for appearing excited, but you know how strong a parental instinct I have when it comes to short titles and how completely I am convinced that system and method in terminology have something of value to contribute to the development of international legislative technique. Alas you will find many loose ends in the Venezuelan Proyecto de Codigo de Trabajo – some of them we just didn't have time to tackle and when I tried to do something about the others they thought I was trying to destroy that reckless latin variety which is the very spice of life beneath a tropical sky.[56]

The consequence of this strategy was to strip labour law of its cultural dimension, which in turn was meant to guarantee its universalisation. Its "success" was largely measured by the technical nature of the discourse produced by Office civil servants, which can be characterised as "devoid of context", i.e. dena-

---

[53] Letter from Jenks to Morellet, July 9, 1938, Active Correspondence (Mission to Venezuela) February–August 1938. FWJ, ILOA.
[54] Robert, C. 2012. "Les dispositifs d'expertise dans la construction européenne des politiques publiques : quels enseignements?", *Éducation et sociétés* 29(1): 60.
[55] Letter from Jenks to Butler, April 29, 1936. FWJ, ILOA.
[56] Letter from Jenks to Morellet, July 9, 1938. FWJ, ILOA.

tionalised and detached from the social struggles that are at the very heart of social development.[57] This discourse trickled its way into the official reports submitted by international civil servants to the government. According to the Office it was imperative that the Venezuelan Labour Code reflect, albeit imperfectly, the universality of the principles on which social rights are built. However, this denationalisation argument also served as a weapon for actors opposed to social reforms.[58] According to an anonymous report on the administrative organisation of social security by the Office submitted to the Ministry of the Interior and shown to Blelloch, "one Venezuelan sitting on a library could evolve a scheme that would be far more applicable to the conditions of the country than any recommendations by foreigners".[59] Jenks' collaboration on the labour code received similar criticism. For instance, the Union of Industrialists of Valencia sent a report to the Office which denounced the experimental and "distorted" nature of the legal provisions, in particular for their overly trade unionist orientation. In their eyes the code was a foreign body, insofar as it was perceived as international interference in the nation's affairs.

Although Office civil servants did succeed in advancing the trade union issue, freedom of association was still not recognised. On this subject, Jenks noted the following:

> Freedom of association is implicitly provided for in that the only restriction is upon the capacity of foreigners to become officers of trade unions. I secured the reduction from ten to five years of the period after which they may do this but failed to secure deletion of a provision that special government approval is required in each individual case.[60]

---

[57] For an application of discourse process analysis to the activities of international organisations, see, in particular, Siroux, J.-L. 2008. "La dépolitisation du discours au sein des rapports annuels de l'Organisation mondiale du commerce", Mots. Les langages du politique 88 | 2008, online since 01 November 2010. URL: http://journals.openedition.org/mots/14223 [last accessed 17.09.2017]. For a study of the discursive mechanisms that structure international language, see Rist, G. ed. *Les Mots du pouvoir : sens et non-sens de la rhétorique internationale*. (Les nouveaux cahiers de l'Institut universitaire d'études du développement 13). Paris : Genève: Presses universitaires de France ; Institut universitaire d'études du développement.

[58] Cussó, R., Gobin, C. 2008. "Du discours politique au discours expert : le changement politique mis hors débat?", *Mots. Les langages du politique* 88: 5–11.

[59] Unfortunately, David Blelloch does not mention the author of this report. Letter dated August 2, 1936 to Harold Butler. XT 63/1/1 "Invitation from Venezuelan Government to send ILO expert in labour legislation. (Blelloch's mission, 1936)", ILOA.

[60] Letter from Jenks to Waelbroeck, May 1, 1938. FWJ, ILOA.

This excerpt sheds light on one particular aspect of the role of Office experts, which consisted of making observations and suggestions.[61] "I have been asked to sit with the Committee and to advise them as they go along".[62] The role of international civil servants was to guide national administrators in the interpretation, scope and difficulties posed by the various legislative provisions. It was therefore not a matter of deciding, so much as persuading. This work of persuasion was facilitated by the social and professional identity of the Venezuelan elites with whom Office civil servants collaborated. Most of them had legal training, acquired at Venezuelan, American or European universities. The Committee with which Jenks collaborated was composed mainly of government lawyers from the National Labour Office: Tito Gutiérrez Alfaro, also Secretary to the Minister of the Interior, José Luis Quintero Garcia, who succeeded Alfaro as Director of the National Labour Office in 1938, and Fernando Amores y Herrera, legal adviser. This common professional sociability facilitated the circulation of ideas and, in particular, the cordial understanding between Jenks, himself a lawyer by training, and the members of the Committee.

During their mission, Office civil servants also stressed the technical challenges and needs associated with the implementation of reforms, in particular in the field of social insurance. Blelloch, who had drafted a first bill on accident insurance in 1936, suggested to Dr. Calatrava, then director of the National Labour Office, that a committee of experts, particularly from Geneva, be appointed. Following this suggestion a technical section was created within the National Labour Office by executive decree on 22 August 1936 to prepare the statistical data needed to calculate the costs of social insurance. Dechamp and Zelenka collaborated with this section in 1938. While in Caracas they produced a preliminary report and a questionnaire intended to clarify the government's "preferences" on a number of aspects relating to the introduction of social insurance.[63] Beyond the seemingly didactic nature of this document, the Dechamp-Zelenka report was strongly oriented. It proposed a system based on the principle of compulsory insurance. Furthermore, agricultural employees were excluded from the proposed model. Dechamp and Zelenka also stressed that, for practical reasons and given

---

[61] For an essay on the typology of the different types of social science expertise missions, see Théry, I. 2005. "Expertises de service, de consensus, d'engagement : essai de typologie de la mission d'expertise en sciences sociales", *Droit et société* 2(60): 311–327.

[62] Letter from Jenks to Butler, September 14, 1938. XT 63/2/1 "Invitation from the Venezuelan Government to send ILO expert in labour legislation (MR. Jenks' Mission, 1938)", ILOA.

[63] Preliminary report of the Office's technical mission: transmitted by Stein to Butler, 30 March 1938. SI 2/63/2 "Technical collaboration with Venezuelan Government concerning social insurance. Jaket I, 1937–1939", ILOA.

the country's limited experience, the application of social security should initially be limited to the Federal District. They suggested the creation of a central federal insurance institute, in charge of supervising health and maternity insurance. It was to be administered by a network of territorial funds, in accordance with the plan drawn up by Stein in Geneva.

The technical difficulties posed by the various aspects of social legislation sometimes far exceeded Office civil servants' technical skills. "I would be expected to be a qualified expert on every special branch of labour legislation – a sort of Carozzi-cum Vaage-cum Stein-cum everyone else." Jenks' first conversations with Gutiérrez Alfaro in Caracas convey his concerns.[64] Work on the code thus led to tense exchanges between Jenks and Office Chiefs of Section.[65] However, it appears that Office civil servants were not always able to provide precise answers, for the simple reason that the Office mainly produced general theoretical studies. During exchanges with the civil servants of the National Labour Office, for instance, the issue of public supervision of trade union funds emerged. This excerpt from Blelloch's letter exposes the fact that the Office had not taken on this particular topic:

> It would be impossible for us to undertake a detailed study of the question with any hope of completing it in time to be of use to you; but I may say at once that, generally speaking, the relevant national legislation does not deal (directly, at any rate) with the public supervision of trade union funds.[66]

Their apparent mastery of the diversity and complexity of social legislation nevertheless gave Office civil servants the legitimacy to oversee national administrators, who lacked experience and knowledge. The persuasive function mentioned above, which is generally devolved to experts, according to Blelloch, also aimed to channel the ambitions of national authorities which "seemed in general rather lacking in the capacity to visualise the practical consequence of their decisions".[67] This discourse, on the scope and function of expertise, thus underlines another central characteristic of the role of international expertise which consist-

---

[64] Correspondence dated April 23, 1938 to Harold Butler, XT 63/2/1 "Invitation form Venezuelan Government to send ILO expert in Labour legislation (Mr. Jenk's mission, 1938), ILOA.
[65] The exchange of correspondence between Jenks and the ILO's technical sections can be found in the file, LE 229/3/1 "Information, documents, publications etc. sent to Mr. Jenks during his mission in Venezuela", ILOA.
[66] Letter from Blelloch, March 17, 1938. FWJ, ILOA.
[67] Letter from Blelloch to Butler, July 17, 1936. XT 63/1/1, ILOA.

ed in "reducing dissonance" and "producing coherence".[68] In the end the work of Office civil servants helped "smooth over" objections that may have arisen within the committee.[69] Another extract from the Blelloch report exemplifies this trend: "As I anticipated, my position throughout has been rather that of an 'advocatus diaboli' trying to prevent the passage of legislation so advanced as to be unworkable."[70]

Misinterpretations and the adoption of inapplicable standards were generally attributed to the lack of a sense of reality among national civil servants. Jenks also wrote: "I constantly found myself in the difficult position of having to call their bluff and force them to admit that the country was not advanced enough to permit of the enforcement of suggestions which they were making."[71] In the Office's vision, interactions built during missions therefore went beyond the mere diffusion of international standards: national elites were also expected to adopt a different mindset.

2.2 Field Surveys

The formulation of the draft labour code and the draft social insurance law was mainly done within the framework of committees. Therefore they were completely untethered by empirical observation, which illustrates local actors' negligence. Office experts made their recommendations from an "ivory tower". Jenks, who had already spent two months in Caracas, wrote the following to a member of Butler's cabinet, Camille Pône: "My work on the code has been very theoretical and there has been no attempt yet to test the text out against the facts and an inapplicable code will not do the Office any good."[72] In Jenks' mind the work done so far remained provisory, requiring "testing" in the field. For this reason he insisted on visiting the country's interior, in order to gain a better understanding of the problems that may arise from the provisions of the labour code: "It has

---

68 Krieg-Planque, A., Oger, C. 2010. "Discours institutionnels. Perspectives pour les sciences de la communication", *Mots. Les langages du politique [Online], 94 | 2010*, online since 06 November 2012. http://journals.openedition.org/mots/19870 [last accessed 17.09.2019].

69 For an analysis of this process in the context of research on institutional communication, see Oger, C., Olivier-Yaniv, C. 2006. "Conjurer le désordre discursif. Les procédés de " lissage " dans la fabrication du discours institutionnel", *Mots. Les langages du politique* 81: 63–77.

70 Letter from Blelloch to Butler, July 17, 1936. XT 63/1/1, ILOA.

71 Letter from Jenks to Butler, September 14, 1938. XT 63/2/1 "Invitation from the Venezuelan Government to send ILO expert in labour legislation (MR. Jenks' Mission, 1938)", ILOA.

72 Jenks Report, May 4, 1938. FWJ, ILOA.

all been done too much in an ivory tower, but I am to leave for the country in a few days and try and spot the main mistakes before a final text has been approved by Congress."[73] The table below summarises the different stages of Jenks' journey during his mission.

Tab. 5: Chronology of the Stages of Wilfred Jenks' Journey

Dates	Steps
15 February 1938	Departure from Geneva
18 February	Departure from Amsterdam
23 February	Stopover in Madeira
1–4 March	Stopovers in Barbados, then Trinidad
6 March	Arrival in La Guaira
Subtotal	**19 days**
6 March–19 May	Caracas
Subtotal	**74 days**
19 May	Trip to the Andes
29–30 May	Merida, Barquisimeto (State of Lara)
Until 5 June	San Cristóbal (State of Táchira)
6 June	Colombia, Cucuta
	From Cucuta to Maracaïbo, by train then by bus
11–12 June	Maracaïbo by boat with stopover on Curaçao
23–30 July	Visit to the mining region in the east of the country
Subtotal	**72 days**
6 August	Departure from Caracas
25 August	Arrival in Geneva
Subtotal	**19 days**

---

73 Letter from Jenks to McNair, May 13, 1938. FWJ, ILOA.

Tab. 5: Chronology of the Stages of Wilfred Jenks' Journey *(Continued)*

Dates	Steps
Total	184 days

Field surveys should have given Office civil servants the knowledge of local conditions they lacked. However, their intellectual background and lack of experience and training came to have a direct impact on the way they understood and analysed Venezuela's economic and social problems. Indeed, these were measured and assessed based on higher international standards.

Studying Jenks' travels within Venezuela provides insight into the state of its economic and social development.[74] This way of looking at travel can be applied to all processes of scientific knowledge construction. As Paul Mercier notes in his history of anthropology: "These ambassadors, these merchants, and then these conquerors and administrators of new worlds, these missionaries, while they had none of the authority of specialised anthropologists, would nonetheless come to gather an enormous and varied documentation".[75] This information gathering work directly contributed to the development of social knowledge, which was essential in building the legitimacy of the Office's action. However, the production of knowledge in the case of the Venezuelan missions was never objective, strongly influenced as it was by the mental framework of its actors.

2.2.1 "Hot, Ragged, Dirty" Venezuela

In his account of his adventures, Jenks relied heavily on a discursive apparatus aimed at highlighting the profound differences between Geneva and "here". He was insistent in his descriptions of the poverty, poor housing and sanitation conditions, along with the various problems he encountered. In Merida, he noted that:

> It is rather like getting out of hot, ragged, dirty, malaria ridden Venezuela altogether. […] The contrast is the pleasanter as we have just come from the Llanos, hot tropical plains, mainly cattle country, with the poorest of roads and a weak and disease ridden population – the sort of place where you always sleep under mosquito net (in the worst hotels this traveller has met) and take quinine tablets twice a day.[76]

---

[74] Veynare, S. 2012. *Panorama du voyage (1780–1920). Mots, figures, pratiques*, 215. Paris: Les Belles Lettres.
[75] Mercier, P. 1966. *Histoire de l'anthropologie*, 23. Paris: PUF. Author's own translation.
[76] Letter from Jenks to his mother, May 29, 1938. FWJ, ILOA.

International missions conveyed an inverted representation of Western civilisation, in which its own modernity was counterpointed by the absence of structures and the pervasiveness of wilderness and poverty. Jenks, who regularly compared Venezuela to Europe – the altitude of Caracas to that of Salève, "Geneva's balcony", the Venezuelan flora to that of Switzerland, the state of the roads to those in Norway – undeniably exposed his insensitivity with regard to the singularity of things and places.[77] His descriptions directly contributed to the construction of a "spurred by the senses",[78] often miserable, representation of Venezuela.[79] Jenks thus imagined Venezuela first and foremost as an exotic country, where life is simple and wild. These stories also reflected the writer's perceptions. Judging what surrounded him based on his own mental framework, Jenks repeatedly resorted to a racist discourse when confronted with Venezuela's indigenous peoples:

> The chauffeur is not completely reliable – I suspect that he has more Indian than Negro blood and the Negro is […] a better driver than the American Indian – but he is a far better driver than we ever found in Chile and Peru.[80]

This discourse was widespread at the time,[81] and resembles that of Butler regarding the native peoples of the colonies he visited in 1937. As a corollary, it draws the line between the "civilised" and the "savage", widely perceived as dangerous. These observations disseminate fantasies of wealth and poverty, generally devolved to distant and wild lands. These kinds of tales directly fed experts' discourse on "underdevelopment" and contributed, alongside direct confrontation with on the ground realities, to justify their action. In an article published in 1961 in the *International Labour Review*, Jef Rens, an international civil servant at the Office who was very involved in ILO technical cooperation projects, including the Colombo project launched in 1950 for economic development in South Asia, summed up this idea perfectly: "Our experts and civil servants feel that they are contributing directly and substantially to the transformation and improvement of the harsh realities of the underdeveloped world".[82] The civil serv-

---

77 For Claude Levi-Strauss, who sought to warn practitioners, this attitude was characteristic of Western science in general. Levi-Strauss, C. 1955. *Tristes tropiques*, 67. Paris: Plon.
78 Veynare, S. 2012. *Panorama du voyage (1780–1920). Mots, figures, pratiques*, 384.
79 Letter from Jenks to his mother, April 10, 1938. FWJ, ILOA.
80 Letter from Jenks to his mother, March 13, 1938. FWJ, ABIT.
81 Todorov, T. 1989. *Nous et les autres. La réflexion française sur la diversité humaine*, 113–151. Paris: Seuil.
82 Rens, J. 1961. "L'Organisation internationale du travail et la Coopération technique internationale", in *Revue internationale du travail* 83(5): 441–466, ILOA.

ants who left for Venezuela were particularly convinced of their positive role in the country's economic development and democratisation process, as shown by Jenks' assertion: "If it [the code] is adopted in anything like its present form it ought to help in the present process of transforming Venezuela from the type of oppressed and oligarchy-ridden slave farm, which it was under Gómez into one of the more democratic and socially advanced of South-American Republics."[83]

Jenks' letters provide some insight into how foreign experts viewed relating to others. Jenks generally insisted on the strangeness of these relationships, where surprise, rejection and admiration mingled. When visiting the interior of the country, he wrote to some of the Office civil servants: "I leave for the mysterious interior next week."[84] "My real ambition of course is to penetrate to the upper waters of the Orinoco (where the savages still use poisoned arrows)."[85] These correspondence excerpts lead us to question the grasp international civil servants had of the culture of the countries requesting their assistance. While, as noted in the 1960s by Maurice Domergue, a French expert at the Organisation for Economic Co-operation and Development, technical assistance was "ultimately the expert's best training",[86] the inexperience of Office civil servants partly explains their difficulty understanding the environment in which they worked. In the interwar period, the hiring of technical assistance agents was not based on moral, psychological or physical fitness criteria, but on an institutional logic. During this early period of international technical assistance, recruiting experts based on a natural willingness to understand the cultures they engaged with was unheard of.[87]

2.2.2 Inequality and Standards of Living

Travels across the country confronted Office civil servants with the heterogeneity of economic and social conditions. Between the Andes in the northeast and the central plains of Llanos and Guaina, different regions of Venezuela were devel-

---

[83] Undated letter from Jenks, in "February-August 1938: Active correspondence (mission in Venezuela)", FWJ, ILOA.
[84] Letter from Jenks to Clottu, May 3, 1938. FWJ, ILOA.
[85] Letter from Jenks to Rao, May 7, 1938. FWJ, ILOA.
[86] Domergue, M. 1973. *Théorie et pratique de l'assistance technique*, 47. Paris: Les Editions ouvrières; Opler, M. E. 1954. *Les Problèmes sociaux de l'assistance technique*. Paris: UNESCO.
[87] Nations Unies. Comité de l'assistance technique; Nations Unies. Conseil économique et social. (1965). *Cent cinquante mille spécialistes en 15 ans : Bilan anniversaire du programme élargi d'assistance technique des Nations Unies*, 15. [New York].

oping at a very different pace. On 27 March 1938, Jenks, who visited the cities of Maracay, Valencia and Puerto Cabello with Dechamp and Zelenka, stressed the problem with attempting to uniformly apply labour laws: "It was certainly a most useful day and helped to get the country in better perspective. [...] The country is very mixed and the application of any uniform labour standards will be very difficult."[88] What Office experts observed above all was the adequacy of social legislation with international standards. In Merida, Jenks thus noted:

> The standard of application of the present laws is pretty poor – our worst cases were one of a sugar factory where the same men had been working continuously for 19 hours when we went in and had still another 5 or 6 hours to finish the job they were working on and tobacco factories where children under and just over ten work (in some cases side by side with their mothers) an eight-hour day on the making of fifty cigars out of raw tobacco.[89]

Highlighting the social conditions of production was a central feature of the Office's technical assistance and the observations of international civil servants generally stressed their inadequacy with international standards. Whether regarding the ILO's eight-hour day or conventions protecting women and children's labour, Venezuela was far from meeting international standards. Civil servants also focused on labour relations and the state of trade union development. In their reports they generally stressed the difficulty of establishing contacts with trade unions and employers' organisations. In 1938 in San Cristobal a meeting was held with the trade unions, which was first and foremost meant to be propaganda for the new labour code. Jenks' account exposes a total lack of preparation for these meetings, which were crucial to successfully involve workers in reform policies: "We had the meeting there with about fifty representatives of the trade unions present. But the lights went out and every effort to set them going again failed. So we continued in the dark and I read sections of the Code by match light with occasional pauses when the match failed to strike at the required moment."[90] Jenks finally took a rather pessimistic look at these different encounters: "If you had heard my speeches in Spanish to Venezuelan trade unionists in the most dead and alive little slums you ever saw you would have been tickled to death [...]. Of twelve meetings with trade unionists in six different states only one had been a doubtful success."[91] Most of these meetings took place in the Lake Maracaibo region, home to a large proportion of the oil companies' activities. Unfortunately, little information on the working conditions in

---

88 Letter from Jenks to his mother, March 28, 1938. FWJ, ILOA.
89 Letter from Jenks to his mother, May 29, 1938. FWJ, ILOA.
90 Letter from Jenks to his mother, June 11, 1938. FWJ, ILOA.
91 Letter from Jenks to a friend in Geneva, June 17, 1938. FWJ, ILOA.

these oil enclaves remains in the international reports.[92] These omissions in the observations made by Office civil servants are problematic and question their real understanding of the social problems of the country into which they had been "catapulted". Their reports show that the ethnic composition of the working classes and the labour relations conflicts it generated, particularly in oil enclaves, was not analysed. However, the organisation of labour in these farms reflected, as Miguel Tinker-Salas notes, "a complex racial division of labor".[93] In these enclaves, Indian, Mexican, Caribbean, Afro-Caribbean, Chinese and Venezuelan workers coexisted.[94] The ethnic origin of workers determined the type of job they occupied and "social, racial, and national distinctions found expression in the wage and salaries paid workers and employees".[95] Foreign companies' wage policies, which reproduced the racism of their society of origin and resembled colonial practices, were never raised by Office civil servants. The fact that Jenks, the only civil servant to visit the *campamentos*, never mentioned this problem is all the more surprising as he spent several days negotiating the provisions of the new labour code with representatives of British companies.

Despite a biased and rather superficial understanding of working conditions in Venezuela, Office civil servants insisted on the objective value of the work they had accomplished: "On the whole our observations have not suggested very many changes in the text submitted to Congress though there are a few points to be rectified and some which in my view ought to be amplified" wrote Jenks on 29 May 1938.[96]

2.3 Oppositions to the Labour Code

Government instability, political oppositions, the influence of oil companies, which seemed to function like states within the state, and international competition over social policies were all obstacles to the smooth adoption of the La-

---

[92] Bermúdez Briñez, N., Rodríguez Arrieta, M. 2012. "Las industrias azucarera y petrolera en el Zulia: formas de ocupación territorial (1913–1935)", Diálogos. Revista Electrónica de Historia 13(1): 90–122. https://dialnet.unirioja.es/servlet/articulo?codigo=5601839 [last accessed 12.09. 2019]
[93] Tinker-Salas, M. 2003. "Races and Cultures in the Venezuelan Oil Fields", in Peloso V. C. ed. *Work, Protest and Identity in Twentieth-Century Latin America*, 143–164. Wilmington Delaware: SR Books.
[94] *Ibid.*, p. 144.
[95] *Ibid.*, p. 154.
[96] Letter from Jenks to his mother, May 29, 1938. FWJ, ILOA.

bour Code and soon threatened the authority of the Office. Jenks was very clearly aware of this:

> Doubtless the technical assistance which Venezuela has recently received should inspire some sort of gratitude; but gratitude is notoriously an unreliable factor on which to count in politics, the history of this technical assistance has not been as free of friction as one would wish, and if we have made any bad mistakes – which would not be surprising in view of the conditions in which the work has been done, but which only time can show – technical assistance may have proved to be a boomerang.[97]

When the first draft labour code drawn up by the National Labour Office in collaboration with David Blelloch went before the Senate in 1936, heated debates took place and various oppositions emerged. On one side stood those who wished to protect the interests of foreign oil companies, hoping to reduce the social benefits provided for by the code. On the other, those who, like Senator Ibrahim Garcia and Deputy Matos Romero of Zulia State, were opposed to the presence of foreign companies and used the draft code to force them out of Venezuela. In this struggle against oil companies, Garcia's amendments, which were unanimously adopted by the Senate, for instance instituted a guaranteed pension for all workers which was twice as generous as the scheme established by the Office.[98]

Jenks' missions reports also shed light on the opposition of oil companies to the draft labour code. The most important points of divergence between Office civil servants and the representatives of oil companies' interests concerned the provisions relating to the special obligation of oil companies to provide good and safe working conditions in the *campamentos*, along with freedom of association. The provisions of the draft labour code on strengthening the role of oil unions sparked outrage in the oil companies. The British Controlled Oilfields Limited operating in Venezuela thus attempted to thwart the Office by seeking to provoke a diplomatic incident with Great Britain.[99]

On other points, however, Office civil servants seem to have provided support to the oil companies. For instance, one of the central points of contention between workers and oil companies concerned the hiring of *contratistas*, i.e. private construction companies or the foreign workers of these companies, who were often more qualified and benefited from better working conditions and re-

---

[97] Correspondence from Jenks to Butler, April 23, 1938. XT 63/2/1 "Invitation du gouvernement vénézuélien à envoyer un expert de l'OIT en législation du travail (mission de M. Jenk, 1938), ILOA.
[98] Letter from David Blelloch to Butler, June 7, 1936. XT 63/1/1.
[99] Jenks Report, 1938. FWJ, ILOA.

muneration.¹⁰⁰ *Contratistas* were mainly called in for construction (aqueducts, wharves, roads, telephone lines, warehouses, hotels, clubs, restaurants, inns and other buildings). These private companies were also exempt from customs duties for the import of machinery, miscellaneous equipment and any other apparatus intended exclusively for oil exploration, exploitation and refining. Perceived as settlers by Venezuelan workers, their presence disrupted the administrative, spatial, economic and social organisation of municipalities.¹⁰¹ In Blelloch's view, the use of *contratistas* contributed to considerably weakening the national social insurance system as a whole.¹⁰² However, despite the problems posed by their presence, Jenks believed that it was impossible to prohibit the use of *contratistas*. Seemingly supportive of oil companies' practices, he insisted on the importance of *contratistas* in the country's economic modernisation process: "To prohibit the use of *contratistas* must therefore be regarded as impracticable and even as indefensible in principle."¹⁰³ From Jenks' point of view, the main concern was to avoid any obstacle to the development of industrialisation, without much consideration for its effects on labour relations.

The most important provisions of the 1936 labour code concern the 8-hour day, paid annual leave, maternity protection in line with the ILO Convention, the general prohibition of night work, freedom of association, the granting of powers to the National Labour Office, established the same year, in matters of health and safety and the setting of minimum wages. According to a letter dated 17 July 1936, Blelloch made a significant contribution "to prevent pregnant women from being forced to leave work without provision being made for their maintenance, to prevent arbitration in labour disputes from being made compulsory, and to secure for trade unions the right to affiliate to international organisations".¹⁰⁴ After the law was passed, Blelloch worked on the organization of the National Labour Office so that its services would ensure the application of the new law. In 1938, a revised version of the law, prepared by Wilfred Jenks,

---

100 Bermúdez Briñez, N., Rodríguez Arrieta, M. 2012. "Las industrias azucarera y petrolera en el Zulia: formas de ocupación territorial (1913–1935)", Diálogos. Revista Electrónica de Historia 13(1): 90–122. https://dialnet.unirioja.es/servlet/articulo?codigo=5601839 [last accessed 12.09. 2019]
101 *Ibid.*, 108–109.
102 Letter from Blelloch to Butler, May 21, 1936. SI 2/63/1 "Social Insurance. General questions. Venezuela", ILOA.
103 Jenks Report, 1938. FWJ, ILOA.
104 Letter from Blelloch to Butler, 17 July 1936. XT 63/1/1 "Invitation from Venezuelan Government to send ILO expert in labour legislation. (Blelloch's mission, 1936) ", ILOA.

was presented to Congress after Jenks departure on 6 August 1938 but not adopted.

Concerning social insurance, a draft law on health, maternity and accident insurance for industrial and commercial workers was introduced in 1938 but was quickly opposed. On 26 May 1938, Senator Rangel Lamus, who had unsuccessfully submitted his own draft law in 1937, obstructed a vote on the text prepared in collaboration with civil servant Dechamp and expert Zelenka, requesting that a committee be set up "to correct defective points".[105] Lamus' action, constituted a direct threat to the adoption of the draft law elaborated with the assistance of the Office. According to Zelenka, when it was read before the Senate the latter had been in favour of extending social insurance to the country as a whole and insurance coverage to agricultural workers. Lamus also recommended that health insurance and accident insurance be completely separated, calling for the creation of two separate institutions. Even more alarming for the Office, Lamus now claimed that accident insurance should not be mandatory for private companies. For the Office this marked the beginning of a period of uncertainty regarding the future of the draft law it had helped develop.

The situation became even more complicated when on 3 February 1939 Cyrille Dechamp received an anonymous letter from Caracas informing him that a certain Otto Paul, attached to the German Social Insurance Service in Berlin, had been hired to revise Zelenka's draft regulation for implementing social insurance. Paul was a former civil servant of the *Reichsarbeitsministerium* and supporter of the Nazi regime.[106] He had worked for two years at the Chilean Social Insurance Fund and for several years travelled extensively around Latin America as a civil servant on secondment. He was a concrete embodiment of German action on this continent, which sought to strengthen its influence by spreading its own social insurance model.[107] Dr. Hector Cuenca, the new Minister of Labour and Communications, who was "dead against everything done by Pietri",[108]

---

105 Letter from Zelenka, 26 May 1938. SI 2/63/2 "Technical collaboration with Venezuelan Government concerning social insurance. Jaket I, 1937–1939", ILOA.
106 Internal note from Stein to Tixier and Director John G. Winant, February 3, 1939. SI 2/63/2 "Technical collaboration with Venezuelan Government concerning social insurance. Jacket I, 1937–1938", ILOA.
107 Some authors have highlighted the existence of an imperialist policy of Nazi Germany in Latin America, where some countries, such as Argentina, have a high rate of German immigrants. Blancpain, J.-P. 1994. *Migrations et mémoire germaniques en Amérique latine*. Strasbourg: Presses universitaires de Strasbourg.
108 Internal note of 3 February 1939 by Dechamp. SI 2/63/2 "Technical collaboration with Venezuelan Government concerning social insurance. Jacket I, 1937–1938", ILOA.

was behind Paul's recruitment. More generally, the attractiveness of the Nazi model reflected the willingness of some members of the Venezuelan political elite to strengthen social order at the expense of protection.[109]

The Office attempted to salvage its social insurance reform project by multiplying contacts with Venezuelan civil servants and by sending, through Para Perez, a critical study of Paul's project. On 31 May 1939, however, the House of Representatives adopted the German counter-proposal. That said, the Office received contradictory information. Indeed, at the June 1939 ILC the Venezuelan government delegate stated that the government wished to present to the next session of Congress the draft law prepared with the assistance of the Office, with minor modifications.[110] Nevertheless, the Office was seeking to absolve itself of responsibility, especially following an article published in the Ecuadorian magazine *Boletin De Prevision Social*, which presented the German project as one resulting from the Office![111] Despite this, Oswald Stein remained optimistic about the Venezuelan government's sinuous attitude. "Common sense and technique are on our side and will eventually prevail," he wrote.[112] Finally, Office civil servants only learned in the summer of 1940, when trans-Atlantic communications were increasingly difficult due to the war, that it was indeed the Dechamp-Zelenka project that had been adopted by the legislative power. The Social Insurance Act moreover mentioned the Office's collaboration and included a list of the international conventions on which it was based. The law on compulsory social insurance of 14 June 1940 was promulgated on 24 July.[113] It was implemented in 1944 through a series of decrees, becoming operational in the Federal District on 9 October 1944.

3 The Work of Experts in Crisis

As we can see, technical assistance could not always rely on open collaboration between foreign experts and domestic actors. Many conflicts and opposition between the various actors involved in fact plagued the missions. They were the

---

[109] Otto Paul's social insurance project, which Stein described as "demagogic improvisation", almost completely eliminated the benefit of insurance in the event of illness. SI 2/63/2, ILOA.
[110] Internal note of 16 June 1939 by Dechamp to Stein, Tixier and Butler, SI 2/63/2, ILOA.
[111] *Ibid.*
[112] Stein's internal note, July 13, 1939. SI 2/63/2.
[113] The law also provided for methods of protection against other risks: old age, disability, death and involuntary unemployment must be studied. Powell, O. M. 1946. "Social Insurance in Venezuela", *International Social Security Association Bulletin*, April: 3.

cause of much unrest and the Office's control over the missions and political decisions was limited. In this last section, I wish to show that the missions of technical assistance also constituted a real physical and professional threat for the civil servants of the International Labour Office. The lack of preparation combined with the constant undermining of their authority led them to question their participation and responsibility in the reform processes.

3.1 Feelings of Exile, Physical and Psychological Constraints

International civil servants were a special category of traveller. Agents in multilateral diplomacy, they traveled as official representatives of the Office. In Chapter 5, I addressed the consequences of this position of representation, where civil servants on a mission were generally the "trusted men" of the Office's Director. They therefore did not choose where they were sent and sometimes travelled for long periods at a time (the longest mission of technical assistance averaged between four and six months) before returning to Geneva. The missions' length represented a serious physical constraint. For some civil servants, crossing the Atlantic was also a new experience leading to sometimes brutal reactions. "The mission entrusted to me is all but a leisure trip! I accepted it through no will of my own, and only at the very urgent request of the Bureau",[114] wrote Cyrille Dechamp before his departure for Caracas.

Civil servants quickly felt isolated during their mission in Venezuela. Far from relatives – with the exception of those accompanied by their wives and who, like Blelloch, obtained permission to bring their children with them for a few weeks – and far from a familiar workspace, they resorted to letter writing to break the isolation. Jenks' first letters to his mother date back to his journey aboard the SS "Simon Bolivar", which operated between Amsterdam and the port of La Guaira. The letters took between two and three weeks to cross the Atlantic, further reinforcing this feeling of loneliness: "I am almost beginning to understand the psychology of exile," Jenks confided in a letter to his mother.[115] To John Winant, a few days before leaving Venezuela, Jenks mentioned his need to go home: "I shall be perfectly all right as soon as I get back to friends and books and wholesome food and such like things".[116] The isolation of Office civil servants was heightened by the fact that none of them, apart from Siewers,

---

[114] SI 2/63/3/1 "Invitation by the Government of Venezuela for technical collaboration in matters of social insurance. Administrative and financial arrangements", ILOA.
[115] Letter from Jenks to his mother, July 23, 1938. FWJ, ILOA.
[116] Letter from Jenks to Winant, July 20, 1938. FWJ, ILOA.

spoke Spanish well. This also prevented them from gaining access to other local sources.

Office civil servants also endured difficult climatic and material conditions. They often mentioned how hostile the environment was. Jenks remembers the upheavals, both experienced and avoided, during his various travels on Venezuelan roads:

I am perfectly well, have escaped typhoid, smallpox, malaria and pneumonia, have not been eaten by either sharks or crocodiles, have not been in the course of a revolution, have travelled 2789 kilometers by Venezuelan roads with a Venezuelan driver in three weeks without breaking my neck, my ribs or even a stray limb, and in short have nothing wrong with me except an immense weariness and fatigue.[117]

Others, like Cyril Dechamp, suffered greatly physically. Upon his arrival in Caracas, Dechamp experienced considerable physical and psychological difficulties in adapting to local conditions. His war scars – let us remember that he was 100 per cent mutilated in the war, indeed could not bear the tropical climate.[118] The Office's decision to send Dechamp to Venezuela clearly shows the institution's lack of preparation and anticipation of the climatic, geographical and material conditions that awaited the civil servants there. It should also be recalled that the missions to Venezuela took place in a context of intense social mobilisation leading to strikes and violence that directly endangered Office civil servants. When he arrived in 1936 Blelloch was directly confronted with the social unrest orchestrated by the various left-wing trade union organisations: "The students' organisation is a force to be reckoned with, and is playing a considerable role under the new regime. Societies, unions and associations of all kinds are springing up like mushrooms. Strikes are frequent."[119]

According to the National Labour Office there were 135 trade union organisations in 1936 but they only represented some 50,000 workers in the export sectors.[120] Daily, the press reported on strikes throughout the country. The government quickly adopted a reactionary attitude and in May 1936 sought to pass a law on public order that provoked massive opposition from public opinion.[121]

---

[117] Letter from Jenks to his mother, June 11, 1938. FWJ, ILOA.
[118] Letter from Jenks to Butler, April 23, 1938. XT 63/2/1, ILOA.
[119] Lettre from Blelloch to Butler, 22 March 1936. XT 63/1/1 "Invitation from Venezuelan Government to send Ilo expert in labour legislation. (Blelloch's mission, 1936)", ILOA.
[120] Alberto J. Pla, *Syndicats et Politique au Venezuela, 1924–1950*, Thèse de doctorat, Paris, 1985, pp. 253–254.
[121] Kelvin Singh, "Oil Politics in Venezuela During the Lopez Contreras Administration (1936–1941)", in *Journal of Latin American Studies*, vol.21, 1989, pp. 89–104.

Demonstrations took place in Caracas on 19 May, shots were fired and a bomb exploded near where Blelloch found himself.

3.2 When the Status of Expert Conflicts with Institutional Loyalty

International civil servants were doubly constrained: on top of their obligation to represent the institution, they also had to take into account the wishes of the government for which they made themselves available. This dual positioning, as an international civil servant at the service of the ILO and as an expert working for a government, posed real difficulties when it came to maintaining the international nature of their mission and ensuring that their work was carried out in accordance with the principles defended by the ILO.

The Office's participation in a non-transparent reform process, for instance, could have jeopardised the foundations of its action. In Caracas, Blelloch, Jenks, Dechamp and Zelenka worked under the close supervision of the National Labour Office. Most of their work was carried out within the framework of Committees set up by the National Labour Office. "The commission meets every afternoon, normally at three, normally a little later, and goes on till 7.30 or eight."[122] The daily proximity with members of this Office sometimes extended beyond working hours, as Jenks and Dechamp stayed with Rafael Caldera, while Zelenka had taken up residence at the Legation of the Czechoslovak Republic. During his mission, Jenks attended 97 meetings in seven weeks, an average of 14 weekly meetings. The Committee met in Gutiérrez Alfaro's country house, "and his chauffeur [drove] the Committee there every afternoon and [brought] us back to town again". [123] Far from the business that was going on at the time at the Miraflores Palace, the Committee therefore operated in a vacuum and Jenks never mentioned the participation of other stakeholders in the discussions. Workers' and employers' representatives were never consulted, which Blelloch had already regretted in 1936.[124] Wishing to pursue objectives that did not reflect the interests or demands of other social or economic powers, the Venezuelan government would have chosen to isolate the actors in the social reform process, both from the interests of the oil companies and from other pressure groups, such as professional organisations and trade unions, and thus to

---

[122] Letter from Jenks to his mother, 20 March 1938, Caracas, FWJ, ILOA.
[123] *Ibid.*
[124] Letter from Blelloch to Butler, April 29, 1936. XT 63/1/1 "Invitation from Venezuelan Government to send ILO expert in labour legislation. (Blelloch's mission, 1936)", ILOA.

protect the reform process from any political incursions.[125] The Venezuelan government considered Office civil servants as private technical experts, with "the ILO coming into the picture as a sort of mysterious providence which in some half understood way has made such things possible".[126] This discourse testifies to the apparent contradiction in which civil servants found themselves and the "complex network of obligations" in which they were locked.[127] Moreover, foreign experts did not have a good reputation. It is undoubtedly for this reason that the field surveys conducted by civil servants were strictly supervised, as Jenks points out in a letter to Butler: "All decisions as to where I was to travel and what was to be left out were taken before I left Caracas by agreement between Pietri [Luis Pietri] and José Luis Quintero Garcia, director of the national labour office."[128]

The various correspondences clearly highlight the difficulties experienced by civil servants in assuming their expert status, as evidenced by this passage from Jenks' report, written shortly after the Minister of Labour Luis Pietri mentioned the possibility of extending his mission:

In no circumstances could I agree to stay here in that capacity. I am prepared to stay as an Office official on mission, with the independence of status which that gives me, if the Office so desires. I am not prepared to stay as one of the numerous experts who are generally regarded, and in some cases with justice, as being in Venezuela for what they can get out of it, and I am not prepared to stay in circumstances under which I have to take orders from any Venezuelan authority in the existing condition of political and administrative life here.[129]

The different constraints that weighed on the expertise process generated a discursive strategy on the part of international civil servants that highlights the fragility of their position as experts. The study of the discourse they produced on the constraints they faced in an environment of contingency and political alternation opens the discussion on their perception of technical assistance, which

---

[125] Facchini, F. 1993. "Pour une critique du modèle technocratique-savoir-marché politique et production de la loi", *Politiques et management public* 11(3): 63–75; Evans, P., Rueschemeyer, D., Skocpol, T. eds 1985. *Bringing the State Back In*. Cambridge: Cambridge University Press; Trimberger E. K. 1977. *Revolution from Above: Military Bureaucrats and Development in Japan, Turkey, Egypt, and Peru*. New Brunswick, N.J: Transaction Books.

[126] Letter from Jenks to Pone, April 30, 1938. XH 7/63/1 "Attitude of Venezuela towards the League of Nations", ILOA.

[127] Krieg-Planque, A., Oger, C. 2010. "Discours institutionnels. Perspectives pour les sciences de la communication", Mots. Les langages du politique [Online], 94 | 2010, online since 06 November 2012. http://journals.openedition.org/mots/19870 [last accessed 17.09.2019].

[128] Letter from Jenks to Butler, September 14, 1938. XT 63/2/1, ILOA.

[129] Report from Jenks to Butler, May 19, 1938. XT 63/2/1.

they ultimately considered as an instrument that risked jeopardising the authority of the Office along with their careers within the institution.

In their correspondence, international civil servants emphasised the lack of consideration they received. In a letter dated 12 April 1936, Blelloch mentioned to Butler that local personalities – such as the director of the National Labour Office, Alonso Calatrava (a lawyer over 60 years old) and his deputy, Rafael Caldera (still a student), who were certainly no labour experts – were unable to help him gather information.[130] Collaborations with members of committees also revealed tensions, signs of the fragility of civil servants' position. In Dechamp's report of 23 May 1938, he states: "The memos we sent on the organisation of insurance have not been answered. [...] Weeks passed without any indication from the Venezuelan administrations regarding the fate of our work.[131]

The insistence with which civil servants depicted the disorder of Venezuela's political life highlights the intrigues, corruption, ignorance and bad faith of the ruling elites. While institutional instability – Blelloch saw three ministers cycle through the Ministry of the Interior during his mission – was a real hindrance to achieving concrete results, the discourse of Office civil servants also aimed to clear them of any responsibility for the failure of reform projects, giving the general impression of chaos.

Difficulties encountered in the field were causing a general state of crisis among civil servants, who felt torn between the institutional loyalty imposed by their status and their inability to fulfil the objectives of their mission.[132] Jenks wrote as follows: "It was even more understood that I took no responsibility for the Code as a whole." Blelloch, on the other hand, evoked a deep aversion to the new code, the drafting of which he did not ultimately wish to be associated with: "A labour Bill – in preparing which I collaborated to some extent, but for which I should hate to accept any serious responsibility, is at present before congress."[133] The tensions generated by action on the ground reinforced

---

130 In this respect, Blelloch emphasised the lack of knowledge and skills exhibited by Calatrava, who he considered close to right-wing conservatives ideas. Letter from Blelloch to Butler, May 19, 1936. XT 63/1/1, ILOA.
131 Excerpt from Dechamp's report, May 23, 1938. XT 62/2/2 "Invitation from Venezuelan Government to ILO to send insurance experts to Venezuela. Dechamp's mission", ILOA.
132 For a similar interpretation in the study on the internationalisation of military expertise, see Oger, C. 2003. "Communication et contrôle de la parole: de la clôture à la mise en scène de l'institution militaire", *Quaderni* 52: 77–92.
133 Letter from Blelloch to Waelbroeck, May 28, 1936. LE 229, Jacket 1 "Labour legislation: invitation from Venezuela for an ILO Expert to cooperate in the preparation of draft legislation, 02.1936–12.1936", ILOA.

their attachment to the institution, or at least the claim to it, as shown in this excerpt of a letter from Jenks to Butler:

> And though I have thoroughly enjoyed having a wider scope than a member of section normally has in Geneva my main interests are still in Geneva and I do not wish to be away for an indefinite period. [...] I have not of course overlooked the attractions of the measure of responsibility and influence which I have been enjoying during the last two months; nor is the building up of a new country where there is rather poor material but a quite genuine desire to build, altogether without attractions in the present state of European and world affairs.[134]

The "contradictory injunctions",[135] to use Alice Krieg-Planque's and Claire Oger's expression, which framed the production of expertise, sometimes led to ruptures likely to call into question the very cohesion of the institution that the civil servants represented. On 22 April 1938, Dechamp sent an alarming telegram to the Office:

> Embarking for Colombia. Urgent health reasons. Preparatory work, including regulations and application completed. Zelenka must embark for Britain. Pietri agreement will later request expert law application. Have warned wife. Avoid worrying. Thank you.[136]

His high-conflict relations with the administrators of the social insurance department, in particular with the head of the department, Dr. Stronak, who Dechamp claimed knew nothing about social insurance, led him to leave Venezuela in a hurry. The following excerpt from a letter written by Jenks, highlights the tensions that profoundly marked Dechamp's mission:

> Dechamp's departure has created here a position of some embarrassment about which I think I ought to write to you in a purely personal way. The situation is of course one in which I should prefer to have no personal concern. [...] Dechamp himself asked me before he left to write and explain the position to you. I cannot do so in a manner, which would be entirely satisfactory to him, because I do not entirely share his point of view but I will try to combine loyalty to the Office with fairness to Dechamp and loyalty to him as a colleague. [...]
>
> Relations between him and them seem to me to have been rather strained from the outset. Dechamp quickly forged a considerable contempt for Venezuela and perhaps he was not successful in concealing this as would have been desirable. He had the impression that

---

134 Letter from Jenks to Butler, May 19, 1938. FWJ, ILOA.
135 Krieg-Planque, A., Oger, C. 2010. "Discours institutionnels. Perspectives pour les sciences de la communication", *Mots. Les langages du politique* 94: 93.
136 Telegram from Dechamp, April 22, 1938. SI 2/63/2, ILOA.

he had been sent here without any preparation of the ground and more at Mr. Arocha's insistence than to meet any genuine demand here for technical assistance in relation with social insurance [...] Dechamp has not been treated with a particular deference of consideration, and naturally has found it quite impossible to tie the Government down to any statement of its intentions. [...] Dechamp began in an excited way by declaring that he must leave the country at once and thrust the medical certificate before the Minister. [...] I should like to stress strongly at his point that Dechamp was at this time overwrought and almost hysterical and that I am quite certain that he had convinced himself that his life was in danger unless he left Caracas at once.[137]

Dechamp knew that his attitude could potentially prevent him from returning to the Office: "If I cannot return to the Office, rest assured that I will have made, in the name of the institution you lead, the greatest effort in my power."[138] Dechamp's loyalty to the institution was intact after all, but his "overflow" had altered the Office's cohesive *façade*.[139] Dechamp returned to the International Labour Office after his mission and then, like many of his colleagues, left it in 1940. After the war he sought to return to the Social Insurance Section, but his attitude during his mission in Venezuela would soon resurface, as would his difficult temperament. He was thus not rehired.[140] This rejection of an actor who had nevertheless accomplished important work for the Office testifies to the potential jeopardising nature of technical assistance for international civil servants who, during a journey, risked seeing their international careers shattered.

Conclusion

The analysis of technical assistance to Venezuela provides a new perspective on the practice of international expertise, well beyond its function. Starting from a focus on experts' discourse, this chapter called the institution itself into question, along with the way it prepared, organised and monitored its civil servants in the field. Advice and assistance provided by civil servants was not anchored in social and cultural literacy, and the civil servants' use of empirical work captured through field surveys was limited at best. While it was possible to make

---

[137] Letter from Jenks to Butler, April 23, 1938. XT 63/2/1, ILOA.
[138] Letter from Dechamp to Butler, April 22, 1938. SI 2/63/2 "Technical collaboration with Venezuelan Government concerning social insurance. Jaket I, 1937–1939", ILOA.
[139] For a sociological analysis of the notion of *façade*, see Codaccioni, V., Maisetti, N., Pouponneau, F. 2012. "Les façades institutionnelles : ce que montrent les apparences des institutions", *Sociétés contemporaines* 4(88): 5–15.
[140] Internal note, 25 October 1946. Cyrille Dechamp's personal file, P 1729, ILOA.

"on the spot" adjustments, depending on the wishes expressed by national politicians and civil servants, it is clear that the action of Office civil servants was essentially aimed at opening up Venezuelan national law to the influence of international labour Conventions. Although it referred to prior instructions, the expertise most often followed three tacit rules: maintaining the international character of the mission, promoting the Office's activities and disseminating international labour standards. This imperative, to function within the limits of an authorised expertise, explains why field experience did not produce a substantial transformation of expert knowledge developed within the Office. However, the change of scale led to a transformation in the professional thinking of civil servants. Those four to six months spent in Venezuela allowed them to better understand the limits of their action. If we can observe no real qualitative change in the way they approached their action, we can clearly see an increased awareness among them regarding the fragility of their expert status.[141]

The internationalisation of expertise made it possible for the Office to project itself in a specific national space for a limited time and, with it, to spread a working culture, with methods and techniques. Technical assistance also made it possible to put internationally trained professionals in contact with professionals who shared a common culture and who were likely to extend the efforts of civil servants over time. That being said, the concrete experience of non-European national spaces imposed obvious limitations on the action of international civil servants. While, in the interwar period, technical assistance allowed ILO action to be deployed in a kind of geographical universality, the missions sent by the Office highlight a permanent tension between a universalist approach and a necessarily pragmatic action, with the models promoted by the ILO subject to permanent negotiation. Although the universality of international labour Conventions was never called into question, Office civil servants de facto relativised the possibility of reconciling social ideals with political and economic realities. In addition, the missions received fragile support and several conflicts emerged.[142] Journeys, and the distance they implied, further weakened the position of international civil servants, and by extension that of the Office. The self-reflective discourse on their activities supports this analysis. If they acted with a

---

[141] However, some research has shown that temporary missions abroad can have a significant role in the evolution of the experts' work. Godard, S. 2014. *Construire le " bloc " par l'économie : configuration des territoires et des identités socialistes au Conseil d'aide économique mutuelle (CAEM), 1949–1989*. PhD Diss., University of Geneva. See Chapter 6 in particular, section II: 423–448.

[142] Théry, I. 2005. "Expertises de service, de consensus, d'engagement : essai de typologie de la mission d'expertise en sciences sociales", *Droit et société* 2(60): 311–327.

missionary vocation, their commitment must be linked to the desire to serve the institution for which they worked. For Office civil servants, technical assistance only made sense insofar as it increased the ILO's authority in the world.

Chapter VIII
Technical Assistance and the Formulation of an International Development Policy During the Second World War

The war put an end to the international regime organised around the League of Nations.[1] The ILO was also forced to leave Geneva and the relocation of the International Labour Office to Montreal in 1940 meant an almost complete break with European governments, employers' and trade union organisations.[2] The Office's new position was both a strength and a weakness. In a conflict-free environment, civil servants, in accordance with the resolutions adopted at the ILO regional conferences in Santiago and Havana, continued to provide advice and assistance in Latin America. The war years, however, were dominated by the United States and its international policy. Latin America's geostrategic importance for the United States and its involvement in the war had the effect of directly linking the Office's technical assistance to the American continental defence programme. The Second World War therefore undoubtedly brought about an evolution in technical assistance. In this particular context it was mobilised in the service of Allied victory.

The 1940s were also a time to prepare for peace. With the emergence of reconstruction plans and new international institutions, in the span of just a few years the new post-war international order was built and international development became institutionalised.[3] Key moments include the following: the Hot Springs Conference in May and June of 1943, where the Food and Agriculture Organisation of the United Nations (FAO) was instated; 9 November 1943, when the

---

[1] For recent analyses of the impact of the Second World War on the League of Nations, see Tournès, L. 2015. *Les États-Unis et la Société des Nations (1914–1946). Le système international face à l'émergence d'une superpuissance*. Bern: Peter Lang; Tournès, L. 2014. "The Rockefeller Foundation and the Transition from the League of Nations to the UN (1939–1946)", *Journal of Modern European History* 12(3): 323–341; Clavin, P. 2013. *Securing the World Economy: The Reinvention of the League of Nations, 1920–1946*. Oxford: Oxford University Press.
[2] Kott, S. 2014. "Fighting the War or Preparing for Peace? The ILO during the Second World War", *Journal of Modern European History* 12(3): 359–376.
[3] Helleiner, E. 2014. *Forgotten foundations of Bretton Woods: International development and the making of the postwar order*. Ithaca; London: Cornell University Press; Helleiner, E. 2009. "The Development Mandate of International Institutions: Where Did it Come From?", *Studies in Comparative International Development* 44(3): 189–211; Rist, G. 2007. *Le Développement: histoire d'une croyance occidentale*, 3ᵉ édition revue et augmentée. Paris: Les Presses de Sciences Po.

United Nations Relief and Rehabilitation Administration (UNRRA) was created; and August 1944, the Dumbarton Oaks Conference, which brought together the United States, China, the USSR and Great Britain in formulating the first draft of the United Nations Charter and the plan for the creation of the Economic and Social Council (CESNU);[4] and lastly, the 1945 San Francisco Conference, where the United Nations Charter was adopted. The ILO's reflections on the foundations of its post-war action led to the adoption of the Declaration of Philadelphia at the 26th Conference of the ILO in Philadelphia in 1944. This text reaffirmed some of the ILO's foundational principles while defining new goals and objectives.[5] Analysing the period between 1939 and 1946 is therefore crucial to understand the impact of the war on the development of technical assistance, and to assess the extent to which it contributed to redefining the ILO's mandate and practices. This chapter will begin with a study of the Office's technical assistance, highlighting its role in supporting the Allied war effort. It will conclude with an analysis of the impact of the Second World War on the formulation of new ideas on economic and social development at the ILO.

1 Between Continental Defence and Regional Development

1.1 The Office Moves to Montreal

The inner workings of the International Labour Office were severely disrupted by the war. Major lay-offs accompanied the relocation of some collaborators to Montreal, at McGill University. Initially, in 1939, the first suspended contracts mainly affected Swiss nationals. In March 1939, Phelan, appointed Deputy Director in 1938, had already begun preparing the first evacuation plans. In February 1939 a Commission outlying the measures to be taken in the event of exceptional circumstances was set up by the Governing Body. It listed possible safe havens, such as France, Ireland, the United States, Spain and Canada, before deciding that ILO activities should be based in Geneva for as long as possible.[6] However,

---

4 The idea of an economic and social council had already been imposed on the League of Nations in 1935. Ghebali, V.-Y. 1972. "Aux origines de l'Ecosoc : l'évolution des commissions et organisations techniques de la Société des Nations", *Annuaire français de droit international* 18: 469–511.
5 Supiot, A. 2010. *L'esprit de Philadelphie : La justice sociale face au marché total*. Paris: Seuil.
6 The Committee on Measures to be Taken in Exceptional Circumstances consisted of four government representatives, two members chosen from the workers' group and two from the employers' group.

in the spring of 1940, under the pressure of events and decisions taken by Switzerland, it became clear to the Office staff that the organisation could no longer remain in Geneva.[7] The tensions generated by the war was captured in 1940 in a letter written by Wilfred Jenks:

> A few days ago an invasion of Switzerland was widely believed to be imminent, and though all immediate danger seems to have passed the Director has decided that, as in the event of an invasion similar to the invasions of Denmark, Norway and Holland he might not be able to evacuate more than a few car-loads with people, the time has come to adopt certain precautionary measures.[8]

M.R.K. Burge, of the London Correspondence Office, wrote Phelan, sure that Lisbon and Dublin could not welcome the Office, and that meanwhile total withdrawal on the other side of the Atlantic would be perceived by the European side as precipitated.[9] In July 1940 arrangements were made with Oxford College to accommodate some civil servants during the summer months.[10] In August 1940 the option of moving to Montreal was confirmed following negotiations initiated by the Office Director, the American John G. Winant, supported in his efforts by Phelan and Jenks. At the same time, the Canadian government officially agreed to the temporary transfer of some of the Office's staff to Montreal.[11] For Winant this geographical position would allow the Office to play a role in the development of cooperation between the United States, Great Britain and the Dominions, while providing direct assistance to Latin American countries during

---

[7] LBO 2-4-1 "London Branch Office: World War: London Office Transfer" Jacket I, ILOA.
[8] Letter from Jenks to his mother, May 19, 1940, FWJ, in ABIT.
[9] Correspondence between Burge and Phelan, June 3, 1940. LBO 2-4-1 "London Branch Office: World War: London Office Transfer" Jacket I. Lisbon was excluded because of the regime, and Dublin because of the impossibility of establishing communications. The occupation in June 1940 ruled out a move to France.
[10] Wilfred Jenks and Maurice Stack stayed there for a few weeks. Letter from Jenks to his mother, July 12, 1940, FWJ, ILOA.
[11] Travel to Montreal was difficult and complicated by the general transport situation in Western Europe, the difficulty of obtaining the necessary visas and the gradual closure of borders. Awaiting the agreement of the League Supervisory Commission on the ILO's budget for 1941, Phelan was one of the last to leave Geneva. Arriving at the Spanish border on 15 August, he was unaware that General Franco had closed the border to League of Nations and ILO staff two days earlier. Anticipating some trouble, he followed a secondary road to a customs post where he presented his Irish passport marked "diplomatic". Thinking he was an Irish minister, the guards let him through. ILO, 2009. *Edward Phelan and the ILO: Life and Views of an International Social Actor*, 31. Geneva: International Labour Organisation.

the war.¹² The Office's activities were therefore to be consolidated in three regions: America, Europe (Geneva as well as London, where the ILO was strengthening the functioning of the correspondence office) and Asia, where the ILO had decided to keep the Delhi and Shanghai offices open. However, maintaining a small group in Geneva, under the direction of Marius Viple, former head of Albert Thomas' cabinet, did not prevent the Office's European activities from being put on hold. Moreover, from October 1941 onwards, correspondence became increasingly difficult and monitored, particularly by the United States.¹³

On 18 August 1940, the Office publicly announced its relocation to Canada. Those civil servants who had been dismissed or whose contracts had been suspended found refuge where they could, mainly in Great Britain, France and Switzerland. Others, such as the British James Nixon, who was unable to leave France, were imprisoned.¹⁴ Finally, a small number of civil servants were mobilised.

Tab. 6: List of Montreal Staff (27 November 1940)

John G. Winant	Mme Munguia
E.J. Phelan	E.F. Penrose
I. Bessling	Mlle G. Rabinowitch
H.T.P. Binet	Mlle M.W. Rankin
D.H. Blelloch	H. Reymond
Mlle K.H. Carew	Mme R. Ryan
W.J. Carlton	E.J. Riches
W.J. Couper	Mlle C. Riegelman
Mme. E. Denhardt	Mlle M. Roberts (future Mrs. Oswald Stein)
Mlle S. Deutschmann (future Mrs Adrien Tixier*)	
Mlle E.P. Dutt	M. de Salis
F.J.A. Faller	A. Stall
Mlle A.M. Fernandez-King	D. Stacey
Mlle M.E. Healy	M.R. Stack
Mlle A.B. Hill	O. Stein
Mlle D.E. Hopkins	Mlle Taylor
C.W. Jenks	D. Vaage

---

12 Letter from Winant to Frederick Keppel, President of the Carnegie Foundation, October 17, 1940. F 100 "Grant from the Carnegie Corporation", ILOA.

13 The State Department reportedly censored certain political correspondence from Marius Viple. Letter from Tixier to Phelan, October 13, 1941. Z/1/1/1/9 "Correspondence between the Acting Director and M. Tixier, 1940–1944", ILOA.

14 James Nixon was held captive until 1944. Guinand, C. 2008. "Un fonctionnaire international en France occupée (1940–1944)", in Heinen, A., Hüser D., Günther, A. *Tour de France. Eine historische Rundreise. Festschrift für Rainer Hudemann*, 391–399. Stuttgart: Franz Steiner.

J.E.A. Johnston	P. Waelbroeck
Mlle H. Lewis	C.W.H Weaver
Mlle L. Long	Mlle M.H. Wood
Mlle E. Mayer (future Mrs. J.E.A. Johnston)	B.M. Woodbury
R.J.P. Mortished	C.M. Wright
M. Osmay	J.N.R. Lee
*Due to his French nationality, Adrien Tixier could not travel to Montreal as Office staff. He therefore acted from the Office's correspondence office in Washington.	A.Turton
	T.N. Elvidge

Although the choice of Montreal was generally well received in Europe, some Latin American countries interpreted this move as a disavowal of the United States. In 1941, while on mission in Mexico, Tixier noted the lack of enthusiasm for the Office's new position, the astonishment at not seeing the Office move to Washington and rumours circulating that President Roosevelt attached little importance to maintaining the Office's activities afloat during the war.[15] One of the tasks that therefore motivated civil servants was to demonstrate to the countries that remained free, particularly in Latin America, that the war had not halted the Office's activities.

1.2 Social Security and Regional Solidarity

The strong influence of the United States on the regional scene led Office's civil servants to become closely associated with the United States' inter-American policies. To guarantee their safety and their economic and political position in this hemisphere during the war, the United States established measures to ensure that the prosperity of Central and South American countries was tied to a web of cooperation and dependent relationships. These activities were implemented as early as the 1930s as part of the US Good Neighbor Policy, and we know the role the ILO played in consolidating inter-American cooperation. This strategy continued during the war.[16] It is reflected in an intensification of relations between the Office and civil servants of the American administration, in particular

---

[15] MI 9 "Missions – Adrien Tixier Mission to Cuba and Mexico, Jacket 1, 09/1940–07/1941", ILOA.

[16] Van Goethem, G. 2010. "Phelan's War: The International Labour Organization in Limbo (1941–1948)", in Van Daele, J., Rodríguez García, M., Van Goethem, G., van der Linden, M. eds. *ILO Histories: Essays on the International Labour Organization and its Impact on the World During the Twentieth Century*, 314–340. Bern: Peter Lang.

the Labor Department, the State Department and the Office of the Coordinator of Inter-American Affairs (OCIAA), set up in 1941 to develop cooperation with Latin American countries and led by Nelson Rockefeller. Between 1939 and 1946 the Office's action in Latin America focused on two fronts: helping states organise their economies by developing a labour policy made all the more necessary by the industrial mobilisation required by war production; and socially orienting the development of Latin America after the war.

National and regional contexts contributed to the Office's activities in Latin America shifting towards the development of social security. As of 1939 social security became a central concept in the Office's thinking. It was the result of a combination of two ideas: protection through social insurance and economic security. The transition from social insurance to social security was influenced by the United States' 1935 Social Security Act and Britain's 1942 Beveridge Plan. Office civil servants Adrien Tixier, Oswald Stein, future Deputy Director of the Office between 1942 and 1943, and Maurice Stack, also a member of the Social Insurance Section, directly participated to the elaboration of these laws and programs.[17] The 1936 and 1939 regional conferences in Latin America also adopted resolutions on the development of social security, which Latin American delegates perceived as a means of combating the effects of the global economic crisis and encouraging industrialisation.[18] Since May 1941, Oswald Stein had been considering an action programme for the Office, particularly in Latin America.[19] In his view the development of social security had to be at the centre of its regional activities. For Stein it was essential for the Office to focus its efforts on the development of compulsory insurance as a method of long-term economic planning and on the dissemination of a tripartite social security management model: "Social security services are conceived as an interdependent whole, called upon to care for, preserve and develop human resources by ensuring

---

[17] Kott, S. 2009. "De l'assurance à la sécurité sociale (1919–1949). L'OIT comme acteur international", draft paper, ILO Century Project. For an analysis of the impact of this reform on the Office's work, namely in Philadelphia in 1944, see Margairaz, M. 2010. "L'OIT et la sécurité du travail. Du rapport Beveridge à la conférence de Philadelphie : l'invention de la Sécurité sociale", in Aglan, A. ed. *Humaniser le travail : régimes économiques, régimes politiques et Organisation internationale du travail (1929–1969)*, 131–148. Brussels; Bern: Peter Lang.

[18] Jensen, J. 2011. "From Geneva to the Americas: The International Labor Organization and Inter-American Social Security Standards, 1936–1948", *International Labor and Working-Class History*, 80(1): 215–240.

[19] Letter from Stein to Tixier, May 29, 1941. MI – 3–7 "Missions – Osvald Stein, 1940–1942", ILOA.

their greatest productivity and a fair share in material progress, even beyond periods of active participation in production."[20]

During the war, the development of social security thus constituted a priority for the Office's technical assistance activities. Social insurance reforms in Latin America were more or less in line with the programme established at the 1936 and 1939 ILO Regional Conferences.[21] In December 1940, a meeting brought together the heads of social security administrations and the diplomatic representatives of ten countries of the Americas.[22] Under the leadership of Winant and the Peruvian Minister of Public Health and Social Insurance, Constantino J. Carvallo, an Inter-American Committee for the Advancement of Social Security was established under the auspices of the ILO.[23] The fruits of this cooperation first materialised in June 1941 in Mexico, with the establishment of a tripartite technical commission to draw up a general social insurance programme.[24] At the 1941 ILO conference, some workers' delegates, such as Argentina's Domenech and Chile's Ibanez, insisted that the Office pursue its work. Stein quickly understood the importance of social security development for America, which he saw as a way to affirm the ILO's role in building democratic continental solidarity: "Social security services are called upon to fulfil vital functions. In planning and developing social security systems, the Latin American countries are strengthening continental solidarity with the active help of workers' and employers' organisations."[25]

The publication of the Beveridge report in 1942 gave a new impetus to the Office's activities. The Inter-American Social Security Conference organised

---

[20] Stein, O. 1941. "Vers la sécurité sociale", *International Labour Review* 44(3): 269. Original quote in French: "Les services de sécurité sociale sont conçus comme un ensemble interdépendant, appelé à soigner, à conserver et à développer les ressources humaines en leur assurant la plus grande productivité et une juste part dans le progrès matériel, au-delà même des périodes de participation active à la production".

[21] Director's Report, 1939, Havana, ILOA. This report is entirely devoted to the ILO's American activities.

[22] "The ILO and economic and social reconstruction". Report of the Acting Director of the ILO, ILO Conference, New York, Montreal, 1941, 52. ILOA.

[23] Cohen, W., J. 1942. "The First Inter-American Conference on Social Security", *Social Security Bulletin*, October: 4–7.

[24] SI 12–61–1 "Social security: correspondence with R. Watt, American Federation of labour, USA, 1943 Conference paper RW on AFL trade union attitude towards the Wagner-Murray-Dingall Bill (social security legislation); 1942 note O. Stein on social security trends in Argentina, Brazil, Chile, Mexico; 1941 Paper RW on social insurance", ILOA.

[25] Note from Stein to Robert Watt, January 22, 1942. SI 12–61–1, ILOA.

from 10 to 16 September 1942, partly thanks to OCIAA funding,[26] testifies to the interweaving of international and regional interests made possible by the active involvement of Office civil servants on both fronts. This conference brought together American social security specialists and experts committed to encouraging the development of relations between American social security institutions and to proposing a post-war agenda for action. The representatives from 21 countries of the Americas met, in addition to representatives from the Pan-American Health Bureau, OCIAA (Nelson Rockefeller personally travelled) and the Office.[27] The United States was represented by Arthur J. Altmeyer, Chairman of the delegation, John Maurice Clark, Director of OCIAA's Cultural Relations Division, and Emil Rieve, former member of the American delegation to the 1937 World Textile Conference. The American Federation of Labor (AFL) also supported the Office's work by sending Robert J. Watt's to the conference. Watt saw the Office's activities as an effective instrument in the fight against fascist and communist influences, which then motivated much of the AFL's action in Latin America. In 1941 he wrote: "The expense of social insurance would be justified as a domestic defense against the subversive influences of fascism, communism or other crackpot schemes."[28] The Office appealed to the AFL beyond its anti-communist ideology. Latin America's raw material production and potential as a new market were important factors. The ILO could thus serve as an instrument to encourage a planned industrialisation of Latin American economies that could be oriented to further the interests of the United States.

The 1942 conference, chaired by the Chilean Minister of Health, Insurance and Social Security, Miguel Etchebarne, adopted a series of resolutions that formed the basis of an inter-American cooperation programme.[29] Latin American experts also prepared a series of technical reports for the conference, outlining the particular problems of social insurance, including its application to agricultural and domestic workers.[30] At this conference social security was put forward as an indispensable factor for continental solidarity, reliant on political under-

---

26 Z 1/61/1/6 "Relations with Nelson Rockefeller, Co-ordinator for Inter-American Affairs, Washington DC (through Mr. Stein), 1942–1943", ILOA.
27 XR 61/1/25 "The Rockefeller Foundation. New York. 1935–1937", in ABIT.
28 Excerpt from an unpublished article by Robert J. Watt. SI 12–61–1, ILOA.
29 1942. "Une structure nouvelle de la sécurité sociale : l'œuvre de la Conférence interaméricaine de sécurité sociale de Santiago du Chili", *International Labour Review* 46(6): 745–778; 1942. *Approaches to Social Security: An international Survey*, Studies and Reports, Series M (Social Insurance), n°18. Montreal: International Labour Office, ILOA.
30 See the report prepared by Chilean experts Julio Bustos Lagos, José Vizcarra and Manuel De Viada (1942): *Extension of Social Insurance Coverage to Agricultural Workers, to the Self-employed and to Domestic Servants*, Montreal: International Labour Office, ILOA.

standing and the continuous and planned development of both industrial and agricultural production and consumption. It would have to include measures to promote employment, increase national income, share it more equitably, and raise living standards. "The health, capacity and well-being of workers across an entire American nation, it was emphasised at the conference, is the concern of all countries in the Americas."[31] The resolutions of this conference, which go beyond the Atlantic Charter's agenda, reflected the syncretism of ideas on social protection and economic development, and the support of American countries to the ILO.[32]

In the summer of 1943 the success of the 1942 conference led the Office to invite a group of American social security specialists to Montreal to draft an "International Social Security Charter". On this point, as Stein remarked, the Office's action was a success: "As the Director knows, we have prevented any Charter or conference on social security from occurring outside the ILO. The Heads of State as well as the experts know that the formulation of future international regulations is in the hands of the Office."[33] Beveridge was present alongside Canada's Minister of Pensions and National Health, Ian Mackenzie, and Leonard Marsh, author of the Canadian Social Security Report. Representatives from Chile, Cuba, Peru, Mexico, Brazil and Ecuador were also in attendance.

The adopted recommendations gave new expression to social security projects and would soon stimulate their implementation in Latin America. In order to carry out the programme established at the Inter-American Conference in 1942, the Office undertook to make its expertise available to the Latin American governments that wished to develop social security programmes. For Stein these activities of technical assistance were now an integral part of the ILO's mandate: "We are well within our role in helping concerned administrations to propose a bold but rational and technically defensible policy."[34] The table below gives an

---

[31] Cohen, W., J. 1942. "The First Inter-American Conference on Social Security", *Social Security Bulletin*, October: 5.

[32] Z 1/61/1/5 "Relations with M. Laurence Duggan. Department of State. Washington (Through Mr. Stein) 1942", ILOA.

[33] Stein's report on the Washington mission, July 27, 1943. MI 3–24 "Mr Stein's mission and Mr. Flores mission to Washington, 19–22 July 1943", ILOA. Original quote in French: "Nous avons bloqué, le Directeur le sait, toute possibilité d'une Charte ou conférence sur la sécurité sociale en dehors de l'OIT. Les chefs d'État et aussi les experts savent que la préparation de la future réglementation internationale est entre les mains du Bureau".

[34] Letter from Stein to Moisés Poblete Troncoso, May 29, 1941. SI 2–0–12–1 "Social Security: Chile–ILO technical cooperation with social security reform; comments on draft social security legislation N°4054, 5802. 11/1940–06/1962", ILOA. Original quote in French: "Nous sommes bien

overview of the Office's main missions of technical assistance in this field between 1939 and 1945.

Date	Country	Expert 1	Expert 2
1939	Ecuador	Emil Schoenbaum (Czech)	
1940	Mexico	Adrien Tixier (French)	
1940	Canada	Oswald Stein (Czech)	
1940	Bolivia	Oswald Stein (Czech)	
1940	Ecuador	Oswald Stein (Czech)	
1941	Mexico	Emil Schoenbaum (Czech)	
1941	Peru	Oswald Stein (Czech)	
1941	Chile	Oswald Stein (Czech)	
1941	Bolivia	Oswald Stein (Czech)	
1943	Mexico	Oswald Stein (Czech)	John J. Corson (American –Social Security Board)
1943	Venezuela	Oswald Stein (Czech)	Oscar Powell (American –Social Security Board)
1944	Haiti	Henri Reymond (French)	Alejandro Flores (Spanish)
1944	Haiti	David Blelloch (British)	Tadeusz Poznanski (Polish)
1945	Central America	R.A Metall (Austrian)	

At the diplomatic level these missions were never carried out without prior notification to the US State Department, and the missions were generally followed by stops in New York or Washington, making the Office "a kind of annex of the US intelligence service".[35] In practice, the Office's technical assistance was essentially based on the intellectual and technical capital of the civil servants who'd been hired in the interwar years. Czech experts and actuaries almost exclusively carried out the social security assignments. Since the 1930s, but with

---

dans notre rôle en aidant ainsi l'administration responsable à proposer une politique audacieuse mais rationnelle et techniquement défendable."

35 Kott, S. 2014. "Fighting the War or Preparing for Peace? The ILO during the Second World War", *Journal of Modern European History* 12(3): 368.

greater intensity during the Second World War, Oswald Stein and Emil Schoenbaum had worked tirelessly at disseminating Czech methods of establishing the actuarial bases of social security in Latin America. Office civil servants also worked closely with American experts. In Chile, Stein worked in collaboration with OCIAA, providing them with information on needs for hospital equipment and pharmaceutical supplies.[36] Stein's missions also highlight collaborations with experts such as John J. Corson from the SSB, funded by OCIAA, for the development of insurance accounting in Mexico in 1943,[37] and Oscar M. Powell, SSB Executive Director, accompanied Stein on his mission to Venezuela in 1943 to provide advice on health and accident insurance.[38]

Until the end of the war, technical assistance continued to operate on the model of the 1930s missions. It combined the development of social legislation, the administrative organisation and the formulation of general guidelines for national social policies as well as information gathering. Despite limited technical personnel the Office succeeded in developing expertise on social security issues in Latin America, publishing many articles in the *International Labour Review* throughout the 1940s.[39] In its staff reduction policy, the Office strongly valued keeping experts in all its sectors of activity in order to be "in a position to answer enquiries as heretofore and on occasion to lend assistance to Governments by way of missions".[40] Nevertheless, while in the 1930s Office civil servants could spend up to six months in the same country, during the war missions rarely lasted more than a few days, perhaps a few weeks. This made information gathering more difficult and limited. Finally, Stein's death in 1943 deprived the Office of its main asset in the field as well as in negotiations with members of the State Department, hence the decline in missions from 1943 onwards.[41]

---

[36] MI 3–12 "Mr. Stein's mission to Chile and Uruguay, July 1942", ILOA.
[37] See Stein's mission files MI 3–17, MI 3–19, MI 3–20, MI 3–21, ILOA.
[38] MI 3–25 "Mr. Stein's Mission to Venezuela, November 1943", ILOA.
[39] Stack, M. 1941. "Les assurances sociales en Amérique latine : leur développement actuel", *International Labour Review* 44(1): 1–33; Allende, S. 1942. "La médecine sociale au Chili", *International Labour Review* 45(1): 28–47; Gonzalez Gail J. 1942. "Les assurances sociales en Argentine : problèmes et perspectives", *International Labour Review* 45(5): 543–553; De Viado, M. 1942. "Les buts et l'application de la loi chilienne sur la médecine préventive", *International Labour Review* 46(2): 139–152; Herrnstadt, E. 1943. "La Colombie et le problème de la sécurité sociale", *International Labour Review* 47(4): 485–512.
[40] Letter from Phelan to Robert Guye, November 5, 1940. MI 11 " Missions – Robert Guy, Jacket 1, 07/1940–12/1944", ILOA._
[41] His sudden death occurred on 28 December 1943, when he left Ottawa, where he met the Minister of the Czechoslovak Legation in Ottawa. He was killed in an accident in Rigaud, aboard the fast Ottawa-Montreal train of the Canadian Pacific. According to press reports, Stein slipped

The activities of Office civil servants demonstrate just how important extending social security was to Latin American countries. While on a mission to Chile in 1941 Stein was asked by the Minister of Health, Salvador Allende, to extend the medical service of health insurance to the members of the insured person's family.[42] Stein also advocated for a complete change in the workers' pension scheme, with the state paying a fixed basic pension. He also proposed the introduction of compulsory accident insurance, managed exclusively by the workers' insurance fund.[43] In Mexico these reforms were driven by the desire to combine economic and social development.[44] Miguel Garcia Cruz, head of the Social Insurance Department, reportedly stated that industrial growth in his country would be "synchronized with the gestation and birth of social security".[45] However, the Office's missions reflect the diversity of national trajectories in the field of social security. The first systems that were set up in the 1940s in Venezuela, Mexico, Costa Rica, Peru and Colombia were, with the exception of Costa Rica, institutionally fragmented and economically fragile. They mainly concerned the military, government civil servants and workers organised in major trade unions.

The war also saw the first actuarial seminars dedicated to the issue of financing social security. Stein wrote to Tixier on 21 June 1941 to inform him of the interest of certain Latin American administrations in collaborating with the Office: "Technically and linguistically, contact will not be simple, but here is an opportunity for the Office to help by proposing the subjects to be studied and understood, taking into account the needs of Latin American administrations."[46] These reflections on the investment of social insurance institutions were not new for the ILO as they dated back to the late 1930s when the first international conferences of experts on the subject were held in Geneva. In July

---

off a door bearing and rolled under the car. However, the train was moving at the time of the accident.

42 SI 2–0–12–1 "Social Security: Chile–ILO technical cooperation with social security reform; comments on draft social security legislation N°4054, 5802. 11/1940–06/1962", ILOA.
43 MI 3–5 "Mission au Chili Janvier 1941", ILOA.
44 "Social security programmes in the Americas". Note from Stein to James Watt, January 22, 1942. SI 12–61–1, ILOA.
45 Jensen, J. 2011. "From Geneva to the Americas: The International Labor Organization and Inter-American Social Security Standards, 1936–1948", *International Labor and Working-Class History*, 80(1): 230.
46 MI 3–7, "Missions to Peru", ILOA.

1943, the Office organised its first seminar in Montreal, followed by another in December 1944.[47]

Thus, the inter-American environment in which the Office was operating led to the development of new instruments of international cooperation, such as Inter-American social security conferences and training seminars for actuaries who wished to participate in the progressive construction of socio-technical networks dedicated to the development of social insurance in Latin America. These seminars bore witness to a movement towards the internationalisation of the mathematical techniques of Czech actuarial science. It is therefore not surprising to find that the 1944 meeting took place under the direction of Emile Schoenbaum. These spaces for the exchange of expertise, set up by the Office, allowed American experts to meet and formulate an inter-American social security policy. It is also out of these seminars that a transnational technocratic class could emerge, under the patronage of the civil servants of the International Labour Office.

1.3 Technical Assistance in Support of the Allied War Effort

The United States' entry into the war and the acceleration of industrial mobilisation from 1942 onwards contributed to intensifying the development of social insurance in sectors that were strategic for war production. The question of access to raw materials became a crucial aspect of economic relations with Latin American countries and the Office's activities reflected this.[48] The intensification of economic relations with certain Latin American countries, most of them pro-Allied and pro-American, took place amid struggles for access to raw material production centres. Half of the world's tin production was in Malaysia, Indonesia, Siam (Thailand) and China.[49] With the capture of Singapore in February 1942,

---

[47] In attendance were Rodolfo Pomeranz, Costa Rican, head actuary of the insurance fund; Gastao Quartin Pinto de Moura, Brazilian, actuary of the Ministry of Labour, Industry and Trade; Guillermo Patino Hurtado, Mexican; Pedro Thullen, Ecuadorian mathematician of German origin; and Bernardino Vila, Chilean chief of the public employees' fund. SI 21, Jacket 1 "Social security: seminars – travel arrangements for meetings of social security administration Board, Washington, 02–03 Jan. 1945; 1944 trends in Latin America as summarised by the Inter-American Committee on Social security; Nov meeting in Montreal of actuarys form Brazil, Chile, Costa Rica, Ecuador, Mexico", ILOA.

[48] Eckes, A., E. 1980. *The United States and the Global Struggle for Minerals*. Austin: University of Texas Press.

[49] Bethell, L., Roxborough, I. 1997. *Latin America Between the Second World War and the Cold War: Crisis and Containment, 1944–1948*, 131. Cambridge: Cambridge University Press.

however, the Allies were cut off from Asia. The United States and Great Britain therefore withdrew to Congo, Nigeria and Bolivia.[50] Bolivia thus became the United States' main supplier from 1942 onwards. The battle for minerals was also strategic to counter Nazi influence in certain countries such as Argentina, which the Office was well aware of and which it sought to limit via its correspondence office in Buenos Aires.[51]

The Office's participation in the development of cooperation between the United States and Bolivia in the field of tin production reflects both the intertwining of labour and trade interests and the ILO's instrumentalisation by the State Department. Indeed, The Labor Department's activities in Latin America were decreasing in favour of the State Department and military agencies, such as the Board of Economic Warfare. In April 1942 ILO activities in South America and technical assistance, were centralised under the authority of the Board of Economic Warfare.[52] The United States' involvement in the war reoriented the Office's action to serve the US government's military strategy. In this new configuration, the Office was quickly given a new purpose: to support the Allied war effort. The members of the State Department, SSB and OCIAA all supported this. Between 31 March and 4 April 1942 Stein was in close contact with the latter:

> The intervening months between now and the Santiago meeting [Inter-American Social Security Conference organised by the ILO in 1942] should be used in order to expand and intensify the protection afforded by several South American institutions to workers engaged in producing raw materials mostly needed for the war effort. [...] The ILO will have to ascertain the essential needs of those social insurance institutions whose members are engaged in war production, to elicit their requests and to refer them to [the Office of the Coordinator of Inter-American Affairs] with proposals for concrete action.[53]

---

50 On competition between the United States and Great Britain, see Saunders, O. 2015. "Preserving the *Status Quo:* Britain, the United States, and Bolivian Tin, 1946–1956", *The International History Review*, 2015. www.tandfonline.com/doi/full/10.1080/07075332.2015.1049643 [last accessed 17.09.2019]
51 Luis Lauzet was the ILO's correspondent in Argentina. In 1942, the ILO commissioned him to carry out a propaganda mission in different regions of Argentina. MI 25 "Missions – Luis Lauzet, Jacket 1, 11/1942–12/1942", ILOA.
52 Letter from the Executive Office of the President, Bureau of the Budget, Washington DC, to Nelson Rockefeller, April 28, 1942. Collection NRA, Record Group (RG) 4, Nelson A. *Rockefeller, Personal* Papers. Series: O, Washington DC, Sub-Series: IAA. Box 1, folder 3: "Washington DC files, CIAA. General, 1942", NRA, RAC.
53 Stein's mission report to Washington, D.C., March 31–April 4, 1942. MI 3–10 "Mr. Stein's mission to Washington, April 1942", ILOA.

As such, the Office's action would focus on improving the protection of those workers employed in the production of strategic materials (tin, copper, raw rubber), in direct contact with the State Department, the OCIAA and the South American embassies in Washington, "by demonstrating that the Office is at the service of the allied nations, and not exclusively of the United States and Britain".[54] However, this newfound collaboration was not self-evident. Indeed, in 1940, Nelson Rockefeller was considering the development of raw materials mainly through the private sector.[55] Stein's intervention with Nelson Rockefeller seems to have been at the root of his interest in using the Office as an instrument to develop and organise the war production in Latin America. The discussions between Stein and Rockefeller show a clear rapprochement. The latter would have told Stein: "We are behind your action."[56] This support first materialised with financial assistance to the ILO for the 1942 Inter-American Social Security Conference.[57] Then, with the consent of Laurence Duggan, political adviser for the State Department in charge of the Latin American Division, Stein and Rockefeller arranged to invite John Maurice Clark to join Stein's missions in Latin America. This proposal by Stein was intended to disarm the State Department, which had expressed some reluctance to collaborate with the ILO, "by demonstrating, through the association of a civil servant who will report to the United States' diplomatic authorities during his mission, that we have absolutely nothing to hide to Washington, quite the contrary".[58] During one of Stein's missions to Washington in June 1942, the core elements of the *modus vivendi* for technical assistance in Latin America were established:

1. Requests and inquiries from insurance institutions are addressed to the Office.
2. After examination, the Office returns material requests (credits, hospital equipment, pharmaceutical stocks, travel grants) to OCIAA.
3. The Office is responsible for guiding the action of insurance institutions, preferably for the war effort.[59]

---

[54] Stein's mission to London, April 27 to May 19, 1942. Z 3/25/1 "Mr. Stein's mission to London (April-May 1942)", ILOA.

[55] Report of a conversation between Nelson Rockefeller and Raymond Rich, August 19, 1940. Collection NRA, Record Group (RG) 4, Nelson A. *Rockefeller, Personal* Papers. Series: O, Washington DC, Sub-Series: IAA. Box 1, folder 1 "Washington DC files, CIAA. General, 1940", NRA, RAC.

[56] *Ibid.*

[57] *Ibid.*

[58] *Ibid.*

[59] Stein Mission Report, June 1942. MI 3-11 "Stein's mission to Washington, 3-4 June 1942", ILOA.

Stein ensured that ILO cooperation with the State Department would guarantee that OCIAA technical and financial assistance was used "for the exclusive benefit of workers engaged in the war effort".⁶⁰ In October 1942, Stein and Rockefeller also agreed to collaborate on extensive urban and rural sanitation programmes in Bolivia, Peru and Chile. The OCIAA had undertaken to submit its plans to the Office for review. The latter had proposed to collaborate on OCIAA health schemes to insurance institutions in the various countries.⁶¹ These were to adapt to American military interests:

> The main purpose of our health and sanitation programme is to safeguard the lives and health of the armed forces of the United States and of the other American Republics around the many naval and air bases established for our mutual defense and also to protect the health of workers engaged in the production of strategic and critical materials needed for our war program.⁶²

The OCIAA then multiplied requests for collaboration with the Office in order to pursue this action in the field.⁶³ Stein's response to OCIAA's invitations was eager and enthusiastic, although he was keenly aware of the Office's position: "What Rockefeller and the State Department are looking for is a social alibi [...]. Still, I don't think we should refuse, because once again those who are absent are always at fault."⁶⁴ Already in 1942 he wrote in one of his reports that "cooperation projects with the various Latin American states are not revolutionary, but they do demonstrate the pervasive inter-American trends of various Department of Labor divisions and offices. If these projects were to multiply, the very *raison d'être* of the Office would be called into question."⁶⁵ The civil serv-

---

60 Original quote in French: "[...] l'OIT s'assurera que l'aide accordée sera utilisée dans la plus grande mesure possible au bénéfice exclusif des travailleurs engagés dans l'effort de guerre". Stein Mission Report, 31 March – 4 April 1942. MI 3–10: "Mr. stein's mission to Washington, April 1942", ILOA.
61 Stein Mission Report, October 27, 1942. MI 3–16 "Mr Stein's Mission to Washington, 23–26 October, 1942", ILOA.
62 Correspondence from Nelson Rockefeller to William Colmer, member of the United States House of Representatives, December 17, 1943. Collection NRA, Record Group (RG) 4, Nelson A. *Rockefeller, Personal* Papers. Series: O, Washington DC, Sub-Series: IAA. Box 1, folder 5 "Washington DC files, CIAA. General, 1944", NRA, RAC.
63 Z 1/61/1/6 "Relations with Nelson Rockefeller, Co-ordinator for Inter-American Affairs, Washington DC (through Mr. Stein), 1942–1943", ILOA.
64 Stein's internal note, September 7, 1943. Z 1/61/1/6, ILOA. Original quote in French: "Je ne crois pas que nous devions dire non, car encore une fois les absents ont toujours tort."
65 Stein's report on his mission to Washington, August 10–12, 1942. MI 3–14 "Suggested mission of Mr. Stein to Washington to confer with various personalities, on questions relating to social social insurance", ILAO.

ants of the Office were also facing competition from the Pan-American Union (PAU) engaged in the fight against Nazi political and economic infiltration on the Latin American continent.⁶⁶ Already in 1941, Tixier wrote Stein that it was imperative to swiftly specify the Office's policy towards Latin America, "where we risk being completely overwhelmed by the United States' pan-Americanist propaganda, which completely omits the Office's existence".⁶⁷ In his response Stein insisted on quickly establishing a division of labour with the PAU and added that: "In spite of everything, we remain technically stronger and can offer something in exchange for political support".⁶⁸

This intensification of US-led cooperation was the subject of much criticism in Latin America. This was particularly the case in Bolivia where members of the revolutionary nationalist movement accused President Enrique Peñaranda of having transformed Bolivia into a colony of the United States.⁶⁹ A cooperation programme for Bolivia's economic development was established by the State Department in June 1940. The 1942 strike in the Bolivian Catavi mines then almost completely paralysed mining activity. This event in turn had spurred the creation of the Joint Bolivian-American Labor Commission, with which the Office would later be associated. This commission was created following a government request from Bolivia, transmitted to the United States government on 2 January 1943.⁷⁰ In an exchange of telegrams between Cordell Hull and Edward Phelan on 26 and 27 January 1943, the State Department requested that an expert from the Office be involved in this commission. The British David Blelloch was chosen to represent the Office and to provide its expertise on labour issues. He had technical assistance experience in Latin America, having led a Bolivian mission in 1940, following which the President of the Republic appointed him Honorary Adviser of Bolivia to the Office as well as Permanent Adviser to members of Bolivian delegations to the ILC.⁷¹ The Bolivian members of the commission hoped Blelloch would be a support for their demands. Indeed, he shared their opinion on the problem posed by the United States' economic influence. At the time, in a report published in Spanish, Blelloch had called attention to the danger

---

66 Lübken, U. 2003. "'Americans All': The United States, the Nazi Menace, and the Construction of a Panamerican Identity", *American Studies*, 48(3): 389–409.
67 Letter from Tixier to Stein, May 22, 1941. MI 3–7, "Missions to Peru", ILOA.
68 Letter from Stein to Tixier, May 29, 1941. MI 3–7, "Missions to Peru", ILOA.
69 Bethell, L., Roxborough, I. 1997. *Latin America Between the Second World War and the Cold War: Crisis and Containment, 1944–1948*, 132. Cambridge: Cambridge University Press.
70 Letter from the Ambassador of Bolivia to Laurence Duggan, January 2, 1943. Magruder Papers, Harvard Law Library, Harvard University.
71 MI 1–1 "Missions David Blelloch, 1940–1941", ILOA.

that dependence on the mining industry and foreign capital, which was not very keen on improving working conditions, represented for the Bolivian economy.[72]

For the Bolivian government several interests were at stake. On the one hand, it hoped that this inter-American cooperation would "be the basis for a future policy of full social and economic development".[73] However, before this could happen the mining business sector and the government wished to obtain an extension of their contract with the United States. In return, they promised to invest in a social development programme.[74] As a reminder, at the 1942 Rio de Janeiro Conference, the United States obtained the freezing of prices on raw materials during the war. However, the resulting increase in the price of other consumer goods that led to the deterioration of living conditions in Bolivia prompted the government to renegotiate the selling price of tin. An international report reiterating the necessity of improving production conditions and social protection for minors would give them leverage to act. However, the State Department wanted to avoid any long-term economic and financial commitments.[75] It clearly forbade the experts who sat on the commission to discuss Bolivian mineral prices.

On the Bolivian side, negotiations were led by Remberto Capriles Rico, *Oficial Mayor* of the Ministry of Labour; Jesus Lozada, member of the Hacienda Advisory Committee, Humberto del Villar, assessor for the Ministry of Economy, and Antonio Bravo, Director of Colonisation at the Ministry of Agriculture.[76] The composition of the American group reflected the diversity of institutions then active in Latin America. Robert J. Watt, member of the AFL, of the ILO Governing Body since 1937 and of the National War Labor Board represented workers' interests. Watt was also a member of the National Silicosis Committee and participated in the 1942 Inter-American Social Security Conference. Charles R. Hook Jr., assistant to the president of the Rustless Iron and Steel Corporation of Baltimore, represented industry interests. Hook worked as a District of Maryland representative in the Training for Industry division of the War Production Board. In June 1942 he was appointed as an employer member of the Mediation Panel of the National War Labor Board.[77] Other American members were Alfred Giardino, Executive

---

72 Blelloch, D. 1940. *Legislación del trabajo en Bolivia*, 12. La Paz: Editorial Fénix.
73 Telegram from Ambassador Luis Guachalla to Cordell Hull, April 9, 1943. Magruder Papers, Harvard Law Library, Harvard University.
74 Letter from Blelloch to Magruder, April 8, 1943. MI 1–2 "Missions – David Blelloch, 1943–1946", ILOA.
75 The *Foreign Relations of the United States (FRUS)* series, volume V, 526–615.
76 Report submitted to the Bolivian Governement by the Joint United States-Bolivian Commission of Labor experts, 13 mars 1943. Magruder Papers, Harvard Law Library, Harvard University.
77 Blelloch mission report, 1943. MI 1–2 "Missions – David Blelloch, 1943–1946", ILOA.

Secretary of the New York State Labor Board, responsible for conducting a study on working conditions in South America for the Labor Department; Robert E. Matthews member of the General Counsel's office of the Board of Economic Warfare and Edward G. Trueblood, Second Secretary of the American Embassy in Mexico, appointed as the mission secretary. Finally, Judge Calvert Magruder – former consul with the National Labor Relations Board between 1934 and 1935, and the Wage and Hour Division of the Labor Department between 1938 and 1939 – chaired the American group.

American members were strictly limited to making suggestions on improving the living and working conditions in Bolivia, with no say on how these reforms might be financed.[78] The joint commission unanimously recommended major economic and labour standard reforms in Bolivia to reduce workers' exploitation and promote collective bargaining. The Office initiated the recommendations on freedom of association, social insurance, working hours and minimum wages. However, the report failed to mention any recommendations on the health of miners. Blelloch never addressed the need to improve hygiene conditions. Finally, the commission suggested drawing on the United States' government and the Office's technical agencies to provide the committee's recommendations with a practical dimension. Despite the adoption of a final report on 11 June 1943, Blelloch concluded that it was impossible to implement its recommendations: "All discussions on the implementation of the report are suspended pending conclusion of the negotiations for the renewal of the tin contracts, and these latter negotiations have reached a deadlock."[79]

Regarding inter-American economic cooperation, commission discussions highlight the divergent positions adopted on both sides, with the Bolivian government prioritising economic development and using this argument to strengthen its position in trade negotiations with the United States. Victor Andrade, director of the Workers' Pension Fund, who decided not to participate in the commission after the United States' refusal to discuss a possible renegotiation of commercial tin contracts, nevertheless sent a study whose main argument was that increasing the price of tin would finance the development programme in Bolivia. The commission's Bolivian members then tried to get American members to bend. In this regard, Blelloch noted: "the Bolivian members of the commission tried hard in the course of the two last sittings of the commission to per-

---

[78] Report submitted to the Bolivian Governement by the Joint United States-Bolivian Commission of Labor experts. Magruder Papers, Harvard Law Library, Harvard University.
[79] Summary by David Blelloch of conversations concerning the application of the Magruder Report, 16 June 1943, MI 1–2, ILOA.

suade their United States colleagues to make some concessions on this point".⁸⁰ The Minister of Labour, Juan Manuel Balcázar, who defended the same position as Andrade, decided not to sign the report in the end.⁸¹ Calvert Magruder summarised his statements as follows:

> He (Juan Manuel Balcázar) said that everybody knew labor conditions in Bolivia were deplorable; that the American mission was not invited down to Bolivia to tell them that, but to devise fundamental solutions; that though the American Government was already rendering some assistance to Bolivia in the direction of improving the conditions of living, this assistance was of minor character; and that the Bolivian Government was utterly without resources to finance the broad program sketched in our report unless the prices of strategic materials needed by the United States was increased.⁸²

The Bolivian government had no illusions about American assistance. According to Magruder, Bolivia "would not be surprised if we dropped her 'like a hot cake' after the war is over and after our need for her minerals and rubber ceases to be a factor".⁸³ The other major disagreement between Bolivia and the United States concerned the retention of labour clauses in United States commercial contracts. Adopting a liberal attitude, the American members, in particular Watt and Hook, opposed the commission's recommendation to insert labour clauses into commercial contracts dealing with strategic materials. For the Office, however, these clauses were important – they encouraged the improvement of working conditions.

While continental solidarity remained a key objective in Washington after 1941 the United States' policy was to prioritise its supply of raw materials rather than to promote equitable development and long-term economic engagement.⁸⁴ The Office's involvement in Bolivia was largely determined by the political decisions of the State Department. Despite insistence on the Office's part, and although the report refers to the ILO's collaboration and its particularly important experience in the development of social legislations in Latin America, no recommendation was made for its use in addressing problems facing Bolivian mine industry during and after the war.

---

80 Blelloch mission report, 1943. MI 1–2, ILOA.
81 Letter from Magruder to Cordell Hull, March 22, 1943. Magruder Papers, Harvard Law Library, Harvard University.
82 *Ibid.*
83 *Ibid.*
84 Telegram from Cordell Hull to Magruder, February 25, 1943, Magruder Papers, Harvard Law Library, Harvard University.

2 The Post-War Social Agenda and Development

2.1 Initial Reflections on Reconstruction

The adaptation of ILO's action to the needs of war was a gradual and continuous process. This being said, since 1938 it also reflected on its role after the war and in reconstruction policies. The civil servants of the Office started to mobilise at the beginning of 1941 to establish the main lines of the ILO's activities during and after the war. Ideas for the ILO's post-war action plan were largely inspired by the reflections, studies and conclusions of the 1930s conferences and technical activities in extra-European countries.

In October 1938, meeting under the threat of a war that had been temporarily delayed by the Munich events, the Governing Body discussed the ILO's role and policy given a prolonged period of crisis or war. At its February 1939 session, it decided to maintain as many Office activities as possible during the war.[85] In June 1939 the Governing Body unanimously supported the Commission on Measures to be Taken in Exceptional Circumstances' official statement on ILO policy in the event of war.[86] This commission stated that the tripartite nature of the ILO would play a central role in maintaining the organisation's activities during the war. In February 1940, the Governing Body approved an action plan for the Office aimed at developing collaboration between employers, workers and governments. ILO member governments were aware that war mobilisation required the support of workers, whose role appeared to be as fundamental as that of soldiers on the front line.[87] For trade union organisations, the survival of the ILO was above all a guarantee for the future, particularly for British and American trade unions, which hoped that workers would be represented in post-war negotiations.[88] However, uncertainty about the ILO's future prevented the formulation of a more concrete action plan at this point, hence the Commission on Measures

---

[85] Minutes of the GB, 86th session, 2–4 February 1939, ILOA. See also Jenks, W. 1969. *The ILO in Wartime*, 11. Ottawa, Canada: Département du travail; Ghebali, V.-Y., Ago, R., Valticos, N. 1989. *The International Labour Organisation: A Case Study on the Evolution of U.N. Specialised Agencies*, 17–20. Dordrecht, Boston [etc.]: M. Nijhoff.
[86] Report of the GB, 88th Session, 6–13 June 1939, ILOA.
[87] Kott, S. 2000. "*World War Two and Labor:* A Lost Cause?", *International Labor and Working Class History* 58: 181–191; Goodrich, C. 1942. "The Effect of the War on the Position of Labor", *The American Economic Review* 32(1): 416–425.
[88] Van Goethem, G. 2010. "Labor's Second Front: The Foreign Policy of the American and British Trade Union Movements During the Second World War", *Diplomatic History* 34(4): 663–680.

to be Taken in Exceptional Circumstances' second report stressing the need to develop the new post-war economic and social policy as soon as possible.

The Governing Body's official position nevertheless engaged the Office in a reflection on the role it would come to play after the war. These reflections were first developed under the leadership of the American John G. Winant. However, President Roosevelt soon appointed him ambassador in London. He resigned from the Office in 1941 and Edward Phelan took over as Acting Director.[89] Edward Phelan (1888–1967), who was considered a liberal socialist, was one of the founding members of the ILO and was part of an intellectual generation that marked the turn of the nineteenth century. Irish by birth, he made his first administrative debut under the direction of Lloyd George whose social policy development programme laid the foundations for the welfare state in Britain.[90] He was chosen to organise the Intelligence Division of the Ministry of Labour. A member of Bruce Lockhart's secret mission to Russia in 1918, as a labour attaché, Phelan was directly involved in Britain's diplomatic action after the war. Back in London, he was seconded to the Foreign Office as a consultant on Russia. Convinced that the Bolshevik regime would survive, he considered how to link labour issues with British foreign policy and drew up a memorandum on "democracy and diplomacy", in which he proposed the creation of a permanent international labour organisation. His career was then entirely dedicated to the development of this project.[91] Appointed by Albert Thomas as head of the Diplomatic Division in 1920, Phelan played a key role in the development of the Office's activities. He took over the Director's responsibilities when Thomas was on the move, and prepared all of his missions abroad.[92] After 1932 he worked under the direction of Harold Butler, who charged him with raising the ILO's profile in the United States and affirming its role in the economic crisis.[93] Winant and Phelan after him were therefore both responsible for formulating the ILO's reconstruction programme and ensuring the organisation's survival during the war.

Clearly influenced by the war, Winant's report presented in Montreal in 1941 stressed the fundamental role of the ILO in rebuilding political, economic and social democracy:

---

89 He was officially appointed Director-General in 1946.
90 See his biography at: http ://www.ilo.org/global/about-the-ilo/who-we-are/ilo-director-general/former-directors-general/WCMS_192734/lang-fr/index.htm [last accessed 17.09.2019].
91 *Edward Phelan and the ILO*, 1.
92 Edward Phelan's personal file, P 108, ILAO.
93 XT 11/1/1 "Missions: Mr. Phelan's visit to Canada, the United States and Mexico", Jacket 1, 1933 and Jacket 2, 1932–1933, ILOA.

Political democracy must be broadened to include economic stability and social security. [...] No opportunity to expand the social heritage of democracy should be lost. No opportunity to strengthen the fundamental social and civil rights of the vast majority of citizens should be overlooked. No opportunity to eliminate the misery and despair of the pre-war period should be ignored. To do so is not only to exercise caution in national defence, but also to practice the tradition of democratic freedom.[94]

In a note published in 1940 in the *International Labour Review*, Winant insisted on the continuity of ILO war-time objectives with the guidelines adopted in the 1930s, in particular on the problem of raising living standards.[95] The assistance the Office could provide, in particular to developing countries, was essentially intended as an accompanying measure in the industrialisation process, forced upon nations by the war. However, there was no consensus within the Office on how to encourage this industrialisation process. For some economists, particularly Americans, the emphasis should be on improving production conditions. Ernest Penrose, an expert in the Office's Economic Section between 1939 and 1942,[96] wrote the following in a draft research programme on reconstruction that he submitted to Phelan:

> The development of industries in what, from the standpoint of industrial development, may be called "infant countries" will constitute one of the major problem of post-war economic recovery and development. [...] But the main emphasis should be not on protection but on improvements in productive methods, not on raising prices of manufactured goods but on lowering their costs of production.[97]

However, the Office's missions of technical assistance in Latin America testify to the centrality of social protection.[98] As previously mentioned, this strategy was

---

[94] Report to the Governments, Employers and Workers of the Member States of the International Labour Organization, Montreal, February 14, 1941, 17: http ://www.ilo.org/public/libdoc/ilo/1941/41B09_1_fren.pdf [last accessed 17.09.2019].
[95] Winant, J. G. 1940. "Le Bureau international du travail regarde vers l'avenir. Une note du Directeur" in *International Labour Review*, 42(4–5): 179–180.
[96] Penrose has been in contact with the ILO since 1937, the date of the World Textile Conference. Ernest Penrose's personal file, P 3425, ILOA.
[97] Report from Penrose to Phelan, May 15, 1941. Z 6/3/7, "Post-War Reconstruction: Notes by E. Penrose for the extension of Economic Activities of the ILO after the war, 1941–1942", ILOA.
[98] However, the productivist orientation found a concrete realisation as early as 1948 with the establishment of the ILO's Manpower Programme. For more information on this programme, see Mecchi, L. 2013. "Du BIT à la politique sociale européenne : les origines d'un modèle", *Le Mouvement social*, 3(244): 17–30.

developed under the influence of experts from the ILO's Social Insurance Section. Adrien Tixier, Deputy Director of the Office since 1937, prepared a draft International Labour Charter in 1941, which was to serve as a basis for a discussion among ILO members on the future direction of its mission.[99] Faithful to Albert Thomas' socialist heritage, Tixier wished to see the ILO and the Office take position in favour of the achievement of true democracy, not merely political but also economic and social, "as one of the aims of war and future peace".[100] In the condensed version sent to Phelan on 17 August 1941 he insisted on the following principles: economic and social security organisation by the state, employment policy development and the right to work. Among the measures to be promoted Tixier deeply valued the establishment of a compulsory social insurance system, a wage policy to guarantee a minimum standard of living, a food and housing policy, the improvement of working conditions by reducing working hours, increasing rest periods, and finally, the participation of professional associations in the social and economic organisation of the state. Tixier's draft Charter, in addition to affirming the role of the state, affirms the individual rights of workers.[101] This draft also reflected new principles, such as the right to work and the participation of workers' representatives in the management of economic life. All these proposals would be included in the Director's 1941 annual report and discussed at the ILC that same year.

2.2 New York 1941 and Philadelphia 1944

It was not until the November 1941 ILO Conferences in New York and Washington that ILO commitment to the Allies was made official. From that moment on, in order to survive, the ILO sacrificed its universalism in favour of the defence of democracy. The ILO was in an exceptional situation. During the war the GB was operating at reduced capacity and international labour conferences would not resume until 1944. The Office was in a similar predicament and Phelan, acting without the support of the GB, did not have the necessary authority to take a firm position against totalitarian regimes. In 1940, while Tixier was in Mexico, he emphasised the astonishment caused by this silence, interpreted as a desire on the part of the United States and Great Britain to put the organisation to sleep

---

99 LE 102 "Labour Legislation: Proposal for a new international Charter of Labour. 01/1941– 06/1942", ILOA.
100 Ibid.
101 Ibid.

during the war.[102] In the spring of 1941, Stein and Tixier urged Phelan to quickly organise an international conference. The ILO was also facing direct competition from American agencies operating in Latin America. For Stein, "if it [the conference] is only to be held in the fall, it will be too late. In the meantime, others will have formulated the anti-totalitarian social program."[103]

For Stein and Tixier an official commitment of the Office against totalitarian countries was not only a way to guarantee the ILO's survival during the war, it would also reflect the struggle in which they themselves felt involved. However, Tixier was well aware that issuing an official statement against totalitarian regimes was no simple thing. By taking a clear stance against these regimes' social doctrines, characterised by the suppression of workers' organisations in Germany, or their subjection to political power in Italy, the Office risked provoking controversy between the conservative and revolutionary members of its ranks and between the neutralist and interventionist factions in the countries having not yet entered the war.[104] A strong position against totalitarian countries could also spark fear of reprisals from Germany in European countries, particularly in Switzerland and Sweden. Finally, it might provoke negative reactions in countries that had until then remained neutral, such as Argentina. Phelan's wait-and-see attitude, as disappointing as it may have been to some civil servants, testifies above all to the Office's dependence on the decisions of the world's major powers.

The first evidence of this was that the 1941 ILO Conference was only organised after the publication of the Atlantic Charter in August. This joint declaration by the United States and Great Britain was the first response of the democratic powers to Hitler's new order and presented itself as a kind of "New Deal for the World".[105] It laid the foundations for the new international order, where the social aspects of economic planning were seen as central elements. This declaration was of direct interest to the ILO, as the improvement of working conditions, economic progress and social security were considered essential elements

---

[102] Report of Tixier's mission to Cuba and Mexico, MI 9 "Missions – Adrien Tixier Mission to Cuba and Mexico, Jacket 1, 09/1940–07/1941", ILOA.

[103] Letter from Stein to Tixier, May 26, 1941. MI 3–7, "Missions to Peru", ILOA. Original quote in French: "si elle [la conférence] ne doit se tenir qu'en automne, ce sera trop tard. Entre temps, d'autres auront formulé le programme social antitotalitaire".

[104] "La position politique de l'OIT". Internal note from Tixier to Phelan, May 29, 1941. Z 1/1/1/9 "Correspondence between the Acting Director and M. Tixier, 1940–1944", ILOA.

[105] Borgwardt, E. 2005. *A New Deal for the World: America's Vision for Human Rights*, 14–45. Cambridge, MA [etc.]: Belknap Press, Harvard University Press.

of the Allies' reconstruction policy. It gave the necessary impetus to organise the ILO Conference in November 1941.

Phelan sought Washington's support first and foremost, meeting with Frances Perkins and then with Secretary of State Cordell Hull.[106] According to Phelan, Perkins and Hull supported the project of an ILO conference because it could publicise the United States' central concerns about its role in post-war reconstruction.[107] Its years-long relative isolation required preparing the American public opinion for the new international responsibilities the United States now wished to assume. Phelan then travelled to Ottawa and met with Prime Minister William Lyon Mackenzie King, who also expressed strong support for the conference. Concurrently, Phelan, who was unable to travel to Europe, asked Burge, from the London correspondence office, to discuss the project with members of the British government. At first, reactions were clearly hostile. The idea of sending high-ranking civil servants across the Atlantic was indeed considered absurd. Employers and workers were against this idea as well. Burge, who was also instructed to meet informally with the exiled governments, informed Phelan of their approval, which helped put into perspective the otherwise entirely negative atmosphere in London at the time. The likely intervention of members of the Roosevelt administration and the Canadian Prime Minister would then have defeated Britain's opposition.[108]

At the conference, the ILO's Governing Body was present, as well as its Chairman, the American Carter Goodrich. Clement Attlee, second spokesman in the House of Commons and leader of the Labour Party, represented the British War Cabinet. Members of the Council of Ministers represented the governments of Belgium, Bolivia, Canada, Chile, Czechoslovakia, Greece, Luxembourg, Mexico, New Zealand, the Netherlands, Norway, Poland and Yugoslavia. Delegates from China, India, Iran and Thailand represented Asia. The Union of South Africa was also represented.[109] On the workers' side, it is worth noting the absence of Léon Jouhaux, who nevertheless sent a letter of support to Phelan.[110] This conference was being placed in the powerful hands of the Roosevelt administration,

---

[106] Z 1/61/1/3 "Correspondence with Miss Frances Perkins, Secretary of Labor, Department of Labor, Washington D.C., 1941–1943", ILOA.
[107] *Edward Phelan and the ILO*, 296–297.
[108] Ibid.
[109] 1942. "L'objectif social en temps de guerre et dans l'œuvre de reconstruction du monde. La conférence de New York de l'Organisation internationale du travail", *International labour Review* 45(1), Montreal: 1–2.
[110] Letter from Jouhaux to Phelan, November 7, 1941. Z 1/22/3/1 "Relations with M. Léon Jouhaux, 1941–1948. Jacket 1", ILOA.

with Perkins elected as president, and the final session of the conference was held at the White House in Washington on 6 November, where President Roosevelt delivered a speech.

This international gathering fuelled the Office's ambitions.[111] It was to determine the ILO's contribution to future peace planning. However, Phelan's report at the conference remained cautious. It was written in collaboration with Tixier and Jenks, who specified that: "It [is] a very prudent [...] document, but its object [is] to secure widespread agreements on certain preliminary steps".[112] Phelan resolutely framed the ILO's future action within "new social thinking", where social policy was seen as an essential component of economic progress. At the conference, consensus emerged: post-war economic policy had to integrate labour policies, economic growth, trade development and social security.

The Phelan report highlights the profound change that took place since the 1930s. In addition to ensuring better working conditions, the organisation had to develop its activities in the field of economic security, as evidenced by this passage from Phelan's report:

> Economic security for the individual in this sense implies more than the old slogans of "the right to work" or "work or relief". It implies more even than "the prevention of unemployment" by such economic measures and policies as may produce that result and thereby eliminate economic insecurity from the life of the average worker. It aims in addition at enabling him to secure, for himself and his family, all that is necessary to enable him in youth, through his working years, and in old age, to enjoy a place of dignity in the life of the community and to make to it whatever contribution his gifts and capacities may render possible.[113]

It is worth noting the influence of Roosevelt's four freedoms speech, in particular the freedom from want. This excerpt also reflects the connections made by the Office between economic security and respect for individual dignity and freedom, which would be enshrined in the 1944 Philadelphia Declaration. For Phelan, however, economic security should not be seen as an end in itself, but as the condition that enables people to enjoy higher living standards and reduces inequalities, requiring economic and social planning at the national and international levels. In one of its resolutions the conference stated that the ILO should

---

111 Clavin, P. 2013. *Securing the World Economy: The Reinvention of the League of Nations, 1920–1946*, 274–278. Oxford: Oxford University Press.
112 Letter from Jenks to his mother, August 30, 1941, FWJ, ILOA.
113 Report by the Acting Director of the International Labour Office to the Conference of the International Labour Organisation New York, October 1941, 93, ILOA.

be involved in "the planning and implementation of reconstruction measures".[114] As early as 1942 the Governing Body allotted an additional million Swiss francs for the development of Office studies on reconstruction.[115] This resolution attests that governments, employers' and trade union organisations still placed their trust in the ILO. In particular, the ILO had the strong support of the Roosevelt administration, as evidenced by his closing speech: "In the planning of such international action, the International Labour Organization, with its representatives of labour and management, its technical knowledge and experience, will be an invaluable instrument for peace. Your Organisation will have an essential part to play in building up a stable international system of social justice for all peoples everywhere."[116] The Roosevelt administration saw the ILO as an instrument to internationalise the principles of the New Deal and support American foreign policy during the war, much like the UN would soon come to be a means of increasing the United States' influence in newly decolonised countries through international development programmes. Roosevelt's speech was also aimed at American citizens. Roosevelt used the conference to shape American public opinion in favour of a new international economic order, in which the United States would take a more active part.

Another resolution adopted in 1941 stipulated that the ILO should be "represented at all conferences on peace and post-war reconstruction".[117] Workers' representatives Jef Rens, Deputy Secretary of the Belgian CGT, Joseph Hallsworth, Secretary of the British Trade Union of Commercial Employees, and Walther Schevenels, General Secretary of the International Federation of Trade Unions (IFTU), insisted that the ILO be placed on an equal footing with future international organisations created to manage reconstruction. However, the effective implementation of this resolution could not be guaranteed. At the 1941 conference, the United States did not officially state how reconstruction activities would be coordinated.[118] The Bretton Woods agreements and the creation of new international organizations would marginalize the ILO's place eventually. While

---

114 "Résolution concernant les mesures à prendre à l'égard des problèmes qui se poseront immédiatement après la cessation des hostilités ainsi que pour l'œuvre de reconstruction". ILC Record of Proceedings, 1941, 167–168.
115 1942. "Vers une "paix du peuple". La réunion de la commission de crise du BIT. Londres, avril 1942", *International Labour Review* 46(1): 46.
116 ILC Record of Proceedings, 1941, 158, ILOA.
117 "Résolution concernant les mesures à prendre à l'égard des problèmes qui se poseront immédiatement après la cessation des hostilités ainsi que pour l'œuvre de reconstruction". ILC Record of Proceedings, 1941, 167–168.
118 Alcock, A. 1971.*History of the International Labour Organisation*, 167. London: Macmillan.

the 1930s and early 1940s birthed a vision of prosperity and progress based on economic planning and social justice, the decision made on 22 July 1944 at the Bretton Woods Conference to establish the International Bank for Reconstruction and Development (IBRD) and the International Monetary Fund (IMF) reflected the United States' commitment to begin addressing economic issues independently of social issues. This was a significant setback for the ILO.[119] Moreover, since 1943 the ILO had been systematically excluded from international discussions. It was not represented at the Hot Springs Conference, nor was it mentioned in the plans presented at Dumbarton Oaks, which provided for the creation of an economic and social organisation (the future ECOSOC). Despite attempts to establish concrete partnerships with UNRRA, the ILO never succeeded in collaborating with the agency.[120] In 1945 Jenks noted that the Office had little to expect from relations with this organisation.[121]

Despite the ILO's clear commitment to actively participating in the reconstruction and development programs after the war, its place in the United Nations system depended largely on the political negotiations of the major powers. The ILO's marginalisation was also due to the USSR, which opposed the ILO for several reasons. Its connection to the League of Nations made it a symbol of prewar European hegemony. Historically, the ILO had also emerged from a desire to fight the expansion of Bolshevism. Finally, the ILO's tripartite structure, which would be maintained after the Second World War, was hardly reconcilable with the USSR's political and social organisation. The latter refused to participate in the Philadelphia Conference and strongly opposed the ILO's participation in the San Francisco Conference. The presence of a small ILO delegation in San Francisco was only possible thanks to the support of the British Minister of Labour, Ernest Bevin, and the British Trades Union Congress.[122]

---

119 Kott, S. 2015. "Organizing World Peace. The International Labour Organisation from the Second World War to the Cold War", in Hoffmann, S.-L., Kott, S., Romijn, P., Wieviorka, O. eds. *Seeking Peace in the Wake of War: Europe, 1943–1947*, 309–310. Amsterdam: Amsterdam University Press.
120 RRA 1000–41–1 "United Nations Relief and Rehabilitation administration – Committee of the Council of Europe Ad-hoc sub-committee"; RRA 1 "UNRRA – Council of the United Nations Relief and Rehabilitation administration – 5th session – Geneva – August 1946", in ILOA. S-1303–0000–5485 (1943–1949); S-1303–0000–5486 (1943–1949); S-1303–0000–5487 (1943–1949); S-1303–0000–5488 (1943–1949); S-1303–0000–5489 (1943–1949). United Nations Relief and Rehabilitation Administration. UNRRA. United Nations Archives. New York.
121 Letter from Jenks to Phelan, February 23, 1945. Z 1/1/1/13 (J.1) "Correspondence between the Director and C.W. Jenks, 1945–1948", ILOA.
122 Van Goethem, G. 2010. "Phelan's War: The International Labour Organization in Limbo (1941–1948)", in Van Daele, J., Rodríguez García, M., Van Goethem, G., van der Linden, M.

The 1944 Philadelphia Conference thus took place in a context of increased institutional competition and testifies to the loss of ILO influence.[123] Nevertheless, the Declaration adopted at this conference provided the basis for the orientation of ILO social policy after the war. It reiterated principles adopted in 1941.[124] Article III established that everyone has the right to a "living wage", "an adequate level of food and housing", insisting on the "collaboration of workers and employers in the development and implementation of social and economic policy"; while Article IV confirmed the ILO's collaboration in the implementation of international policies aimed at "a more complete and wider use of the world's productive resources".[125] The Declaration of Philadelphia was the first to clearly set out the ILO's objective of positioning itself as an organisation for the control and regulation of international economy. It stipulated that the ILO would study the social implications of economic and financial policies, while cooperating fully with international organisations yielding large and steady volumes of international trade. However, the Declaration of Philadelphia did not fundamentally alter the scope of ILO action, as defined in its 1919 Constitution.[126] It actually reaffirmed a set of principles, such as the notion that "labour is not a commodity", trade liberalisation and raising living standards. These reflect the ILO's European social democratic and liberal roots. New principles were nevertheless adopted, such as respect for human rights, the struggle for "full employment", and the "cooperation of management and labour in the continuous improvement of productive efficiency", which reflect, according to Jason Guthrie, the growing influence of American liberalism and its industrial relations model.[127]

The Declaration of Philadelphia would be annexed to the 1946 ILO Constitution and its principles would guide ILO development programmes after the war.

---

eds. *ILO Histories: Essays on the International Labour Organization and its Impact on the World During the Twentieth Century*, 314–340. Bern: Peter Lang.
123 Kott, S. 2014. "Fighting the War or Preparing for Peace? The ILO during the Second World War", *Journal of Modern European History* 12(3): 359–376.
124 Supiot, A. 2010. *L'Esprit de Philadelphie. La justice sociale face au marché total*. Paris: Seuil.
125 Declaration adopted by the Conference, Appendix XIII, Record of Proceedings, International Labour Conference, 26th session, Philadelphia, Montreal, 1944, 621 and following; Lee, E. 1994. "The Declaration of Philadelphia: Retrospect and Prospect", *International labour Review* 133(4): 467–84.
126 Tortora, M. 1980. *Institution spécialisée et organisation mondiale : étude des relations de l'OIT avec la SDN et l'ONU*, 215–216. Bruxelles: E. Bruylant.
127 Guthrie, J. 2012. "The ILO and the International Technocratic class, 1944–1966", in Droux, J., Kott, S. eds. *Globalizing Social Rights: The International Labour Organization and Beyond*, 115–136. Basingstoke, Palgrave Macmillan, International Labour Office.

Interestingly, however, in the ILO's new constitution, technical assistance was still not officially part of the ILO's mandate. That said, the idea was implicit in Article 10, paragraph 2, sub-paragraph b, which provided for the possibility of assisting governments for labour inspection in the preparation of social legislation. This predicament for technical assistance is surprising, to say the least, given its steady growth since the 1930s. After all, by the end of the war the Office's missions of technical assistance had spread worldwide, covering various sectors: social insurance, migration, labour legislation and vocational training.

Conclusion

The ILO's official position to side with the Allies in 1941 and the integration of the Office's activities into the inter-American defence programmes placed the development of social policies in the context of the fight against totalitarian regimes. From this vantage point the Office's technical assistance activities were meant to support Allied war policy. The positioning of the ILO "in the shelter of one power bloc" partly explains its survival during and after the war.[128] The expertise it gained from technical assistance in several countries in Latin America also explained its survival during the war and the speed with which it succeeded in setting guidelines for the social development after the war. From 1946 onwards, Office civil servants were regularly called upon to attend Pan-American conferences and UN regional economic commissions meetings. In the immediate post-war period, missions of technical assistance were called upon to renew the official relations that had been shattered by war[129] and were essential in establishing reconstruction and development programmes, first in Latin America and then worldwide. In 1947, missions of technical assistance were sent to Baghdad, Iraq, to prepare for the implementation of a social insurance plan. Iraqi Djamalzadeh, a former member of the non-European countries section, was sent the same year to Iran to collaborate with the government on labour legislation.[130] An important mission involving seven Office civil servants was also sent to Greece in autumn 1947 to assist the government in the revision of labour legislation and trade union legislation.[131]

---

[128] Haas, E. B. 1964. *Beyond the Nation-State: Functionalism and International Organization*, 436. Stanford California: Stanford University Press.
[129] MI 75/1 "Missions – Rudolf A. Metall. 04/1946–06/1951", ILAO.
[130] Annual report of the Director, ILC Record of Proceedings, 1947, 124, ILOA.
[131] The civil servants mobilised were Miss Natzio, member of the Official Relations Section, I. Bessling, member of the Labour Legislation and Labour Relations Section, Anton Zelenka, mem-

The war, like the crises of the 1930s, provided an important intellectual and institutional framework for the ILO's commitment into international development projects. The Declaration of Philadelphia that allowed this transition was not derived from entirely new principles and some of them had already been claimed before the war. The ILO officially adopted its first development programme in 1948, under the influence of the new Office Director, the American David Morse. However, the orientation of ILO's activities towards technical assistance and development quickly raised debates and opposition between those who considered that the core of ILO action should remain the production of international labour standards, like stressed by workers delegates, and those who considered that these same standards were an obstacle to economic development.[132] From 1947 onwards, this debate also reflected the evolution of the geopolitical context and the domination of the United States in guiding the activities of the United Nations. While in 1945 Phelan could still define technical assistance as an instrument "to make the work of the ILO more widely known throughout the world and base its activities on an intimate and continuous touch with the conditions, preoccupations and aspirations of widely differing regions",[133] the emergence of the Cold War placed the ILO in front of new challenges, and marked the end of the first phase in the history of development at the ILO.

---

ber of the Social Security Section, J.D. Kingsley, Head of Section, John Price, Head of the Industry Committees Section, and Marguerite Thibert, former civil servant until January 1947, who acted as external consultant. Annual Report of the Director, ILC Record of Proceedings, 1948. See the section "Missions of an advisory nature".

132 At the 1948 ILC, Léon Jouhaux expressed his concerns about the future of the ILO, the main focus of which should remain, in his view, the development of international labour standards. ILC Record of Proceedings, 1948, 177, ILOA.

133 Annual Report from the Director, ILC Record of Proceeding, 1945, 128, ILOA.

General Conclusion

At the end of this analysis one conclusion that arises with utmost clarity is that during the 1930s the ILO developed a series of ideas and practices that foreshadowed development thinking as it would emerge after the Second World War. This evolution was closely linked to the period's particular context, one marked by a dual crisis ripping through the international economy on the one hand, and the social state on the other. Through the study of ILO activities, this book therefore offers a historical reinterpretation of the origins of international development and the policies that gave rise to it.

One cannot begin to understand the ILO's perspective on economic and social development without taking into account the concurrent evolution of economic thinking in the 1930s and implementation of innovative national policies which led to increased state interventionism in the economy, particularly in the United States. By systematically taking into account the evolution of international contexts, institutional logics and the specific practices of international civil servants, my analysis allowed for a reflection on the importance of the ILO as a forum for debating the functioning of the capitalist economy. In particular I have shown that the ILO became an essential platform where heterodox economic ideas could be expressed and recommendations on the international organisation of the economy and on economic and social planning could be formulated on a global scale.

As for the Office, it played a central role in this process of intellectual construction. Albert Thomas, who had followed the evolution of economic thought very closely, had also, in some ways, anticipated it. I underlined the importance of the European reformist movement, of which he was one of the proponents, and the American progressive movement, which he helped internationalise, as matrices of ideas on social modernisation and planning. I also stressed the importance of the First World War as a laboratory for worldwide planist experimentation and cooperation between the state, industry and workers, of which Thomas was one of the main architects in France. In the early 1930s Thomas was an active promoter of planning. According to him the survival of democracies depended entirely on economic and social organisation. To that end, the Office's activities were deployed to help spread this notion. Ideas on economic and social planning were then incorporated into the 1944 Philadelphia Declaration. From this standpoint the economic principles that guided post-war international social policy must be viewed less as a revolution than as an evolution, rooted in the analyses initiated in the wake of the 1930s.

The dynamics at work in the 1930s led to an evolution in the ILO's very perception of labour, along with its scope of action. In the 1920s its main activity was to produce international standards to protect workers and to disseminate them mainly throughout Europe's industrialised nations. However, the economic crisis of the 1930s led to an awareness of the limits of conventional international action. In addition, the international civil servants developed the idea that social policies have an economic role and that their objective is not only to protect workers, in particular from unemployment, but also to boost consumption, a prerequisite for economic development. In this book I stressed the catalytic role of the 1929 economic crisis in raising awareness of the importance of labour regulation in the expansion of the global economy. In this regard the ILO stressed the need to organise economic and social progress in less developed regions in order to ensure greater price stability and revive international trade. However, these issues quickly became the subject of ideological competition, embodied in the withdrawal of Nazi Germany from the ILO in 1933, fascist Italy in 1937 and Japan in 1938. In this context, the construction of a discourse on development appears to be an attempt by democratic countries to counter the growing influence of totalitarian regimes. The role played by the Office, in particular the solutions it advocated for and the expertise it developed, testifies to the agility with which it managed to navigate these opposing forces, understanding them as signs of the growing need for social justice all over the world.

The Office's research and economic studies also stimulated the development of a reflection on the validity of harmonising social policies as a condition for global economic development. They helped formulating burgeoning ideas on productivity gains as prerequisites for further social progress, especially in less developed economies.[1] Experience acquired and techniques developed in the 1930s would come to be mobilised after 1945, in particular through productivity and development programmes.

The growing interest in finding solutions to the global economic crisis accompanied the geographical expansion of the Office's activities. By becoming the first "universal" problem since the First World War, the crisis had brought the world to the ILO's doorstep. The United States was undoubtedly one of the key actors in this decentralisation of ILO's activities from Europe. After becoming a member of the organisation in 1934 its involvement played an important role in the evolution of the Office's activities in the economic field, providing models of economic and social organisation that could be applied to different countries.

---

[1] This idea came to the fore after 1945. Mecchi, L. 2013. "Du BIT à la politique sociale européenne : les origines d'un modèle", *Le Mouvement social* 3(244): 17–30.

The United States' influence at the ILO increased in the late 1930s and became evident during and after the Second World War. As for the role the United States played in international relations, there may be less of a rupture between the interwar period and the post-1945 period.

The United States' entry to the ILO was not the only sign of the globalisation process the organisation was undergoing. During this period the ILO developed a form of technical diplomacy based on the economic and social expertise of less developed regions. In the course of my analysis I have shown that various actors from Central and Eastern Europe, non-European countries and the colonies sought, through the ILO, to renegotiate and reimagine the internationalism inherited from the 1920s to adapt it to their demands. Within this movement the participation of Latin American countries, in particular Brazil, Venezuela and Chile, was significant, leading to changes in the ILO's institutional structure and to social expertise being extended to the economic conditions of less developed countries. In particular I stressed the importance of the work of Office civil servants, who were regularly sent on missions to collect information, give advice, produce reports and contact influential figures to initiate transnational collaborations. The growing interest in less developed economies led to a wider dissemination of international labour Conventions in Latin America, particularly in the field of social insurance. It also helped to advance international cooperation in certain areas, such as migration for colonisation or social insurance financing. This ability of the ILO to build and disseminate expertise explains its survival during the Second World War.

Probing ILO activities in Asia showed how the ILO responded to economic competition from emerging powers such as Japan and India. The end of the 1930s was also a favourable time to revive the question of colonial reform. The Office took advantage of this context to promote the idea of economic and social recovery policies in these territories. This discourse was based on a particular view of development as combining industrialisation policy, the liberalisation of international trade and the improvement of living and working conditions. The discourse of Office civil servants on the need to raise the standard of living was not only born of a humanist discourse, but also responded to the desire to fight against unfair competition, to expand the world consumer market and to integrate all territories, in particular colonies, into the international economy. The problems facing the colonies were thus analysed from a global perspective. This led to a reflection on the internal structural imbalances of the colonies, such as poverty and overpopulation, which prevented their economic and social development. However, this discourse was not at odds with the framework of colonial thinking. While Office civil servants developed an awareness of the issues posed by the colonies' dependence on the metropoles' markets, they did not as such consider the colonies' independence, instead prioritising a strengthening of relations within the empire's framework. The Second World War inhibited any major advances in the formulation of an international colonial social policy. The 1944 ILO Conference in Philadelphia adopted nothing more than declarations of principle and general obligations for the improvement of social conditions in the colonies. The adopted recommendations nevertheless stressed the responsibility of the colonial powers to create favourable economic conditions for the application of international social protection standards, in line with the ideas formulated by the Office at the end of the 1930s.

It is against this backdrop of tensions in international relations, a slowdown in economic activity and a change in economic thinking that the organisation of the Office's technical assistance took place. The latter, which I examined in the second part of this book, reflect the important changes that took place at the ILO. They highlight the close link that was then being established between the adoption of modern social policies, international expertise and the growing involvement of the state in the organisation of economic life. This book shows that these missions were first organised in Europe. If we take the case of the ILO, technical assistance was therefore not originally designed as an instrument of North-South co-operation, but one serving European integration, through social policies.

Technical assistance practices were based on the recognition of an enormous gap between ILO policies and the economic and social realities of less industrialised countries, where economic and social structures simply did not exist in the same ways, where the institutionalisation of social policies were still inchoate and where there was little to no tradition of social dialogue. At the Office, technical assistance was conceived from the outset as a means of filling these gaps. By seeking to organise labour markets in less industrialised countries, the Office was an important player in the globalisation of social modernisation. On several occasions between 1930 and 1946 the Office collaborated with the governments of the member states in the drafting of new labour laws and, more generally, in the formulation of social policy programmes. Thus, since the 1930s, the ILO has offered an original perspective on development, with social engineering as its main tool. The ILO's engagement with the Allies at the beginning of the Second World War redefined the challenges of technical assistance. This period highlighted both the versatility of the notion of "development" along with its crystallisation around issues of economic security.

My analysis of how missions were organised and the type of expertise mobilised for technical assistance was combined with a study of their reception in national spaces. The results of the latter are limited, however, by my methodological decision to prioritise understanding the main thrust of the ILO's action. That said, I highlighted three essential functions. First, I underscored technical assistance's obvious diplomatic function. In 1931 Albert Thomas clearly expressed the idea that it was an original way for the Office to play the role of a "family council".[2] In the context of a fragile diplomatic balance, technical assistance appeared as a means of developing political relations, based on an exchange of expertise. Technical assistance also helped the Office find new support by raising awareness of its activities in countries that were generally not very active on the international scene. In this respect, between 1930 and 1946, the Office was most successful in Latin America.

Secondly, technical assistance allowed for technical knowledge transfers to occur. The global economic crisis undoubtedly fostered a growing interest in the activities of international organisations, whose knowledge and resources constituted "turnkey" solutions for governments. However, the dynamics of technical assistance reflect the contested and negotiated nature of these knowledge transfers. Once again, the reasons behind these oppositions are complex and manifold. Summarising them as nothing more than rivalling national and international interests seems far too simplistic. The social interactions that played out reflect the equally important weight of individual actors' personal strategies (who often acted for their own prestige), or even the competition between international organisations.

Thirdly, technical assistance had a political function. It is clear from the Office's archives that the use of international expertise was presented by government actors as a strategy for legitimising public and state action, particularly in the face of opposing economic interests and the mobilisation of workers demanding new social rights. The vast majority of missions took place amid social crises marked by revolts, strikes and violence against workers in certain branches of industry. From the ILO's perspective, technical assistance was fundamentally linked to its mission to ensure that member states ratify international labour conventions. It was also a means of encouraging a democratic process of social change. However, on this issue, the results are mixed. While the archives I consulted did not prove that social actors other than the state were excluded, in countries where social dialogue was not widely practised, the political tensions surrounding the projects and the way in which civil servants worked led me to posit that the Office's presence did not favour this dialogue. To my knowledge, the civil servants of the Office never collaborated with workers' or employers' organisations during their missions of technical assistance. This finding more gen-

---

[2] Letter from Albert Thomas to Jacques Reclus, December 22, 1931. CAT 5–19–1 "Relations et informations. Chine." ILOA. Original quote in French: "conseil de famille."

erally reflects the limits of tripartism in the 1930s when it comes to national economic development, which also applies to Europe.

What did the Office's technical assistance amount to? First, these activities directly contributed to strengthening the role of the state. Technical assistance was and continues to be directed towards stabilising and strengthening the nation-state as the only viable framework within which economic and social progress is possible. Second, technical assistance, which was prompted by government request, reflects the role of the state as an actor in the international circulation of social policy models. Incidentally some missions directly hired experts from foreign national institutions. Within the limits of sources available to me I sought to specify the stakes of these technical collaborations, but also the interests and motivations of the agents involved, and to expose the representations that existed among various actors. The other contribution of this analysis is to demonstrate that social construction processes at the national level are central to the development of collaboration between states and the ILO. From this observation it follows that each mission of technical assistance constitutes a collaboration of a particular type. Taking into account the socially constructed dimension of technical assistance then appears as a necessary condition to restore the complexity of the interactions it both generates and requires. Third, technical assistance, essentially modelled after European experiences and designed around the skills of European civil servants (having moreover undergone a process of professionalisation in European social reform networks), directly contributed to the global dissemination of Western conceptions of social justice. That said, it should be stressed that by the end of the Second World War, the generation that had hitherto carried out the Office's activities gradually disappeared, paving the way for a more critical understanding of the professionalisation and socialisation processes that shaped the new actors involved in technical assistance and development activities. An analysis of the practices of international civil servants and external experts, recruited more systematically after 1945, would help deepen our understanding of the modalities of building development practices by examining the models of social modernisation valued by the Office and reinvested in the implementation of international technical cooperation programmes, while a sociological study would specify the profile of the actors selected in this undertaking. This social approach would thus lead to a renewed view of this period, focusing more on how Western powers and, through them, experts, invested in international organisations to promote their own development model.

Given my willingness to question the Office's operating logic, it is above all on the question of what practices are engendered by technical assistance that my contribution is most significant. First of all it should be noted that until 1948 there were no development programmes as such. Involvement in this type of activity during the 1930s must therefore be understood as the result of the Office's ability to adapt to a new international context, rather than as the result of a clearly defined strategy. Second, it emerges from the analysis of these missions that Office civil servants had a very limited knowledge of the land they invested in and a biased understanding of national economic and social problems. They mainly collaborated with national elites and contact with other local sources was almost non-existent. Despite these limitations the Office built a culture of action through technical assistance and contributed to the emergence development aid as a practice fundamentally based on field experience. For a long time this direct confrontation with reality in the field would justify the development action of international organisations. Finally, the discourse of Office civil servants demonstrates that field experience did not generally lead to a profound transformation of the knowledge developed within the Office in the interwar period. The missions, above all, allowed the civil servants to layer their discourse with a kind of "geographical universality".

As indicated in the introduction to this book, using the ILO as an observation site for the emergence of ideas and practices of development raises concerns with several issues in historiography, including its chronological framework and ideological origins. This book has, I hope, demonstrated the value and need for further studies on the subject. Historical work is still sparse, and results require further development. However, and this is a crucial point, historical research should emphasise the careful study of actors working in and around international organisations, along with the dynamics behind knowledge and expertise exchange and circulation. In light of my own work this seems crucial to better understand the processes driving the internationalisation of development.

Images

Photo 1: 1936, ILO Regional Meetings – 1st American Regional Conference with Harold Butler. ILO historical archives. From left to right: Maurice Thudichum, Moisés Poblete Troncoso, David Blelloch, Stephen Lawford Childs, Harold Butler, Kenneth McKinlay, George Johnston, Lewis Lorwin, Oswald Stein, Robert Lafrance, C. Wilfred Jenks, Enrique Siewers, Winifred Duncan et Geneviève Laverrière. ILO historical archives. Ref: e46218.

https://doi.org/10.1515/9783110616323-015

Photo 2: 1936, ILO Regional Meetings – 1st American Regional Conference, Arturo Alessandri Palma, President of Chile, and Harold Butler, ILO Director-General (centre), leaving the inaugural sitting of the Labour Conference of American Member States of ILO (Santiago de Chile). ILO historical archives. Ref: e46219.

Photo 3: 1928, Albert Thomas (Japan). ILO historical archives. Ref: e46089

Photo 4: 1928, Maurice Viple and Albert Thomas (Japan). ILO historical archives. Ref: e46120

Photo 5: Reception of M. F. Maurette (in front) at the Ministry of Foreign Affairs, Japan , 7th April 1934. ILO historical archives.

Photo 6: The World Textile Conference. From left to right: Harold B. Butler, Conference Secretary; Henry A. Wallace, Secretary of Agriculture; Cordell Hull, Secretary of State; and John G. Winant, Conference President, April 12, 1937. ILO historical archives.

Photo 7: Arrival of the chartered aeroplane of the Royal Netherlands Indies Airways at Djokjakarta with Mr. Harold Butler and party of the "Bureau international du travail", Geneva, on the 24th. November 1937. Just after landing. From left to right: An official of the Royal Netherlands Indies Airways, Mrs. Butler, Mr. Martin, Mr. Harold Butler, Woudstra and Mr. E.A.C. den Hamer, Hear of the Labour-office of the Government of the Dutch Eat Indies. Source: ILO historical archives.

Photo 8: Harold Butler's Visit to the Headquarters of the National Trade Union Federations, Bombay. 1937. ILO historical archives.

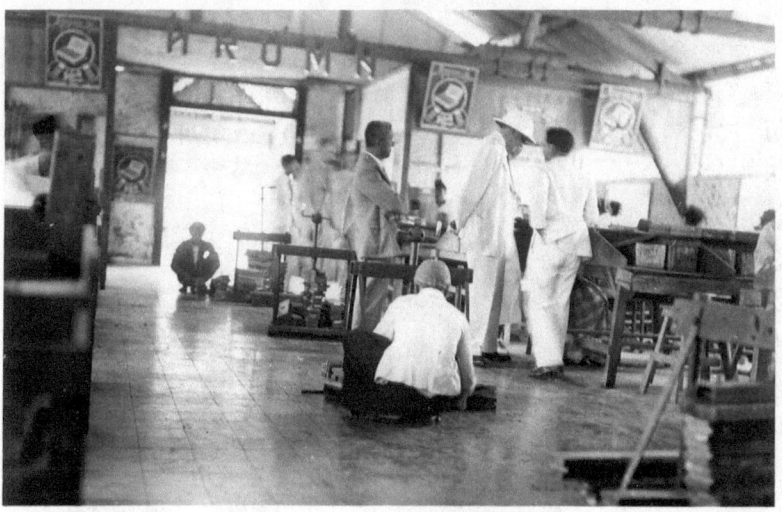

Photo 9: Harold Butler, Director of the International Labour Office, visits the cigar factory "Aroma" near Magelang, Java. 1937. ILO historical archives.

Photo 10: Staff of the International Labour Office, 1935. ILO historical archives. The chair in the centre may have been left empty in memory of Albert Thomas.

Photo 11: 1940–09, a group of ILO officials and their spouses waiting to board a ship to Lisbon (From the private collection of Carol Riegelman Lubin). ILO historical archives. Ref: e9835.

Unprinted Materials

Archives of the International Labour Office
Given the considerable number of ILO files consulted, only the titles of the funds are given. The reader may refer to the detailed quotations in the book.

Cabinet Files:
Albert Thomas papers
Harold Butler papers
Cabinet John G. Winant + Edward Phelan papers
David Morse papers
Private papers of Wilfred Jenks

ILO Division and Technical Services files:
Series C: Correspondent
Series CO: Cooperatives
Series D: Diplomatic Division
Series E: Emigration
Series EP: "Economic problems"
Series F: Finance
Series FO: Field Office
Series FS: Fellowships
Series G: General
Series GB: Governing Body
Series HY: Hygiene
Series LBO: London Branch Office
Series LE: Legislation
Series MI: Missions
Series MP: Manpower
Series N: Trade Union Movement
Series RL: Relations
Series RRA: United Nations Relief and Rehabilitation administration
Series SI: Social insurance
Series T: Statistics
Series TA: Technical assistance

Personal files (Series P):
Harold Butler, P 7
Camille Pône, P 9
Maurice Thudichum, P 14
Percival Martin, P 19
Roger Plissard, P 82
Harold Grimshaw, P 131
Royal Meeker, P 192
Adrien Tixier, P 217
Luigi Carozzi, P 506
Christie Tait, P 752
David Blelloch, P 760
Maurice Stack P1188
Fernand Maurette, P 1720
Oswald Stein, P 1289
Carlos Garcia-Palacios, P1299
Cyrille Dechamp, P 1729
Xavier Bueno, P 1848
Charles Becker, P 1947 a)
John Edward Riches, P 1998
Moisés Poblete Troncoso, P 2037
Enrique Siewers, P 2122
Jaroslav Drbohlav, P 2231
Wilfred Jenks, P 2597
Hans Staehle, P 2446
Ryoichi Kojima, P 2942
Anton Zelenka, P 3611
Emil Schoenbaum, P 3926

Archives of the League of Nations, Palais des Nations, Geneva

ONUG, ASDN, R 3995, 5B/5867/1226: Collaboration of the Government of China the work of Intellectual Cooperation. Discussion at the 15th session of the CICI. July 1933.

United Nations Archives, Palais des Nations, Geneva

ONUG, G.X. " Affaires économiques " (CEE), 18/11/1/1 "Manpower. EECE Documentation. Study by ECE, IRO, and ILO concerning Manpower position in Europe".

Archives of the International Institute for Intellectual Cooperation (UNESCO), Paris

AUNESCO, AG 1 – International Institute of Intellectual Co-operation, IICI, AI (Direction), 135 (Relations with the Government of China), 1932–1946.

AUNESCO, AG 1 – International Institute of Intellectual Co-operation, IICI, AIII (Correspondence), 55 (China), 1933–1946.

United Nations Archives and Records Centre (ARC), New York, USA

ARC, United Nations Relief and Rehabilitation Administration UNRRA, Lake Success Office, S-1303–0000–5485 (1943–1949); S-1303–0000–5486 (1943–1949); S-1303–0000–5487 (1943–1949); S-1303–0000–5488 (1943–1949); S-1303–0000–5489 (1943–1949).

Rockefeller Archive Center, Pocantico Hills, New York, USA

RG 1.1 (Projects), Series 100 S (International – Social Sciences):

- Box 108, Folder 973: International Labor Office, 1936–1940.
- Box 108, Folder 974: International Labor Office – Armament Program Study, 1939–1941.
- Box 108, Folder 975: International Labor Office – Armament Program Study, 1939–1941.
- Box 108, Folder 977: International Labor Office – Migration, 1941–1942.
- Box 108, Folder 978: International Labor Office – Migration, 1941–1942.
- RG 1.2 (Projects), Series 100 E (International – Fellowships, Scholarships):
- Box 35, Folder 260: Training Awards, (Fellowships – Administration and Policy) – Stipend, 1935–1961.

Collection NAR, Record Groupe (RG) 4, NELSON A. ROCKEFELLER, PERSONAL PAPERS. Series: O, Washington DC, Sub-Series IAA:

- Box 1, Folder 1 and 2: Washington DC files, CIAA. General, 1940.
- Box 1, Folder 3: Washington DC files, CIAA. General, 1942.
- Box 1, Folder 4: Washington DC files, CIAA. General, 1943.
- Box 1, Folder 5: Washington DC files, CIAA. General, 1944.
- Box 3, Folders 18–24: Latin America post-war planning, 1941–1945.

Collection NAR, Record Groupe (RG) 4, NELSON A. ROCKEFELLER, PERSONAL PAPERS. Series: A, Personal Activities:

- Box 144, folders 1565–1573: Trips South America. Itineraries, Guest lists, 1937).

National Archives and Records Administration (NARA), College Park, Maryland, USA

RG 174: General records of the Department of Labor, 1907–1986
174.3.1 Records of Secretaries.

- Box 45: Office of the Secretary. Secretary Frances Perkins. General Subject File, 1933–1941. Conferences.
- Box 46: Office of the Secretary. Secretary Frances Perkins. General Subject File, 1933–1941. Conferences.
- Box 50: Office of the Secretary. Secretary Frances Perkins. General Subject File, 1933–1941. Conferences to Embargo.
- Box 74: Office of the Secretary. Secretary Frances Perkins. General Subject File, 1933–1941. International Labor Office.
- Box 75: Office of the Secretary. Secretary Frances Perkins. General Subject File, 1933–1941. International Labor Office to Japanese Trade Union Congress.
B- ox 92: Office of the Secretary. Secretary Frances Perkins. General Subject File, 1933–1941. Resettlement Administration to Social Security Board.

Columbia University Rare Books and Manuscript Library, New York City, USA

Lewis Lorwin Papers.

Seeley G. Mudd Rare Books and Manuscript Library, Princeton, USA

David Morse Papers.

Harvard Law School Library & Historical and Special Collections, Cambridge, USA

Calvert Magruder Papers.

Leeds University Library Special Collections, Leeds, UK

David Blelloch Papers.

Columbia Center for Oral History, Butler Library, Columbia University, New York, USA

Oral History interviews with David A. Morse, Oral History Research Office, Columbia University 1981. Conducted par Peter Jessup, Columbia University, Washington DC, 19 July, 25 July, 2 August, 9 August, 11 October, 25 October 1980 and 11 January, 7 March 1981.

Private Records

Personal Papers of Maurice Thudichum, held by is grand-son Pierre Roehrich, Geneva.

Printed Materials, Archives of the International Labour Office

Studies and Reports

The Workers's Standard of Life in Countries with Depreciated Currency, Studies and Reports, Series D, n°15, Geneva, International Labour Office, 1925.
Les Méthodes d'enquête sur les budgets familiaux, Studies and Reports, Series N, n° 9, Geneva, International Labour Office, 1926.
Les Relations industrielles aux États-Unis, Studies and Reports, Series A, n°27, Geneva, International Labour Office, 1927.
An international Enquiry into Costs of living. A Comparative Study of Workers' Living Costs in Detroit (USA) and Fourteen European Cities, Studies and Reports, Series N, n°17, Geneva, International Labour Office, 1931.
Contribution à l'étude de la comparaison internationale du coût de la vie, Studies and Reports, Series N, n°17, Geneva, International Labour Office, 1932.
International Comparison of Food Costs, Studies and Reports, Series N, n°19, Geneva, International Labour Office, 1934.
Three Sources of Unemployment: The Combined Action of Population Changes, Technical Progress and Economic Development, Studies and Reports, Series C, Geneva, International Labour Office, 1936.
Problèmes de travail en Indochine. Studies and Reports, Series B, n°26, Geneva, International Labour Office, 1936.
Quelques aspects sociaux du développement présent et futur de l'économie brésilienne, Studies and Reports, Series B, n°25, Geneva, International Labour Office, 1937.
La coopération internationale technique et financière en matière de migrations colonisatrices. Conférence technique d'experts, Studies and Reports, Series O, n°7, Geneva, International Labour Office, 1938.
Le Standard de vie des travailleurs, Studies and Reports, Series B, n°30, Geneva, International Labour Office, 1938.
Problème de travail en Orient. Études et documents, Studies and Reports, Series B, n°29, Geneva, International Labour Office, 1938.
L'investissement des fonds des assurances sociales, Studies and Reports, Series M, n°16, Geneva, International Labour Office, 1939.
Technique actuarielle et organisation financière des assurances sociales, Studies and Reports, Series M, n°17, Geneva, International Labour Office, 1940.

International Labour Review

1933. "Le programme de redressement économique aux États-Unis" 28(6): 799–815.
1938. "Les travaux publics, facteur de stabilisation économique" 38(6): 793–825.
1942. "Vers une "paix du peuple" La réunion de la commission de crise du B.I.T. Londres, avril 1942" 46(1): 1–48.
Belshaw, H. 1933. "La main-d'œuvre agricole en Nouvelle-Zélande" 28(1): 27–50.
Butler, H. 1931. "Les répercussions sociales de la crise économique en Amérique du Nord" 23(3): 309–333.
Butler, H. 1934. "L'œuvre de redressement économique aux USA" 29(1): 1–20.
Idei, S. 1930. "Japan's Migration Problem" 22(6): 773–789.
Idei, S. 1930. "The Unemployment Problem in Japan" 22(4): 503–523.
Lorwin, L. 1936 "L'Organisation internationale du travail et la politique économique mondiale" 33(4): 485–498.
Lorwin, L. 1936. "The Present Phase of Economic and Social Development in the USSR" 33(1): 5–40.
Martin, W. P. 1929. "La technique de l'équilibre économique. Son rôle dans la prospérité américaine" 20(4): 521–540.
Maurette, F. 1933. "La conférence préparatoire pour la semaine de quarante heure" 27(3): 315–343.
Johnston, G.A. 1930. "L'industrialisation dans les pays du Pacifique" 21(6): 811–829.
Riches, J. 1937. "Le planisme et les salaires dans l'agriculture en Nouvelle-Zélande" 35(3): 309–349.
Tixier, A. 1935 "Le développement des assurances sociales en Argentine, au Brésil, au Chili et en Uruguay" I and II 32(5): 646–673 and 32(6): 797–827.
Weaver, C.W.H. 1933. "Notes sur un voyage en Inde, en Irak, en Perse et en Turquie" 28(4): 491–527.
Woytinsky, W. 1932. "Un remède à la crise : La création d'emploi par une action internationale" 25(1): 1–23.

Bibliography

2008. "Albert Thomas, société mondiale et internationalisme. Réseaux et institutions des années 1890 aux années 1930", *Les Cahiers Irice* 2(2), Special Issue, 195 pages.
2009. *Edward Phelan and the ILO: Life and views of an international social actor.* Geneva, International Labour Office.
2012. "L'anthropologie des organisations internationales", *Critique internationale,* Special Issue: 54(1).
Aamir, A. 1969. "Fifty Years of the ILO and Asia", *International Labour Review* 99(3): 347–361.
Abélès M., Bellier, I. 1996. "La Commission européenne. Du compromis culturel à la culture politique du compromis", *Revue française de science politique* 46(3): 431–456.
Abélès, M. 1998. "Homo coconmmunautarius", in Kastoryano, R. ed. *Quelle identité pour l'Europe ? Le multiculturalisme à l'épreuve,* 43–63. Paris: Presses de Sciences Po.
Adler, E., Haas, P. M. 1992. "Conclusion: Epistemic Communities, World Order, and the Creation of a Reflective Research Program", *International Organization* 46(1): 367–390.
Aglan, A. 2008. "Albert Thomas, historien du temps présent", *Les Cahiers Irice* 2(2), Special Issue: 23–38.
Aglan, A., Feiertag, O., Kevonian, D. eds. 2011. *Humaniser le travail. Régimes économiques, régimes politiques et Organisation internationale du travail, 1929–1969.* Brussels, Bern: PIE Lang.
Akami, T. 2002. *Internationalizing the Pacific: The United States, Japan and the Institute of Pacific Relations, 1919–1945.* London: Routledge Studies in Asia's Transformations.
Alcock, A. 1971. *History of the International Labour Organisation.* London: Macmillan.
Aldcroft, D. H. 2006. *Europe's Third World: the European Periphery in the Interwar Years,* 42. Aldershot, Hants, England; Burlington, Vt.: Ashgate.
Alexander, R. J. 1982. *Rómulo Betancourt and the Transformation of Venezuela.* New Brunswick and London: Transaction Books.
Alexander, R. J., Parker, E. M. 2009. *International Labor Organizations and Organized Labor in Latin America and the Caribbean: A History.* Santa Barbara, Denver, Oxford: ABC-CLIO.
Allen, R. D. G. 1933. "On the Marginal Utility of Money and Its Application", *Economica* 40 (May, 1933): 186–209.
Alvarez García, M. 2007. *Líderes Políticos del Siglo XX en América Latina.* Santiago, Chili: Lom Ediciones.
Amrith, S. 2006. *Decolonizing International Health India and Southeast Asia, 1930–65.* UK: Palgrave Macmillan.
Anastasiadou, I. 2011. Constructing Iron Europe: Transnationalism and Railways in the Interbellum. Amsterdam: Amsterdam University Press.
Andrade, J. C. Y. 2014. *L'OIT et l'Amérique du Sud (1919–1939). La construction d'un laboratoire social regional.* Phd diss. Paris, École des hautes études en sciences sociales.
Apostolakou, L. 1997. "'Greek' Workers or Communist 'Others': The Contending Identities of Organized Labour in Greece", *Journal of Contemporary History* 32(3): 409–424.
Backouche, I. 2006. "Expertise", *Genèses* 65(4): 2–3.
Barber, W. J. 1988. *From New Era to New Deal: Herbert Hoover, the Economists, and American policy, 1921–1933.* New York: Cambridge University Press.

Barnett M. N., Finnemore, M. 1999. "The Politics, Power, and Pathologies of International Organizations", *International Organization* 53(4): 699–732.

Barnett, M. N., Finnemore, M. 2004. *Rules for the World: International Organizations in Global Politics*. Ithaca: Cornell University Press.

Barona, J. L. 2008. "Nutrition and Health. The International Context during the Inter-War crisis", *Social History of Medicine* 21(1): 87–105.

Batou, J., David, T. eds. 1998. *Le Développement inégal de l'Europe (1918–1939). L'essor contrarié des pays agricoles*. Genève: Droz.

Becker, J.-J. 2008. "Albert Thomas, d'un siècle à l'autre. Bilan de l'expérience de guerre", *Les Cahiers Irice* 2(2), Special Issue: 9–15.

Béguin, B. 1959. *Le Tripartisme dans l'Organisation internationale du travail*. Genève: Droz.

Bel, C., Lewis, C. M. eds. 1993. *Welfare, Poverty and Development in Latin America*. London: The Macmillan Press.

Bellier, I. 1995. "Une culture de la Commission européenne ? De la rencontre des cultures et du multilinguisme des fonctionnaires", in Mény, Y., Muller, P., Quermonne, J.-L. eds. *Politiques publiques en Europe*, 49–60. Paris: L'Harmattan.

Bérard, Y., Crespin, R. eds. 2010. *Aux frontières de l'expertise, dialogues entre savoirs et pouvoirs*. Rennes: PUR.

Berend, I. T. 1982. *The European Periphery and Industrialization, 1780–1914*. Cambridge: Cambridge University Press.

Berend, I. T. 1986. The Crisis Zone of Europe An Interpretation of East-Central European History in the First Half of the Twentieth Century. Cambridge: Cambridge University Press.

Berend, I. T. 2006. *An Economic History of Twentieth-Century Europe*. Cambridge: Cambridge University Press.

Berend, I. T. and Ranki, G. eds. 1974. *Economic Development of East-Central Europe in the 19th and 20th Centuries*. New York: Columbia University Press.

Berger, F. 2006. "Les milieux économiques et les États vis-à-vis des tentatives d'organisation des marchés européens dans les années trente", in Bussière, É., Dumoulin, M., Schirmann, S. eds. *Europe organisée, Europe du Libre-échange (Fin XIXe siècle–Années 1960)*, 71–105. Brussels: Peter Lang.

Berger, M. T. 2000. "A Greater America? Pan Americanism and the Professional Study of Latin America, 1890–1990", in Sheinin, D. ed., *Beyond the Ideal: Pan Americanism in Inter-American Affairs*, 79–94. Westport, Conn.: Greenwood Press.

Bermúdez Briñez, N., Rodríguez Arrieta, M. 2012. "Las industrias azucarera y petrolera en el Zulia: formas de ocupación territorial (1913–1935)", *Diálogos. Revista Electrónica de Historia* 13(1): 90–122. https://dialnet.unirioja.es/servlet/articulo?codigo=5601839

Berquist, C. 1986. *Labor in Latin America. Comparative Essays on Chile, Argentina, Venezuela and Columbia*. Stanford: Stanford University Press.

Bertrams, K. 2008. "Une inspiration tout en contrastes. Le New Deal et l'ancrage transnational des experts du planning, 1933–1943", *Genèses* 71(2): 64–83.

Bessis, J. 1981. La Méditerranée *fasciste*: l'Italie mussolinienne et la Tunisie. Paris: Ed. Karthala.

Bethell, L., Roxborough, I. 1997. *Latin America Between the Second World War and the Cold War: Crisis and Containment, 1944–1948*. Cambridge: Cambridge University Press.

Beyers, J. 2005. "Multiple Embeddedness and Socialization in Europe: The Case of Council Officials", *International Organization* 59(4): 899–936.
Beyersdorf, F. 2011. "'Credit or Chaos'? The Austrian Stabilisation Programme of 1923 and the League of Nations", in Laqua, D. ed. *Internationalism Reconfigured. Transnational Ideas and Movements between the World Wars*, 135–157. London: Tauris.
Biard, J.-F. 1985. *Le Socialisme devant ses choix : la naissance de l'idée de plan*. Paris: Publication de la Sorbonne.
Blancpain, J.-P. 1994. *Migrations et mémoire germaniques en Amérique latine*. Strasbourg: Presses universitaires de Strasbourg.
Blelloch, D. 1940. *Legislación del trabajo en Bolivia*. La Paz: Editorial Fénix.
Blelloch, D. 1957. "*Bold New Programme: A Review of United Nations Technical Assistance*", *International Affairs* 33(1): 36–50.
Blelloch, D. 1958. *Aid for Development*, Fabian Research Series, 195, The Fabian Society.
Bollé, P. 2012. "La *Revue internationale du travail*, le BIT, l'OIT: fragments d'une histoire", *International Labour Review* 152, Special Issue: 1–14.
Bonnecase, V. 2008. *Pauvreté au Sahel. La construction des savoirs sur les niveaux de vie au Burkina Faso, au Mali et au Niger (1945–1974)*. Phd diss., University of Paris 1, École doctorale d'histoire, Centre d'études des mondes africains.
Bonvin, J.-M. 1998. *L'Organisation internationale du travail. Étude sur une agence productrice de normes*. Paris: PUF.
Borgwardt, E. 2005. *A New Deal for the World: America's Vision for Human Rights*. Cambridge, MA [etc.]: Belknap Press, Harvard University Press.
Boris, G. 1950. "*Assistance technique et point IV: origine, principe, buts*", *Politique étrangère* 15(5/6): 533–550.
Borowy, I. 2009. *Coming to Terms with World Health: The League of Nations Health Organisation, 1921–1946*. Frankfurt a.M., Bern [etc.]: Peter Lang.
Bose, S. 1998. "*Instruments and Idioms of Colonial and National Development. India's Historical Experience in Comparative Perspective*", in Cooper, F., Packard, R. eds. *International Development and the Social Sciences: Essays on the History and Politics of Knowledge*, 45–63. Berkeley, Los Angeles [etc.]: University of California.
Bourdieu, P. 1997. "De la maison du roi à la raison d'État. Un modèle de la genèse du champ bureaucratique", *Actes de la recherche en sciences sociales*, 118(3): 55–68.
Buchet de Neuilly, Y. 2009. "Devenir diplomate multilatéral", *Cutltures & Conflits* 75(3): 75–98.
Burkman, T. W. 2008. *Japan and the League of Nations: Empire and World Order, 1914–1938*, 18. Honolulu: University of Hawaii Press.
Bussière, E. 2005. "*Premiers schémas européens et économie internationale durant l'entre-deux-guerres*", *Relations internationales* 123(3): 51–68.
Butler, H. 1941. *The Lost Peace: A Personal Impression*. London: Faber and Faber.
Cabanes, B. 2014. *The Great War and the Origins of Humanitarianism, 1918–1924*. Cambridge: Cambridge University Press.
Carrupt, R. *Un processus d'internationalisation entre la rue d'Ulm et les bords du Léman : Fernand (1878–1937) et Marie-Thérèse Maurette (1890–1989)*. PhD thesis in progress, University of Geneva.
Cassasus-Montero, C. 1984. *Travail et travailleurs au Chili*. Paris: La Découverte.

Cayet, T. 2007. "Le Bureau International du travail et la modernisation économique dans les années 20: esquisse d'une dynamique institutionnelle", in "Centenaire du ministère du Travail. Première partie," Special Issue, *Travail et Emploi* 110, April-June: 15–27.
Cayet, T. 2010. *Rationaliser le travail, organiser la production: le Bureau international du travail et la modernisation économique durant l'entre-deux-guerres*. Rennes: PUR.
Cayet, T. 2011. "Le planning comme organisation du travail", in Lespinet-Moret, I., Viet, V. eds. *L'Organisation internationale du travail : origine–développement–avenir*: 79–89. Rennes: PUR.
Cayet, T. 2011. "Regards croisés sur une adhésion : l'Organisation internationale du travail et le New Deal", in Aglan, A., Feiertag, O., Kevonian, D. eds. 2011. *Humaniser le travail. Régimes économiques, régimes politiques et Organisation internationale du travail, 1929–1969*, 39–54. Bruxelles ; Bern: PIE Lang.
Centeno, M. A., Silva, P. 1998. "The Politics of Expertise in Latin America: Introduction", in Centeno, M. A., Silva, P. eds. *The Politics of Expertise in Latin America*, 1–12. Basingstoke: Macmillan Press.
Cerami, A., Stanescu, S. 2009. "Welfare State Transformations in Bulgaria and Romania". In Cerami, A. and Vanhuysse, P. eds. *Post-Communist Welfare Pathways. Theorizing Social Policy Transformations in Central and Eastern Europe*, 112–126. Basingstoke: Palgrave Macmillan.
Chandavarkar, R. 1994. *The origins of Industrial Capitalism in India: Business Strategies and the Working Classes in Bombay, 1900–1940*. Cambridge [England]: Cambridge University Press.
Chaudron, G. 2012. *New Zealand in the League of Nations: The Beginnings of an Independent Foreign Policy, 1919–1939*. Jefferson, NC: McFarland & Company.
Checkel, J. T. 2005. "International Institutions and Socialization in Europe: Introduction and Framework", *International Organization* 59(4): 801–826.
Chen, Y. 2016. "ILO, Extraterritoriality and Labour Protection in Republican Shanghai", in Liukkunen, U., Chen, Y. eds. *Fundamental Labour Rights in China. Legal Implementation and Cultural Logic*, 83–116. Cham: Springer International Publishing.
Claude Jr., I. L. 1964. *Swords into Plowshares: The Problems and Progress of International Organization*. New York: Random House.
Claude, M. 2015. "Lewis L. Lorwin and "The Promise of Planning": Class, Collectivism, and Empire in U.S. Economic Planning Debates, 1931–1941". Phd diss., Georgia State University. https://scholarworks.gsu.edu/history_theses/88
Clavin, P. 2000. *The Great Depression in Europe, 1929–1939*. London: Macmillan Press.
Clavin, P. 2005. "Defining Transnationalism", *Contemporary European History* 14(4): 421–439.
Clavin, P. 2013. *Securing the World Economy: The Reinvention of the League of Nations, 1920–1946*. Oxford: Oxford University Press.
Clavin, P. and Wessels, J.-W. 2005. "Transnationalism and the League of Nations: Understanding the Work of its Economic and Financial Organisation", *Contemporary European History* 14(4): 465–492.
Clavin, P., Patel, K. K. 2010. "The Role of International Organisations in Europeanisation: The Case of the League of Nations and the European Economic Community", in Conway, M., Patel, K. K. eds. *Europeanisation in the Twentieth Century: Historical Approaches*, 110–131. Basingstoke: Palgrave Macmillan.

Clavin, P., Sunil, A. 2013. "Feeding the world: Connecting Europe and Asia, 1930–1945", *Past and Present* 218 (suppl. 8): 29–50.
Cobble, D. S. 2015. "Japan and the 1919 ILO Debates over Rights, Representation and Global Labour Standards", in Lichtenstein, N., Jensen, J. M. *The ILO from Geneva to the Pacific Rim – West meets East*, 55–79. International Labour Organization, Palgrave Macmillan, ILO Century Series.
Codaccioni, V., Maisetti, N., Pouponneau, F. 2012. "Les façades institutionnelles : ce que montrent les apparences des institutions", *Sociétés contemporaines* 4(88): 5–15.
Cohen, A. 1968. *Belle du Seigneur*. Paris: Gallimard.
Cohen, Y., Baudouï, R. eds. 1995. *Les Chantiers de la paix sociale (1900–1940)*. Fontenay/Saint-Cloud: ENS.
Conrad, C. 2004. "Observer les consommateurs. Études de marché et histoire de la consommation en Allemagne, de 1930 aux années 1960", *Le Mouvement social* 1(206): 17–39.
Constantine, S. 1984. *The Making of British Colonial Development Policy, 1914–1940*. London: Routledge.
Cooper, F. 1997. "Modernizing Bureaucrats, Backward Africans, and the Development Concept", in Cooper, F. and Packard R. eds. *International Development and the Social Sciences*, 64–192. Berkeley: University of California Press.
Cooper, F. and Packard, R. eds. 1997. *International Development and the Social Sciences: Essays on the History and Politics of Knowledge*. Berkeley; Los Angeles [etc.]: University of California Press.
Cooper, F. 2008. *Decolonization and African Society: The Labor Question in French and British Africa*. Cambridge: Cambridge University Press.
Cox, R. W. et al. 1974. *The Anatomy of Influence: Decision Making in International Organization*. New Haven: Yale University Press.
Croes González, H. 2011. *Transformations économiques et formes d'État au Venezuela : un siècle de "capitalisme pétrolier" (1908–2008)*, PhD dissert., University Paris I.
Cullather, N. 2000. "Development? It's History", *Diplomatic History* 24(4): 641–653.
Cussó, R., Gobin, C. 2008. "Du discours politique au discours expert : le changement politique mis hors débat ?", *Mots. Les langages du politique* 88: 5–11.
Dab, S. 1999. "Bienfaisance et socialisme au tournant du siècle: la Société des Visiteurs, 1898–1902", in Topalov, C. ed. *Laboratoires du nouveau siècle. La nébuleuse réformatrice et ses réseaux en France, 1880–1914*, 219–235. Paris: EHESS.
Dabène, O. 2003. *L'Amérique latine à l'époque contemporaine*. Paris: Armand Colin.
Dard, O. 1995. "Voyage à l'intérieur d'X-Crise", *Vingtième siècle* 3(47): 132–146.
Dard, O. 2003. "Technocrates et architectures européennes durant les années Trente", in Schirmann, Sylvain ed. *Organisations internationales et architectures européennes, 1929–1939: actes du colloque de Metz, 31 mai-1er juin 2001*, 269–284. Metz: Centre de recherche Histoire et civilisation de l'Europe occidentale de l'Université de Metz.
Daughton, J. P. 2013. "ILO Expertise and Colonial Violence", in Kott, S. Droux, J. eds. *Globalizing Social Rights: The International Labour Organization and Beyond*, 85–97. Basingstoke: Palgrave Macmillan, ILO.
David, T. 2009. *Nationalisme économique et industrialisation: l'expérience des pays d'Europe de l'Est (1789–1939)*. Genève: Droz.

De Grazia, V. 2005. *Irresistible Empire: America's Advance Through Twentieth-Century Europe*. Cambridge, MA [etc.]: Belknap Press of Harvard University Press.

Decorzant, Y. 2011. *La Société des Nations et la naissance d'une conception de la régulation économique internationale*, Bruxelles: Peter Lang.

Delaisi, F. 1929. *Les Deux Europes* : Europe industrielle et Europe agricole. Paris: Payot.

Delaisi, F., Mousset, A., Clerc, H., von Beckerath, H., Hantos, E., Osuski, S. 1933. *L'Europe centrale et la crise*. Paris: Publications de la conciliation internationale, Centre Europe de la Dotation Carnegie.

Desrosières, A. 1989. "Comment faire des choses qui tiennent: histoire sociale et statistique", *Histoire & Mesure* 4(3–4): 225–242.

Desrosières, A. 2000. *La Politique des grands nombres. Histoire de la raison statistique*. Paris: La Découverte.

Desrosières, A. 2003. "Historiciser l'action publique: l'État, le marché et les statistiques", in Trom, D., Laborier, P. eds. *Historicités de l'action publique*, 207–222. Paris: PUF.

Desrosières, A. 2005. "Décrire l'État ou explorer la société: les deux sources de la statistique publique", *Genèses* 1(58): 4–27.

Desrosières, A. Kott, S. 2005. "Quantifier", *Genèses* 1(58): 2–3.

Devin, G. 2008. "Que reste-t-il du fonctionnalisme international ? Relire David Mitrany (1888–1975)", *Critique internationale* 1(38): 137–152.

Dhermy-Mairal, M. 2015. "Les Sciences sociales et l'action au Bureau international du travail (1920–1939) ", PhD diss., EHESS, Paris.

Dhermy-Mairal, M. 2015. "Durkheimisme scientifique et durkheimisme d'action. François Simiand et le Bureau international du travail (1920–1930)", *Revue Française de Sociologie*, 4(56): 673–696.

Domergue, M. 1973. *Théorie et pratique de l'assistance technique*. Paris: Les Editions ouvrières.

Dominique, G., Amy, J. 2002. "Biology-inspired Sociology of the Nineteenth Century: A Science of Social 'Organization'", *Revue française de sociologie* 43(1): 123–155.

Douglas, P. H., Wolff Douglas, D., Smith Joslyn, C. 2009 [1921]. *What Can a Man Afford*. United States, Montana: Kessinger Publishing.

Downey, K. 2009. *The Woman behind the New Deal*. New York: Knopf Doubleday Publishing Group.

Downs, L. L. 1995. *Manufacturing Inequality: Gender Division in the French and British Metalworking Industries, 1914–1939*. Ithaca: Cornell University Press.

Downs, L. L. 2003. "Les marraines élues de la paix sociale ? Les surintendantes d'usine et la rationalisation du travail en France (1917–1935)", in Prost, A. ed. *Guerres, paix et sociétés : 1911–1946*, 219–242. Paris: Éditions de l'Atelier.

Droux, J. 2011. "L'internationalisation de la protection de l'enfance: acteurs, concurrences et projets transnationaux (1900–1925)", *Critique internationale* 3(52): 17–33.

Dubois, V., Dulong, D. eds. 1999. *De l'invention d'une figure aux transformations de l'action publique*. Strasbourg: Presses Universitaires de Strasbourg.

Duchêne, A. 2004. "Construction institutionnelle des discours. Idéologies et pratiques dans une organisation supranationale", *TRANEL (Travaux neuchâtelois de linguistique)* 40: 93–115.

Duffield, M. and Hewitt, V. 2009. *Empire, Development & Colonialism: The Past in the Present*. Suffolk: Boydell & Brewer.

Dupuy, M. 1956. *L'Assistance technique et financière aux pays insuffisamment développés*. Ed. A. Pedone: Paris.
Dupuy, P., Gallois, L. 1938. "Fernand Maurette (1879–1937)", *Annales de Géographie* 47(266): 199–202.
Eckert, A., Malinowski, S. and Unger, C. 2010: "Modernizing Missions: Approaches to "Developing" the Non-Western World after 1945", *Journal of European Modern History*, 8(1).
Eckes, A., E. 1980. *The United States and the Global Struggle for Minerals*. Austin: University of Texas Press.
Ekbladh, D. 2009. *The Great American Mission: Modernization and the Construction of an American World Order*. Princeton: Princeton University Press.
Ellner, S. 1979. "The Venezuelan Left in the Era of the Popular Front, 1936–1945", *Journal of Latin American Studies* 11(1): 169–184.
Endres, A. M., and Fleming, G. A. 2002. *International Organizations and the Analysis of Economic Policy, 1919–1950*. Cambridge: Cambridge University Press.
Endres, A. M., Fleming, G. A. 1996. "International economic policy in the interwar years: The special contribution of ILO economists", *International Labour Review* 135(2): 207–225.
Engerman, D. C. and Unger, C. R. 2009. "Introduction: Towards a Global History of Modernization", *Diplomatic History* 33(3): 375–385.
Escobar, A. 1995. *Encountering Development. The Making and Unmaking of the Third World*. Princeton, Oxford: Princeton University Press.
Evans, P., Rueschemeyer, D., Skocpol, T. eds 1985. *Bringing the State Back In*. Cambridge: Cambridge University Press.
Evans, R. 2007. "The Successor States", in Gerwarth, R. ed. *Twisted Paths: Europe 1914–1945*. Oxford: Oxford University Press.
Ewell, J. 1996. *Venezuela and the United States: From Monroe's Hemisphere to Petroleum's Empire*. Athens, GA [etc.]: University of Georgia Press.
Facchini, F. 1993. "Pour une critique du modèle technocratique-savoir-marché politique et production de la loi", *Politiques et management public* 11(3): 63–75.
Feiertag, O. 2008. "Réguler la mondialisation: Albert Thomas, les débuts du BIT et la crise économique mondiale de 1920–1923", *Les Cahiers Irice* 2(2), Special Issue: 127–155.
Feiertag, O. 2011. "Humaniser la crise économique (1929–1934): l'expertise du BIT dans la crise de mondialisation des années 1930", in Aglan, A., Feiertag, O., Kevonian, D. *Humaniser le travail. Régimes économiques, régimes politiques et Organisation internationale du travail, 1929–1969*, 19–38. Brussels, Bern: PIE Lang.
Feuer, L. S. 1962. "American Travelers to the Soviet Union 1917–1932: The Formation of Component of New Deal Ideology", *American Quarterly* 14(2): 119–149.
Fine, M. 1977. "Albert Thomas: a reformer's vision of modernization, 1914–1932", *Journal of Contemporary History* 12(3): 545–564.
Fink, L. 2015. "A Sea of Difference: The ILO and the Search for Common Standards, 1919–45", in Lichtenstein, N., Jensen, J. M. *The ILO from Geneva to the Pacific Rim – West meets East*, 15–32. International Labour Organization, Palgrave Macmillan, ILO Century Series.
Finnemore, M. and Sikkink, K. 1998. "International Norm Dynamics and Political Change", *International Organization* 52(4): 887–917.

Fior, M. 2008. *Institution globale et marchés financiers. La Société des Nations face à la reconstruction de l'Europe (1918–1931)*. Bern: Peter Lang.

Fischman, M., Lendjel, E. 2000. "La contribution d'X–Crise à l'émergence de l'économétrie en France dans les années trente", *Revue européenne des sciences sociales* 38(118): 115–134.

Fiti Sinclair, G. 2017. *To Reform the World: International Organizations and the Making of Modern States*. Oxford: Oxford University Press.

Fiti Sinclair, G. 2016. "International Social Reform and the Invention of Development". SSRN: https://ssrn.com/abstract=2842441

Fiti Sinclair, G. 2017. "A Civilizing Task: The International Labour Organization, Social Reform and the Genealogy of Development", *Journal of the History of International Law* 20(2): 1–53.

Flandreau, M. ed. 2003. *Money Doctors: The Experience of International Financial Advising, 1850–2000*. London: Routledge.

Forclaz, A. R. 2011. "A New Target for International Social Reform: The International Labour Organisation and Working and Living Conditions in Agriculture in the Interwar Years", *Journal of Contemporary European History* 20(3): 307–329.

Fourcade, M. 2006. "The Construction of a Global Profession: The Transnationalisation of Economics", *American Sociology* 112(1): 145–194.

Fraser, S., Gerstle, G. eds. 1989. *The Rise and Fall of the New Deal Order: 1930–1980*. Princeton: Princeton University Press.

Fridenson, P., Griset, P. eds. 2018. *L'industrie dans la Grande Guerre: colloque des 15 et 16 novembre 2016*. Paris: Comité pour l'histoire économique et financière de la France.

Fritzsche, P., and Hellbeck, J. 2009. "The New Man in Stalinist Russia and Nazi Germany", in Fitzpatrick, S. and Geyer, M. eds. 2009. *Beyond Totalitarianism. Stalinism and Nazism Compared*, 302–344. Cambridge: Cambridge University Press.

García Belaunde, D., & Antillón Montealegre, W. 1992. *Los sistemas constitucionales iberoamericanos*. Madrid: Dykinson.

Georgakakis, D. 2010. "Comment les institutions (européennes) socialisent", in Michel, H., Robert, C. *La Fabrique des Européens : Processus de socialisation et construction européenne (Sociologie politique européenne)*, 129–167. Strasbourg: Presses universitaires de Strasbourg.

Georgakakis, D., de Lassalle, M. 2007. "Genèse et structure d'un capital institutionnel européen. Les très hauts fonctionnaires de la Commission européenne", *Actes de la Recherche en Sciences Sociales*, 39–53. Paris: Editions du Seuil.

Gernignon, B. 2004. "La liberté syndicale et les missions sur place de l'OIT", in Javillier, J.-C., Gernignon, B., Politakis, G. eds. *Les Normes internationales du travail : un patrimoine pour l'avenir. Mélanges en l'honneur de Nicolas Valticos*. Geneva: International Labour Office.

Gerwarth, R. ed. 2007. *Twisted Paths: Europe 1914–1945*. Oxford: Oxford University Press.

Ghebali, V.-Y. 1975. *Organisation internationale et guerre mondiale. Le cas de la société des nations et de l'organisation internationale du travail pendant la seconde guerre mondiale*. PhD. dissert., Science politique, Grenoble 2.

Ghebali, V.-Y., Ago, R., Valticos, N. 1989. *The International Labour Organisation: A Case Study on the Evolution of U.N. Specialised Agencies*. Dordrecht, Boston [etc.]: M. Nijhoff.

Ghebali, V.-Y. 1972. "Aux origines de l'Ecosoc : l'évolution des commissions et organisations techniques de la Société des Nations", *Annuaire français de droit international* 18(1): 469–511.

Ghebali, V.-Y., Ago, R., Valticos, N. 1987. *L'Organisation internationale du travail*. Geneva: Georg.

Gilbert, N. 2004. "La solidarité agricole européenne: des congrès d'agriculture à la politique agricole commune", in Canal, J., Pécout, G., Ridolfi, M. eds. *Sociétés rurales du xxe siècle: France, Italie et Espagne*, Collection de l'École française de Rome 331, 310–326. Rome: École française de Rome.

Gilman, N. 2003. *Mandarins of the Future: Modernization Theory in Cold War America*. Baltimore: Johns Hopkins University Press.

Gobin, C., Deroubaix, J.-C. 2010. "L'analyse du discours des organisations internationales. Un vaste champ encore peu exploré", *Mots. Les langages du politique*, [Online], 94 | 2010, online on 06 November 2012. URL: http://journals.openedition.org/mots/19872

Godard, S. 2014. *Construire le " bloc " par l'économie. Configuration des territoires et des identités socialistes au Conseil d'Aide Économique Mutuelle (CAEM), 1949–1989*. PhD diss., University of Geneva.

González Oquendo, L. J. 2008. "Bolívar y la constitución del discurso nacionalista en Venezuela", *Amérique Latine. Histoire et Mémoire*. Les Cahiers ALHIM [On line], 16 | 2008, online on 04 November 2009. URL: http://journals.openedition.org/alhim/3060

Goodrich, C. 1942. "The Effect of the War on the Position of Labor", *The American Economic Review* 32(1): 416–425.

Grabas, C. and Nützenadel, A. 2014. *Industrial Policy in Europe after 1945: Wealth, Power and Economic Development in the Cold War*, Basingstoke: Palgrave Macmillan.

Gross, S. G. 2015. *Export Empire: German Soft Power in Southeastern Europe, 1890–1945*. Cambridge: Cambridge University Press.

Guérin, D. 1996. *Albert Thomas au BIT 1920–1932: de l'internationalisme à l'Europe*. Genève: Euryopa.

Guieu, J.-M. 2009. "L'"insécurité collective'. L'Europe et la Société des Nations dans l'entre-deux-guerres", *Bulletin de l'Institut Pierre Renouvin*, 2(30): 21–43.

Guinand, C. 2008. "Un fonctionnaire international en France occupée (1940–1944)", in Heinen, A., Hüser D., Günther, A. *Tour de France. Eine historische Rundreise. Festschrift für Rainer Hudemann*, 391–399. Stuttgart: Franz Steiner.

Guthrie, J. 2013. "The ILO and the International Technocratic Class, 1944–1966", in Kott, S., Droux J. eds. *Globalizing Social Rights. The International Labour Organization and Beyond*, 115–136. ILO Centuries Series. Basingstoke: Palgrave Macmillan.

Guy, D. 1998. "The Pan American Child Congresses, 1916 to 1942: Pan Americanism, Child Reform, and the Welfare State in Latin America", *Journal of Family History* 23(3): 272–291.

Haas, E. B. 1964. *Beyond the Nation-State: Functionalism and International Organization*. Stanford: Stanford University Press.

Haas, P. M. 1992. "Introduction: Epistemic Communities and International Policy Coordination", *International Organization* 46(1): 1–35.

Halperin, S. 1996. *In the Mirror of the Third World: Capitalist Development in Modern Europe*, Ithaca and London: Cornell University Press.

Hardach, G. 1977. "La mobilisation industrielle en 1914–1918: production, planification et idéologie", in Fridenson, P., Becker, J., & Berstein, S. *1914–1918: L'autre front* (Cahiers du "Mouvement social" 2), 81–109. Paris: Les Ed. ouvrières.
Havinden, M. A., Meredith, D. 1993. *Colonialism and Development: Britain and its Tropical Colonies, 1850–1960*, 173. London and New York: Routledge.
Helleiner, E. 2009. "The Development Mandate of International Institutions: Where Did It Come From?", *Studies in Comparative International Development* 44(3): 189–211.
Helleiner, E. 2014. *Forgotten foundations of Bretton Woods: International development and the making of the postwar order*. Ithaca; London: Cornell University Press.
Hennebicque, A. 1977. "Albert Thomas et le régime des usines de guerre", in Fridenson, P., Becker, J., & Berstein, S. *1914–1918 : L'autre front* (Cahiers du "Mouvement social" 2), 126–130. Paris: Les Ed. ouvrières.
Herren, M. 2013. "Global corporatism after World War I, the Indian case", in Kott, S. and Droux, J. eds. *Globalizing Social Rights. The International Labour Organization and Beyond*, 137–152. ILO Centuries Series, Basingstoke: Palgrave Macmillan.
Herrera León, F. 2011. "México y la Organización Internacional del Trabajo: Los orígenes de una relación, 1919–1931", *Foro Internacional*, 204: 336–355.
Herrera León, F. and Wehrli, Y. 2011. "Le BIT et l'Amérique latine durant l'entre-deux-guerres: problèmes et enjeux", in Lespinet-Moret, I. and Viet, V. eds. *L'Organisation internationale du travail : origine, développement, avenir*, 157–166.
Hettne, B. 2009. *Thinking about Development*. London: Zed Books.
Hidalgo-Weber, O. 2017. *La Grande-Bretagne et l'Organisation internationale du travail (1919–1946) : Une nouvelle forme d'internationalisme*. Paris: L'Harmattan.
Hobsbawm, E. 2008. L'Âge des *extrêmes* : histoire du court xxe siècle : 1914–1991. Bruxelles: André Versaille.
Hodge, J. M. 2010. "British Colonial Expertise, Post-Colonial Carreering and the Early History of International Development", *Journal of Modern European History*, Special Issue on "Modernizing Missions: Approaches to 'Developing' the Non-Western World after 1945" 8(1): 24–46.
Hodge, J. M. 2015. "Writing the History of Development (Part 1: The First Wave)", *Humanity Journal* 6(3): 429–463.
Hodge, J. M. 2016. "Writing the History of Development (Part 2: Longer, Deeper, Wider)", *Humanity Journal* 7(1): 125–174.
Hoehtker, D., Kott, S. eds. 2015. *À la rencontre de l'Europe au travail. Récits de voyages d'Albert Thomas (1920–1932)*. Paris, Genève: Publications de la Sorbonne, Bureau international du travail.
Hofstetter, R., Schneuwly, B. 2013. "The International Bureau of Education (1925–1968): a platform for designing a 'chart of world aspirations for education'", *European Education Research Journal* 12(2): 215–230.
Hooghe, L. 2005. "Several Roads Lead to International Norms, but few via International Socialization. A case study of the European Commission", *International Organization* 59(4): 861–898.
Hu, A. 2015. "China's Early Labor (Social Insurance) Legislation: The Role of the International Labor Organization, 1910s–1928", in Hu, A. ed. *China's Social Insurance in the Twentieth Century: A Global Historical Perspective*, 51–75. Leyde: The Brill Academic Press.

ILO, 2009. *Edward Phelan and the ILO: Life and Views of an International Social Actor.* Geneva: International Labour Organisation.

Inglot, T. 2008. *Welfare States in East Central Europe, 1919–2004.* Cambridge: Cambridge University Press.

Iriye, A. 2004. *Global Community, The Role of International Organizations in the Making of the Contemporary World.* Berkeley: University of California Press.

Iriye, A. and Saunier, P.-Y. eds. 2009. *The Palgrave Dictionnary of Transnational History. From the mid-19th Century to the Present Day.* Basingstoke: Palgrave.

James, H. 2001. *The End of Globalizazion. Lessons from the Great Depression.* Harvard: Havard University Press.

Javillier, J.-C., Gernignon, B., Politakis, G. eds. *Les Normes internationales du travail : un patrimoine pour l'avenir. Mélanges en l'honneur de Nicolas Valticos.* Genève: International Labour Office.

Jenks, W. 1969. *The ILO in Wartime.* Ottawa, Canada: Département du travail.

Jensen, J. 2011. "From Geneva to the Americas: The International Labor Organization and Inter-American Social Security Standards, 1936–1948", *International Labor and Working-Class History*, 80(1): 215–240.

Jervis, R. 1998. "Realism in the Study of World Politics", *International Organization* 52(4): 971–991.

Johnston, G. 1970. *The International Labour Organisation. Its Work for Social and Economic Progress.* London: Europa Publications.

Jolly, R., Emmerij, L. and Ghai, D. P. eds. 2004. *UN Contributions to Development Thinking and Practice.* Bloomington: Indiana University Press.

Jousse, E. 2008. "Du révisionnisme d'Eduard Bernstein au réformisme d'Albert Thomas (1896–1914)", *Les Cahiers Irice* 2(2): 39–52.

Keck, M. E. and Sikkink, K. 1998. *Activists beyond Borders: Advocacy Networks in International Politics.* Ithaca; London: Cornell University Press.

Kettunen, P. 2013. "The ILO as a Forum for Developing and Demonstrating a Nordic Model", in Kott, S. and Droux, J. eds. *Globalizing Social Rights. The international Labour Organization and Beyond*, 210–230.

Kettunen, P., Petersen K. eds. 2011. *Beyond Welfare State Models: Transnational Historical Perspectives on Social Policy.* Cheltenham: Edward Elgar Publishing; Albert, M., Bluhm, G., Helmig, J., Leutzsch, A., and Walter, J. eds. 2009. *Transnational Political Spaces. Agents-Structures-Encounters*, 7–31. Frankfurt, New York: Campus Verlag.

Kévonian, D. 2005. "Enjeux de catégorisations et migrations internationales", *Revue européenne des migrations internationales* 21(3): 95–124.

Kevonian, D. 2008. "La légitimation par l'expertise: le Bureau international du travail et la statistique internationale", *Les Cahiers Irice* 2(2): 81–106.

Kevonian, D. 2008. "La légitimation par l'expertise: le Bureau international du travail et la statistique internationale", 86.

Kideckel, D. 2004. "Miners and Wives in Romania's Jiu Valley: Perspectives on Postsocialist Class, Gender, and Social Change", *Identities* 11(1): 44.

Kirby, W. C. 2000."Engineering China: Birth of the Developmental State, 1928–1937", in Yeh, W.-H. ed. *Becoming Chinese: Passages to Modernity and beyond*, 147–148. Berkeley: University of California Press.

Knight, F. 1923. *The Ethics of Competition and Other Essays*. New York and London: Harper & Bros.

Kotkin, S. 2000. "*World War Two and Labor:* A Lost Cause?", *International Labor and Working Class History* 58: 181–191.

Kott, S. 2008. "De l'assurance à la sécurité sociale (1919–1949): L'OIT comme acteur international": 1–29. Geneva: International Labour Organization, Working paper for the ILO Century Project.

Kott, S. 2008. "Une 'communauté épistémique' du social? Experts de l'OIT et internationalisation des politiques sociales dans l'entre-deux-guerres", *Genèses* 2(71): 26–46.

Kott, S. 2010. "Constructing a European Social Model: The Fight for Social Insurance in the Interwar Period", in Van Daele, J. et al. eds. *ILO Histories. Essays on the International Labour Organization and Its Impact on the World During the Twentieth Century*, 173–196. Bern: Peter Lang.

Kott, S. 2011. "Dynamiques de l'internationalisation : L'Allemagne et l'Organisation internationale du Travail (1919–1940)", *Critique internationale* 3(52): 69–84.

Kott, S. 2011. "Les organisations internationales, terrains d'étude de la globalisation. Jalons pour une approche socio-historique", *Critique internationale* 3(52): 9–16.

Kott, S. 2011. "Par-delà la guerre froide. Les organisations internationales et les circulations Est-Ouest (1947–1973) ", *Vingtième Siècle. Revue d'histoire* 1(109): 129–143.

Kott, S. 2011. "Une autre approche de la globalisation : socio-histoire des organisations internationales (1900–1940)", *Critique internationale* 3(52).

Kott, S. 2014. "Fighting the War or Preparing for Peace? The ILO during the Second World War", *Journal of Modern European History* 12(3): 359–376.

Kott, S. 2014. "From Transnational Reformist Network to International Organization: The International Association for Labour Legislation and the International Labour Organization (1900–1930s)", in Rodogno, D., Struck, B., Vogel, J. eds. *Shaping the Transnational Sphere: Experts, Networks and Issues from the 1840s to the 1930s*, 239–258. New York: Berghahn Books.

Kott, S. 2015. "Organizing World Peace. The International Labour Organisation from the Second World War to the Cold War", in Hoffmann, S.-L., Kott, S., Romijn, P., Wieviorka, O. eds. *Seeking Peace in the Wake of War: Europe, 1943–1947*, 309–310. Amsterdam: Amsterdam University Press.

Kott, S. 2018. "OIT, justice sociale et mondes communistes. Concurrences, émulations, convergences", *Le Mouvement Social* 263(2): 139–151.

Krieg-Planque, A., Oger, C. 2010. "Discours institutionnels. Perspectives pour les sciences de la communication", *Mots. Les langages du politique [Online], 94 | 2010*, online since 06 November 2012. http://journals.openedition.org/mots/19870.

Lagendijk, V. 2008. *Electrifying Europe*: The Power of *Europe* in the Construction of Electricity Networks. Amsterdam: Aksant.

Lake, M. 2016. "The ILO, Australia and the Asia–Pacific Region: New Solidarities or Internationalism in the National Interest?", in Lichtenstein, N., Jensen, J. M. *The ILO from Geneva to the Pacific Rim – West meets East*, 33–54. International Labour Organization, Palgrave Macmillan, ILO Century Series.

Latham, M. E. 2011. *The Right Kind of Revolution: Modernization, Development, and U.S. Foreign Policy from the Cold War to the Present*. Ithaca: Cornell University Press.

Latouche, S. 2005. *L'Occidentalisation du monde. Essai sur la signification, la portée et les limites de l'uniformisation planétaire.* Paris: La Découverte.

Latouche, S. 2010. "Standard of Living", in Sachs, W. ed. 2010. *The Development Dictionary. A Guide to Knowledge as Power,* 250–263. London and New York: Zed Books.

Lee, J. M., Petter, M. 1982. *The Colonial Office, War, and Development Policy: Organisation and the Planning of a Metropolitan Initiative, 1939–1945.* University of London, Institute of Commonwealth Studies, Commonwealth Papers, number 22. London: Maurice Temple Smith, for the Institute.

Legouté, J. R. 2015. "Définir le développement : historique et dimensions d'un concept plurivoque", *Economie politique internationale. Cahier de recherche* 1(1): 1–43.

Legro, J. W. 1997. "Which Norms Matter? Revisiting the "Failure' of Internationalism", *International Organization* 51(1): 31–63.

Lengyel, P. 1960. "Le rôle de l'assistance technique dans le développement économique", *Tiers Monde* 4: 461–490.

Léon, P. 1969. *Économies et sociétés de l'Amérique Latine. Essai sur les problèmes du développement à l'époque contemporaine, 181–-1967.* Paris: Regards sur l'Histoire.

Lespinet-Moret, I. 2004. "Justin Godart et le Bureau international du travail", in Wieviorka, A. ed. *Justin Godart: Un homme dans son siècle (1871–1956),* 81–86. Paris: CNRS Ed.

Lespinet-Moret, I. 2007. "Le vivier de la Direction du travail et du ministère du Travail au sein de l'Organisation internationale du travail, 1919–1932", in Chatriot, A., Join-Lambert, O., Viet, V. eds. *Les Politiques du Travail (1906–2006). Acteurs, institutions, réseaux:* 241–257. Rennes: PUR.

Lespinet-Moret, I. and Viet, V. eds. 2011. *L'Organisation internationale du travail* : origine, développement, *avenir.* Rennes: PUR.

Lespinet-Moret, I., Liebeskind-Sauthier, I. 2008. "Albert Thomas, le BIT et le chômage: Expertise, catégorisation et action politique internationale", *Les Cahiers Irice* 2(2): 157–179.

Lespinet-Moret, I., Viet, V. eds. 2011. *L'Organisation internationale du travail* : origine, développement, *avenir.* Rennes: PUR.

Levi-Strauss, C. 1955. *Tristes tropiques.* Paris: Plon.

Lewis, C. M 1993. "Social Insurance: Ideology and Policy in the Argentine, c.1920–1966", in Bel, C., Lewis, C. M. eds. *Welfare, Poverty and Development in Latin America,* 175–200. London: The Macmillan Press.

Lewis, J. 2005. "The Janus Face of Brussels: Socialization and Everyday Decision Making in the European Union", *International Organization* 59(4): 937–971.

Lichtenstein, N., Jensen, J. M. 2015. *The ILO from Geneva to the Pacific Rim – West meets East.* International Labour Organization, Palgrave Macmillan, ILO Century Series.

Liebeskind-Sauthier, I. 2005. "L'Organisation internationale du travail face au chômage: entre compétences normatives et recherche de solutions économiques, 1919–1939". PhD diss., University of Geneva.

Liebig, G. 1997. "How the German trade unions could have stopped Hitler", *Executive Intelligence Review,* 24(16): 20–39.

Lindsay, S. M. 1934. "The *Problem* of *American Cooperation*", in Shotwell, J. T. ed. *The Origins of the International Labor Organization,* 331–367. New York: Colombia University Press.

Lockman, Z., Beinin, J. 1987. *Workers of the Nile: Nationalism, Communism, Islam and the Egyptian Working Class (1882–1954)*. Princeton: Princeton University Press.

Lorenz, E. C. 2001. *Defining global justice: The History of U.S. International Labor Standards Policy*. Notre Dame, Ind.: University of Notre Dame Press.

Lorwin, L. L. 1933. "Economic Nationalism and World Cooperation", *Pacific Affairs* 6(7): 361–372.

Lorwin, L. L., Wubnig, A. 1935. *Labor Relations Boards*, Washington: The Brookings Institution.

Lorwin, L. L. 1945. *Time for Planning: A Social-Economic Theory and Program for the Twentieth Century*. New York: Harper.

Lorwin, L. L. 1972. *The American Federation of Labor*. New Jersey: Augustus M. Kelley Publishers.

Louis, M. 2018. "Le parent pauvre de la gouvernance économique mondiale ? L'OIT face aux crises de 1929 et de 2008", *Le Mouvement Social* 263(2): 45–59.

Love, J. L. 1996. *Crafting the Third World: Theorizing Underdevelopment in Rumania and Brazil*. Palo Alto, California: Stanford University Press.

Lübken, U. 2003. "'Americans All': The United States, the Nazi Menace, and the Construction of a Panamerican Identity", *American Studies*, 48(3): 389–409.

Luyten, D. 2005. "Un corporatisme belge, réponse à la crise du libéralisme", in Dard, O., Deschamps, É. eds. *Les Relèves en Europe d'un après-guerre à l'autre. Racines, réseaux, projets et postérités*, 197–213. Bruxelles: Peter Lang.

Lyon-Bowley, A. 1923 [1915]. *The Nature and Purpose of the Measurement of Social Phenomena*. London: P.S. King.

MacKenzie, D. C. 2010. *A World Beyond Borders: An Introduction to the History of International Organizations*. North York: University of Toronto Press.

Maier, C. S. 1970. "Between Taylorism and Technocracy: European Ideologies and the Vision of Industrial Productivity in the 1920s", *Journal of Contemporary History* 5(2): 27–61.

Margairaz, M. 2010. "L'OIT et la sécurité du travail. Du rapport Beveridge à la conférence de Philadelphie : l'invention de la Sécurité sociale", in Aglan, A. ed. *Humaniser le travail : régimes économiques, régimes politiques et Organisation internationale du travail (1929–1969)*, 131–148. Brussels; Bern: Peter Lang.

Margherita, Z. 2007. "Exporting Development: The League of Nations and Republican China", *Comparative Studies in Society and History* 49(1):143–169.

Marinakis, A. 2008. "The role of the ILO in the development of minimum wages", ILO Century Project Paper. https://www.ilo.org/global/topics/wages/minimum-wages/definition/WCMS_180793/lang-en/index.htm

Maris, B. 2002. "Légitimation, autolégitimation, discours expert et discours savant", in Maris, B. ed. *La Légitimation du discours économique*, 109–121. Toulouse: Presses universitaires du Mirail.

Martin, L. L. and Simmons, A. B. 1998. "Theories and Empirical Studies of International Institutions", *International Organization* 52(4): 729–757.

Matsaganis, M. 2005. "Greece-Fighting with Hands Tied behind the Back. Anti-Poverty Policy without Minimum Income", in Ferrera, M. ed. *Welfare State Reform in Southern Europe: Fighting Poverty and Social Exclusion in Italy, Spain, Portugal and Greece*, 24–64. New York: Routledge. EUI Studies in the Political Economy of the Welfare State

Maul, D. 2007. "The International Labour Organization and the Struggle against Forced Labour", *Labour History* 48(4): 477–500.
Maul, D. 2012. *Human Rights, Development and Decolonization: The International Labour Organization, 1940–70.* Basingstoke, Palgrave Macmillan. Geneva: International Labour Organization.
Maurette, F. 1934. *Tour du Pacifique.* Paris: Librairie Hachette.
Mazower, M. 2011. "Reconstruction. The Historiographical Issues", in Mazower, M., Reinisch, J., Feldman, D. eds. *Post–war Reconstruction in Europe. International Perspectives, 1945–1949,* 17–28. Oxford: Oxford University Press.
McBeth, B. S. 2002. *Juan Vicente Gómez and the oil companies in Venezuela, 1908–1935.* Cambridge [etc.]: Cambridge University Press.
McCook, S. G. 2000. *States of Nature: Science, Agriculture, and Environment in the Spanish Caribbean, 1760–1940.* Austin: University of Texas Press.
McKillen, E. 2010. "Beyond Gompers: The American Federation of Labor, the Creation of the ILO, and US Labor Dissent", in Van Daele, J. et al. eds. 2010. *ILO Histories,* 41–66.
McPherson, A. and Wehrli, Y. 2015. *Beyond Geopolitics: New Histories of Latin America at the League of Nations.* New Mexico: University of New Mexico Press.
Mecchi, L. 2013. "Du BIT à la politique sociale européenne : les origines d'un modèle", *Le Mouvement social* 3(244): 17–30.
Mercier, P. 1966. *Histoire de l'anthropologie.* Paris: PUF.
Métral, A. 1931. *Deux conceptions économiques: Europe ou États-Unis?.* Paris: Nouvelles Editions Latines.
Meyer, J.-B., 1997. *Experts en mission : les coulisses d'un transfert de technologie.* Paris: Karthala-ORSTOM.
Michael E. L. 2000, *Modernization as Ideology: American Social Science and "Nation Building" in the Kennedy Era,* Chapel Hill, University of North Carolina Press.
Micu, C. 2012. *From Peasants to Farmers? Agrarian Reforms and Modernisation in Twentieth Century Romania.* Frankfurt am Main: Peter Lang.
Mitchell, T. 2002. *Rule of Experts: Egypt, Techno-Politics, Modernity.* Berkeley: University of California Press.
Mitrany, D. 1943. *A Working Peace System*: An Argument for the Functional Development of International Organization. London: The Royal Institute of International Affairs.
Mokyr, J. 2005. "The Intellectual Origins of Modern Economic Growth", *The Journal of Economic History* 65(2): 285–351.
Molineu, H. 1986. *US Policy toward Latin America: from Regionalism to Globalism.* Colorado: Westview Press.
Moynihan, D. 1960. *The United States and the International Labor Organization, 1889–1934.* Medford, Mass.
Murphy, N. C. 2006. *The United Nations Development Programme: A Better Way?* Cambridge: Cambridge University Press.
Myers, J. 1933. "American Relations with the International Labour Office, 1919–1932", *Annals of the American Academy of Political and Social Science* 166: 135–145.
Nations Unies, *Comité de l'assistance technique. (1965). Cent cinquante mille spécialistes en 15 ans : Bilan anniversaire du programme élargi d'assistance technique des Nations Unies.* [New York].

Nay, O. 2011. "Éléments pour une sociologie du changement dans les organisations internationales", *Critique internationale* 4(53): 9–20.

Nemo, P. 2013. *Histoire des idées politiques aux Temps modernes et contemporains*. Paris: PUF.

Norel, P. 1986. *Nord-Sud: Les enjeux du développement*. Paris: Syros.

Nyland, C. 2001. "Critical Theorising, Taylorist Practice, and the International Labor Organization", CMS Conference, Manchester School of Management, UMIST, England. Unpublished.

Oger, C., Olivier-Yaniv, C. 2006. "Conjurer le désordre discursif. Les procédés de " lissage " dans la fabrication du discours institutionnel", *Mots. Les langages du politique* 81: 63–77.

Opler, M. E. 1954. *Les Problèmes sociaux de l'assistance technique*. Paris: UNESCO.

Osterhammel, J. 1979. "Technical Co-Operation between the League of Nations and China", *Modern Asian Studies* 13(4): 661–680.

Ostrower, G. B. 1975. *"The American Decision to Join the International Labor Organization"*, *Labor History* 16(4): 495–504.

Owen, D. 1950. "The United Nations Expanded Program of Technical Assistance – A Multilateral Approach", *The Annals of the American Academy of Political and Social Science* 323, 25–32.

Owen, D. 1950. "The United Nations Program of Technical Assistance", *The Annals of the American Academy of Political and Social Science* 270, 109–117.

Paddle, S. 2001. "For the China of the Future': Western Feminists, Colonization and International Citizenship in China in the Inter-War Years", *Australian Feminist Studies* 16(36): 325–329.

Pedersen, S. 2006. "The Meaning of the Mandates System: An Argument", *Geschichte und Gesellschaft* 32(4): 569.

Pedersen, S. 2007. "Back to the League of Nations: Review Essay", *American Historical Review* 112(4): 1091–1117.

Pernet, C. 2011. "L'OIT et la question de l'alimentation en Amérique latine (1930–1950): Les problèmes posés par la définition internationale des normes de niveau de vie", in Lespinet-Moret, I., Viet, V. eds. *L'Organisation internationale du travail*, 167–178. Rennes: PUR.

Pernet, C. 2013. "Developing Nutritional Standards and Food Policy: Latin American Reformers Between the ILO, the League of Nations Health Organization, and the Pan-American Sanitary Bureau", in Droux, J., Kott, S. eds. *Globalizing Social Rights. The International Labour Organization and Beyond*, 249–261. Basingstoke: Palgrave Macmillan.

Pestre, D. 1995. "Pour une histoire sociale et culturelle des sciences. Nouvelles définitions, nouveaux objets, nouvelles pratiques", *Annales. Histoire, Sciences Sociales*, 50(3): 487–522.

Peterson, M. D. 1999. *Coming of Age with the New Republic, 1938–1950*. Columbia: University of Missouri.

Petmesidou, M. 2006. "Tracking Social Protection: Origins, Path Peculiarity, Impasses and Prospects", in Petmesidou, M., Mossialos E. eds. *Social Policy Developments in Greece*, 25–54. Burlington: Ashgate.

Phelan, E. J. 1936. *Albert Thomas et la création du BIT*. Paris: Grasset.

Picón, D. 1999. *Historia de la Diplomacia Venezolana 1811–1985*. Caracas : Universidad Catolica Andres.

Pla, A. J., 1985. *Syndicats et Politique au Venezuela, 1924–1950*, PhD diss., University of Paris.

Plata, V. 2013. "La difusión de las normas internacionales del trabajo en Venezuela, 1936–1939: una práctica de cooperación técnica internacional en la OIT", in Herrera León, F., Herrera González, P., & Wehrli, Y. *América Latina y la Organización Internacional del Trabajo: Redes, cooperación técnica e institucionalidad social (1919–1950)*, 127–160. (Colección encuentros. UMSNH 14). Morelia: Universidad Michoacana de San Nicolás de Hidalgo – Instituto de Investigaciones Históricas.

Plata, V. 2014. "Le Bureau international du travail et la coopération technique dans l'entre-deux-guerres", *Relations internationales* 157(1): 55–69.

Plata-Stenger, V. 2015. "To Raise Awareness of Difficulties and to Assert their Opinion". "The International Labour Office and the Regionalization of International Cooperation in the 1930s", in McPherson, A., Wehrli, Y. eds. *Beyond Geopolitics: New Histories of Latin America at the League of Nations*, 97–113. New Mexico, University of New Mexico Press.

Plata-Stenger, V. 2016. "Europe, the ILO and the wider world (1919–1954)", EGO | European History Online: http://ieg-ego.eu/en/threads/transnational-movements-and-organisations/international-organisations-and-congresses/veronique-plata-stenger-europe-the-ilo-and-the-wider-world-1919–1954.

Plata-Stenger, V. 2017. "L'OIT et l'assurance sociale en Amérique latine dans les années 30 et 40: enjeux et limites de l'expertise internationale", *Revue d'histoire de la protection sociale*, 10(1): 42–61.

Plata-Stenger, V. 2018. "L'OIT et le problème du sous-développement en Asie dans l'entre-deux-guerres", *Le Mouvement Social* 263(2): 109–122.

Plata-Stenger, V. 2019. "'Mission civilisatrice', réforme sociale et modernisation : l'OIT et le développement colonial dans l'entre-deux-guerres", *Relations internationales* 1(177): 15–29.

Plata-Stenger, V., Schulz, M. 2019. "Décolonisation et développement : genèses, pratiques et interdépendances. Introduction", *Relations internationales* 1(177): 3–13.

Plata, V. 2010. *Le Recrutement des fonctionnaires du Bureau international du travail en 1920 : Une approche prosopographique*. Master diss., University of Geneva.

Plata, V. 2014. "Le Bureau international du travail et la coopération technique dans l'entre-deux-guerres", *Relations internationales* 2(157): 55–69.

Polanyi, K. 1944. *La grande transformation : aux origines politiques et économiques de notre temps*. Paris: Gallimard.

Racianu, I. 2012. "La mission de Charles Rist en Roumanie (1929–1932)", in Feiertag, O., Margairaz, M. eds. *Les Banques centrales à l'échelle du monde. L'internationalisation des banques centrales des débuts du XXe siècle à nos jours*, 59–78. Paris: Presses de Sciences Po.

Rasmussen, A. 2001. "Tournant, inflexions, ruptures : le moment internationaliste", *Mil neuf cent. Revue d'histoire intellectuelle* 1(19): 27–41.

Reagan, P. D. 1999. *Designing a New America. The Origins of the New Deal Planning, 1890–1943*. Amherst: University of Massachusetts Press.

Rebérioux, M., Fridenson, P. 1974. "Albert Thomas, pivot du réformisme français", *Le Mouvement social* 87: 85–97.

Reinalda, B. 2009. *Routledge History of International Organizations: From 1815 to the Present Day.* London: Routledge.
Rens, Jef. 1959 "Latin America and the International Labour Organisation. Forty years of collaboration 1919–1959", in *International Labour Review* 80(1): 1–25.
Rens, J. 1961. "L'Organisation internationale du travail et la coopération technique internationale", *Revue internationale du travail* 83(5): 441–466.
Revel, J. 1996. *Jeux d'échelles : la micro-analyse à l'expérience.* Paris: Le Seuil.
Reynaud, E. 2017. "The International Labour Organization and the Living Wage: A Historical Perspective", 1–37. International Labour Office, Inclusive Labour Markets, Labour Relations and Working Conditions Branch. – Geneva: ILO.
Ribi Forclaz, A. 2011. "A New Target for International Social Reform: The International Labour Organization and Working and Living Conditions in Agriculture in the Inter-War Years", *Contemporary European History* 20(3): 307–329.
Richard, A.-I. 2012. "Competition and Complementarity: Civil Society Networks and the Question of Decentralising the League of Nations", *Journal of Global History* 7(2): 233–256.
Rist, G. 2002. *Les Mots du pouvoir. Sens et non-sens de la rhétorique international.* Genève: Nouveaux Cahiers de l'IUED.
Rist, G. 2007. *Le Développement : Histoire d'une croyance occidentale*, Paris: Presses de la Fondation nationale des sciences politiques.
Ritschel, D. 1991. "A Corporatist Economy in Britain? Capitalist Planning for Industrial Self-Government in the 1930s", *The English Historical Review* 106(418): 41–65.
Rivas, R. 1995. "Venezuela, petróleo y la Segunda Guerra Mundial (1939–1945): Un ejemplo histórico para las nuevas generaciones", *Economía* 10: 163–179.
Robert, C. 2010. "Être socialisé à ou par " l'Europe " ? Dispositions sociales et sens du jeu institutionnel des experts de la Commission européenne, in Michel, H., Robert, C. *La fabrique des " Européens " : processus de socialisation et construction européenne.* Chapter 10. Strasbourg : Presses universitaires de Strasbourg.
Robert, C. 2010. "Les groupes d'experts dans le gouvernement de l'Union européenne. Bilans et perspectives de recherche", *Politique européenne* 3(32): 7–38.
Robert, C. 2012. "Les dispositifs d'expertise dans la construction européenne des politiques publiques : quels enseignements ?", *Éducation et sociétés* 29(1): 57–70.
Roberts, R. S. 1962. Economic Development, *Human Skills* and Technical Assistance: A Study of I.L.O. Technical Assistance in the Field of Productivity and Management Development. Genève: Droz.
Rodan, G. ed. 1996. *Political Oppositions in Industrialising Asia.* London, New York: Routledge.
Rodger, G., Swepston, L., Lee, E., Van Daele, J. 2009. *The International Labour Organization and the Quest for Social Justice, 1919–2009.* Geneva: ILO.
Rodgers, D. T., 1998. *Atlantic Crossings: Social Politics in a Progressive Age.* Cambridge Mass., London: The Belknap Press of Harvard University Press.
Rodgers, G. et al. 2009. *The International Labour Organization and The Quest for Social Justice, 1919–2009.* Ithaca: ILR Press.
Rodgers, G. 2011. "India, the ILO and the Quest for Social Justice since 1919." *Economic and Political Weekly* 46(10): 45–52.

Rodgers, G., Lee, E., Swepston, L., Van Daele, J. 2009. *The International Labour Organization and the Quest for Social Justice 1919–2009*. Geneva-Ithaca: ILO-Cornell University Press.

Rodogno, D., Gauthier, S., and Piana, F. 2013. "What Does Transnational History Tell Us about a World with International Organizations?", in Reinalda, B. ed. 2013. *Routledge Handbook of International Organizations*, 94–105. Routledge: London.

Rodríguez–Piñero, L. 2005. *Indigenous Peoples, Postcolonialism, and International Law. The ILO Regime (1919–1989)*. Oxford: Oxford University Press.

Roger, A. 2002. *Fascistes, communistes et paysans. Sociologie des mobilisations identitaires roumaines (1921–1989)*. Bruxelles: éditions de l'Université de Bruxelles.

Rosenberg, E. 1999. *Financial Missionaries to the World: The Politics and Culture of Dollar Diplomacy, 1900–1930*. Cambridge: Harvard University Press.

Rosenstein-Rodan, P. N. 1944. "The International Development of Economically Backward Areas", *International Affairs* 20(2): 157–165.

Rosenthal, P.-A. 2006. "Géopolitique et État-providence. Le BIT et la politique mondiale des migrations dans l'entre–deux–guerres", *Annales. Histoire, Sciences Sociales* 1(61): 99–134.

Rostow, W. W., 1960. *The Stages of Economic Growth. A Non-Communist Manifesto*. London; New York: Cambridge University Press.

Rothermund, D. 1993. *An Economic History of India from PreeColonial Times to 1991*. London; New York: Routledge.

Rowntree, B. S. 1942. *Poverty and Progress. A Second social survey of York*. London: Longman.

Rowntree, B. S., Lavers, G. R. 1951. *Poverty and the Welfare State: A Third Social Survey of York Dealing only with Economic Questions*. London: Longmans.

Sachs, W. ed. 2010. *The Development dictionary. A Guide to Knowledge as Power*. London and New York: Zed Books.

Sacriste, G., Vauchez, A. 2005. "Les 'bons offices' du droit international : la constitution d'une autorité non politique dans le concert diplomatique des années 1920", *Critique internationale* 1(26): 101–117.

Saunders, O. 2015. "Preserving the *Status Quo:* Britain, the United States, and Bolivian Tin, 1946–56, *The International History Review* 38(3): 551–572.

Saunier, P.-Y. 2004. "Circulations, connexions et espaces transnationaux", *Genèses* 4(57): 110–126.

Saunier, P.-Y. 2008. "Les régimes circulatoires du domaine social 1800–1940 : projets et ingénierie de la convergence et de la différence", *Genèses* 2(71): 4–25.

Saunier, P.-Y. 2010. "Borderline Work: ILO Explorations onto the Housing Scene until 1940", in Van Daele, J., Rodríguez García, M., Van Goethem, G., Van der Linden, M. *ILO Histories. Essays on the International Labour Organization and its Impact on the World during the Twentieth Century*, 197–221. Bern: Peter Lang.

Saunier, P.-Y. 2013. *Transnational History. Theory and History*. Basingstoke: Palgrave.

Scelle, G. 1930. *L'Organisation internationale du travail et le BIT*. Paris: M. Rivière.

Schaper, B. W. 1960. *Albert Thomas, trente ans de réformisme social*. Paris: PUF.

Schirmann, S. 2000. *Crise, coopération économique et financière entre États européens, 1929–1933*. Paris: Comité pour l'histoire économique et financière de la France.

Schot J., Lagendijk, V. 2008. "Technocratic Internationalism in the Interwar Years: Building Europe on Motorways and Electricity Networks", *Journal of Modern European History* 6(2): 196–216.

Schoultz, L. 2003. *Beneath the United States: A History of U.S. Policy Toward Latin America.* Cambridge Massachusetts: Harvard University Press.

Scott, J. C. 1998. *Seeing Like a State: How Certain Schemes to Improve the Human* Condition Have Failed. New Haven: Yale University Press.

Scott, M. N. 2010. *Free Trade and the New Deal: The United States and the International Economy of the 1930s.* Phd diss., Graduate College, Iowa State University.

Seekings, J. 2008. "The ILO and Social Protection in the Global South, 1919–2005". CSSR Working Paper No. 238. ILO Century Project: 1–50.

Seekings, J. 2010. "The ILO and Welfare Reform, in South Africa, Latin America, and the Carribbean, 1919–1950", in Van Daele, J. et al. eds. *ILO Histories. Essays on the International Labour Organization and Its Impact on the World During the Twentieth Century*, 145–172. Bern: Peter Lang.

Seidel, R. N. 1972. "American Reformers Abroad: The Kemmerer Missions in South America, 1923–1931", *The Journal of Economic History* 32(2): 520–545.

Sen, A. 1985. *Commodities and Capabilities*. Amsterdam and New York: North-Holland.

Sen, A. 1987. *The Standard of Living*. The Tanner Lectures, Clare Hall, Cambridge: Cambridge University Press.

Sergiu, D. 2014. "The welfare-state as a means of nation-building in interwar Romania, 1930–1938", 46. Master of Arts. Budapest: Hungary.

Sharp, W. 1953. "The Institutional Framework for Technical Assistance", *International Organization* 7(3): 342–379.

Sheinin, D. ed. 2000. *Beyond the ideal: Pan Americanism in Inter-American affairs*. Westport, Conn.: Greenwood Press.

Shipper, F. 2008. *Driving Europe: Building Europe on Roads in the Twentieth Century*. Amsterdam: Aksant.

Shotwell, J. T. 1934. *Origins of the International Labour Organization*, New York: Columbia University Press.

Singaravélou, P. 2009. "Le moment 'impérial' de l'histoire des sciences sociales (1880–1910)", *Mil neuf cent. Revue d'histoire intellectuelle* 1(27): 87–102.

Singh, K. 1989. "Oil Politics in Venezuela During the Lopez Contreras Administration (1936–1941)", *Journal of Latin American Studies* 21(1–2): 89–104.

Singleton, L. 2013. "The ILO and Social Security in Latin America, 1930–1950", in Herrera León, F., Herrera González, P. eds. *América Latina y la Organización Internacional del Trabajo: Redes, coopéracion técnica e institucionalidad social, 1919–1950*, 243–74. México City: UMSNH, UM, UFF.

Siroux, J.-L. 2008. "La dépolitisation du discours au sein des rapports annuels de l'Organisation mondiale du commerce", *Mots. Les langages du politique* 88 | 2008, online since 01 November 2010. URL: http://journals.openedition.org/mots/14223

Skocpol, T. 1985. "Bringing the State Back In: Strategies of Analysis in Current Research", in Evans, P., Rueschemeyer, D., Skocpol, T. eds. *Bringing the State Back In*, 3–43. New York: Cambridge University Press.

Sluga, G. 2011. "Editorial – The Transnational History of International Institutions", *Journal of Global History* 6(2): 219–222.

Smith, J. 2000. "The First Conference of American States (1889 –1890) and the Early Pan American Policy of the United States", in Sheinin, D. ed. *Beyond the Ideal: Pan Americanism in Inter-American Affairs*, 19 –32. Westport: Greenwood press.
Smith, J. 2000. "The First Conference of American States (1889 –1890) and the Early Pan American Policy of the United States", in Sheinin, D. ed. *Beyond the Ideal: Pan Americanism in Inter-American Affairs*, 19 –32. Westport, Conn.: Greenwood Press
Smith, J. 2005. *The United States and Latin America. A history of American diplomacy, 1776 –2000*. New York: Routledge.
Smith, P. H. 2000. *Talons of the Eagle: Dynamics of U.S.-Latin American Relations*. New York: Oxford University Press.
Société des amis d'Albert Thomas, 1957. *Un grand citoyen du monde : Albert Thomas vivant. Études, témoignages, souvenirs*. Genève: Bureau international du travail.
Speich Chassé, D. 2008. "Traveling with the GDP Through Early Development Economics History", *Working Papers on the Nature of Evidence: How Well Do Facts Travel?*", n°33. http://eprints.lse.ac.uk/22501/1/3308Speich.pdf.
Staples, A. 2005. *The Birth of Development: How the World Bank, Food and Agriculture Organization, and World Health Organization Changed the World, 1945 –1965*. Kent: Kent State University Press.
Steffen, K. and Kohlrausch, M. 2009. "The Limits and Merits of Internationalism: Experts, the State and the International Community in Poland in the First Half of the Twentieth Century", *Revue européenne d'histoire* 41, EUI Working Paper RSCAS: 715 –737.
Steiner, Z. 2005. *The Lights That Failed. European International History, 1919 –1933*. Oxford: Oxford University Press
Steiner, Z. 2011. *The Triumph of the Dark. European International History, 1933 –1939*. Oxford: Oxford University Press.
Stepan, A. C. 1978. *The State and Society: Peru in Comparative Perspective*. Princeton: Princeton University Press.
Stokke, O. 2009. *The UN and Development*. Bloomington: Indiana University Press.
Stolte, C. 2012. "Bringing Asia to the world: Indian trade unionism and the *long road* towards the Labour Congress, 1919 –37", *Journal of Global History* 7(2): 257 –278.
Storrs, L. R.Y. 2012. *The Second Red Scare and the Unmaking of the New Deal Left*. Princeton: Princeton University Press.
Sun, Y., Hein, C., Song, K. 2017. "Planning of public housing in modern Tianjin (1928 –1945). Planning Perspectives" 34(3): 439 –462.
Supiot, A. 2010. *L'Esprit de Philadelphie. La justice sociale face au marché total*. Paris: Seuil.
Szikra D., Tomka, B. 2009. "Social Policy in East Central Europe: Major Trends in the Twentieth Century", in Cerami, A. and Vanhuysse, P. eds. *Post-Communist Welfare Pathways. Theorizing Social Policy Transformations in Central and Eastern Europe*, 17 –34. Basingstoke: Palgrave Macmillan.
The Development of International Co-operation in Economic and Social Affairs. Special Committee on the Development of International Cooperation in Economic and Social Affairs, 1939. Geneva: League of Nations.
Theodorou, V., Karakatsani, D. 2008. "Health Policy in Interwar Greece: The Intervention by the League of Nations Health Organisation", *Dynamis* 28: 53 –75.
Théry, I. 2005. "Expertises de service, de consensus, d'engagement : essai de typologie de la mission d'expertise en sciences sociales", *Droit et Société* 2(60): 311 –329.

Thomann, B. ed. 2015. *La naissance de l'État social japonais. Biopolitique, travail et citoyenneté dans le Japon impérial (1868–1945)*. Paris: Presses de Sciences Po (P.F.N.S.P.).

Thomas, A. 1947. *Politique sociale internationale*. Genève : Bureau international du Travail.

Thomas, A. 1959. *À la rencontre de l'Orient. Notes de voyage, 1928–1929*. Genève: la Société des amis d'Albert Thomas.

Thurston, A. 2008. *Sources for Colonial Studies in the Public Record Office*. London: HMSO.

Tinker-Salas, M. 2003. "Races and Cultures in the Venezuelan Oil Fields", in Peloso V. C. ed. *Work, Protest and Identity in Twentieth-Century Latin America*, 143–164. Wilmington Delaware: SR Books.

Todorov, T. 1989. *Nous et les autres. La réflexion française sur la diversité humaine*. Paris: Seuil.

Topalov, C. ed. 2009. *Laboratoires du nouveau siècle*: la nébuleuse réformatrice et ses réseaux en France, 1880–1914. Paris: Éditions de l'EHESS.

Tortora, M. 1980. *Institution spécialisée et organisation mondiale : étude des relations de l'OIT avec la SDN et l'ONU*. Bruxelles: E. Bruylant.

Tosstorff, R. 2010. "Albert Thomas, the ILO and the IFTU", in Van Daele, J. et al. eds. *ILO Histories. Essays on the International Labour Organization and Its Impact on the World During the Twentieth Century*, 91–114. Bern: Peter Lang.

Touraine, A. 1988. "L'évolution du syndicalisme en Amérique latine", *Revue française de sociologie* 29(1): 117–142.

Tournès, L. 2006. "L'institut scientifique de recherches économiques et sociales et les débuts de l'expertise économique en France (1933–1940), *Genèses* 4(65): 49–70.

Tournès, L. 2012. "La philanthropie américaine, la Société des Nations et la coproduction d'un ordre international (1919–1946)", *Relations internationales* 3(151): 25–36.

Tournès, L. 2013. "Philanthropic foundations and the exportation of development". Conference paper presented at the "International organisations and the politics of development: historical perspective". Conference organised by the Geneva Graduate Institute and the Fondation Pierre du Bois in collaboration with the University of Geneva. Geneva, 6–7 December 2013.

Tournès, L. 2014. "The Rockefeller Foundation and the Transition from the League of Nations to the UN (1939–1946)", *Journal of Modern European History* 12(3): 323–341.

Tournès, L. 2015. *Les États-Unis et la Société des Nations (1914–1946). Le système international face à l'émergence d'une superpuissance*. Bern: Peter Lang.

Trépos, J.-Y. 1996. *La Sociologie de l'expertise*. Paris: PUF.

Trimberger E. K. 1977. *Revolution from Above: Military Bureaucrats and Development in Japan, Turkey, Egypt, and Peru*. New Brunswick, N.J: Transaction Books.

Unesco. 1961. *Coopération internationale et programmes de développement économique et social*. Bibliographie commentée par Jean Viet, Comité international pour la Documentation des sciences sociales, Unesco.

Unger, C. R. 2010. "Histories of Development and Modernization: Findings, Reflections, Future Research", http://hsozkult.geschichte.hu-berlin.de/forum/2010–12–001.

Urquijo, J. I. 2000. *El Movimiento Obrero de Venezuela*. Caracas: Universidad Catolica Andres.

Van Daele, J. 2005. "Engineering Social Peace: Networks, Ideas, and the Founding of the International Labour Organization", *International Review of Social History* 50(3): 435–466.

Van Daele, J. 2008. "The International Labour Organization (ILO) in Past and Present Research", *International Review of Social History* 53(3): 485–511.
Van Daele, J. et al. 2010. *ILO Histories. Essays on the International Labour Organization and Its Impact on the World During the Twentieth Century*. Bern: Peter Lang.
Van Goethem, G. 2010. "Labor's Second Front: The Foreign Policy of the American and British Trade Union Movements During the Second World War", *Diplomatic History* 34(4): 663–680.
Van Goethem, G. 2010. "Phelan's War: The International Labour Organization in Limbo (1941–1948)", in Van Daele, J. et al. eds. 2010. *ILO Histories. Essays on the International Labour Organization and Its Impact on the World During the Twentieth Century*, 314–340. Bern: Peter Lang.
Van Meurs, W. 1999. "Land Reform in Romania – A Never-Ending Story", *South-East Europe Review for Labour and Social Affairs* 2(2): 109–122
Vernon, J. 2007. *Hunger: A Modern History*. Cambridge Mass.: The Belknap Press of Harvard University Press.
Veynare, S. 2012. *Panorama du voyage (1780–1920). Mots, figures, pratiques*. Paris: Les Belles Lettres.
Walter-Busch, E. 2006. "Albert Thomas and scientific management in war and peace, 1914–1932", *Journal of Management History* 12(2): 222.
Webster, D. 2011. "Development Advisors in a Time of Cold War and Decolonization: The United Nations Technical Assistance Administration, 1950–1959", *Journal of Global History* 6(2): 249–272.
Wehrli, Y. 2003. *"Créer et maintenir l'intérêt" : la liaison entre le Secrétariat de la Société des Nations et l'Amérique Latine (1919–1929)*, Master diss., University of Geneva.
Wehrli, Y. 2010. "L'Amérique latine à la Société des Nations : le rêve de Bolívar réalisé ?", paper presented at the conference "Les Amériques latines : héritages et mirages des indépendances (1810–2010)", IHEID, Geneva, 18–19 March 2010.
Wehrli, Y. (2016). *Etats latino-américains, organismes multilatéraux et défense de la souveraineté : Entre Société des Nations et espace continental panaméricain (1919–1939)*, PhD diss., University of Geneva.
Weindling, P. ed. 2007. *International Health Organisations and Movements, 1918–1939*. Cambridge: Cambridge University Press.
Weinstein, B. 1996. *For Social Peace in Brazil Industrialists and the Remaking of the Working Class in Sao Paulo, 1920–1964*. Chapel Hill: University of North Carolina Press.
Wilcox, F. O. 1950. "The United Nations Program for Technical Assistance", *Annals of the American Academy of Political and Social Science* 268, 45–53.
Williams, M. 2005. *Mussolini's Propaganda Abroad: Subversion in the Mediterranean and the Middle East, 1935–1940*. London: Routledge.
Wolfgang, S. ed. 2010. *The Development Dictionary. A Guide to Knowledge as Power*. London; New York: Zed Books.
Wonik, K. 2007. "Social Insurance Expansion and Political Regime Dynamics in Europe, 1880–1945", *Social Science Quarterly* 88(2): 494–514.
Wright, W. R. 2003. *Café Con Leche: Race, Class, and National Image in Venezuela*. Ann Arbor: UMI Books.

Yeo, E. J. 2003. "Les enquêtes sociales aux 18ᵉ et 19ᵉ siècles", in Porter, T. M., Ross, D. eds. *The Cambridge History of Science*, Volume 7. *The Modern Social Sciences*, 83–99. Cambridge: Cambridge University Press.

Yifeng, C. 2014. "The International Labour Organisation and Labour Governance in China 1919–1949", in Blanpain, R., Liukkunen, U., Yifeng, C. eds. 2014. *China and ILO fundamental principles and rights at work*, 19–54. Netherlands: Wolters Kluwer.

Zanasi, M. 2007. "Exporting Development: The League of Nations and Republican China", *Comparative Studies in Society and History* 49(1): 143–169.

Index

Al-Shamsi, Ali 183
Alessandri Palma, Arturo 74, 292
All-India Trade Union Congress 98
Allen, Roy George Douglas 151
Allende, Salvador 262
Altmeyer, Arthur J. 259
American Federation of Labor 47, 259, 269
Andler, Charles 24, 25
Andrade, Victor 270, 271
Argentina 66, 67, 70, 72–73, 75–76, 79, 86–87, 102, 131, 258, 265, 276
Armstrong, Timothy H. 112
Arocha, Manuel Juan 183, 219–221, 225–226, 249
Association of National Unions of Mutual Benefit Societies and Health Insurance Funds 173, 199
Attlee, Clement Richard 277
Australia 132, 145
Austria 173, 190, 193, 212
Avenol, Joseph 41, 220
Bach, Federico 73
Balcázar, Juan Manuel 270–271
Bandeira de Mello, Affonso 67, 77, 85, 183
Bank for International Settlements (BIS) 41
Barbados 233
Becker, Charles 297
Belgium 32, 52, 139, 277
Bernstein, Eduard 24–25
Bétancourt, Romulo 221
Bevin, Ernest 280
Blatchford, Robert 174
Blelloch, David 159, 161, 163, 165, 168, 172, 174–175, 183, 187, 214, 217, 223–224, 226–232, 239–241, 243–248, 255, 261, 268, 270, 291, 297
Blum, Léon 33, 136
Board of Economic Warfare 265, 269
Bolivia 87, 261
Booker, Leon C. 223
Borges, Esteban Gil 183, 217
Bourgin, Hubert 27
Bravo, Antonio 269

Brazil 66–67, 72–73, 75, 77, 84–88, 102, 158, 177, 181, 183, 224–225, 260, 286
Bretton Woods 87, 279–280
Briand, Aristide 38, 64
British Controlled Oilfields Limited 240
Brookings Institution 51–53, 55
Bueno, Xavier 76, 297
Bulgaria 147, 189, 196–197, 212
Burge, M.R.K. 150, 254, 277, 285
Butler, Harold 1, 10, 22–23, 44–51, 54–58, 67–68, 70, 73–77, 85, 101–102, 104, 111, 115–117, 125, 141, 151, 158, 166, 170–171, 180, 183–185, 221, 225–227, 232, 235, 246–248, 273, 291–292, 294–295, 297
Butler, R. A. 117
Cahen-Salvador, Georges 208
Caldera, Rafael 218, 223, 245, 247
Canada 77, 87, 132, 145, 159, 161, 178, 183, 253, 255, 260–261, 277
Capriles Rico, Remberto 269
Carnegie Endowment European Centre in Paris 41
Carozzi, Luigi 159, 169, 178, 231, 297
Carvallo, Constantino J. 258
Central Prisoners of War Agency of the Red Cross 186
Ceylon 115
Chagas, Carlos 66
Chalmers, Ellison 106
Charron, René 147
Chatterjee, Atul Chandra 43
Childs, Stephen Lawford 68, 75–76, 117, 291
Chile 142, 159, 167, 170, 177, 183, 224, 227, 235, 258, 260–262, 267, 277, 286, 292
China 10, 72, 91, 93, 96, 100–102, 118–121, 145, 151, 158, 163, 175–177, 182–183, 253, 264, 277
Clark, John Maurice 55, 259, 266
Clemenceau, Georges 28
Cohen, Albert 164

Colombia 72, 87, 142, 217, 227, 233, 248, 263
Colombo 236
Commission for Relief in Belgium 52
Commission on International Labour Legislation 127, 166–167
Commission of Enquiry for European union (CEEU) 38, 48
Condliffe, John Bell 120, 144
Confederation of Mexican Workers 72
Corson, John J. 261–261
Costa Rica 263
Cruchaga Tocornal, Miguel 183
Cuba 72, 142, 158–159, 177, 179, 183, 260
Cuenca, Hector 242
Curaçao 233
Czechoslovakia 173, 193, 195–196, 198–200, 209–210, 212, 277
Day, Edmund 56–57
Dechamp, Cyrille 158, 162, 167, 170, 172, 175, 179–180, 185, 214, 223, 225–227, 230–231, 237, 241–245, 247–249, 297
Delaisi, Francis 38, 41
Djamalzadeh, Mohammad Ali 282
Dominican Republic 87
Douglas, Paul H. 152
Doyle, William T. 223
Drbohlav, Jaroslav 297
Drummond, Éric 135
Duggan, Laurence 266
Eastman, Mack 170
Economic and Financial Organisation (EFO) 57, 146, 148–149
Economic and Social Council (CESNU) 59, 253
Ecuador 72, 87, 178, 184, 260–261
Egypt 1, 10, 158–159, 162, 177–178, 182–185
El–Bindari, Mohamed Kamel 183
Elbel, Paul 147
Eleazar López Contreras, José 221–222
Engels, Friedrich 24
Escalante, Diogénes 217
Etchebarne, Miguel 259
Fabian Society 174
Filene, Edward Albert 133–137, 139, 147
Flores, Alejandro 261

Fontaine, Arthur 24, 27
Food and Agriculture Organisation (United Nations) 252
Ford, Henri 133–139, 147
Foreign Policy Association 53
Fortoul, José Gil 219
Fosdick, Raymond B. 57
France 23–25, 33, 44–45, 50, 106, 131–132, 139–141, 151, 167, 253, 255, 284
French Section of the Workers' International 25, 33, 173
Fuenmayor, Juan B. 221
Fuss, Henri 162
Garcia Cruz, Miguel 263
Garcia, Ibrahim 239
Garcia, Oldini 74
Garcia-Palacios, Carlos 297
General Agreement on Tariffs and Trade (GATT) 9
Germany 3, 25–26, 30, 32, 40, 43, 52, 69, 101, 128, 130, 139, 150, 168, 186, 212, 276, 285
Giardino, Alfred 269
Gil Borges, Esteban 183, 217
Godart, Justin 106
Gómez, Juan Vicente 216–217, 220–222
Goodrich, Carter 46, 277
Great Britain 26, 32, 45, 96, 106–107, 140, 150, 174, 240, 253–255, 264, 275–276
Graves, R.M. 182
Greece 158, 177, 182, 189, 191, 198, 200, 202–204, 208, 210–213, 277, 282
Greenwood, Ernest 46
Grimshaw, Harold Atheling 179, 297
Gutiérrez Alfaro, Tito 183, 218, 226, 230–231, 245
Guye, Robert 145
Haiti 261
Halbwachs, Maurice 27, 131, 151
Hall, Noel 147–148
Hallsworth, Joseph 279
Hamer, E.A.C den 294
Hamilton, Walton H. 105
Hanson, Alice 153
Haţieganu, Emil 206
Hawaii 145
Health Organisation (HO) 148

Herr, Lucien 24
Hook, JR Charles R. 269, 271
Hoover, Herbert 141
Horthy, Miklós 196
Hungary 39, 193, 195–196, 200, 212
Hull, Cordell 67, 140, 268, 277, 294
Hunt, Edward Eyre 52
India 72, 90–92, 94–101, 107–108, 115–117, 131, 142–143, 151–153, 162, 170, 277, 286
Indochina 142
Indonesia 264
International Association for Labour Legislation (IALL) 125, 127, 150
International Bank for Reconstruction and Development (IBRD) 280
International Chamber of Commerce (ICC) 29
International Committee of the Red Cross (ICRC) 186
International Congress of Economic and Social Sciences 42
International Congress of Health Insurance Funds 209
International Federation of Health Insurance Funds 209
International Federation of Trade Unions (IFTU) 62, 279
International Institute of Agriculture 42
International Institute of Intellectual Cooperation (IIIC) 120–121
International Law Association 173
International Management Institute (IMI) 34, 134–137
International Monetary Fund (IMF) 150, 176, 280
Institute of Pacific Relations (IPR) 55, 142–143
Iran 91, 277, 282
Ireland 253
Italy 3, 30–31, 107, 150, 186, 276, 285
Japan 30, 69, 72, 91, 92, 93, 96, 100–103, 107–109, 120, 131, 142, 144–145, 150–152, 162, 285–286, 292–293
Jaurès, Jean 24
Java 295

Jenks, Wilfred 69, 90, 159, 161, 164, 169, 175–176, 179, 187, 214, 218, 221, 223, 225, 228–241, 243–249, 254–255, 272, 278, 280, 291, 297
Johnston, George 291
Joint Committee of Cotton Trade Organizations 107
Joshi, Narayan Malhar 98–99
Jouhaux, Léon 40, 43, 136, 277
Kanellopoulos, Panajotis 211
Keynes, John Meynard 32, 45, 54
Kittredge, Tracy Barrett 58
Knight, Frank 153
Kojima, Ryoichi 297
Kung, H. H. 182
Kupers, Evert 75, 128
Labor Department (US) 16, 47, 256, 265, 269–270
La Follette, Robert 55
Lafrance, Robert 291
Lall, Diwan Chaman 98
Lambert – Ribot, Alfred 136
Lamus, Rangel 241
Laura Spelman Rockefeller Memorial 35
Lazard, Max 197
League of Nations 102, 112, 118, 120, 126–127, 134, 140, 143–144, 146–148, 151, 164, 169, 176, 182, 183, 190–191, 197, 202, 204, 211, 217, 219, 224, 252, 280
Lederer, Emile 32
Lewis, John 57
Lindsay, Samuel McCune 46
Linlithgow, Lord 117
Lithuania 193–194, 198–199
Lloyd George, David 26, 273
Lockhart, Bruce 273
Lorwin, Lewis 49–58, 104, 107, 144, 147–149, 151–153, 291
Loveday, Alexander 48, 147–148
Lozada, Jesus 269
Mackenzie, Ian 260
Mackenzie King, William Lyon 277
Magnusson, Leifur 46
Magruder, Calvert 269, 271
Man, Henri de 33
Maniu, Iuliu 202
Manpower Programme 186

Marino, Sylvio 201
Marsh, Leonard 260
Martin, Percival 35, 56–58, 103, 152, 294, 297
Marx, Karl 24, 201
Masaryk, Jan 173
Matthews, Robert E. 269
Maurette, Fernand 24, 44, 86, 102–105, 120–121, 136, 158, 167, 172, 175–176, 178, 293, 297
McDougall, Frank Lidgett 147–148
McKinlay, Kenneth 291
Meeker, Royal 46, 129, 297
Metall, Rudolf A. 261
Mexico 65–68, 70, 72–73, 76, 90, 142, 225, 256, 258, 260–263, 269, 275, 277
Michelis, Giuseppe de 42
Migone, Raul 74
Milhaud, Edgard 24, 135
Millan Delpretti, Vicente 218
Miller, Frieda 106
Mitchell, Wesley C. 35
Mitra, Bhupendra Nath 98
Mochanoff, Stoitcho 198
Mody, Homusji 98, 109, 115, 117
Morse, David 186, 283, 297
Mortished, Ronald James Patrick 256, 106
Murray, Albert Victor 174
Netherlands 128, 277, 294
New Deal 35, 45–47, 51, 54–55, 140, 276, 279
New School for Social Research 35
Newman, George 174
New Zealand 111–114, 132, 144, 277
Nicholson, Edward Max 151
Nixon, James 129, 136, 148–152, 255
Normano, John F. 55
Norway 69, 132, 235, 254, 277
Obolensky-Ossinsky, Valerian 36
Office of the Coordinator of Inter-American Affairs (OCIAA) 256, 258–259, 262, 265–267
Oldini, Garcia 74
Organisation for Economic Co-operation and Development 236
Oualid, William 27

Pan American Union (PAU) 65, 217, 267–268
Parra Pérez, Caracciolo 183, 219
Paul, Otto 241
Penrose, Ernest 255, 274
Perkins, Frances 47, 67, 106–107, 277–278
Permanent Mandates Commission (PMC) 94, 112
Peru 72, 83–84, 87, 227, 235, 260–261, 263, 267
Perry, Percival 135
Person, Harlow S. 36
Phelan, Edward 75, 90, 106, 163, 253–255, 268, 273–278, 283, 297
Pietri, Luis 217, 242, 246, 248
Pillai, Purushottama Padmanabha 92
Plissard, Roger 159, 162, 168, 297
Poblete Troncoso, Moisés 74–76, 84, 159, 162, 167, 170–171, 178, 29, 297
Poland 195–196, 199–200, 212, 277
Political and Economic Planning Group (PEP) 32, 151
Pône, Camille 158, 166, 172, 175, 232, 297
Powell, Oscar M. 261–262
Poznanski, Tadeusz 261
Pribram, Karl 129
Quintero Garcia, José Luis 230, 246
Răducanu, Ion 182, 201–202, 207
Rajchman, Ludwik 153, 203–205
Rasminsky, Louis 87
Rathenau, Walther 26
Rens, Jef 33, 236, 279
Reymond, Henri 255, 261
Ribot, Alexandre 28
Richardson, J. H. 136
Riches, John Edward 255, 297, 56, 111–114, 297
Riddell, Walter 77, 136
Rieve, Emil 106, 259
Rist, Charles 33
Rockefeller Foundation 56–58, 153
Rockefeller, John D., Jr. 57
Rockefeller, Nelson 256, 259, 266, 267
Rodríguez, Abelardo L. 68
Romania 18, 39, 158, 177, 182, 189–191, 196, 200–202, 205–207, 209, 212–213
Romero, Matos 239

Roosevelt, Franklin Delano 35, 45–49, 57, 67, 105, 107, 223, 256, 273, 277–279
Roques, Mario 27
Rostow, Walt Whitman 8
Rowntree, Seebohm 130
Royal Dutch Shell 222
Russell Sage Foundation 36
Russia 50, 173, 273
Saint-Simon, Claude Henri de Rouvroy de 24
Samoa 111–114
Sandys, Duncan 150
Schevenels, Walther 279
Schüller, Richard 87
Shanmukham Chetty, Ramasamy Kandasamy 99
Schoenbaum, Emil 200, 210, 261–262, 264, 297
Shotwell, James T. 46, 53, 144
Siam (Thailand) 96, 264
Sidqi, Ismaïl 1, 182
Siewers, Enrique 86, 88, 159, 169, 180, 215, 244, 291, 297
Simiand, François 27
Singapore 264
Slovenia 196
Smith, Adam 24
Soares, Macedo 85
Social Science Research Council (SSRC) 52, 133, 153
Social Security Board (SSB) 16, 106, 183, 261, 262
Solis Solis, Luis 78–79
Soublette, Félix 217
Spain 253
Stack, Maurice 160, 162, 164, 170, 255, 257, 297
Staehle, Hans 56, 137, 147, 149–152, 297
Stamboliyski, Alexandre 197
Standard Oil Company 222–223
Stein, Oswald 81–82, 159, 164, 169, 172–173, 175–176, 178, 200, 204, 209, 212, 226–227, 231, 242, 255, 257–258, 260–263, 265–268, 276, 291, 297
Stoppani, Pietro 41, 87, 146–147
Sweden 69, 276
Switzerland 219, 235, 254–255, 276

Tait, Christie 159, 162, 164, 168, 297
Taylor Society 34, 36
Thailand 91, 96, 264, 277
Thomas, Albert 1, 6–7, 17, 21–43, 45–46, 49, 59–62, 65, 68, 70, 84–85, 93, 98–99, 110, 119–120, 128–130, 134–138, 143, 163–164, 171–173, 178, 182, 191–199, 204–205, 207–208, 214, 255, 273, 275, 284, 288, 292–293, 296–297
Thudichum, Maurice 76, 159, 168, 186, 217, 291, 297
Tixier, Adrien 68–70, 72–75, 80–81, 83, 158, 164, 166, 172–173, 176, 178, 181–182, 189, 201–202, 204–211, 213, 226–255–257, 261, 263, 267, 275–276, 278, 297
Tracy, Martin 105
Trinidad 233
Trueblood, Edward G. 269
Truman, Harry S. 8
Tunisia 159, 178, 183
Turkey 159–160, 178, 183
Twentieth Century Fund 52, 133, 135
Unesco 16
Union of Soviet Socialist Republics (USSR) 3, 30, 31, 36, 51, 253, 280
Union of South Africa 277
United Nations (UN) 280, 283, 297
United Nations Relief and Rehabilitation Administration (UNRRA) 253, 280
United States 8–9, 12, 16, 23, 26, 31, 33–36, 38, 44–50, 52, 55–58, 60 –61, 67, 71, 75–77, 82, 92, 101, 104–107, 117, 129, 132–136, 140, 144, 150, 152, 158, 161, 177, 183, 217, 223 –224, 252–257, 259, 264–271, 273, 275–277, 279–280, 283–286
Unsain, Alejandro 75
Uruguay 63, 72–73, 75, 86–87, 132, 142, 179
Urwick, Lyndall 136
Van Kleeck, Mary 36, 53
Van Sickle, John 57–58
Varlez, Louis 84, 197
Vasconcellos, Henrique Doria de 86, 88, 215

Venezuela 18, 63, 66, 72, 77, 84, 87–89, 158, 159, 176, 177, 178, 180, 183, 214–250, 261–263, 286
Venizélos, Eleuthérios 198, 203, 205, 208
Villar, Humberto del 269
Viner, Jacob 151
Viple, Marius 27, 255, 293
Voldemaras, Augustinas 194, 198
Vourloumis, P. 208
Waelbroeck, Pierre 255
Waline, Pierre 106
Walters, Frank 220
Watt, Robert J. 259, 269, 271
Wilson, Woodrow 129
Winant, John G. 106, 152, 183, 244, 254–255, 258, 273–274, 294, 297
Woytinsky, Wladimir 32
Wubnig, Arthur 50, 55, 106
Yepes, Luis 77
Yugoslavia 39, 186, 277
Zakkas, Andreas 182, 208–211
Zelenka, Anton 210, 214, 223, 225–226, 230–231, 237, 241–242, 245, 248, 297
Zumeta, César 219

www.ingramcontent.com/pod-product-compliance
Lightning Source LLC
Chambersburg PA
CBHW031754220426
43662CB00007B/404